THE
GOUZENKO
TRANSCRIPTS

Edited by Robert Bothwell
and J.L. Granatstein

THE GOUZENKO TRANSCRIPTS

The Evidence Presented to the Kellock-Taschereau Royal Commission of 1946

Canadian Cataloguing in Publication Data

Main entry under title:
The Gouzenko transcripts

ISBN 0-88879-069-4

1. Canadian Spy Trials, 1946 — Sources. 2. Espionage, Russian —
Canada — History — Sources. I. Bothwell, Robert, 1944–
II. Granatstein, J.L., 1939– III. Canada. Royal Commission to
Investigate the Facts Relating to and the Circumstances Surround-
ing the Communication, by Public Officials and Other Persons in
Positions of Trust of Secret and Confidential Information to
Agents of a Foreign Power.

FC583.G6G68   327.1'2'0947   C82-090051-6
F1034.2G68

©Deneau Publishers & Company Ltd.
 281 Lisgar Street
 Ottawa, Ontario K2P 0E1

Cover design by Heather Walters

Printed in Canada by Webcom Ltd.

Contents

PREFACE

In September 1945, a young and very frightened cipher clerk left the Soviet Embassy in Ottawa carrying with him a substantial number of documents that proved beyond doubt that the Soviet Union was engaging in espionage against Canada, one of its wartime allies. In February 1946, the Canadian government created a Royal Commission under two justices of the Supreme Court of Canada to inquire into the evidence Gouzenko had brought and to take testimony from him and from those his material implicated. The Royal Commissioners presented their report in July 1946 by which time a number of trials had already been held. The courtroom events were not concluded until 1949.

The Gouzenko Case was a great sensation of its day, an event that many consider one of the first of the Cold War. And ramifications of the case were widespread, implicating major figures in the United States and the United Kingdom. As late as 1981, allegations that the one-time head of MI-5 in Britain had been fingered by Gouzenko in 1946 drew world-wide headlines.

Astonishingly, however, all the evidence taken by the Royal Commission in 1946 was made public only in late 1981, more than 35 years after Gouzenko's defection. This book is the first to present the crucial sections of the Kellock-Taschereau Commission testimony.

Since that testimony is more than 6000 pages long, we have had to be very selective. We have tried to present every bit of relevant information that Gouzenko offered, and this makes up more than half the book. Then we have tried to show how the Commissioners operated, some of the legal problems they — and the suspected spies — faced, and substantial portions of testimony from and about the major figures. We have also corrected minor spelling errors and standardized spelling and capitalization. Quoted material, however, was left untouched. There are some gaps. Alan Nunn May, the British atomic scientist, was tried in England and did not appear before the Royal Commission. Sam Carr fled Canada and was not captured until 1949. Fred Rose, aided by skillful counsel, managed to avoid testifying. Some others involved were so unforthcoming in their testimony that they added little to the story. Notwithstanding these problems, there is much of interest here on the techniques of espionage and the recruitment of agents, on the uses of study groups as an entrapment device, and on the reasons why rather average Canadians betrayed their country.

We have been assisted in our work by a number of friends. Mr. Jerry O'Brien and Mr. Jim Whalen of the Public Archives of Canada provided assistance that facilitated our task. We are most grateful to them. Mr. Norman Hillmer, Mr. Dave Fransen, and Mr. Jim Littleton also assisted us, and we owe them our gratitude.

RB/JLG

INTRODUCTION

The first week of September, 1945 was the first week of peace. The Japanese Empire formally surrendered to the Allies, American troops took over the administration of their defeated enemy, and around the Pacific the armies that had assembled for the invasion of Japan began to get ready to go home.

Allied victory had been assured for some time, but it had been expected that the Japanese military would put up a fierce resistance to any invading force, despite the overwhelming odds against them. Suddenly, and unexpectedly, the Americans increased the odds. On August 6th, 1945, a B-29 bomber dropped a bomb of unprecedented power on the Japanese city of Hiroshima. It was, the Allies announced, an atomic bomb. Three days later, on August 9th, a second bomb was dropped, this time on the city of Nagasaki. Finally convinced of the futility of further resistance, the Japanese government announced its willingness to surrender on the Allies' announced terms.

The revelation that the American government had successfully developed an atomic bomb was not quite the surprise it initially seemed. True, there had been little in the way of public or press speculation during the war, and there had been a curious absence of scientific publications in an area that had been the centre of intense research prior to 1939. But the "secret" of the atomic weapon had been shared among three governments, the British, the American and the Canadian. The British had had most to do with the initial stages of atomic research. The Americans had had the money and the expertise to carry it out. The Canadians, blessed with some money and, most importantly, real estate far from the range of the German air force, had provided a haven for British scientists in laboratories in Montreal. Canada also provided uranium, the essential ingredient of the atomic bomb, and refined Belgian uranium at the only remaining commercial uranium refinery outside occupied Europe.

The basic scientific knowledge that helped to create the bomb was no secret. German, British, Russian, French and American physicists had all made notable progress in atomic physics before the war. It was known (and widely known) that an atomic explosion was a theoretical possibility, and that uranium was the essential ingredient in such an explosion. But it was not widely known that the Americans had invested billions of dollars in developing an atomic device, nor that such a device had been successfully tested in the New Mexico desert at the end of July. That knowledge, it was believed, was restricted to the members of the American, British and Canadian atomic teams, to a few ranking members of the military, and to even fewer members of the three governments. All those who knew had to have a reason to know, and their knowledge was protected by security clearances, secrecy classifications, and loyalty oaths.

Not surprisingly, it came as a great shock to the Canadian Prime Minister, William Lyon Mackenzie King, to learn on the morning of September 6th, 1945 that something had gone terribly wrong. The Under-Secretary of State for External Affairs, Norman Robertson, had distressing news. A man had turned up, with his wife, at the office of the minister of justice. He asked to see the minister. He said he was from the Russian embassy. So far nothing startling, though just a trifle unusual. But the Russian's message was highly unusual: the Russian democracy was different from ours. To prove it the Soviet official, Igor Gouzenko, had brought a sheaf of documents from the embassy. The story they told, coupled with his own, was damning. A Soviet spy ring was operating in Canada, and their objective was nothing less than the secret of the atomic bomb.

THE BACKGROUND

It is, in retrospect, curious that the Canadian government should have been so surprised that the Soviet Union took a clandestine interest in events in Canada. For many years the Canadian Communist Party had maintained a close connection with Moscow, and Canadian authorities were known to take a jaundiced interest in home-grown Bolsheviks whose pockets were stuffed with Soviet gold. In the early 1930s, under the Conservative regime of R.B. Bennett, the Communist party was outlawed and its leaders imprisoned. The Liberal government of Mackenzie King had changed that in 1936, but to redress the balance the government of Quebec had renewed the attack on communism by passing a Padlock Law that required the padlocking of any premises used for the purpose of propagating communism.

Bennett's repression, and the controversy that attended the Padlock Law, helped to make communism a civil liberties' issue in Canada. It was not difficult to be sympathetic towards Communists whose fate seemed to be determined by the persecution of the heavy hand of bourgeois authority. That authority, in any case, had lost much of its legitimacy in the eyes of the Left by its failure to solve the grievous economic problems of the Great Depression. The capitalist system had failed, and of those who opposed it only the Communists promised to do a thorough job of replacing capitalist injustice by scientific, humanitarian socialism. And for those who worried about the course of events in Europe and were concerned with the rise of Hitler to power in Germany, communism seemed to offer an answer to those problems too. Only the Soviet Union had replaced the obsolete forms of capitalism with a universal system of social justice, so the argument ran, and only the Soviet Union was prepared to oppose fascism outright. The half-hearted compromises and evasions of bourgeois governments, especially those of Britain and Canada, were perceived as ignoble, futile and ultimately foolish.

The attraction of the Soviet Union, as model and leader for the world's progressive forces, was accordingly strengthened throughout the 1930s. The same applied to the leader of the Soviet Union, the general secretary of the Soviet Communist party, Josef Stalin. Delegations of foreign Communists and Communist sympathizers trekked to Moscow to view the Soviet miracle at first hand. With rare exceptions they reported, in the classic phrase of the period, that they had seen the future, and it worked. Travellers through the Soviet Ukraine in the early thirties found no evidence of famine. Foreign correspondents, writers, and even some politicians and diplomats discerned nothing strange in Stalin's purge trials in the mid-1930s. And, indeed, even opponents of the Soviet regime would have found it hard to credit the truth about Stalin's archipelago of concentration camps or the mass starvation that accompanied the imposition of collectivized agriculture. Some overseas boosters of the Soviet system might even have found the ruthlessness and brutality of the Russian government attractive; at least in Moscow there were no half-measures and no timidity.[1]

Naturally, when the Soviet government denounced Hitler, or when it proclaimed its support of the Spanish republican government in its civil war against an army uprising backed by fascists, its actions appeared to be firm and decisive. A generation of young idealists applauded these actions and many did more, such as volunteering for the International Brigades fighting in Spain or, like Dr. Norman Bethune of Canada, applying their talents to help behind the lines. Although some participants in the Spanish civil war noted the presence of Communist influence and commented on the heavily political nature of Russian aid to Spain, their complaints and queries were ignored in an understandable preoccupation with the greater good of the cause of the Spanish republic.

Matters became somewhat more complicated on the outbreak of the Second World War in September 1939. Britain and France declared war on Hitler's Germany on September 3, and Canada did so on September 10. But the Soviet Union at first remained aloof and then, in mid-September and thereafter, actively assisted in the destruction of Poland. The conclusion of a non-aggression pact between Nazi Germany and Communist Russia on August 23, 1939 had guaranteed the Germans the luxury of a one-front war, once the hapless Poles were polished off. In addition to eastern Poland, the Soviet Union absorbed Lithuania, Latvia and Estonia and, after a short and bloody war, parts of Finland as well.

Stalin's actions in forming a tacit alliance with Hitler were defended abroad as a tactical necessity. In any case, the western imperialist powers were no better than the Nazis, so Soviet propaganda claimed, and it was entirely in the Soviet Union's interest to let the capitalists fight among themselves. Communists in other lands who found this a difficult proposition to swallow left the Party, but many remained to oppose the war and to mobilize "working class" sentiment against the belligerent governments of Britain, France — and Canada.

The allied governments responded by banning the Communist party in their respective countries. In Canada the government began by prohibiting Communist publications and then, in June 1940, it banned the Communist party itself, and began rounding up all its leaders. The experience of one prominent Communist, Pat Sullivan, has been recorded:

> And so it came about that on the morning of June 19th, 1940, the R.C.M.P. visited me in my room in the St. Regis Hotel in Toronto, and told me that an inspector of the Force wanted to talk to me, adding that I would be back in the hotel in an hour or so. . . . The hour or so stretched from June 19th, 1940, to March 20th, 1942.[2]

In internment, Canadian Communists shared quarters with Canadian fascists while those leaders who had escaped the R.C.M.P. net struggled to mobilize opinion around the Party's slogan for war: "Withdraw Canada from the Imperialist War." "It would be an exaggeration," party leader Tim Buck wrote, "to say that the slogan of the Communist Party of Canada . . . has become the slogan of the masses."[3]

As a consequence of the Communists' official banning, Communist cells or study groups ceased to meet, except, of course, in the internment camps, while the party's popularity with "the masses" plumbed new depths. Thus, when the Germans invaded the Soviet Union in June 1941, Canadian Communists were ill-prepared doctrinally and organizationally to rally support for the Soviet Union and its new allies, the imperialist warriors of the previous day.

At least the Party no longer had to follow the politically suicidal line of opposing the war against Hitler, and in the course of time the various official prohibitions on its activities were withdrawn. The Communist party was not refounded, however. Instead, a Dominion Communist-Labour Total War Committee made its appearance in August 1942. This was, as a historian of the Communist party has pointed out, a makeshift arrangement, and a year later the Communists took the final step and re-established an official, legal party. But the party was not to be called Communist since that name, apparently, still held too many negative connotations. It was as the Labour-Progressive party that the Communists approached the electorate.[4] Some Communists denied that the old Communist party and the new Labour Progressive party were one and the same, and formally they were not. Informally, it was a sign of great political naiveté to believe that there was, or could be, any difference.

That the Labour-Progressive strategy was successful to some extent cannot be denied. Communist representatives regularly appeared in respectable, official surroundings, on platforms with bourgeois politicians and even in elected office. "Almost every major city west of Montreal had at least one alderman either belonging to the LPP or closely associated with it," one historian has written. In a Montreal by-election for the federal House of Commons in August 1943 the Labour-Progressive candidate, Fred Rose, was elected. Although the democratic socialist party, the Co-operative Commonwealth Federation or CCF, remained stiffly aloof from the Communists, many left-leaning Canadians could not understand why an alliance of democratic and progressive forces should not take place, especially when the over-riding issue was the victory of the Allies over Hitler's Germany.[5]

Utilizing their strength in some sections of the trade union movement, Communists reinforced their political position with useful labour muscle. In some areas a tacit alliance with the governing Liberals was talked about, and in fact the Labour-Progressives lent the Liberals their rhetorical endorsement on several occasions between 1943 and 1945. But however vocal Communist spokesmen might be, their real voting strength was a great deal less than the party believed. At the end of the war a federal election was called for June 11, 1945. In the result, only one Communist candidate, Fred Rose in Montreal-Cartier, was elected, and the party garnered less than 2% of the total vote. It could be anticipated that the party's political importance, not to mention its overall political significance, was on the decline.

But if domestic communism was of slight and diminishing importance, the overseas variety was of ever-greater significance for the Canadian government. Canada had never had formal diplomatic relations with the Soviet Union, viewing the Soviet government as ideologically incompatible and, even more important, fearing the Soviet Union as a formidable trade rival. The German invasion of Russia in 1941 changed all that. A friendlier attitude towards the Soviets immediately became apparent. At the end of 1942 Canada and the U.S.S.R. announced that they would exchange diplomatic missions, and in the spring of 1943 the Russians began to arrive, taking up quarters in an old mansion on Ottawa's Charlotte Street, overlooking the Rideau River.

Among the new arrivals was a cipher clerk on the staff of the military attaché, Igor Gouzenko. Born in 1919, Gouzenko had received a superior education and trained as an architect, but in the war he was naturally swept up into military service, which in his case meant military intelligence. In 1942, Gouzenko (by then a junior officer) received instruction in ciphering, which prepared him for service abroad. Abroad, in Gouzenko's case, was to mean Canada, where he arrived in June 1943 via Siberia and the North-West Staging Route across Alaska and western Canada.[6]

A life of deprivation in the Soviet Union had not prepared Gouzenko for what he would find in Canada. He was, for example, "not prepared for the wealth of food in the Edmonton hotel where we stayed, nor the abundance of clothing, candies and luxuries of all kinds in such windows as those of the huge Hudson's Bay store on the main street." He and his Russian companions were even less ready for the luxury of uninhibited conversation with ordinary Canadians. On the train from Edmonton to Ottawa one of the Russian officers was asked, as he reported to his incredulous companions, "if we have freedom of speech in Russia."

"What did you say?"

"I said we do."[7]

Difficult though it was to credit the ignorance of ordinary Canadians on Soviet affairs, the naiveté that existed even among the ostensibly well-informed guaranteed a friendly reception for the new Soviet mission. Soviet diplomats and officers were much sought-after in Ottawa, where they struck their hosts as amiable, entertaining and, above all, free with their unrationed liquor — no small thing in a town squirming under the cumulative effects of wartime rationing. On one famous occasion Russian hospitality was so effective as to cause the Deputy Minister of finance to pass out at an embassy reception celebrating the latest Canadian Mutual Aid gift to the U.S.S.R.[8]

The entertaining was by and large left to the senior diplomats and military officers. At Gouzenko's level in the hierarchy there was little official socializing, so that despite his officer's rank — which, of course, was not officially admitted — his existence was, by Ottawa standards, comparatively humble and obscure. Gouzenko's wife Anna joined him in October, and the two of them — there was soon a son Andrei — settled down to a life of unbelievable relaxation and affluence by Soviet standards. Russians were not generally well-informed on the subject of life in Canada or on life in the West as a whole. Most of their preconceptions were quickly proven false or misleading, not only about material welfare, but about social conditions, and political freedoms unimaginable in a police state. As Gouzenko's testimony would later reveal, he was astonished by the relative freedom of the Canadian elections of 1945, by comparison with which the liturgy of Soviet politics seemed more than ever ludicrous and deceitful.

ATOMIC SECRETS

One of the principal objects of the Soviet embassy in Ottawa was the discovery of information useful to the Soviet Union. In this respect Soviet embassies do not differ from those of other countries, but in reference to the 1940s it is reasonable to argue that the balance within Soviet missions abroad was somewhat unusual.

Equally unusual, as far as most Canadians were concerned, was the possibility that Canada might have something worth stealing. Prior to 1939 Canadian science was systematically starved by cost-conscious governments, while Canadian engineering was in an equally parlous state. As a partial consequence, Canadian research and development during the Second World War took a back seat to the technical innovations of Canada's richer and better equipped partners, Great Britain and the United States. But Canada's sheltered location and the gradual accumulation of engineering and scientific knowledge did, eventually, have an impact. In the fields of explosives, optics and radar, Canadian technology was impressive. Organized through the National Research Council, headquartered in and around Ottawa, Research Enterprises Limited, a Crown corporation located just outside Toronto, and in various army research establishments, it enabled Canadian scientists and technicians to soon make an important contribution to the collective allied war effort.

In the spring of 1942 Canada was asked to help with another allied project. Great Britain and the United States had agreed to collaborate in devising an atomic bomb. Canada had reserves of uranium and, more important, a uranium refinery. It had ample hydroelectric power, and its government's treasury was not quite as constrained as that of the British. It seemed natural to ask Canada to contribute laboratories and other facilities to bring the British half of the atomic enterprise physically closer to the American and a project which, it was hoped, would have important scientific and engineering benefits for all three countries.

A team of British scientists was transported to Montreal where they took up residence in some unused buildings at the Université de Montréal. There, their Canadian counterparts joined them. Unfortunately for the hopes of the British team, the Americans imposed tight security controls on their part of the atomic bomb project, forbidding the transmittal of information except on the most rigorous "need to know" basis. As a result, the British-Canadian team was excluded from all American information except that which was strictly essential for the success of the heavy water reactor experiments which would take place in Canada. Those experiments were largely successful, and it was decided to take matters one step further by building a reactor on the Ottawa River upstream from Ottawa at a tiny hamlet called Chalk River. When the war ended in September, 1945 that reactor was well underway, but had not yet begun to function.[9]

Understandably the Soviet embassy soon demonstrated an intense, unofficial interest in what it could learn about the progress of Canadian research in explosives, radar, and, above all, atomic experimentation. More routinely, it sought whatever political information it could find, although in the nature of things that information could not hope to be more than mildly titillating to Soviet intelligence (Canada being excluded from the highest inter-allied exchanges between Britain and the United States).

By September, 1945 Soviet espionage in all the above fields was well-established. There was much to reveal, and the immediate reaction of the embassy authorities to Gouzenko's disappearance seems to have been a well-justified panic. That of the Canadian government was, initially, quite different.

THE GOUZENKO CASE: FIRST STAGES

When Igor Gouzenko left the Soviet embassy on September 5, 1945, he had had little contact or experience with the attitudes and procedures of the Canadian government. But he seems to have acquired a regard for the workings of a free press in a democracy, and his first steps on the road to freedom took him to the newsroom of the Ottawa *Journal*, the better and coincidentally the more conservative of Ottawa's two English-language newspapers. But by the time the hapless Gouzenko got to speak to anyone, the senior staff had packed up and gone home for the night. The increasingly panic-stricken Russian was told to come back in the morning or, better yet, to go directly to the Royal Canadian Mounted Police. When Gouzenko desperately tried to hold the *Journal* city editor's attention, the latter responded, "Sorry, I'm busy" and walked away.

Gouzenko's next stop was the office of the Minister of Justice. But by then it was almost midnight and the minister and his staff were long gone. "Come back in the morning," he was told. Morning was no better. With his wife at his side, Gouzenko made a fruitless tour of the offices of the Minister of Justice, Louis St. Laurent. Rebuffed there, he turned once again to the Ottawa *Journal* where he was predictably told to go away. Despairing, the Gouzenkos returned home only to notice that their apartment was being watched by two men sitting in a park opposite.[10]

By evening on September 6, a fair number of people knew that something had gone wrong with Gouzenko. There was the Minister of Justice, of course, and the members of his staff. There was the Under-Secretary of State for External Affairs, Norman Robertson, and his Associate Under-Secretary, Hume Wrong, and the Prime Minister, the Right Honourable William Lyon Mackenzie King.

Mackenzie King, when Igor Gouzenko entered his life, was seventy years old and had been Canada's prime minister for more than eighteen years. He had achieved this eminence through a careful cultivation of the domestic concerns and prejudices of his fellow-countrymen. He was a strong believer in the negative virtues of an active foreign policy, never more uneasy than when Canada was asked to step out in front of its allies on an important issue of foreign policy. And now an employee of the Russian embassy was asking him to do just that. The alternative, King was told, was suicide. Perhaps, King mused, that was inevitable. Let Gouzenko's apartment be watched. "If suicide took place let the city police take charge and secure whatever there was in the way of documents, but on no account for us to take the initiative." In any case, King told his diary, he did not believe Gouzenko.[11]

Thus it came about that the two men sitting in a park opposite Gouzenko's apartment were none other than Mackenzie King's agents and not those of the Soviet embassy. That was no consolation to Gouzenko, who had taken refuge with his wife and family in the apartment of a neighbour. They were safe there when the representatives of the embassy finally came to call, breaking down Gouzenko's door in the process. That attracted the attention of the Ottawa city police, who asked the R.C.M.P. what they should do. The R.C.M.P. in turn phoned Norman Robertson. Robertson, who had passed the evening with Sir William Stephenson of British intelligence, ordered that Gouzenko be brought in the next morning.

The evidence that Gouzenko presented to the R.C.M.P. on the morning of September 7th persuaded the Canadian government that they faced a domestic espionage ring with ramifications extending across the border into the United States and across the Atlantic to Great Britain. Gouzenko and his wife and child were spirited out of Ottawa to a tourist camp while the mass of information he had brought was sorted and translated.

Back in Ottawa appearances were preserved. While attending a garden party at the British High Commission, King encountered the Soviet ambassador who, he noted, "had a very anxious look on his face." The British High Commissioner, Malcolm MacDonald, was a great favourite of Mackenzie King's; MacDonald, along with the American ambassador, Ray Atherton, was the next to know. The news had a special piquancy for MacDonald, because one of the spy ring, Kay Willsher, was located inside his own office. To assist MacDonald, the British secret service sent two agents (one of whom was Roger Hollis of MI-5) to Ottawa to aid in the investigation, in which they were joined by what King described as "F.B.I. representatives."[12]

As the investigation proceeded Mackenzie King preferred to bide his time. In discussion with Sir William Stephenson on September 17th, King advised caution and cooperation between Canada, the United States and Great Britain in handling Gouzenko's revelations so as "to prevent further developments," by which King presumably meant a worsening of relations with the Soviet Union. To help shape western reactions, King decided that he would go personally to see President Truman in Washington and Prime Minister Attlee in London. On September 29 King and Robertson flew to Washington, where the Canadian ambassador, Lester Pearson, was let into the secret. The next morning, when King and Truman met, the two men explored the ramifications of what Gouzenko had revealed. The Russian defector, King told Truman, had alleged "that an assistant secretary of the Secretary of State's Department was supposed to be implicated although," the Canadian prime minister cautiously added, "I made perfectly clear this was only what Corby* had said but I had no information to back it up."[13]

Dean Acheson, an assistant secretary of state who was present, remarked that King's report "had reference to an assistant to an assistant secretary." The discussion between King and Truman nevertheless seems to have been curiously inconsequential. Truman later remarked to Edward Stettinius that "although the Russians were clearly working on a bomb, he was not as concerned as Mackenzie King. There was no 'precious secret' which the United States could withhold from other countries" because the American monopoly of the atomic secret would, in the nature of things, disappear within the next five to ten years.[14]

King's next stop was London where he arrived on October 7th. Gouzenko was still uppermost in his mind. Discussing the case with Clement Attlee, King urged "the view that the President held, with which Attlee said he was much in agreement, namely that as much information should be secured both in the U.S. and here before the case was opened to the public." The consequences and implications of Russia's espionage were much in King's mind as he reviewed the future of international control over atomic energy with British ministers and officials. Throughout his visit King worked to temper British anxiety to arrest the nuclear physicist Dr. Alan Nunn May, identified by the code name "Primrose" in Gouzenko's documents. King was disposed to put off any decisive action over Gouzenko until a tripartite meeting on atomic energy between Attlee, Truman and himself scheduled for the middle of November.[15]

Although King's diary for most of November and December is missing, it is well known that the November conversations between the three English-speaking

---

*Corby was the code name assigned to the whole Gouzenko case, or sometimes to Gouzenko alone, as here."

leaders produced little of lasting importance except an agreement to continue with atomic cooperation as far as American self-interest allowed. In Canada, police investigation into the Gouzenko affair secretly continued, although intelligence activity was temporarily suspended for the birth of a child to Anna Gouzenko. (British intelligence contributed a layette). As late as February 1, when Truman's chief of staff, Admiral Leahy, visited Ottawa and lunched with Mackenzie King, nothing had been done. Leahy told King that "he felt we ought to go on with our inquiry if it involved our own civil servants. He also agreed that it might have far-reaching repercussions."[16] How far-reaching neither man suspected.

THE ROYAL COMMISSION

The long delay in government action to deal with the espionage activities of the Soviet embassy came to an end because of a leak from an unlikely source. Drew Pearson was a slightly scurrilous and sensationalist American print and radio columnist, who told his radio audience on February 4, 1946 that Prime Minister King had advised President Truman of a Soviet spy ring in Canada. Some Washington official must have been anxious to precipitate a crisis in Ottawa — and Washington. Mackenzie King decided to act. The next day he told his assembled Cabinet for the first time about the Gouzenko case. "I said little about the source of the discovery but mentioned that we had the documentary evidence." King then read out the text of an Order in Council appointing two Supreme Court of Canada justices, Robert Taschereau, a professor of Law at Laval until his elevation to the Supreme Court in 1940, and R.L. Kellock, a Torontonian appointed to the Supreme Court in October 1944, as commissioners to take evidence. The Cabinet agreed, and also accepted that the Royal Commission would begin its operations in secret the next day.[17] E.K. Williams, a distinguished Winnipeg lawyer and the president of the Canadian Bar Association, an earlier adviser to the government on the legalities of the Gouzenko affair, was named counsel. He was to be assisted by Gerald Fauteux, an able Montreal lawyer, and by D.W. Mundell of the Justice Department.

From February 6 to 13, the Royal Commission functioned behind closed doors, reviewing the evidence brought by Gouzenko from the Soviet embassy. Gouzenko's oral evidence began on February 13 in sessions that proceeded through the day and into the evening; by February 14, the commissioners had heard enough to justify advising the government that many of those named in the documents and testimony should be taken into custody. "I can see where a great cry will be raised," the Prime Minister wrote in his diary, "having had a Commission sit in secret, and men and women arrested and detained under an order in council passed really under War Measures [Act] powers. I will be held up to the world as the very opposite of a democrat."[18] The arrests were made at 7 a.m. in the morning of February 15, the arrested twelve men and women being taken to the Rockcliffe barracks of the R.C.M.P. Among those picked up were Dr. Raymond Boyer, an explosives' expert with the National Research Council; two engineers with the N.R.C., S.W. Mazerall and Durnford Smith; J. Scott Benning, an official in the Department of Munitions and Supply; Emma Woikin, a code clerk in External Affairs; Gordon Lunan, an army officer on loan to the Wartime Information Board; and Kathleen Willsher, the deputy registrar in the British High Commission in Ottawa. Further arrests followed as evidence was taken.

That day, Mackenzie King informed the Leader of the Opposition, John Bracken, of the government action and, King recorded, "He made no adverse criticism of anything."[19] Neither did two representatives of the Soviet embassy, Belokhvostikov, the chargé d'affaires, and Pavlov, the second secretary. Evidence at the Royal Commission would reveal Pavlov to be the N.K.V.D. officer at the embassy and a man with a spy ring of his own. Finally on February 15, a very dramatic day, Mackenzie King's first public statement on the Gouzenko affair was released to the public. "Information of undoubted authenticity has reached the Canadian Government which establishes that there have been disclosures of secret and confidential information to unauthorized persons, including some members of the staff of a foreign mission in Ottawa." The Soviet Union was not mentioned, a tactful gesture that seemed completely unnecessary. King's statement continued by advising the nation of the creation of the Kellock-Taschereau Commission and of the arrests made that day. "It is the intention of the Government that, after the Report of the Royal Commissioners has been received, prosecution will be instituted in cases in which evidence warrants it." No names of those arrested were revealed, but the statement noted, accurately enough, that some of the detainees "appear to have been far more deeply and consciously involved than others. Some will probably be found to be more or less innocent instruments in furthering activities much more serious than they may have imagined."[20]

Five days later, the Information Bureau of the Soviet Union in Moscow passed to the Canadian Chargé there the first official Russian response to the case. To everyone's surprise, the Russians "after appropriate investigation" stated that "certain members of the staff of the Soviet Military Attaché in Canada received, from Canadian nationals with whom they were acquainted, certain information of a secret character which did not, however, present great interest for the Soviet organization." That was an admission of guilt. The Soviet statement downplayed the significance of the information "in view of more advanced technical attainment in the U.S.S.R.," maintaining that much of the material received was already available in published works on radar and atomic energy. Despite this, the Information Bureau noted, the military attaché, Colonel Zabotin, had been recalled home as a result of his misconduct. On the other hand, the Russians said, "it must also be borne in mind that the Soviet Ambassador and other members of the staff of the Soviet Embassy in Canada had no connection with this."[21] The ambassador may in fact have been clean; innumerable other members of the embassy staff, as the evidence of the Royal Commission makes clear, were not.

The Soviet admissions had, no doubt, been prompted by a full awareness of the extent of the documentation spirited away by Gouzenko. The public received its first intimations of the evidence when the Kellock-Taschereau Commission issued an interim report under the date of March 2, 1946. This report named the principal members of Zabotin's staff who had conducted espionage in Canada — Lt.-Col. Motinov, the chief assistant military attaché, Lt.-Col. Rogov, the assistant air attaché, Maj. Sokolov of the commercial counsellor's staff, Lt. Angelov, a secretary to the military attaché, and other officers. It pointed out that evidence had been sought about the atomic bomb, the production of explosives and chemicals, the ways to recruit agents, and about allied troop movements. And the report stated flatly that Mrs. Emma Woikin, Gordon Lunan, Edward Mazerall and Kathleen

Willsher "have communicated directly or indirectly secret and confidential material to representatives of the U.S.S.R. in violation of the *Official Secrets Act . . .*" The interim report then briefly described the nature of the evidence against the four public servants.[22]

A further report on March 14 told the public that 48 witnesses had been heard in 44 sittings of the Commission and laid out more of the evidence against the Canadian suspects. Dr. Raymond Boyer, H.S. Gerson, Matt Nightingale, and David Shugar were all named, and for the first time actual evidence in the form of telegrams to and from Moscow and biographical files from the Soviet embassy were printed.[23] A third interim report gave more evidence, including a mailing list sent by Zabotin to Moscow that detailed the information passed along by Eric Adams of the Bank of Canada. Yet another detainee named in this report was Israel Halperin, a mathematician who had worked at the Canadian Army Research and Development Establishment on artillery problems, explosives and other secret matters. Durnford Smith of the National Research Council and Scott Benning of the Department of Munitions and Supply drew substantial attention as well, the commissioners offering evidence of their assignments, of the information they supplied, and of their contacts with others in the group of arrested Canadians. Finally, F.W. Poland, an R.C.A.F. officer, was mentioned, the report alluding to the rather tenuous evidence linking him to the spy ring and noting that he had refused to be sworn or to answer questions.[24]

The final *Report of the Royal Commission*, a thick volume of 733 pages, was dated June 27, 1946 and released to the public on July 15. This was a very full account of the Gouzenko case, one that reviewed the Commission's history and procedures, the general pattern of Soviet espionage in Canada since 1924, and the various undercover networks operated from the Soviet embassy. There was, the *Report* observed, one network operated by Zabotin as well as a parallel military network, a political network, a naval intelligence network, and a N.K.V.D. ring. Full information had been secured only about Zabotin's ring, but there was evidence, some of which appears herein, that Zabotin's net was linked to others in the United States and Britain. Particular attention was paid in the *Report* to the ways in which agents were recruited and to the use of the Communist party as a base for this operation. The creation of study groups — the commissioners considered them to be cells — was important as a way of finding likely recruits, and the evidence demonstrated that secret members of the Party helped place others in positions of strategic importance.

Most revealing of all, in the views of Justices Kellock and Taschereau, was that the agents had not been motivated by pecuniary reasons (although small payments often were made) but by a desire to serve the interests of "humanity," embodied in the professed goals of the Soviet Union and Marxist ideology. Some of the others involved had spied because they believed that the U.S.S.R., an ally, should have access to every invention and device that would speed victory over Hitler; others were Jews, motivated by resentment against the anti-Semitism they found in Canada; and others became involved out of a desire for intellectual companionship.

Most striking, perhaps, was the *Report's* evidence that declared Fred Rose, the member of Parliament for Montreal-Cartier and a representative of the Labour-Progressive party, to have been active in the spy ring as a recruiter and transmitter of information. Along with Sam Carr, the organizing secretary of the L.P.P. (and one of the suspects who fled to evade arrest), Rose apparently had found recruits, passed them their tasks, and carried their information to Zabotin or his officers. Fred Rose had been arrested on March 14, a delicate operation as the government was concerned that he might try to shelter behind parliamentary immunity.[25]

Others not previously mentioned in the interim reports as linked to the espionage, were also cited: Samuel Sol Burman, an army officer alleged to have carried messages overseas; Alan Nunn May, a high level British atomic scientist who had worked in Montreal on A-bomb research; Agatha Chapman of the Bank of Canada; and Freda Linton of the Wartime Information Board who had escaped before she could be arrested. These, and all those named in the interim reports, the Royal Commission stated, had been connected with the illegal activities of the Soviet embassy and either disclosed information themselves, conspired to do so, or were aware that others were doing so. A number of other persons were named as potential recruits in various stages of cultivation, as willing spies so imprudent that the Russians refused to employ them, or as people mentioned in the documents but against whom no hard evidence existed.

Justices Kellock and Taschereau spoke at length about Igor Gouzenko. They had been impressed — as undoubtedly will be readers of this book — with the manner in which he gave his evidence, and they stated that they had no hesitation whatever in accepting his evidence as factual. They provided details of Gouzenko's motives, his flight from the embassy, his adventures before he was taken in hand by the Canadian government, and the efforts of the embassy staff to discover his whereabouts. This was a spy novel become reality.

The commissioners also discussed the thorny legal questions they had faced in their inquiry, justifying their sometimes extraordinary actions on the grounds of the hostility of some of the witnesses and on the necessity of nipping the Soviet espionage system in Canada before it could infect healthy parts of the body politic.[26] They then presented the government with their recommendations for the coordination of security measures to prevent infiltration by Communists into positions of trust, and they also recommended that information presented before the Royal Commission not be revealed. More than 35 years were to pass before the Canadian government decided to open the transcripts of the evidence to public scrutiny; even then, exhibits and other material collected by the committee of officials that shaped the government's response to the Gouzenko disclosures remained sealed.

Of the major figures named in the *Report*, only Raymond Boyer, H.S. Gerson, Scott Benning, Gordon Lunan, Alan Nunn May (who was tried in Britain), Edward Mazerall, Durnford Smith, Kathleen Willsher, Emma Woikin, Sam Carr (after his arrest in the United States in 1949) and Fred Rose were found guilty and sentenced to penitentiary terms. Others were acquitted on appeal — and Eric Adams, Israel Halperin, Fred Poland, and David Shugar, among others, won their cases in court. Did acquittal verdicts throw doubt on the evidence brought by Gouzenko? Probably not. There were some legal problems in accepting as evidence stolen embassy materials,[27] the government was not always able — or willing — to introduce in court the evidence presented in secret to the Royal Commission, and if the accused did not make full and voluntary confessions there was often little evidence that the courts could use. Readers can judge for themselves weight-iness of the evidence.

As for Mackenzie King, a man who had had serious doubts about the path that Gouzenko's flight had set the Canadian government, in the end he had few doubts about Igor Gouzenko. When he met the young Gouzenko for the first time on July 16, 1946, he told him that "I thought that he had done a great service and wanted him to know that I appreciated his manliness, his courage and standing for the right."[28]

THE RESPONSE TO THE GOUZENKO CASE

The Canadian public was stunned by the revelation that the Soviet Union had been engaged in espionage in Canada. The Russians had been widely admired in the country since the Nazi invasion of the U.S.S.R. in June 1941 and the stout defence it had met, and a wide variety of Soviet-Canadian friendship societies had come into existence, as had organizations to send aid to the U.S.S.R. In June 1943, the Canadian Institute of Public Opinion had asked people if they thought Russia could be trusted "to cooperate with us when the war is over," and in substantial numbers Canadians indicated their good will. In Ontario, 62 percent trusted the Soviets and only 17 percent did not; nationally, the figures were 51 and 27 percent respectively, and in Quebec, the one province that retained its pre-war suspicions of the Communists, the figures were 30 and 44 percent respectively.[29] But after the deterioration in relations between the West and the Russians that followed V-E Day and after the Gouzenko case broke, opinion began to reverse very quickly. A poll in June 1946 asked Canadians if Russia sought to be the world's ruling power or simply sought protection against attack; 58 percent chose the first and forbidding option and only 29 percent selected the second. An earlier poll in April had found 52 percent with unfavourable attitudes to the U.S.S.R. and only 17 percent sympathetic to it.[30]

This shift in opinion from trust and good-will to fear and suspicion of the Soviet Union had been led by the press, at home and abroad. Unquestionably the Gouzenko affair was the greatest news story in years to emerge from Canada, and reporters from the United States, Britain, France and the Soviet Union flocked to Ottawa. At a press conference on February 21, 1946 at the Department of External Affairs, there were representatives of 32 newspapers, agencies or wire services in attendance — about four times as many as usually attended briefings there.[31] The Canadian media, naturally enough, gave much prominence to the story and to the interim and final *Reports* of the Kellock-Taschereau Royal Commission. The *Globe and Mail*, like other newspapers, was harsh on Communists who put "loyalty to party above loyalty to country" and argued that the wartime efforts at friendly relations with Moscow had deluded Canadians into a false perception of the Soviet Union's sincerity and good faith.[32] Later, the Toronto paper warned Canadians of the "sinister agencies" at work in their midst,[33] while Montreal's *Le Devoir* argued that the spy cases showed that the U.S.S.R. was in the process of destroying diplomacy, that its revolutionary communism was a danger to the world.[34] There seemed little desire anywhere — outside of the Communist press — to disagree with those kinds of comments.

There was also something approximating unanimity in the press and in Parliament in the response to the questions of civil liberties involved in the case.

The Leader of the Opposition denounced the government in the House of Commons on March 15, 1946 for denying the suspected spies access to *habeas corpus*. Canada, he said, was behind the government in its desire to punish crimes against the state, but the people "are not in sympathy with departure from the regular proceedings of the courts."[35] The *Globe and Mail* and the *Winnipeg Free Press* repeatedly argued in a similar vein, the *Globe* asking if the Royal Commission hearings were, in reality, "secret trials"[36] and accusing the government of gross violations of fundamental human rights.[37] The *Free Press* questioned the legality of government actions in using the War Measures Act as the basis of its conduct, telling its readers that "there are very strict limits beyond which a democratic government cannot and must not go."[38]

Did the Royal Commission exceed those limits? There is no doubt that the Justices and the Commission counsel dealt with witnesses in a peremptory fashion, and there is ample evidence of that in this book. On the other hand, it may seem clear to some readers that witnesses' near-total absence of recall amounted to amnesia, even when confronted with chapter and verse about their own activities. Facing such hostile witnesses, the counsel occasionally behaved more like prosecutors than as lawyers assisting the commissioners in assembling the evidence. Sometimes Justices Kellock and Taschereau dropped their impartiality and also pressed witnesses very sternly. Those of the suspects who withstood this type of questioning, who denied everything, and who on occasion even refused to be sworn, faced the commissioners with a difficult problem. So too did those who insisted on the right to counsel before testifying. Again, the text of this volume indicates some of these tussles.

Less defensible perhaps were the fishing expeditions that the counsel and commissioners regularly pursued, trying to determine who knew whom and whether that person was or was not sympathetic to leftist beliefs.[39] Where witnesses knew others connected with the espionage cases, this was understandable and proper; where names were sought of individuals who legally belonged to a political party or who held a particular set of beliefs, this verged on the unconscionable. On the other hand, as Justice Kellock's son angrily wrote to the *Globe and Mail* on November 12, 1981 when that newspaper sharply criticized the conduct of the 1946 inquiry, the commissioners were acting properly and in accord with the federal Inquiries Act. One standard source quoted by Kellock observed that a Commission "may be and ought to be a searching investigation — an inquisition as distinct from the determination of an issue." And the letter writer also made the point that witnesses under Canadian law do not have the right to refuse to answer questions on the grounds that the response might incriminate them. Finally, Kellock reminded the newspaper editors that the Royal Commission was investigating treason and had the duty to seek out the truth. There is much to be said for that position, too.

When the suspects complained of their treatment prior to their appearances before the Commission, Mr. Justice Kellock or his colleague invariably maintained that this was the responsibility of the Justice Department or the R.C.M.P. This was true, and there is less defence for the way the suspects were treated by those agencies of government. The suspects were arrested under the terms of a secret Order in Council, were held incommunicado, denied access for long periods to their families or their lawyers, and refused the right of *habeas corpus*. Before being tried, let alone found guilty, the suspects were denied the rights of citizenship. And after the interim reports and final *Report* of the Royal Commission appeared, their names were spread across the country, their reputations smeared — again, in many cases, before they were tried in court. The government's defence of its early actions was that if the suspects had been allowed to receive visitors they would also have been given orders not to talk. That may have been true, but it is questionable if the end in this case justified the means. There is even less to say for the government's decision to release the *Report* before all the cases had been heard in court. It is difficult to avoid the conclusion that the Canadian government, confronted with an extraordinary situation, reacted with arbitrary and harsh measures that threatened to ape the standards of the society that the Soviet spies were serving.

Ironically, Prime Minister Mackenzie King agreed with this position more than the public. Repeatedly King wrote in his diary of his efforts to hasten the Commission process so that the suspects could be dealt with immediately. Time after time, King expressed his concern over the breaches of civil liberties the commissioners were countenancing. On February 27, "I said that I thought it was wrong that those who are suspected should be detained indefinitely and that some way should be found to shorten the enquiry and give them the full rights of protection. . . ." King did more than merely grumble. On the same day he met with the Commission's counsel to press his position, but two weeks later he wrote that he and his Minister of Justice, Louis St. Laurent, "feel very indignant at the length of time the Commissioners are taking in detaining men; also we were both astonished that Kellock was going to adjourn sittings for some days to keep some engagements with a Y.M.C.A. meeting. . . . It seems to me that everybody is going crazy these days."[40] Possibly everyone was. An opinion poll on May 15 found that 93 percent of Canadians had heard of the cases and that 61 percent of those who had heard agreed that the government had handled the spy question in all its aspects wisely. Only 16 percent disagreed. King may have been troubled by the breaches of civil liberties; his electorate was not.[41]

Outside Canada, the press gave substantial attention to the sensational aspects of the case. "Editors of Communist, anti-Communist, nationalist or other persuasions cited each official statement and report as further proof of the wisdom of their own editorial policy," a summary of press comment prepared by the Department of External Affairs observed. The Communist press denounced Canada for its international political motives; the Soviet press stressed Russian technical superiority, downgrading the information received, and later reports accused Canada of creating a new *Reichstag* fire, a reference to the Nazi use of the burning of the parliament buildings in Berlin in 1933 as an excuse to crush the Communist party. In the United States, there were calls for purges of Reds in high places and demands for more stringent security against subversion.[42]

In official circles, the response was similar if less hysterical. Men like Norman Robertson and Hume Wrong of External Affairs were anxious to maintain good relations with the U.S.S.R. if possible and to prevent a witch-hunt in Canada.[43] On the other hand, both men became convinced advocates of the need for better security measures in Canada and anxious to ensure that friendly governments understood the lesson the Gouzenko case had taught. The Royal Commission's *Report* was circulated widely in Britain and the United States, and books based upon it were permitted and encouraged. Furthermore, a darker view of Soviet world intentions gained credence in the East Block. Russian actions in eastern Europe, at the United Nations Conference on International Organization at San Francisco, and at other international conferences had already spread concern, as had reports from the Canadian embassy in Moscow. The Gouzenko case fed the flames. Even so, Hume Wrong could still write in a top secret paper in June 1946 that while there were dangers from Moscow, "Soviet policy is defensive." Wrong expected recurrent crises, general insecurity, and the risk of local outbreaks in some parts of the world; he did not expect war for the foreseeable future.[44]

In Britain, the Gouzenko case was taken very seriously. The government encouraged publicity of the revelations of Soviet spying and drew the proper implications for its own security.[45] The High Commissioner in Ottawa sent long reports, stressing the way civil servants had been subverted, the use of Communist study groups to entrap the unwary, and the methods employed by Soviet diplomats in committing espionage. "It might be an interesting speculation," the High Commissioner noted, "to assess what might have been the effect of the spy enquiry in Canada on relations with Soviet Russia if that enquiry had not occurred at a time of steadily deteriorating relations between Russia and the Anglo-Saxon powers; as it was, however, the results of the enquiry were revealed in an atmosphere that was already vitiated and the events in Canada merely fitted into the general pattern as minor pieces in the game."[46]

In fact, some skeptics on the Left still believe that the Gouzenko case was an elaborate ruse designed to encourage the advent of the cold war. There is no evidence that this is so or that the Canadian government eagerly seized on the role that had been given to it to play. Indeed, there is some ground for believing that Canadian politicians and officials considered suppressing the Gouzenko evidence for fear that its release would worsen relations with the U.S.S.R.[47] The Drew Pearson broadcast that forced action on Canada may have been inspired by a Washington faction whose motives, although truth-seeking, were undoubtedly also anti-Soviet. But since Gouzenko's documents and recollections pointed the finger at senior officials in the Treasury and State Departments, there were probably sound reasons behind the leak to Pearson.[48] Certainly the Gouzenko case caused a "hullabaloo" in Washington, one that eventually played into the hands of "those everywhere," one writer later noted, "who were advocating a hard line toward Moscow."[49] The cold war was in creation, and the Gouzenko case had briefly put Ottawa on the map as one of its hot spots.

THE GOUZENKO CASE AND CANADIAN SECURITY

Inevitably, the Gouzenko case had implications for the way Canada treated security questions. In the Second World War the R.C.M.P. had carried out cursory "vetting" of applicants for civil and military posts, brief checks into antecedents, relatives and friends. That those checks were cursory surely was proven by the Royal Commission's evidence that demonstrated that active Communists held positions of trust. Perhaps there was some excuse for this. It was assumed that all Canadians wanted to see the defeat of the Axis and that only a relatively small number of German, Italian and Japanese nationals or naturalized Canadians were opposed to this national purpose. In the circumstances, vetting only rarely looked at ideological questions. But the Gouzenko affair made it clear to the Canadian government that such an attitude could no longer protect the secrets of the state and that ordinary Canadians, even those who had sworn an oath to serve Canada, could be attracted to Marxism and, while that in itself was not illegal, could be induced to pass information to the U.S.S.R.

As we have seen, the *Report* of the Royal Commission had recommended that the government take steps to improve security and prevent Communist infiltration. Even before the *Report* was received, in fact, government officials had begun studying the problem of security. In the late winter of 1946, the Cabinet Defence Committee considered such questions and a proposal submitted by the Army's Chief of the General Staff, Charles Foulkes, for an elaborate intelligence and security organization. That proposal was rejected; instead the ministers opted for a proposal of Norman Robertson's, one that established a Security Panel under the Clerk of the Privy Council and Secretary to the Cabinet, Arnold Heeney. The Under-Secretary of State for External Affairs' idea would bring together representatives of External Affairs, the R.C.M.P., the intelligence directors of the armed services, and the Director-General of Defence Research as a guiding and directing body on all matters of intelligence and security.[50]

The Security Panel was soon in operation and it quickly created a subcommittee charged with preparing recommendations on security for government departments. Each department was to appoint a security officer, each was to categorize certain positions as sensitive, and civil servants filling those posts would have to be screened. The R.C.M.P. clearly was about to expand its role — and its strength.[51] By the beginning of 1947 the Cabinet had approved the Security Panel's proposals.[52] Henceforth, the political views held by individuals could be deemed sufficient reason for firings, shiftings to less sensitive posts, or decisions to deny employment in the civil service.

If that sounded harsh and as an invasion of the civil liberties of the individual, the government position was that the state had both the right and the duty to protect itself from those whose goal was to subvert it. It also must be noted that the Canadian practice was less harsh than that in the United States, and designedly so. A Cabinet directive in March 1948 noted that "The establishment of precise and rigid standards for determining the 'loyalty' of government employees, along the lines adopted in the United States, is open to serious objection on grounds of principle and would not in fact ensure that only individuals reliable from the security standpoint are employed in the government service."[53] That was a sensible attitude, one that fitted in well with the normal attitudes of Canadians. And although some people — most notably in the National Film Board — were fired or made to resign, and although some officials — Herbert Norman of the Department of External Affairs comes most prominently to mind — ran into serious difficulties because of past political associations or beliefs, the effects of security screening in Canada generally were benign. Whether or not they were effective remains unknown.

There was another aspect of security that similarly arose out of the Gouzenko case — Canadian intelligence activities against the U.S.S.R. and its allies. During the war, the government had created the "Examination Unit" in the National Research Council, a team of cryptanalysts and wireless interceptors to watch, among other things, the activities of the Vichy French legation in Ottawa. By early

1945 as the war was drawing to its close, the future of the unit was in doubt.[54] But in December 1945, not long after Gouzenko's defection, a meeting of officials from External Affairs, the army and the N.R.C. decided to keep the unit functioning. By March 1946, plans were in hand to have almost 500 servicemen manning 100 high-speed monitoring positions. Their target, almost certainly, was the wireless traffic of the Soviet embassy. Soon other intelligence operations were being launched, directed at the U.S.S.R.'s northern radio communications. As L.B. Pearson, the Under-Secretary of State for External Affairs, wrote in February 1947, the purpose of "these stations is to intercept traffic upon which the cryptographers here, in London and in Washington work" and Canada, because of its relative closeness to the Soviet Arctic, was a useful base for such activity. The cost in 1947 was $3 million a year, all hidden in the estimates of the Defence Research Board. There was also no doubt that Canada was cooperating closely with the U.S. and U.K. in this work; there was even a wireless station at Oshawa, Ont., codenamed "Hydra", that linked the British Wireless Intelligence Service with that of the two North American nations.[55] The Gouzenko affair had helped to push Canada into areas in which it had never ventured before.

THE CONTINUING NATURE OF THE GOUZENKO CASE

There is a tendency today to assume that the information brought to the Canadian government by Gouzenko was relatively insignificant, that it revealed little more than that some Canadians were interested in seeing the U.S.S.R. get its fair access to the secrets its wartime allies were perfidiously keeping from it. In our view, the evidence presented to the Royal Commission and digested here does not support that interpretation. The U.S.S.R. had created at least one widespread spy network in the Canadian civil service and that network had produced significant information on industrial processes, scientific research, military matters, and atomic information. Equally important, had Gouzenko's defection not revealed the presence of spies, further information unquestionably would have made its way to the Soviet embassy. The other networks of which Gouzenko was aware were not uncovered; what they produced — and continue to produce — is unknown.

Gouzenko's evidence also pointed the finger at Soviet spies in the United States and the United Kingdom. In the United States, the Alger Hiss case of great notoriety sprang from Gouzenko's testimony; in Britain, Gouzenko's tales of papers he had seen suggested that a British "mole" codenamed "Elli" worked in MI-5. Just who Elli may have been is unclear, and there has been much written about this in 1981. According to Chapman Pincher in his *Their Trade is Treachery* (London, 1981), Elli was Sir Roger Hollis, the man who eventually rose to head MI-5 and who, ironically, had been sent to Canada to assist the R.C.M.P. and the government in handling the Gouzenko case. According to Pincher's account (and we do not find it very convincing), Hollis gave the British authorities misleading accounts of Gouzenko's information to protect himself. This sounds unlikely because, as we have seen, Norman Robertson and the prime minister had carried a full report of Gouzenko's evidence to London in the fall of 1945. If Hollis was Elli, and if Hollis tried to protect himself by distorting the Gouzenko evidence, then

Robertson's conversation with MI-5 would have caught him out. If Elli was not Hollis, who was he (or she)? That remains completely unclear, although given the presence of Soviet spies in high places in Britain — Burgess, Maclean, Philby, Blunt — there seems little reason to doubt Gouzenko.[56]

Finally, there is one Canadian footnote to this. The author Ian Adams in 1977 and 1981 produced a novel called *S: Portrait of a Spy* which was an account of a double agent inside the R.C.M.P. and the security service in the 1960s and 1970s. That novel, which became a civil liberties *cause célèbre* for reasons that need not concern us here, was clearly based on a wide knowledge of security questions, operations and personnel. In its concluding chapter, Adams has one of his characters refer to the "Taschereau Papers", the records of the Kellock-Taschereau Royal Commission:

> The Taschereau Papers? Some military intelligence type in the PM's office has spent the last year laundering the documents: destroying evidence, erasing names; generally rewriting history under the protection of our security laws.

We have uncovered no evidence of this laundering of evidence. If it had been skillfully done, however, we would not be able to do so. Fortunately, perhaps, novels, even non-fiction novels, are not the best of sources for history.

There is one final note to this story. Igor Gouzenko, whose revelations of Soviet spying had such fateful implications, died suddenly at his home near Toronto while this book was in the final stages. Gouzenko's death, while apparently of natural causes, was in some ways as mysterious as his life since September 1945 had been. In the first place, the date of his death was given variously as Monday, June 28, 1982 or at some time over the preceding weekend. Secondly, Gouzenko was buried in haste before any announcement was made. And finally, the newspapers printed photographs — unmasked — of Gouzenko and his wife, photos that they had apparently taken earlier but had not published. The mysterious Gouzenko saga at last seemed to have come to its end. Only assessments remain.

NOTES

1. See the analysis in David Caute, *The Fellow-Travellers* (London, 1973)
2. Pat Sullivan, *Red Sails on the Great Lakes* (Toronto, 1955), 71.
3. Quoted in I. Avakumovic, *The Communist Party in Canada: A History* (Toronto, 1975), 144.
4. *Ibid.*, 152.
5. *Ibid.*, 156.
6. Igor Gouzenko, *This Was My Choice* (Toronto, 1948), 213.
7. *Ibid.*, 215.
8. Interview with Senator Carl Goldenberg, a witness.
9. Margaret Gowing, *Britain and Atomic Energy, 1939–1945* (London, 1964), chapter 10.
10. Gouzenko, *Choice*, chapter 21; see also his testimony, below, 00–00.
11. J.W. Pickersgill and D.F. Forster, eds., *The Mackenzie King Record*, III (Toronto, 1970), 9.
12. *Ibid.*, 15; J.L. Granatstein, *A Man of Influence* (Ottawa, 1981), 173.
13. Pickersgill and Forster, *King Record*, III, 41.
14. J.L. Gaddis, *The United States and the Origins of the Cold War 1941–1947* (New York, 1972), 252–3.

15. Pickersgill and Forster, *King Record*, III, chapter 3.
16. *Ibid.*, 133.
17. *Mackenzie King Record*, III, 135.
18. *Ibid.*, 136.
19. *Ibid.*, 139.
20. *Documents on Canadian External Relations*, Vol. XII, 1946 (Ottawa, 1977), 2040.
21. *Ibid.*, 2041-2. There is some suggestion that Zabotin was executed for his failures in Canada. Public Record Office, London, Foreign Office Records, F0371/54705, Clutterbuck to Addison, 17 Aug 46. The 17 officials of the embassy eventually cited in the *Report of the Royal Commission* were withdrawn from Canada by the U.S.S.R. *Mackenzie King Record*, III, 281.
22. Printed with the *Report of the Royal Commission* as Appendix A.
23. Appendix B in *ibid.*
24. Appendix C in *ibid.*
25. Public Archives of Canada, W.L.M. King Papers, Diary, 14 Mar 46.
26. One critique of the commissioners' actions is M.H. Fyfe, "Some Legal Aspects of the Report of the Royal Commission on Espionage," *Canadian Bar Review*, XXIV (November, 1946).
27. See, e.g., "The Canadian Spy Case: Admissibility in Evidence of Stolen Embassy Documents," *University of Chicago Law Review*, XV (Winter, 1948).
28. *Mackenzie King Record*, III, 282.
29. *Public Opinion Quarterly*, (Fall, 1943), 505.
30. *Ibid.*, (Summer, 1946), 264-5.
31. PAC, Laurent Beaudry Papers, Press Conference Transcript, 21 Feb 46.
32. *The Globe and Mail*, 18 Feb 46.
33. *Ibid.*, 16 Mar 46.
34. *Le Devoir*, 19, 20 février 46.
35. House of Commons *Debates*, 15 Mar 46, p. 8.
36. *The Globe and Mail*, 21 Mar 46.
37. *Ibid*, 3 Apr 46.
38. *Free Press*, 11 Apr 46.
39. See *Globe and Mail*, 17 Oct 81 and the letter from B.H. Kellock in *ibid.*, 12 Nov 81.
40. *Mackenzie King Record*, III, 148, 150.
41. *Public Opinion Quarterly* (Summer, 1946), 265.
42. Beaudry Papers, Circular Letter, 1 Jun 46.
43. Department of External Affairs, John Holmes interview, 27 Jul 77.
44. PAC, Hume Wrong Papers, vol. 4, file 20, "The Possibility of War with the Soviet Union," 28 Jun 46.
45. Docs on Foreign Office Records, FO 371/56912-3.
46. *Ibid.*, FO 371/54705, Clutterbuck to Addison, 17 Aug 46.
47. J.W. Holmes, *The Shaping of Peace: Canada and the Search for World Order, 1943-57* (Toronto, 1982), II, 24ff.
48. See on the U.S. connection, James Barros, "Alger Hiss and Harry Dexter White: The Canadian Connection," *Orbis*, XXI (Fall, 1977). See also PAC, Department of External Affairs Records, vol. 2156, file C-1/3-3, vol. 2, Minute by Wrong, 3 Jul 53.
49. Robert Donovan, *Conflict and Crisis* (New York, 1977), pp. 171, 187.
50. Department of External Affairs, Records, file 50207-40, Memo Heeney to Robertson, 27 Apr 46 and Memo to Cabinet Defence Committee, 4 May 46. See also Granatstein, *A Man of Influence*, pp. 180ff.
51. Department of External Affairs file 50207-40, Memo for Security Panel, 16 Sep 46; Memo, G.G. Crean to Robertson, 12 Sep 46; Minutes of Security Panel, 23 Sep 46.
52. *Ibid.*, Memo, Heeney to Prime Minister, 6 Jan 47; Memo to Security Panel, 22 Jan 47; Memo to Security Panel, 15 May 47.
53. *Ibid.*, Cabinet Directive, 5 Mar 48.
54. Granatstein, pp. 190-1.
55. Based on docs in PAC, Privy Council Office Records, file C-30, PARC box 287330; file I-50-5, PARC box 287417.
56. See *Globe and Mail*, 6 Apr, 15 Oct 81.

THE GOUZENKO TRANSCRIPTS

THE TESTIMONY OF IGOR GOUZENKO

*In the Matter of an Inquiry under Part (I) of the
Inquiries Act, Chapter 99, R.S.C. 1927,
pursuant to Order in Council P.C. 411,
dated the 5th day of February, 1946.*

Present:

HON. R. TASCHEREAU, *Commissioner*
HON. R.L. KELLOCK, *Commissioner*
E.K. WILLIAMS, K.C., *Counsel*
GERALD FAUTEUX, K.C., *Counsel*
D.W. MUNDELL, *Counsel*
W.K. CAMPBELL, *Clerk*

February 13, 1946.

    MR. COMMISSIONER TASCHEREAU   Mr. Campbell, will you please read the Order in Council appointing the Commissioners
    MR. CAMPBELL   (Reads)

"P.C. 411 Certified to be a true copy of a Minute of a Meeting of the Committee of the Privy Council, approved by His Excellency the Governor General on the 5 February, 1946.

"The Committee of the Privy Council have had before them a report dated 5th February, 1946, from the Right Honourable W.L. Mackenzie King, the Prime Minister, representing:

"That it has been ascertained that secret and confidential information has been communicated directly or indirectly by public officials and other persons in positions of trust to the agents of a Foreign Power to the prejudice of the safety and interests of Canada;

"That by Order in Council P.C. 6444 dated the 6th day of October, 1945, the Acting Prime Minister and the Minister of Justice were authorized to make an Order that any such person be interrogated and/or detained in such place and under such conditions as the Minister might from time to time determine if the Minister were satisfied that it was necessary so to do;

"That it now seems expedient in the public interest that a full and complete inquiry be made into all the facts relating to and the circumstances surrounding the communication by such public officials and other persons in positions of trust of such secret and confidential information to the agents of a Foreign Power.

"The Committee, therefore, on the recommendation of the Prime Minister, advise that the Honourable Robert Taschereau, a Judge of the Supreme Court of Canada, and the Honourable R.L. Kellock, a Judge of the Supreme Court of Canada, be appointed Commissioners under Part I of the Inquiries Act, Chapter 99, Revised Statutes of Canada, 1927, and any other law thereto enabling, to inquire into and report upon such public officials and other persons in positions of trust or otherwise who have communicated, directly or indirectly, secret and confidential information, the disclosure of which might be inimical to the safety and interests of Canada, to the agents of a Foreign Power and the facts relating to and the circumstances surrounding such communication.

"The Committee further advise,—

"1. That for all such purposes and all purposes properly incidental thereto the said Commissioners shall without limiting the powers conferred upon them by the said Part I of the said Inquiries Act, have and possess the power of summoning and that they be empowered to summon before them any person or witness and of requiring them to give evidence on oath or affirmation, orally or in writing, and of requiring them to produce such documents and things as the Commissioners deem requisite to the full investigation of matters into which they are appointed to examine;

"2. That the said Commissioners be directed that a record shall be made of all the evidence which shall be given or produced before them as to the matters of the said inquiry and that the oral evidence of witnesses before the said Commissioners shall be taken in shorthand by a shorthand writer, approved and sworn by the said Commissioners or one of them and shall be taken down question and answer and it shall not be necessary for the evidence or deposition of any witness to be read over to or signed by the person examined and said evidence shall be certified by the person or persons taking the same as correct;

"3. That the said Commissioners may adopt such procedure and method as they may deem expedient for the conduct of such inquiry and may alter or change the same from time to time;

"4. That the said Commissioners be empowered in their discretion from time to time to make interim reports to the Governor in Council on any matter which in their judgment is the proper subject of such a report together with the evidence then before them and their findings thereon;

"5. That the said Commissioners be authorized to engage the services of such counsel and of such technical officers, and experts, and other experienced clerks, reporters and assistants as they may deem necessary and advisable; and

"6. That all the privileges, immunities and powers given by Order in Council, P.C. 1639 passed on the 2nd March, 1942, shall apply.

"(Sgd) A.D.P. Heeney
Clerk of the Privy Council.". . .

MR. WILLIAMS   With the approval of the Commissioners I would suggest that Mr. Gouzenko be sworn and that we proceed with the taking of his statement.

IGOR ZERGEVICH GOUZENKO, *called*

MR. COMMISSIONER TASCHEREAU   Do you wish to be sworn on that Bible?
GOUZENKO   Yes.
TASCHEREAU   The one you have there?
GOUZENKO   Yes.

The witness sworn

MR. WILLIAMS   Mr. Gouzenko, you both read and write the English language?
IGOR GOUZENKO   Yes.
WILLIAMS   And your native language is Russian?
GOUZENKO   Russian.
WILLIAMS   We have sworn Mr. Black as interpreter so that if there is anything that should come up where you would feel you would like to have the assistance of Mr. Black in translating technical names into English, or where there are any questions that are not entirely clear to you, he will help you out. We desire to take your evidence in English to as great an extent as possible. I shall be putting questions to you but if they are not entirely clear will you please tell me so?

The gentlemen at the head of the table are two judges of the Supreme Court of Canada. They have been appointed by the Governor in Council as Royal Commissioners to investigate the matters that arise out of your story and out of the documents you have produced.

The gentleman in front of you is taking down the whole proceedings in shorthand and that will be typed out later on. The evidence will be in permanent form.

The three of us at the table at which I am sitting have been appointed lawyers to assist the Commission. We will ask you questions from time to time, and either of the Commissioners will ask you questions as matters occur to him or ask us to ask you questions. I take it that you understand what is going on here.
GOUZENKO   I understand quite clearly.
WILLIAMS   That is splendid. We shall proceed. If I go too fast you tell me. First of all I understand that you were born in 1919?
GOUZENKO   That is right.
WILLIAMS   And in Russia?
GOUZENKO   Yes.
WILLIAMS   That is the Union of Socialist Soviet Republics?
GOUZENKO   That is right.
WILLIAMS   And in what part of Russia were you born?
GOUZENKO   It is near Moscow, the village of Rogochen.
WILLIAMS   Would you spell that for us?
GOUZENKO   I think it would be better to write it.
WILLIAMS   Did you live continuously in Russia until you came to Canada?

GOUZENKO   That is right.

WILLIAMS   You came to Canada when?

GOUZENKO   In 1943, in June. . . .

WILLIAMS   How did you come?

GOUZENKO   I came by plane through Moscow and through Fairbanks to Edmonton and from Edmonton to Ottawa by train; that is all.

WILLIAMS   Since you came to Ottawa have you been outside of Ottawa or have you lived here continuously?

GOUZENKO   Continuously inside Ottawa.

WILLIAMS   Will you just tell the commissioners the education that you had in Russia before you came here?

GOUZENKO   The first education was primary school; then secondary school, ten classes; then I started in the Architectural Institute in Moscow. Then I went to several schools and then I went to the Academy of Engineering in Moscow. I stayed there about two months and then a special commission was sent there to choose the best people for a special secret academy or school. This was a school of the Red Army. At that time we did not know actually it was a school. Only certain people was chosen for this purpose and until we was confirmed we did not know about it. It was a so-called high school, nobody knows about it here, but it is on the level of an academy. It is the higher school of the Red Army, it is a branch of the general staff of the Red Army.

WILLIAMS   It is some school maintained by a branch of the general staff?

GOUZENKO   To cover all branches of investigation of these cases and others.

WILLIAMS   I understood you to say it was a special secret school at which you got training in branches of investigation?

GOUZENKO   Yes. Everybody who was chosen for this school was investigated without his knowledge. I know I filled out several forms, the story of my birth, my parents and my friends. All the friends I know during this time. All this evidence was to go into these forms and later on was investigated to make sure I am a trusted man.

MR. COMMISSIONER KELLOCK   May I ask whether you are a member of the Communist party?

GOUZENKO   No, I am a member of the Young Communists. . . .

MR. KELLOCK   When did you enter it?

GOUZENKO   1936 I entered those Young Communists. . . .

MR. WILLIAMS   Is that what is called Komsomol?

GOUZENKO   Yes. . . .

WILLIAMS   Because of a lack of manpower after the war they allowed members of the Komsomol to enter these secret schools?

GOUZENKO   That is right.

WILLIAMS   And you entered one?

GOUZENKO   During about, I think two months, when the investigation was continued I just spent time in the barracks waiting the decision. So several men was rejected finally and a small group was entered. Finally we had the decision and we went to the school under Major General Krylov. Then I was told which class I was to go to. In this group there was men taken from the group of the engineering academy. We were sent to two classes, first decoding and coding groups. But this was not the last stage because the people who was allowed

26

to go in the coding group were waiting about five months for the decision of the N.K.V.D. to give them access to secret work.

WILLIAMS   What is the N.K.V.D.

GOUZENKO   That is the Department of Internal Affairs; previous it was called the O.G.P.U., but now it is the N.K.V.D. . . .

MR. COMMISSIONER TASCHEREAU   Is it a secret police?

GOUZENKO   Yes, it is a police. . . .

At this point an interpreter was engaged.

GOUZENKO   Each institution, school, plant, industrial plant, the Red Army and even the branches of the government, all have an official representative of the N.K.V.D. in the organization. He has a special room set apart, a secret room, where he does his business. And then he has his secret agents moving around amongst the workers, amongst the students, the school students, the school children, and amongst the employees of the various institutions in government and civil life. . . .

MR. WILLIAMS   Then at this stage I understand that N.K.V.D. are really the initials of four words?

GOUZENKO   Yes.

WILLIAMS   What are those four words?

GOUZENKO   It means People's Commissariat of Internal Affairs.

WILLIAMS   And it was the N.K.V.D. that investigated you before you were allowed to go into this secret school?

GOUZENKO   Yes; not only me, but everybody who was sent, and for everybody in the Red Army.

WILLIAMS   And then you, with some of the others from this school cf engineering
that you were attending, were admitted into the secret school?

GOUZENKO   Yes in the class, the deciphering class.

WILLIAMS   That is, you were taught to code and decode? . . .

GOUZENKO   For five months the students at this school were not allowed to engage themselves with the actual work of ciphering and deciphering, until final results of the investigations by the N.K.V.D. had come forward showing them trustworthy; and then they were allowed to engage in the work, they were given access to the ciphering. They were given access to secret work, but still not to the ciphering work. After five months they were given access to the cipher work, and during that five months several of the students were eliminated from the class.

WILLIAMS   When you were given access to the cipher work, did that mean that you were given access to the codes that you would use?

GOUZENKO   During the time they were learning the cipher work they were given access to old codes that were not in use at the present time, for training purposes.

WILLIAMS   How long did you spend in this school altogether?

GOUZENKO   Altogether it is about nine months. As they were being prepared for this code work for the front they were at the same time also taught tactical subjects and being prepared for such positions as commander of a division and so on, and practical work along statistical lines for later use at the front.

WILLIAMS   When you completed your course in the school, where were you sent?

GOUZENKO   From the school a group of the students were sent to the main intelligence division of the Red Army in Moscow.

WILLIAMS   Were you one of those?

GOUZENKO   Yes. At that time the front required a large number of cipher workers, at the front. There was a sort of pool through which those students passed in quick succession and were sent off to the front. . . .

WILLIAMS   How long did you remain there?

GOUZENKO   It is about one year. . . . Towards the end of 1942 they began to select cipherers for sending abroad, and they had also decided to send me abroad, but they had not determined which country I was to be sent to. My documentation took approximately half a year before they decided to send me abroad. The documentation consists of filling in forms, which forms again are investigated by the N.K.V.D. until they are satisfied that the individual who is being selected for this job is trustworthy. The documentation goes through the different departments until finally the final stage is the central executive committee of the Communist party, with the signature of the official in the central executive committee. That is the final signature on the documentation, which practically gives sanction to this individual to be sent abroad.

There is a branch of the central executive committee known as the foreign branch, the head of which is a man called Malenkov, and his signature is required on persons of importance who are being sent abroad. Persons of less importance are attended to by a man whose name is Gussarov. He is at present in Ottawa at the Russian embassy. My documentation was signed finally by Gussarov in Moscow. All those who are sent abroad receive a legend composed for the purpose of covering the fact that they are employed in intelligence work.

WILLIAMS   You use the term "legend." Would that be what we would call a certificate? What is it? Will you describe it?

GOUZENKO   This legend consists of a fictitious biography of the individual, showing that he was born at a certain place, that he received a certain education, that he received certain training, all with the object of covering up the fact that he is engaged in intelligence work. Another object of compiling this legend is so as to make it impossible for the representatives of foreign powers in Moscow to check up on the data given about the individual.

MR. COMMISSIONER KELLOCK   I suppose to complete that, what happens to it? Does he carry it on his person? Do you carry it on your person, or what happens to it?

GOUZENKO   No. The individual must learn this legend by heart. The document itself is kept in a secret safe in the military intelligence division.

MR. COMMISSIONER TASCHEREAU   In Moscow?

GOUZENKO   Yes. All documents which are required to be filled in and signed for travel abroad are filled in from the data in this legend. In the beginning of 1943 the staff for the military attaché in Ottawa had already been prepared for sending to Ottawa.

MR. COMMISSIONER KELLOCK   I do not understand that. . . .

GOUZENKO   The military attaché's office was established in Ottawa on my arrival with the military attaché, Colonel Zabotin.

MR. WILLIAMS   How many of you came at that time, when you and Colonel

Zabotin arrived? Were there others on the military attaché's staff who came with you?

GOUZENKO   At that time Colonel Zabotin, the military attaché arrived, and Major Romanov, his secretary, and myself.

WILLIAMS   So there were three of you?

GOUZENKO   Yes, the first time; and the rest of the employees arrived approximately two months later by ship.

MR. COMMISSIONER KELLOCK   That would be August of 1943?

GOUZENKO   Yes. . . .

MR. WILLIAMS   When you arrived in Ottawa were you a married man?

GOUZENKO   Yes.

WILLIAMS   Did your wife accompany you?

GOUZENKO   No, she didn't accompany me, because the wives of the personnel of the military attaché arrived later, on a ship. They arrived with the balance of the staff.

WILLIAMS   What year were you married?

GOUZENKO   1943. . . .

WILLIAMS   And what are the names of your wife?

GOUZENKO   Svetlana Gouzenko.

WILLIAMS   And did you have a family when you came to Ottawa?

GOUZENKO   No, I did not.

WILLIAMS   But since then you have had two children?

GOUZENKO   Yes.

WILLIAMS   The older is how old?

GOUZENKO   The oldest is now two years and two months old, and the younger one is two months old. One is a boy; the older one is a boy, and the baby is a girl.

WILLIAMS   When you left Russia did you speak any English?

GOUZENKO   I spoke a little, but poorly.

WILLIAMS   You had received instruction in English in the Russian schools?

GOUZENKO   Yes, the school of preparation.

WILLIAMS   And had you received instruction in any other languages? Do you speak any other languages than Russian and English?

GOUZENKO   I read in German, but I speak very badly in German. I also learned that at school.

WILLIAMS   You were brought here, then, to be a cipher clerk in the military attaché's department?

GOUZENKO   That is right. . . .

WILLIAMS   Were you the only cipher clerk in the military attaché's department during the time you were here?

GOUZENKO   Yes.

MR. COMMISSIONER KELLOCK   Did you hold any military rank when you came here?

GOUZENKO   Yes, but it was not an official title. I held a military rank, but it was not on the documents.

KELLOCK   What was the rank?

GOUZENKO   Lieutenant.

MR. WILLIAMS   In the Russian army?

GOUZENKO   Yes.

WILLIAMS   When you took over your duties as cipher clerk, were you given a new code to work with?

GOUZENKO   The code was handed over to me by the first secretary of the embassy, who was the chief intelligence officer of the embassy prior to the arrival of the military attaché.

WILLIAMS   What was his name?

GOUZENKO   Koudriavtzev.

WILLIAMS   Had you been familiar with the code that he gave you, before?

GOUZENKO   Yes.

WILLIAMS   Where did you do your work in the Russian embassy?

GOUZENKO   On the second floor, in the so-called secret cipher branch.

WILLIAMS   And that is in the embassy building at 285 Charlotte Street in Ottawa?

GOUZENKO   That is right.

MR. COMMISSIONER TASCHEREAU   Did you live there yourself?

GOUZENKO   No, I lived on Somerset Street, 511.

MR. WILLIAMS   You drew up a little sketch showing the location in the Russian embassy of the secret cipher room in which you worked?

GOUZENKO   Yes. . . .

WILLIAMS   You were in room 12?

GOUZENKO   Yes.

WILLIAMS   Your duties as cipher clerk were carried out entirely in room 12, were they?

GOUZENKO   Yes.

WILLIAMS   And how was that room equipped? What was there in it?

GOUZENKO   A table; four chairs; a safe; a wooden filing cabinet. That is all. The safe was steel.

WILLIAMS   Now will you just briefly describe your duties as cipher clerk?

GOUZENKO   My duties were to cipher the telegrams that were sent by Colonel Zabotin, and to decipher telegrams that arrived from Moscow to Colonel Zabotin.

MR. COMMISSIONER KELLOCK   Zabotin did not know this cipher?

GOUZENKO   No. Zabotin was obliged to knock on the door before he could enter the room where I work, and if I wanted I could refuse to allow him to enter.

MR. WILLIAMS   Where were your code books kept?

GOUZENKO   The code books were kept in a sealed bag, which I handed to the chief of that division, Aleksashkin. . . .

MR. COMMISSIONER TASCHEREAU   In Ottawa?

GOUZENKO   Yes.

MR. WILLIAMS   At the embassy?

GOUZENKO   Yes.

WILLIAMS   Do you mean you received them from him in the morning and handed them to him at night?

GOUZENKO   The procedure was as follows. I would ring the secret bell and a little aperture in the steel door would be opened and Aleksashkin would look through. I would then ask him if there were any telegrams, and if there were any telegrams I would get him the sealed sack with the code and the telegrams. If Colonel

Zabotin wished to send some telegrams to Moscow, I would ask him for the bag, the sealed sack. . . .

WILLIAMS   And when you had finished your coding, what would you do with the code?

GOUZENKO   I placed the code back in the sack and sealed it with my seal and took the sack back to Aleksashkin.

WILLIAMS   And what would you do with the originals of the telegrams or other communications that you had coded?

GOUZENKO   The originals were placed in a file and the file, along with the code, was placed in the pouch, the sealed pouch.

WILLIAMS   So that when you had finished your work and turned the pouch back to Aleksashkin you had no documents yourself, and no code?

GOUZENKO   No code.

WILLIAMS   And would the same process be followed when cables or telegrams had come in from outside to be decoded?

GOUZENKO   Yes, the same.

WILLIAMS   Did you keep anything at all in room 12, then?

GOUZENKO   Yes, there were very secret things kept in that room; reports from agents and reports on contacts with agents; also Colonel Zabotin's secret diary wherein he noted contacts with agents. The safe was sealed with my seal in addition to the usual combination, which I knew and Colonel Zabotin knew.

WILLIAMS   Could the safe be opened by either of you, or did the two of you have to be present to open it?

GOUZENKO   I could open it alone, because I had the seal.

WILLIAMS   Was it a seal or combination; which?

GOUZENKO   The combination was just the handle combination.

WILLIAMS   And was it only your seal that was put on when the safe was closed?

GOUZENKO   Yes, that is the only one.

WILLIAMS   Not Colonel Zabotin's?

GOUZENKO   No.

WILLIAMS   So that if the safe were closed by yourself, with your seal put on it, could Colonel Zabotin open it without you being there?

GOUZENKO   He couldn't, because he would have to break my seal.

WILLIAMS   How was your seal put on; what kind of seal was it?

GOUZENKO   My seal was made of bronze with the figure of a church on it.

WILLIAMS   And how was it attached to the safe? How was it put on?

GOUZENKO   The seal was placed on the top left-hand corner.

WILLIAMS   Just a moment; we have to get this so it can be taken down. You placed your seal on the upper left-hand corner of the door of the safe; is that right?

GOUZENKO   That is right.

WILLIAMS   And how did you place it; did you screw it in or how?

GOUZENKO   Wax.

WILLIAMS   So you put wax on the place where you were going to put the seal, and then impressed your bronze seal on that wax?

GOUZENKO   Yes.

WILLIAMS   And the safe could not be opened without breaking that seal? Did you have any duties in connection with the destruction from time to time of any of the telegrams or other documents in room 12?

GOUZENKO   Yes. From time to time I would ask Colonel Zabotin what documents he wished to have destroyed, and he would mark the documents that were to be destroyed, after which I compiled a list of the documents that were to be destroyed showing that they had been destroyed, and after each document Colonel Zabotin and myself would place our initials, and then after that Colonel Zabotin and myself would go and destroy the documents.

WILLIAMS   Are these documents that you are talking about ones that were kept in the safe in room 12, or were they kept elsewhere?

GOUZENKO   This refers only to telegrams which had been in the pouch, in the secret pouch.

WILLIAMS   Let us go over this just a little more. When a telegram was to be sent to Moscow it would be given to you for coding. You would get it from Colonel Zabotin?

GOUZENKO   Yes. . . .

WILLIAMS   Then when you had to code that telegram, you would get the code book from Aleksashkin?

GOUZENKO   Yes.

WILLIAMS   When you had translated it from Russian into the code, you would give the original telegram to whom?

GOUZENKO   The procedure was as follows. Colonel Zabotin would write out the telegram in Russian, and after that he could go, he could leave the room. I would code this telegram and hand the coded telegram to Aleksashkin for sending by the usual channels, through the cable office. After that I would put the original telegram and the coded copy back into the pouch and give it back to Aleksashkin, sealed.

WILLIAMS   So you kept nothing at all; you did not keep the original written by Colonel Zabotin?

GOUZENKO   In that room?

WILLIAMS   Yes.

GOUZENKO   No.

MR. COMMISSIONER KELLOCK   As I follow it up to this moment, if it is important, Zabotin wrote out the telegram and handed it to the witness. The witness wrote out another document, which was the telegram in code. Was that one copy or two copies?

MR. WILLIAMS   (To the witness)   How many copies of the coded telegram?

GOUZENKO   Only one.

KELLOCK   All right. Then what went to the cable office?

THE INTERPRETER   The code.

MR. WILLIAMS   (To the witness)   Everything you had you gave to Aleksashkin?

KELLOCK   But before that the witness said that something went to the cable office.

GOUZENKO   That is right.

KELLOCK   (To the witness)   What was that?

GOUZENKO   It is the finished coded telegram, on the Canadian Pacific or Canadian National telegraphs, in a series of letters or figures.

KELLOCK   As I understand it, then, the witness copied in code on a piece of paper on the typewriter from the document that was handed him. That is right?

GOUZENKO   That is right.

KELLOCK   Then he had two pieces of paper, one of Zabotin's and one made by the witness. Then what happened?

GOUZENKO   The document which was written by Zabotin was placed in the pouch along with the code.

KELLOCK   Both documents, the one prepared by Zabotin and the one prepared by the witness were put in this pouch?

GOUZENKO   No, Colonel Zabotin wrote out the telegram in Russian and I coded that telegram, making a draft copy first, and then typed it out on Canadian Pacific or Canadian National telegraph forms, which went to Aleksashkin for despatch to the telegraph company. Colonel Zabotin's original telegram or document was placed in the bag, in the sealed bag, and handed to Aleksashkin.

KELLOCK   And what happened to the draft which was prepared?

GOUZENKO   It was burned.

MR. COMMISSIONER TASCHEREAU   Did you keep any copies of the coded telegrams which you prepared?

GOUZENKO   Sometimes I kept a copy of the original telegram, but sometimes there were questions about these and then he could always check up on his copy. . . .

MR. WILLIAMS   When you had done your work of coding and turned over the pouch, you had nothing left in Room 12. These documents which you destroyed from time to time, what were they and where were they kept?

GOUZENKO   They were kept also in the same pouch.

WILLIAMS   I do not mean the ones you destroyed at the time you were coding or decoding, but you were telling us about the destruction of documents, about Colonel Zabotin having said to destroy certain documents. Where were those documents kept that were to be destroyed?

GOUZENKO   In the same sack, where the telegrams were kept.

WILLIAMS   Let us take it this way. When you came to the Mounted Police last September for their protection you had certain documents with you?

GOUZENKO   Yes.

WILLIAMS   If I may just have those telegrams I will get you to explain them. You had with you when you came a number of blue sheets upon which were written telegrams that would be handed to you for decoding?

GOUZENKO   That is right.

WILLIAMS   I show you the first one. This document is written in Russian and is in whose handwriting?

GOUZENKO   Zabotin's.

WILLIAMS   It is the first draft of the telegram, and is dated what day?

GOUZENKO   July 12, 1945.

WILLIAMS   This was a telegram to be sent to whom?

GOUZENKO   It is to the nickname of the chief of the first intelligence headquarters, Major General Bolshakov.

WILLIAMS   At the bottom is a signature?

GOUZENKO   Yes.

WILLIAMS   What is that?

GOUZENKO   It is Grant, the nickname of Colonel Zabotin.

WILLIAMS   This document came to you in this form from Colonel Zabotin?
GOUZENKO   Yes. . . .
WILLIAMS   You said nickname, do you mean code name?
GOUZENKO   I do not know the translation; the literal translation is nickname.
WILLIAMS   It is the name that is used to disguise the real person?
GOUZENKO   That is right.
WILLIAMS   This would be one that would have come to you on this date, July 12, 1945. Would you get it from Colonel Zabotin and would you turn it into code?
GOUZENKO   Yes. . . .
WILLIAMS   Then would you first of all make your coded telegram by writing it out in handwriting or how did you do it, did you immediately type it on the typewriter?
GOUZENKO   I made a draft by hand.
WILLIAMS   You would write it out by hand but in code?
GOUZENKO   There are three stages; it was done in three stages, and the final stage was when it was translated into the letters or figures.
WILLIAMS   Then when you had got your code complete you would then type it on the typewriter, would you?
GOUZENKO   Yes. . . .
WILLIAMS   Then you would put this blue document, the typewritten document, and the code into the pouch?
GOUZENKO   That is right.
WILLIAMS   And you would usually destroy the draft of your codification?
GOUZENKO   That is right.
WILLIAMS   But sometimes you would keep it?
GOUZENKO   Yes.
WILLIAMS   Then this blue document and the typewritten document and the code would go back to Aleksashkin?
GOUZENKO   Yes.
WILLIAMS   In the pouch?
GOUZENKO   In the sealed pouch.
WILLIAMS   Now then, when you later on got these blue documents, where did you get them from? Where were they when you got them?
GOUZENKO   They were also in the sealed pouch, but I took the pouch to my room; that is all.
WILLIAMS   What I wanted to ask you was this: This blue document was one you had with you when you came to the police for protection?
GOUZENKO   Yes.
WILLIAMS   What I wanted to know is when you got it to bring it with you?
GOUZENKO   This particular document is different from the others.
WILLIAMS   I am just using this one as an example. What I wanted to find out was what happened to it after it passed out of your possession. When you coded them where did they go to so that you could get them later on and bring them with you? Do you understand what I want to get at?
GOUZENKO   Yes.
WILLIAMS   I am just using this as an example.
GOUZENKO   From the same pouch.

WILLIAMS   Does that mean that all of the blue documents would be kept in one pouch, or are there different pouches?

GOUZENKO   The same pouch. . . .

WILLIAMS   They are kept in that pouch how long?

GOUZENKO   It depends on when Colonel Zabotin would tell me to destroy them.

MR. COMMISSIONER KELLOCK   (*To Mr. Williams*)   I am not following that. I understood that when the witness was through with his coding and he put this document into the pouch with the code book, that he then handed the pouch back to Aleksashkin.

WILLIAMS   Yes.

KELLOCK   Where was Aleksashkin?

WILLIAMS   (*To the witness*)   Where did Aleksashkin take the pouch to?

GOUZENKO   There is a big safe where Aleksashkin kept all the documents belonging to the — all the sacks belonging to the military intelligence in the embassy and N.K.V.D. and the political branch, and there was also a big incinerator for destroying documents.

MR. COMMISSIONER KELLOCK   Where was this safe and incinerator?

GOUZENKO   Room 14 the safe was, and the incinerator was in the same room. . . .

MR. WILLIAMS   In order to get these blue documents, the first one of which I have shown you, you would need to go to Room 14?

GOUZENKO   No, I have no right to go to Room 14. The only one who has the right to go into that room is Aleksashkin, chief of the secret division, but I can ask him for my pouch, the sealed sack and he will give me the sack.

WILLIAMS   That is how you did it; that is how you got these blue documents, of which I have shown you one?

GOUZENKO   Yes.

WILLIAMS   You asked Aleksashkin for the sack?

GOUZENKO   For work; I asked for work. . . .

WILLIAMS   When you did destroy documents were you and Zabotin together?

GOUZENKO   Yes.

WILLIAMS   Did there have to be the two of you?

GOUZENKO   He simply stood by and watched while I threw the documents into the incinerator, but he was very inattentive in watching the process. . . .

WILLIAMS   The incinerator is the one in Room 14, is it?

GOUZENKO   That was the same incinerator. In Room 17 there was a smaller incinerator. That is where we destroyed our documents because we have not access to Room 14.

WILLIAMS   Did Aleksashkin have the right to look into the pouch in which the code book and the telegrams were?

GOUZENKO   No, absolutely no; he cannot break my seal.

WILLIAMS   When you put the coded telegrams into the sack, the one that was to be sent, and handed it to Aleksashkin he would have to take it to somebody else, would he, to send it to the telegraph office?

GOUZENKO   He takes the coded telegram from my hand.

WILLIAMS   It does not go into the sack?

GOUZENKO   No.

WILLIAMS   And Aleksashkin cannot get into the sack without breaking your seal?

GOUZENKO   Yes. . . .

WILLIAMS   You said that you would describe the set-up of the various departments in the military attaché's department and so forth. We have charts which have been made up from the information that you have furnished us and I think probably it would be simpler if we put one of these charts in front of you and have you explain it to the Commissioners. . . . On the right-hand side of this chart is shown the set-up of the office of the Russian military attaché at Ottawa?

GOUZENKO   That is right.

WILLIAMS   And at the head of that department is Colonel Zabotin to whom reference has been made already?

GOUZENKO   Yes.

WILLIAMS   You and he came to Ottawa at the same time?

GOUZENKO   And Romanov, the three men.

WILLIAMS   Then Colonel Zabotin has as chief assistant, Motinov?

GOUZENKO   Yes. . . .

WILLIAMS   He came after you, did he?

GOUZENKO   In August, 1943.

WILLIAMS   Then there is shown on the chart two assistants, one is just marked assistant and under-assistant, on the left-hand side?

GOUZENKO   Those are vacant places.

WILLIAMS   Where no name is indicated the position is vacant?

GOUZENKO   Right.

WILLIAMS   Then on the right side is shown Assistant Air Force, with the name L.C. Rogov, and an under-assistant with the name vacant?

GOUZENKO   Vacant.

WILLIAMS   How long has Rogov been in that position?

GOUZENKO   I think he came in the beginning of 1944.

WILLIAMS   Then there is an adjutant, and that position is vacant?

GOUZENKO   Vacant.

WILLIAMS   Below the adjutant is shown a secretary where the name has been filled in with Lieutenant Angelov?

GOUZENKO   Angelov.

WILLIAMS   And the shading in that block marked "Secretary" indicates what, the difference in the shading?

GOUZENKO   That indicates that it is my opinion that he is the agent of the N.K.V.D. in the military attaché's organization.

WILLIAMS   Then next are the interpreters, only one of which is filled in, and there is reference there to Under-Lieutenant Levin?

GOUZENKO   Under-Lieutenant.

WILLIAMS   Then there is Chief Guard with no name; does that mean — ?

GOUZENKO   That is vacant. The same as interpreter and under-assistant.

WILLIAMS   Then there is a door guard, Captain Galkin?

GOUZENKO   Yes.

MR. COMMISSIONER KELLOCK   Is he a captain in the Red Army?

GOUZENKO   Yes, but he is a civilian official, of course, here. . . .

MR. WILLIAMS   Then there is a door guard shown as Lieutenant-Technical Gouseev?

GOUZENKO   I do not think that is Gouseev; that is mistake. Gouseev is an agent.

WILLIAMS   We are dealing with the door guard, Lieutenant-Technical Gouseev, and it is possible that he may be an N.K.V.D. man.

GOUZENKO   Yes.

WILLIAMS   Then we come to two drivers, one marked Lieutenant Gourshkov. That marking indicates what?

GOUZENKO   Also possibly an N.K.V.D. man.

WILLIAMS   Then there is another driver, Under-Lieutenant Louvrentyev. Then there is a cook, and a typist, Mrs. Gourshkov, who is the wife of Lieutenant Gourshkov the driver?

GOUZENKO   Yes.

WILLIAMS   Then there are waiters and a charwoman, who is shown as Mrs. Galkin, who is the wife of Captain Galkin, the door guard?

GOUZENKO   Yes. . . .

MR. COMMISSIONER TASCHEREAU   Do all these people live in the same house?

GOUZENKO   No, they work in the same house.

TASCHEREAU   They work in the same house?

GOUZENKO   But live in separate houses in Ottawa.

TASCHEREAU   Oh, yes. Is that the place where they work?

GOUZENKO   14 Range Road.

MR. WILLIAMS   When did Under-Lieutenant Levin come, was that before or after you came to the embassy?

GOUZENKO   After.

WILLIAMS   How long after, do you know?

GOUZENKO   I think it was the middle of the summer of 1944.

WILLIAMS   Then Captain Galkin, the door guard, when did he come, do you recall?

GOUZENKO   Before Levin.

WILLIAMS   Then Lieutenant Gouseev, did he come after you?

GOUZENKO   Yes, he came after me.

WILLIAMS   Can you recall when?

GOUZENKO   I think the winter of 1944, the beginning of 1944.

WILLIAMS   Then Lieutenant Gourshkov; did he come before or after you?

GOUZENKO   After me; he came in August, 1943.

WILLIAMS   And the star beside his position indicates what? . . .

GOUZENKO   He has been marked important because the car that he is using, that he drives, is used for making contacts with agents and he would therefore know the agents by sight and possibly recognize them.

WILLIAMS   That is, he would have to recognize those people. . . .

GOUZENKO   Yes. As far as I know he has no right to know those, because he is only a driver, but he would see.

WILLIAMS   He would drive some other people from the embassy to meet agents; is that the idea?

GOUZENKO   Yes.

WILLIAMS   And the result would be that Gourshov would recognize the people?

GOUZENKO   Some.

WILLIAMS   But it was not his part to know who they were, what their real names were or their nicknames?

GOUZENKO   He just drives. . . .

MR. COMMISSIONER TASCHEREAU   Occasionally Zabotin goes to the embassy for the purpose of sending telegrams?

GOUZENKO   That is right.

TASCHEREAU   That is the only reason why he goes there, on business?

GOUZENKO   Of course, he may go to have a talk with the ambassador or he may go there for dinner.

TASCHEREAU   I mean for business, for the purpose of business?

GOUZENKO   That is the only business.

TASCHEREAU   You were under Zabotin?

GOUZENKO   Yes.

TASCHEREAU   How is it that you are not on this chart if you were working for Zabotin?

GOUZENKO   The top part of the chart is the embassy, and from Zabotin down is the military attaché. I work in the embassy.

MR. WILLIAMS   If your name appeared on this chart in what position would it be?

GOUZENKO   Here (indicating).

WILLIAMS   In other words, going up on the right-hand side we see the square Military with Lieutenant Koulakov or Angelov?

GOUZENKO   Yes.

WILLIAMS   Lieutenant Koulakov was designated as your successor?

GOUZENKO   That is right.

MR. COMMISSIONER KELLOCK   Is the Angelov there the same Angelov that is shown down below under Zabotin?

GOUZENKO   That is right.

KELLOCK   So that all these people may work at Range Road or they may be in the embassy?

GOUZENKO   Yes. . . .

MR. WILLIAMS   Some time in 1945 you received instructions to return to Moscow. I understand that your successor was designated and was sent to Ottawa before you were supposed to leave?

GOUZENKO   Yes.

WILLIAMS   What was the name of your successor?

GOUZENKO   Lieutenant Koulakov.

WILLIAMS   Do you recall when you received word that you were returning to Moscow?

GOUZENKO   Yes. The first time it was received, I think in the summer of 1944 or in the late fall, 1944, but Colonel Zabotin requested Moscow to leave me in Canada because I was a good worker and knew the English language. Moscow left me on the same work as before. Lieutenant-Colonel Zabotin asked Moscow to give him an assistant and suggested that Angelov be my assistant, that he had done this work before. Moscow decided in favour of the proposal and allowed Angelov to have access to the secret files and documents in the sack. But Angelov never actually went into the office because there was not sufficient work and he was being held in reserve. I take that Angelov's name

38

on the chart as having access to the secret information, although he may not actually be engaged in that work as Koulakov was also.

WILLIAMS   We are coming down now to the time when you got notice to report back to Moscow in 1945; what was that date?

GOUZENKO   Moscow asked the second time to have me sent back to Russia in May, 1945, and Zabotin replied to Moscow that it would not be convenient to hand my work over to Angelov as Moscow had suggested, that it would be better to await my replacement, and the arrival of my replacement, Lieutenant Koulakov before handing over the affairs of my work.

WILLIAMS   In May, when Moscow suggested that you be recalled they notified Ottawa at the same time that Koulakov would succeed you, did they?

GOUZENKO   That time they did not, not in May.

WILLIAMS   When did you first hear that Koulakov was to succeed you?

GOUZENKO   Around May 17 they advised from Moscow that my replacement Koulakov would be leaving Moscow.

WILLIAMS   And when did Koulakov arrive in Ottawa?

GOUZENKO   I do not know exactly; in July, 1945, I think.

WILLIAMS   And did you instruct him as to what you had been doing so that you could turn it over to him?

GOUZENKO   He waited approximately for a month before Moscow gave him permission to enter the room where this work was being carried on. . . .

WILLIAMS   After he was given permission to enter the room did you continue to enter it and work with him?

GOUZENKO   During that time I did the work and he looked on and saw how the work was being performed.

MR. COMMISSIONER KELLOCK   He was not in the room?

GOUZENKO   That was after the fortnight. We also prepared the necessary forms for transferring the documents to Koulakov.

MR. WILLIAMS   Then you received definite instructions as to the time you were to leave for Moscow, did you?

GOUZENKO   Several times Moscow demanded that I should be sent home and Colonel Zabotin, under various pretexts, put off the departure and alleged that it took a long time to hand over all business to my replacement, and then I myself drew the whole thing out as much as possible because I wished to find out why Moscow wanted me back in Russia.

WILLIAMS   So finally a definite date was fixed when you were told you must go?

GOUZENKO   Yes, Moscow finally sent a telegram. I was to leave in company with Zheveinov and with the son of Zabotin.

WILLIAMS   That Zheveinov is the man shown under Tass on Exhibit 15?

GOUZENKO   Yes.

WILLIAMS   And was a definite date fixed for that departure?

GOUZENKO   No, there was no definite date set because there was no available steamer. In the meantime the war with Japan complicated things and they were awaiting available accommodation on the steamer.

WILLIAMS   Were you making your preparations to leave to go back to Moscow?

GOUZENKO   Yes, as soon as the first telegram came I began to make preparations for departure to Moscow.

WILLIAMS   What was the nature of those preparations?

GOUZENKO   Buying of foodstuffs and clothing and all kinds of things of which there were none in Russia. . . .

WILLIAMS   Now, you came to the Mounted Police with a request for protection in the month of September 1945?

GOUZENKO   That is right.

WILLIAMS   Do you recall the date?

GOUZENKO   It was September 7.

WILLIAMS   And at that time you had with you a number of documents. That is right, is it not?

GOUZENKO   That is right.

WILLIAMS   And among the documents that you had was one which I am showing you now, which is a typewritten document, typed in Russian. You recognize that?

GOUZENKO   Yes. . . .

WILLIAMS   And the title in Russian, translated into English, reads how?

GOUZENKO   "A list of materials sent to the address of the director in January (5th) 1944."

WILLIAMS   I will mark this now, because I want to ask a number of questions about it . . .   (*To the witness*)   The month is written in handwriting?

GOUZENKO   That is right.

WILLIAMS   Do you know whose handwriting that is?

GOUZENKO   I think it is Lieutenant-Colonel Motinov.

MR. COMMISSIONER KELLOCK   When he says he thinks, does he know or does he not?

WILLIAMS   Do you know Lieutenant-Colonel Motinov's writing?

GOUZENKO   Yes, I know it very well.

WILLIAMS   And can you think it would be anybody else's writing, other than his?

GOUZENKO   I don't think so. It is too short; there is not enough writing to be able to say definitely.

WILLIAMS   (*To Mr. Kellock*)   I may say there will be other writing.

KELLOCK   I just wondered if I understood what the witness meant. Sometimes when a witness says he thinks, he really knows; but this witness means that he thinks.

WILLIAMS   Yes, because there is very little of it.   (*To the witness*)   And this is a form which is filled in from time to time, is it not?

GOUZENKO   That is right.

WILLIAMS   And I draw your attention to the date, 1944. Would that be a form prepared in 1944 but used in 1945?

GOUZENKO   I think so.

WILLIAMS   Where was this document at the time you got it to bring with you?

GOUZENKO   That document was in the safe in room 12.

WILLIAMS   And you obtained it on what day; the day you came to the police or the day before?

GOUZENKO   I obtained this the day before I came to the police, September 5.

WILLIAMS   You took it on the evening of September 5?

GOUZENKO   Yes.

WILLIAMS   I will connect up these a little later on. This is a document that was prepared in the Russian embassy?

40

GOUZENKO   I don't think so. This was prepared in the house of the military attaché. . . .

WILLIAMS   And was it customary to keep these documents in the safe in No. 12?

GOUZENKO   Yes. In view of the fact that the mail takes about three months' time, they keep copies of these lists in the safe in case there is any question asked concerning documents that have been sent.

WILLIAMS   Then across the top of Exhibit 16 there are seven headings, and would you translate into English those headings, 1 to 7 across the page?

GOUZENKO   1. "Numbers in succession." 2. "Source." 3. "From where and under what circumstances were the materials obtained." 4. "The name of the material." 5. "The date and number." 6. "The number of sheets." 7. "Mark."

WILLIAMS   That is intended to indicate the marks that are on the particular documents?

GOUZENKO   Yes.

WILLIAMS   Whether they are secret or not secret, or any other distinguishing mark?

GOUZENKO   Yes, sir.

WILLIAMS   Now let us take the first items, translating from the Russian into English, going across the page. You have first of all, under the number column, the number 105?

GOUZENKO   That is right.

WILLIAMS   And the next word is "Green."?

GOUZENKO   Yes.

WILLIAMS   Then in column 3?

GOUZENKO   That is from the Department of Munitions and Supply, the engineering department.

WILLIAMS   And under 4?

GOUZENKO   "A drawing."

WILLIAMS   Would "plan" be a good translation, too?

GOUZENKO   No, I don't think so. It is a technical drawing.

WILLIAMS   And under the date heading, the fifth column?

GOUZENKO   "The 3rd of the eleventh, 1944."

WILLIAMS   That would be November 3, 1944?

GOUZENKO   Yes.

WILLIAMS   That would be the date of the drawing?

GOUZENKO   Yes.

WILLIAMS   Then under column 6, that gives the number of sheets, one?

GOUZENKO   Yes.

WILLIAMS   And in column 7?

GOUZENKO   "Without designation." That is, without mark.

WILLIAMS   Take first of all the second column, where we have as the source "Green." Do you know who Green was?

GOUZENKO   I know the name of Green. I don't know his real name, but I know that he worked in Montreal in the locomotive works as a draughtsman on construction. . . .

WILLIAMS   How do you know that?

GOUZENKO   From conversations; from telegrams and documents that were sent by Colonel Zabotin to Moscow.

MR. COMMISSIONER TASCHEREAU   Is "Green" the real name or a code name?

GOUZENKO   As far as I know it is his code name.

MR. WILLIAMS   Then I would like to take the fourth item. The number is 108. The source is Debouz. The material, under column 3, is "Notes." The name of the materials under column 4, "Conversation with the Professor on the decisions of the secret session of parliament." And it has no date?

GOUZENKO   Yes. . . .

WILLIAMS   The number of pages, one?

GOUZENKO   Yes.

WILLIAMS   The mark?

GOUZENKO   No mark.

WILLIAMS   Do you know whether Debouz is a cover name or a real name?

GOUZENKO   It is a cover name.

WILLIAMS   Do you know for whom it is a cover name?

GOUZENKO   It is a member of Parliament, Fred Rose.

WILLIAMS   How do you know that?

GOUZENKO   From telegrams Colonel Zabotin sent to Moscow.

WILLIAMS   And telegrams which you decoded?

GOUZENKO   That is right.

WILLIAMS   During the time you were here all the telegrams sent to Moscow would be coded by yourself?

GOUZENKO   Of course.

MR. COMMISSIONER KELLOCK   Colonel Williams, does the witness mean by that that in these telegrams sent to Moscow the man's real name would be used and not the so-called nickname, Debouz?

WILLIAMS   (*To the witness*)   How would you answer that?

GOUZENKO   Usually in sending telegrams the cover name would be used, but in this case the original cover name of this man was Fred. Moscow decided that this was not correct, because his Christian name was Fred. On the suggestion of Zabotin the cover name was changed from Fred to Debouz. In the course of this interchange of telegrams his full name was mentioned, his proper name, "Rose," was mentioned. . . .

WILLIAMS   May I ask you now, would this document Exhibit 16 cover only one day's mail?

GOUZENKO   That only covers one parcel of mail. In one delivery of mail there might be more than one parcel; there might be several.

WILLIAMS   Now I draw your attention to No. 109 —

MR. COMMISSIONER TASCHEREAU   Before you go to 109, on the fourth line of 108 you have "professor."

WILLIAMS   Yes; I am sorry.   (*To the witness*)   Is "professor" a code name, a cover name?

GOUZENKO   Yes.

WILLIAMS   Do you know to whom that refers?

GOUZENKO   In this case that applies to Professor Boyer of McGill University.

WILLIAMS   How do you know that? Where did you get that information?

GOUZENKO   Usually this agent was referred to as "the professor" only, but on one occasion when there was a discussion about the atomic bomb and the professors' came up in the discussion, Colonel Zabotin mentioned Professor Boyer.

MR. COMMISSIONER TASCHEREAU   Is he a professor at the university?

GOUZENKO   Yes.

TASCHEREAU   At McGill?

GOUZENKO   Yes.

TASCHEREAU   Did he ever work here in Ottawa with the government?

GOUZENKO   As far as I know he worked in Montreal at McGill University.

TASCHEREAU   But was he ever connected with the government? . . .

GOUZENKO   The telegrams here mentioned he was connected as a specialist on explosives, one of the greatest specialists on explosives on the North American continent. . . .

MR. COMMISSIONER KELLOCK   This discussion you mention, when Boyer's name was mentioned, was that a discussion between you and Zabotin?

GOUZENKO   No. Colonel Zabotin did not discuss things like that with me. It was a discussion between Colonel Zabotin and Lieutenant-Colonel Motinov in my presence, in room 12. . . .

MR. WILLIAMS   Now I come to item 109. The source is given as "Ellie." Under item 3 the word "copy" appears?

GOUZENKO   Yes.

WILLIAMS   Under item 4, which is "name of materials," what is that?

GOUZENKO   "Letter of Wilgress to King."

WILLIAMS   Date and number?

GOUZENKO   "No. 386, of the 3rd November, 1944."

WILLIAMS   Number of pages?

GOUZENKO   Two.

WILLIAMS   Marks?

GOUZENKO   "Secret."

WILLIAMS   Is Ellie a cover name?

GOUZENKO   Yes, it is a nickname.

WILLIAMS   And do you know whose nickname it is?

GOUZENKO   Yes, Miss Kay Willsher, the secretary of the British High Commissioner in Canada.

WILLIAMS   How do you know that?

GOUZENKO   I know that from reading the file on Kay Willsher, a personal file showing her origin and nickname and position and so on.

WILLIAMS   Where was that file at the time you read it?

GOUZENKO   In the safe.

WILLIAMS   In room 12?

GOUZENKO   That is right.

WILLIAMS   To which you had access?

GOUZENKO   Yes.

WILLIAMS   And in that safe were there other files on other people?

GOUZENKO   That is right.

MR. COMMISSIONER TASCHEREAU   Prepared by whom?

GOUZENKO   This particular file was filled by Gouseev. He had compiled this file.

MR. WILLIAMS   That is, he had compiled the file on Miss Willsher?

GOUZENKO   Yes.

WILLIAMS And it gave her cover name, her nickname as you call it, and her real name and the particulars about her?

GOUZENKO That is right.

WILLIAMS Then the "materials" are referred to as a "Letter of Wilgress to King," with the number of the letter. Do you know who Wilgress is?

GOUZENKO Yes.

WILLIAMS Who is that?

GOUZENKO The Canadian Ambassador to Moscow.

WILLIAMS And do you know who King is?

GOUZENKO It is the Prime Minister of Canada.

MR. COMMISSIONER KELLOCK Did the witness see the documents mentioned in this list, or did he just see the list?

WILLIAMS Did you see any of the documents mentioned on this list?

GOUZENKO I did not see them.

WILLIAMS What I am proposing to do, Messrs. Commissioners, is to take each item where there is a new source name and deal with that particular item, and then put in a translation of the whole document, if that meets with your approval.

Then we come to No. 111. The source given there in Exhibit 16 is Foster. Under paragraph 3 the document is described how?

GOUZENKO "Manuscript."

WILLIAMS Then the name of the material?

GOUZENKO "Canadian-British relations."

WILLIAMS And the date is December 4, 1944?

GOUZENKO Yes.

WILLIAMS And the number of pages or sheets?

GOUZENKO Three.

WILLIAMS And the marking?

GOUZENKO Without mark.

WILLIAMS Do you know who Foster is? Is that a cover name or a nickname?

GOUZENKO A nickname.

WILLIAMS And do you know whose nickname it is?

GOUZENKO Scott Benning.

WILLIAMS How do you know that Foster was Scott Benning?

GOUZENKO I read the file compiled on him by Gouseev.

WILLIAMS And that file was also in the safe in Room 12?

GOUZENKO That is right.

WILLIAMS And that disclosed the real name and the cover name?

GOUZENKO Yes.

WILLIAMS The file would be kept under which, the real name or the cover name?

GOUZENKO Always the nickname.

WILLIAMS On the cover of the file?

GOUZENKO Yes. . . . .

WILLIAMS Do you know what Scott Benning did or does?

GOUZENKO As far as I know he is working in the Department of Munitions and Supplies. He was also working at the same time in a bank, in the Department of Economic Planning.

MR. COMMISSIONER TASCHEREAU   In the bank?

GOUZENKO   Not at the same time. The data he obtained was very disrupted; it was not very full.

MR. COMMISSIONER KELLOCK   The data that he obtained?

GOUZENKO   That I obtained.

KELLOCK   The witness?

GOUZENKO   Yes.

MR. WILLIAMS   I draw your attention to No. 174. . . . The next cover name in the list is 174. You will notice on this list that Foster had supplied a large quantity of documents because his name goes right down to the end of 173.   (*To the witness*)   In 174 we have the source translated as Sam?

GOUZENKO   Sam.

WILLIAMS   And then the place from which the document was obtained is given as?

GOUZENKO   "Translation from the English."

WILLIAMS   And the name of the material under 4?

GOUZENKO   "Biography of statesmen of Canada."

WILLIAMS   Could that be translated as prominent people?

THE INTERPRETER   Prominent people would be more correct.

WILLIAMS   Members of the government?

GOUZENKO   Yes.

WILLIAMS   And the date under the heading 5?

GOUZENKO   No date.

WILLIAMS   And the number of pages or sheets?

GOUZENKO   46.

WILLIAMS   And the markings?

GOUZENKO   No mark.

WILLIAMS   Is Sam a cover or nickname?

GOUZENKO   It is a nickname.

WILLIAMS   And for whom is it the nickname?

GOUZENKO   Sam Carr.

WILLIAMS   Do you know who Sam Carr is?

GOUZENKO   He is national organizer of the Communist party in Canada.

WILLIAMS   Do you know him personally?

GOUZENKO   No.

WILLIAMS   The next is 175, and the source is given as?

GOUZENKO   "Nora". . . .

WILLIAMS   Do you know whether the name Nora is a real name or cover name or nickname?

GOUZENKO   It is a nickname.

WILLIAMS   Do you know whose nickname it is?

GOUZENKO   Emma Woikin.

WILLIAMS   How do you know that was a real name?

GOUZENKO   All the correspondence concerning her enlistment into this work passed through my hands while I was working there.

WILLIAMS   Do you know where she was employed?

GOUZENKO   She was working as a cipher clerk in the Ministry of Foreign Affairs. . . .

WILLIAMS	Whereabouts, in Canada?
GOUZENKO	Canada.
WILLIAMS	Did you ever see the dossier in the safe?
GOUZENKO	There was no dossier compiled on her.
WILLIAMS	Then 180, the source in the second column is translated as what?
GOUZENKO	"Ernst."
WILLIAMS	And the place from where it was obtained or under what circumstances is given as?
GOUZENKO	"Cable."
WILLIAMS	Could that be translated as "review"?
GOUZENKO	Yes.
WILLIAMS	"Summary?"
GOUZENKO	"Summary" is good.
WILLIAMS	And the fourth, the name of the material?
GOUZENKO	"Despatch of armies to England."
WILLIAMS	Would "munitions" be a better translation?
GOUZENKO	Yes, "munitions."
WILLIAMS	"Despatch of munitions to England," and the date?
GOUZENKO	"November."
WILLIAMS	And the number of sheets or pages?
GOUZENKO	Three.
WILLIAMS	And the markings.
GOUZENKO	Without markings.
WILLIAMS	Do you know whether Ernst was a nickname or cover name or real name?
GOUZENKO	It is a nickname.
WILLIAMS	Do you know for whom it is a cover name or nickname?
GOUZENKO	It is Eric Adams.
WILLIAMS	How do you know that?
GOUZENKO	There was a file compiled by Gouseev.
WILLIAMS	And was that in the safe in Room 12?
GOUZENKO	That is right.
WILLIAMS	And you read that?
GOUZENKO	Yes.
WILLIAMS	And do you know where Eric Adams worked?
GOUZENKO	I do not know exactly.
WILLIAMS	Then we will come to 196. The source there is given as what?
GOUZENKO	Gray.
WILLIAMS	And in column 3, from where and under what circumstances the materials were obtained. What does that say?
GOUZENKO	I would say it means copies. It looks like 1-1.
WILLIAMS	You cannot say just what that is?
GOUZENKO	I suppose instead of putting copies, the marks appear in the other part of the column.
WILLIAMS	It does not mean anything to you in Russian?
GOUZENKO	Yes, it does not.
WILLIAMS	And the name of the material?
GOUZENKO	"Corrections."

WILLIAMS   And the date?

GOUZENKO   "7th December, 1944."

WILLIAMS   And the number of pages or sheets?

GOUZENKO   One.

WILLIAMS   And the marking?

GOUZENKO   "Secret."

WILLIAMS   Now do you know whether Gray is the name of an individual or merely a cover name?

GOUZENKO   It is a cover name.

WILLIAMS   What you call a nickname?

GOUZENKO   Yes.

WILLIAMS   Do you know whose nickname or cover name it is?

GOUZENKO   It is Gerson.

WILLIAMS   How do you know that?

GOUZENKO   I know that from telegrams and documents wherein he was mentioned and also from his file.

WILLIAMS   There was a file on Gerson?

GOUZENKO   Yes.

WILLIAMS   In the safe in Room 12?

GOUZENKO   Yes.

WILLIAMS   And you had an opportunity of seeing that and did see it?

GOUZENKO   And seen it. . . .

WILLIAMS   That would be H. Gerson so far as you know?

GOUZENKO   Yes.

WILLIAMS   Do you know what he did, what his occupation was?

GOUZENKO   He was working in Munitions and Supply in the Department of Statistics.

WILLIAMS   You will have noted, Mr. Commissioners, that we have now a certain number of code or nicknames and actual names. Here is a list on which those names as well as other names appear. I think I will give it to you now and the other names will be coming in as the documents are brought in. . . .   (*To the witness*)   In answer to a question I think you have said already — a question by one of the Commissioners — that you did not see the documents that are referred to in this list?

GOUZENKO   No.

WILLIAMS   Take for instance 109; that is one we dealt with where Ellie passed over the document said to be a letter from Mr. Wilgress to Mr. King. Would you have any idea of how that document would come into Ellie's possession?

GOUZENKO   As far as I know she was working as secretary for the High Commissioner in Ottawa and she had access to documents and could therefore take the documents from the files and hand them over to the Intelligence.

MR. COMMISSIONER TASCHEREAU   From the files of the High Commissioner's office?

GOUZENKO   From the files of the High Commissioner's office. . . .

WILLIAMS   How would these documents go out; have you any information on that?

GOUZENKO   Yes. . . . The documents are placed first in one envelope or package which is sealed with five seals on one side and on the other side it is addressed to the director and marked, "Top Secret." Then that is covered by a second covering and sealed again with five seals on the back and on the other side addressed, "Personal — Secret," to the secretary. It is covered with a third covering or envelope, likewise with five seals on the back, and addressed, "To the People's Commissary on Foreign Affairs, not to be opened by anybody else but Novikov."

MR. COMMISSIONER TASCHEREAU   Is that a nickname?

GOUZENKO   There is no such person as Novikov. It is merely an indication that the material in that parcel referred to Intelligence work.

MR. WILLIAMS   These letters and communications are not sent through the ordinary mail, are they?

GOUZENKO   These parcels or packages are placed in a bag and are sealed and are sent by diplomatic mail.

WILLIAMS   Through the Canadian post office?

GOUZENKO   Diplomatic mail is sent by two couriers. One is on duty and the other sleeps or rests. They are armed.

MR. COMMISSIONER TASCHEREAU   Is that sent by air or do they go to Moscow by boat?

GOUZENKO   Only by steamer.

TASCHEREAU   The two couriers from Ottawa will go to Moscow?

GOUZENKO   They are Moscow couriers, they are employees of N.K.V.D.

TASCHEREAU   And they come to Ottawa?

GOUZENKO   They come here as diplomatic couriers; they have immunity as diplomatic couriers.

MR. WILLIAMS   That is the way all this mail is passed backward and forward?

GOUZENKO   Yes. . . .

WILLIAMS   How often does the mail go forward?

GOUZENKO   That depends on the availability of the steamships and transports from America. It is usually twice a month.

WILLIAMS   And how long does it take mail, for instance, to reach you here from Moscow?

GOUZENKO   The same; all depends on the steamer.

WILLIAMS   From two weeks to a month?

GOUZENKO   Yes. During the war even five months.

WILLIAMS   Then at the end of Exhibit No. 16 — would you just translate the two lines at the end?

GOUZENKO   "Textbooks and programs in the English language, 18 copies, and map of Canada, one copy, sent by heavy mail". . . .

WILLIAMS   You had nothing to do with the preparation of this document, Exhibit No. 16? . . .

GOUZENKO   Nothing to do with the preparation.

WILLIAMS   It is a genuine document from the files of the Russian embassy in Ottawa?

GOUZENKO   Oh, yes, it is genuine.

WILLIAMS   Are you a typist?

GOUZENKO   No.

WILLIAMS   You could not have typed this document yourself?

GOUZENKO   No.

WILLIAMS   Were you ever present when any document similar to this list of correspondence was being prepared?

GOUZENKO   Oh, yes.

WILLIAMS   In Colonel Zabotin's office?

GOUZENKO   Yes.

WILLIAMS   Just describe to the commissioners how he would do it. Would he have notes and dictate to the typist or what would he do?

GOUZENKO   Usually Lieutenant-Colonel Motinov, who is responsible for the operative work, would make a rough list, written by hand, leaving a space for the date and signature. He gives that to Mrs. Gourshkov, who types the list and Motinov supervises the work. Then she would return to him the rough note and he would burn it. . . .

MR. COMMISSIONER TASCHEREAU   On that list at the extreme right you have the word "Marked." Was that "marked" put on by Colonel Zabotin? . . .

GOUZENKO   By the Canadian authorities.

TASCHEREAU   By the person from whom the document has been stolen?

GOUZENKO   That is right.

MR. WILLIAMS   Mr. Commissioner, let us take as an example 109. No. 109 is the letter from Mr. Wilgress to Mr. King. The number of the letter is given and the date. Exhibit No. 16 shows that that carried the mark "Secret." That mark "Secret" might have been put on before it got into the hands of the person who took it. In other words, the original document would be marked "Secret."

TASCHEREAU   That would be put on by Mr. Wilgress or by Mr. King?

WILLIAMS   I think that is correct.

GOUZENKO   That is correct. . . .

WILLIAMS   You have referred to files that were in the safe in Room 12. When you came to the police you brought with you three of those files, did you not?

GOUZENKO   Yes.

WILLIAMS   I show you one which on the face of it has a piece of paper with the name "Back" in quotation marks typed on it. This is one of the files which you took out of the safe in Room 12 and brought with you?

GOUZENKO   That is right.

WILLIAMS   It is an original file from the records of the Russian embassy in Ottawa?

GOUZENKO   Yes.

WILLIAMS   This file on "Back" consists of a number of sheets or pages pinned in a folder. Is "Back" the name, the real name or is it a nickname or cover name?

GOUZENKO   It is a nickname.

WILLIAMS   And it is a nickname for whom?

GOUZENKO   Lunan.

WILLIAMS   Do you know his first name, offhand? This file I am showing you is exactly in the condition it was in when you took it out of the safe?

GOUZENKO   Yes.

WILLIAMS   At the same time you took these other documents? The first sheet shows the real name as Lieutenant G. Lunan?

GOUZENKO   Yes.

WILLIAMS   While a great part of the page is in Russian, the actual name is typed in in English?

GOUZENKO   Yes.

WILLIAMS   And the Russian words preceding that are?

GOUZENKO   "Family name and christian name and patronymic."

WILLIAMS   Then the second item?

GOUZENKO   "Pseudonym."

WILLIAMS   That is what we have been calling nickname or cover name?

GOUZENKO   Yes.

WILLIAMS   That shows that the pseudonym of Lieutenant G. Lunan was "Back"?

GOUZENKO   Yes.

WILLIAMS   And the other files that you have referred to which you did not bring with you but which you read were compiled on exactly the same basis as this one?

GOUZENKO   On exactly the same basis.

WILLIAMS   Then the third item on the first page?

GOUZENKO   "Length of time in the net."

WILLIAMS   That means the length of time he has been acting as an agent for Russia?

GOUZENKO   Yes.

WILLIAMS   And it is followed by a date. What is that date and what does it mean?

GOUZENKO   "From March, 1945."

WILLIAMS   Then the fourth item in Russian says?

GOUZENKO   "Address."

WILLIAMS   Then next (a)?

GOUZENKO   "Service."

WILLIAMS   Or "business"?

GOUZENKO   "Business."

WILLIAMS   Sparks Street. That is in English, "Sparks Street, Canadian Affairs" and "telephone 9-7621". Then (b)?

GOUZENKO   "Home."

WILLIAMS   In English, "337 Elgin, Apartment 7, telephone 5-71-20." The balance of the page is in Russian?

GOUZENKO   Yes.

WILLIAMS   The fifth item is translated into English?

GOUZENKO   "Place of business and duties."

WILLIAMS   And opposite that has been filled in at another time or in different type the words which translated into English mean?

GOUZENKO   "Editorial staff, military journal Canadian Affairs. He works in the position of correspondent."

WILLIAMS   In the capacity?

GOUZENKO   Capacity of correspondent.

WILLIAMS   Then without translating the balance of that page, which we will come back to, I will go to the second page. It is all in English with the exception of the heading which is in Russian. What does the heading say?

GOUZENKO   "Scheme of the group of 'research'."

WILLIAMS   "Research" is in quotation marks. The balance has evidently been cut off a slightly larger sheet and was originally in English. Could you say, with your knowledge, whether or not those things which are put together on the second sheet would likely be prepared by Lunan himself?

GOUZENKO   I do not know. . . .

WILLIAMS   Then when we come to the third page we find that it is a form with typewritten title and heading?

GOUZENKO   "Course of meetings."

WILLIAMS   Then the typewritten part contains first of all, the numbers?

GOUZENKO   Numbers.

WILLIAMS   Then another heading?

GOUZENKO   "Contents of meetings."

WILLIAMS   Could that be translated as "substance of the meetings"?

GOUZENKO   Meetings, yes.

WILLIAMS   And at the head of the third column?

GOUZENKO   "Notes."

WILLIAMS   Then the rest of the third page is in somebody else's handwriting?

GOUZENKO   Yes.

WILLIAMS   Do you know whose that it?

GOUZENKO   Yes.

WILLIAMS   Whose is it?

GOUZENKO   Lieutenant-Colonel Rogov.

WILLIAMS   His name appears as Assistant — Air Force on Exhibit 15?

GOUZENKO   That is right. . . .

WILLIAMS   The fourth page is one with identical typewritten headings and the balance again is in the handwriting of somebody?

GOUZENKO   Yes.

WILLIAMS   Whose handwriting is the second page in?

GOUZENKO   Rogov. . . .

WILLIAMS   Then there are two blank pages and we find pinned in a number of typewritten documents. These are in English, but a heading is written on each in Russian. The first one is headed, "Ottawa, March 28", and purports to be a letter addressed: "Dear Mother and Father" and is signed on the typewriter "Back."

GOUZENKO   Yes.

WILLIAMS   What does the Russian heading mean on that?

GOUZENKO   Organization letter about group in research from "Back." . . .

WILLIAMS   We have now identified "Back" as Lunan. On the second page there is a scheme of a group given, and the top name in the group is "Jan." Do you know who "Jan" would be?

GOUZENKO   I don't know, but I think Lieutenant-Colonel Rogov was "Jan", not "Brent."

WILLIAMS   You think that for Lunan, Lieutenant-Colonel Rogov was known as "Jan"? . . .

GOUZENKO   That is my suggestion, my suspicion.

WILLIAMS   Then this scheme gives Lunan with his nickname, and it also gives the name of Isadore [Israel] Halperin, with the nickname Bacon?

GOUZENKO   Yes.

WILLIAMS   Had you known who Bacon was before you read this file on "Back", which is Exhibit 17?

GOUZENKO   Yes, I know him from telegrams. . . .

WILLIAMS   Do you know who Halperin is, what he does?

GOUZENKO   I think he is working in the Research Council, or he can also be a mathematician or a teacher. I don't know exactly.

WILLIAMS   And the next name is written here as Doriuforth Smith, with the nickname Badeau. I may say that we will run across this name again, and it is spelled in different ways, but the proper spelling seems to be Durnford Smith. . . . It shows that his nickname was Badeau. Had you known before you saw the file, Exhibit 17, that Badeau was the nickname of Durnford Smith?

GOUZENKO   Yes; also from the telegrams.

WILLIAMS   And did you know what Durnford Smith did?

GOUZENKO   I think he is a radio engineer in the Research Council.

WILLIAMS   Then the next number, and the last number shown in Exhibit 17 on page 2, is a man named Ned Mazerall, whose nickname or cover name is given as Bagley. Did you know before you saw this document, Exhibit 17, that Bagley was the cover name or nickname of Mazerall?

GOUZENKO   Yes, sir.

WILLIAMS   How did you learn that?

GOUZENKO   From telegrams.

WILLIAMS   The telegrams which you had coded or decoded? And did you know what Mazerall did?

GOUZENKO   He is working in the Research Council.

WILLIAMS   Then on the third page the handwriting starts off and I want to translate this. What is that first line?

GOUZENKO   "Urgent call by telephone."

WILLIAMS   And the next line?

GOUZENKO   "Dial No. 9-7621 and ask for Lieutenant Lunan."

WILLIAMS   And the next?

GOUZENKO   "After this Brent asks 'Can you tell me when your next magazine will be published?' "

WILLIAMS   Those last words are written here in English?

GOUZENKO   Yes.

WILLIAMS   Just let us stop there for a moment. Who is Brent?

GOUZENKO   Lieutenant-Colonel Rogov. . . .

MR. COMMISSIONER TASCHEREAU   I thought Rogov was "Jan"?

WILLIAMS   For the one purpose. That is his suggestion. Rogov, as we will see, had several names. Some of them had several names, but for the purpose of the one scheme there is a "Jan" and the only explanation the witness can give is that he was "Jan" for that; but "Brent" is also definitely Rogov. (*To the witness*)   Then the second item on this third page has the date 28/3/45 which is the 28th of March, 1945. How does the rest of it read; what is the translation into English?

GOUZENKO   "Regular (meeting) everything is normal. Regular. The 18th of April, 1945; reserve, 21st of April, 1945; time, 21 o'clock."

WILLIAMS   Does that mean that the regular meeting was to take place on the 18th at 21 o'clock, but that if for any reason that did not take place, the emergency or reserve meeting would take place on the 21st, three days later, at the same time?

GOUZENKO   Yes.

WILLIAMS   Then the next line?

GOUZENKO   "Place, the corner of Waverley and Macdonald."

WILLIAMS   Then we come to "Remarks." What is that, translated?

GOUZENKO   "Given out: $190.00. Of them, Back, $100.00; Bacon, $30; Badeau, $30; Bagley, $30."

WILLIAMS   Can you tell the Commission anything about these payments of moneys; who would make them in this particular case, and where the money would be got?

GOUZENKO   Lieutenant-Colonel Rogov handed out this money. He took it from the funds of the operative work, from the branch, for payment of sources.

MR. COMMISSIONER TASCHEREAU   Was that reported to Moscow by telegram, the payments made?

GOUZENKO   Sometimes, yes.

TASCHEREAU   And you put those telegrams in code?

GOUZENKO   Yes.

MR. WILLIAMS   I would suggest that there are translations which are in this. We have just left them loose in the pages at the present time, and it might be well to leave them; but the translations might be considered to be marked as Exhibit 17-A. Perhaps Mr. Campbell would mark the first page, and eventually they could be all pinned together. . . .   (*To the witness*)   Then another of the documents which you brought with you and which came out of the safe in room 12 to which we have already referred was the file marked "Badeau"?

GOUZENKO   Yes. . . .

WILLIAMS   And this is the file marked on the front "Frank" in quotation marks; and that is the cover name or nickname for whom?

GOUZENKO   It is the cover name for Sam Carr. . . .

WILLIAMS   The first page is a typewritten form similar to the first page in the other two files, Exhibits 17 and 18, and it contains a picture. Do you know Sam Carr to see him?

GOUZENKO   No, I don't.

WILLIAMS   It is evidently a picture cut out of a newspaper. It gives his pseudonym as "Frank"; his address as 14 Montrose, Toronto, and then item 5 reads how?

GOUZENKO   "Place of his service or duty: Labour-Progressive party. Political activities."

WILLIAMS   Then 6?

GOUZENKO   "Material conditions. Materially he is secure or independent but takes money. It is necessary to help him sometimes."

WILLIAMS   Then the second page is on a similar form to those in the other two files, a typewritten heading and the rest is in the handwriting of some person. Do you recognize the handwriting?

GOUZENKO   Yes, it is Lieutenant-Colonel Rogov. . . .

WILLIAMS   Then there are two blank pages, and then a page with a heading in Russian which reads what?

GOUZENKO   "Task No. 1, of the 16th of December, 1945[sic]."

WILLIAMS   That is queried?

GOUZENKO   Yes.

WILLIAMS   Then there is another heading in red pencil?

GOUZENKO   "To Sam for Shugar."

WILLIAMS   That means instructions to Sam to give to Shugar?

GOUZENKO   Yes, that is right.

WILLIAMS   Then who is Shugar?

GOUZENKO   That is the real name of an agent who was suggested by Sam. . . .

MR. COMMISSIONER KELLOCK   He is not on this list.

WILLIAMS   You will find him under "Prometheus," but his real name is Shugar.   (*To the witness*)   Do you know what his initials are?

GOUZENKO   I don't know.

WILLIAMS   Do you know what he was doing, who he was?

GOUZENKO   He was working in the Naval Department. He is a specialist in anti-submarine protection; asdic.

WILLIAMS   And are you aware that he also had a nickname or a cover name?

GOUZENKO   Later he was given a nickname, Prometheus or Promety, in Russian. . . .

WILLIAMS   Then the next page bound in is on ruled paper, lined paper that has been pasted on a white sheet. I do not know whether or not that shows in the other copies, but you see how it has been put in. This is written in Russian; and can you say whose writing this is?

GOUZENKO   Lieutenant-Colonel Motinov.

WILLIAMS   That is Lieutenant-Colonel Motinov?

GOUZENKO   Yes; this is him.

WILLIAMS   And it is headed up?

GOUZENKO   "Various."

WILLIAMS   And next?

GOUZENKO   "Sam."

WILLIAMS   "Sam" in English, and the street address?

GOUZENKO   Yes.

WILLIAMS   And this reads how?

GOUZENKO   "On the 14th June, 1944, Commander met Sam and arranged with him about meeting with Leon once in three months."

WILLIAMS   Who is "Commander"?

GOUZENKO   That is the nickname for the assistant chief of first intelligence headquarters at Warsaw; Milstein.

WILLIAMS   And was he in Canada?

GOUZENKO   Yes.

WILLIAMS   At this time?

GOUZENKO   Yes.

WILLIAMS   And who is Leon?

GOUZENKO   That is the nickname for the first secretary of the embassy, Koudriadtzev. He is now in London. . . .

WILLIAMS   Do you know anything of an Inspector Milsky; does that name mean anything to you?

GOUZENKO   Yes.

WILLIAMS   That would not be the Commander?

GOUZENKO   This is the Commander.

WILLIAMS   It is the Commander. Just explain why there is Colonel Milstein and Inspector Milsky?

GOUZENKO   Colonel Milstein arrived in Canada under cover of diplomatic courier with the name of Milsky. He came in company with another courier for the purpose of checking up on the whole agency system on the American continent.

MR. COMMISSIONER TASCHEREAU   That is Milsky?

WILLIAMS   Alias Milstein.

GOUZENKO   His companion was obviously working on the line of the N.K.V.D. and his purpose was to check up the N.K.V.D. system of agency work on the American continent.

WILLIAMS   Do you know the name of his companion?

GOUZENKO   No.

WILLIAMS   Did you see Milsky?

GOUZENKO   No.

WILLIAMS   Do you know how long he was in Ottawa?

GOUZENKO   About half a month or fifteen days. . . .

WILLIAMS   Then there is a reference to a Dr. Harris. Will you read the sentence in which Dr. Harris' name appears? The next line is in English.

GOUZENKO   "I wanted to say hello to Frank."

WILLIAMS   Translate this part?

GOUZENKO   "The password Leon rings on the telephone Midway-9553, Dr. Harris, 279 College Street, Toronto." Then in quotations, "I want to say Hello to Frank."

WILLIAMS   Hello is spelled "H-a-l-l-o-w." Do you know anything about Dr. Harris? Is that a real name or is it a code or cover name or nickname?

GOUZENKO   I understand this is his real name.

WILLIAMS   We already have identified Leon. Now there is a reference here to Frank. It says, "I want to say hello to Frank." Who is Frank?

GOUZENKO   Frank is Sam Carr.

WILLIAMS   That is another cover name for Sam Carr?

GOUZENKO   That is right.

WILLIAMS   Then after the English words "I want to say hello to Frank," will you translate the next three lines?

GOUZENKO   "After this Leon comes out to the meeting in Eaton's store, corner College and Yonge. Eric calls through Skelton."

WILLIAMS   Who is Eric?

GOUZENKO   In this case I think maybe it is Eric Adams.

WILLIAMS   Who went under the name of Ernst?

GOUZENKO   Ernst.

WILLIAMS   It may be. That is all you are able to say about that?

GOUZENKO   Yes.

WILLIAMS   Do you know anything about [Alex] Skelton?*

*Alex Skelton was research director of the Bank of Canada and was seconded during the war to a number of important posts involving manpower and reconstruction planning. The Commissioners found nothing improper in his relations with Eric Adams or any others connected with the Soviet embassy.

GOUZENKO   Only one time I met him; only once. . . .

WILLIAMS   This is the only time you have seen his name?

GOUZENKO   Yes.

WILLIAMS   Do you know who it would be?

GOUZENKO   I think that phrase should be understood as Eric calls Sam Carr through Skelton.

WILLIAMS   That is just supposition on your part?

GOUZENKO   Yes.

WILLIAMS   Then there is an item further down on that page under the date 5-12-44; will you read that?

GOUZENKO   "5 December, 44, he asked for meetings through Foster."

WILLIAMS   And Foster is the undercover name for Benning?

GOUZENKO   Yes.

WILLIAMS   Then at the very bottom of the page there are two words — what are those in English?

GOUZENKO   "On the 8th December, 1944, I departed; I met on the 11th of December, 1944, and made appointment for meeting on the 16th of December in my town at 21 hours." Then there are two abbreviations, which might mean Somerset and that might mean Bay. Is there a Bay Street in Ottawa?

MR. COMMISSIONER TASCHEREAU   Yes.

GOUZENKO   I am sure that is Somerset and Bay Streets. . . .

WILLIAMS   Will you translate what is written on the note with the exception of the little sketch? First of all, will you translate the portion covered by the note?

GOUZENKO   "I handed over two hundred dollars. Passport has been detained. Forms were badly filled in. On the 16th December he will give new ones. On the 16th December at 21 hours we met normally. He gave new forms. We agreed on transfer of Ernst. He gave meeting Matt Nightingale. I made him acquainted with Dr. Harris Henry." Just a minute, I think there should be a correction. In this case there may be a little doubt as to who met whom because in Russian the personal pronoun is not written down. It is difficult to say whether Motinov made Sam acquainted with the doctor or whether Motinov made the acquaintance of the doctor. Most probably the translation is that Sam Carr made Motinov acquainted with the doctor. "I set the date for the next meeting on 20th January, 1945, at 21 hours at the old place at the hospital. If he is not there Dr. Harris will take his place."

WILLIAMS   That is somewhat different from this, but it will all be checked. First of all, let me ask you this: This refers to Dr. Harris Henry. The practice in Russia, as I understand it, is to write the last name first?

GOUZENKO   Yes.

WILLIAMS   We have already had reference to a Dr. Harris?

GOUZENKO   Yes.

WILLIAMS   And there is a reference to a Dr. Harris Henry?

GOUZENKO   Yes.

WILLIAMS   Is it right to say that it is Dr. Henry Harris?

GOUZENKO   Motinov wrote that in English but used the Russian way of doing it. . . .

WILLIAMS   Then you have referred to Nightingale; you have translated the word as Nightingale although it is written slightly differently, is it not? It is written as Nantingale?

GOUZENKO   Yes.

WILLIAMS   Is there any doubt in your mind as to what the writer intended, whether he intended Nightingale?

GOUZENKO   That is just writing and that is a mistake.

WILLIAMS   Do you know who Nightingale is?

GOUZENKO   Oh, yes.

WILLIAMS   Who is he?

GOUZENKO   It is the real name of some agent. . . .

WILLIAMS   Do you know whether the agent Nightingale has a nickname or cover name?

GOUZENKO   Yes.

WILLIAMS   What was it?

GOUZENKO   Leader.

WILLIAMS   How did you learn that?

GOUZENKO   From telegrams.

WILLIAMS   Do you know who Nightingale was; what was his position; what was he doing?

GOUZENKO   Squadron Leader in the air force and he worked in the Bell Telephone Company.

WILLIAMS   How did you learn that?

GOUZENKO   From telegrams. . . .

WILLIAMS   Then still dealing with the back page of the lined sheet — first of all, the note is in Motinov's writing?

GOUZENKO   That is right.

WILLIAMS   Will you translate the first sentence of the note?

GOUZENKO   "Urgent call of Sam is conducted through doctor, through the optical doctor Harris Henry, living at 279 College Street, Toronto. Lamont calls doctor on the telephone, Midway-9553."

WILLIAMS   That reference to Lamont is a reference to whom?

GOUZENKO   Motinov; it is a nickname. . . .

WILLIAMS   Then passing on from the ruled sheet. The next sheet is in handwriting with the figure 1 at the top and with a title. Will you translate the title?

GOUZENKO   "Task No. 2 on the 15th June, 1945."

WILLIAMS   And that is in the handwriting of whom?

GOUZENKO   Of Rogov.

WILLIAMS   The handwriting of Rogov. Will you read the first sentence?

GOUZENKO   "On the basis of previous received data about A.M. Veale (Englishman) we know that up to 1942 he worked in meteorological service of the R.A.F. in Cambridge. . . ."

WILLIAMS   Will you tell the commissioners what you know about Veale? Is that his real name?

GOUZENKO   Yes, that is the real name.

WILLIAMS   What do you know about him?

GOUZENKO   Sam Carr told Motinov that a certain Veale had applied to him for work, and that he was a member of the Communist party in England; he said he was a member of the Communist party, and he showed Carr a certificate written by a Communist who had been arrested in England.

WILLIAMS   Where did you get this information?

GOUZENKO   From a telegram that Colonel Zabotin sent to Moscow, writing about this meeting of Motinov with Carr.

WILLIAMS   That was a telegram which you had coded in the course of your duties?

GOUZENKO   Yes.

WILLIAMS   Then I would like you to translate the note on the side of this page with which we have just been dealing?

GOUZENKO   "The details will be cleared through Engineer Chubb, a chemist, a friend of Sam's and also through Debouz, both on the line of trade unions."

WILLIAMS   Do you know anything about Chubb?

GOUZENKO   No.

WILLIAMS   And Debouz you have already told the Commission was the cover name or nickname for —

GOUZENKO   Fred Rose. . . .

WILLIAMS   Then we come to a sheet of ruled paper, and would you translate the heading of that sheet?

GOUZENKO   "Task No. 3 of the 1st August, 1945."

WILLIAMS   And in whose handwriting is this sheet?

GOUZENKO   Colonel Zabotin.

WILLIAMS   Then the last page in this file is written in Russian, by whom?

GOUZENKO   Lieutenant-Colonel Rogov.

WILLIAMS   And what is the heading?

GOUZENKO   "Task which was given by me on the 16th August, 1945."

WILLIAMS   Will you translate the first paragraph?

GOUZENKO   "To write a report on the technique of documentation for passports and other documents, pointing out who is concretely engaged from your side (Frank) with this work."

MR. COMMISSIONER KELLOCK   Does "concretely" there mean "actually"?

GOUZENKO   Yes.

MR. WILLIAMS   And the name in brackets, "Frank" is one of the cover names or nicknames of Sam Carr?

GOUZENKO   Yes.

WILLIAMS   Then will you read the third paragraph, and translate it?

GOUZENKO   "To give full characterization on Prometheus, pointing out his service or occupation in the department in which he works in the navy," or the naval department; "also to write the main biographical data; his home address and the address he works, and telephones."

WILLIAMS   And Prometheus or Promety you have already told the Commission is the cover name or nickname of Shugar?

GOUZENKO   Yes.

WILLIAMS   Then will you translate the fourth paragraph?

GOUZENKO   "The proposed place of work of Prometheus in case of his demobilization." . . .

WILLIAMS   We have already looked at one of the original outgoing telegrams, which has been marked as Exhibit 14?

GOUZENKO   Yes.

WILLIAMS   And you brought with you, in addition to the one that we have already looked at, a large number of others?

GOUZENKO   Yes.

WILLIAMS   And these blue documents were taken by you out of the pouch?

GOUZENKO   Yes.

WILLIAMS   At the time you took the ones that you brought with you, were there any other blue documents, original telegrams, in the pouch?

GOUZENKO   Yes.

WILLIAMS   So you did not remove everything out of the pouch?

GOUZENKO   No.

WILLIAMS   How big is the pouch? Is it like a mail sack?

GOUZENKO   It is made of green canvas.

WILLIAMS   And how wide would it be? You indicate a space of about 12 to 16 inches?

GOUZENKO   Yes.

WILLIAMS   How deep would it be?

GOUZENKO   About this (indicating).

WILLIAMS   That is about two feet deep?

GOUZENKO   Yes.

WILLIAMS   And it would contain, I gather, a very large number of documents?

GOUZENKO   Yes. . . .

WILLIAMS   And on some occasion while you had the pouch in your possession, having got it from Aleksashkin, you removed these blue documents?

GOUZENKO   Yes.

WILLIAMS   How long did you do that before you came to the police for protection? . . .

GOUZENKO   During the course of about half a month I examined the materials so as to select the best ones that would disclose the operative work, leaving the informational telegrams on one side; that is, without taking account of the informational telegrams. The telegrams which I wished to take out I marked by bending over slightly one of the corners, so it would not be noticed by Colonel Zabotin. All the telegrams must lie in their proper order by serial numbers. I did that, so that when I decided finally to take the documents I would lose no time by having to read the telegrams, as I had them all marked and I could take them out with the least possible loss of time, in two or three minutes. . . .

WILLIAMS   I am showing you a bundle of original telegrams, outgoing telegrams on the blue sheets, and asking you whether these are all in Colonel Zabotin's handwriting. There are twenty-two of them?

GOUZENKO   Yes.

WILLIAMS   These are all in Colonel Zabotin's handwriting?

GOUZENKO   Yes.

MR. COMMISSIONER KELLOCK   My question is this: When did he start to gather these documents with the idea of taking them?

GOUZENKO   I think this was all about a month, or maybe a little more I think about this of making preparations like this in case I would not be allowed to enter this secret room. I made preparation approximately for one month, and

I took the first document because I was afraid I would not be allowed to enter this room again. The other documents I took when I left. . . .

WILLIAMS   Then I show you five pages of blue paper, and ask you whose handwriting that is in?

GOUZENKO   Lieutenant-Colonel Rogov.

WILLIAMS   And what is this; what do these five pages represent?

GOUZENKO   They are notes by Lieutenant-Colonel Rogov.

MR. COMMISSIONER TASCHEREAU   Is it not a telegram?

GOUZENKO   No. They were in his brief case which was in the safe. . . .

WILLIAMS   So that Exhibit 21, this document we have just been discussing, is not a telegram and was not in the pouch?

GOUZENKO   No.

WILLIAMS   It was in Colonel Rogov's brief case?

GOUZENKO   That is right.

WILLIAMS   And where was it?

GOUZENKO   In the safe.

WILLIAMS   And you took it at the same time that you took — ?

GOUZENKO   When I left, on the 5th. . . .

WILLIAMS   Now looking at Exhibit 14, I will read you a translation. You will follow this, and tell me if it is correct?

GOUZENKO   Yes.

WILLIAMS   The number at the top is 209. The date is 12/7/45, and it reads: "To the director on No. 8393. 1. Debouz obtained data from conversations with officers who had taken part on the western front. The data were obtained from conversations with the latter."

GOUZENKO   That is right.

WILLIAMS   And Debouz is the cover or nickname for Fred Rose?

GOUZENKO   Yes.

WILLIAMS   "2. Debouz was re-elected for the second time as a member of the federal parliament in the latest elections. Sam and Tim Buck were not elected, although they were balloted for the federal parliament. Thus from the corporators there is one member of the federal parliament."

GOUZENKO   That is right.

WILLIAMS   "The first session of parliament meets 26th August."

GOUZENKO   That is right.

WILLIAMS   And the signature to that is "Grant"?

GOUZENKO   That is right.

WILLIAMS   And down in the left-hand corner again appears the date, 12/7/45?

GOUZENKO   That is right. . . .

MR. COMMISSIONER KELLOCK   Would the witness explain what is meant by "on No. 8393" in the opening phrase?

WILLIAMS   (To the witness)   Will you explain to the Commissioners, please?

GOUZENKO   That is a reply to the director of his telegram No. 8393.

KELLOCK   That is in reference to his telegram?

GOUZENKO   Yes, that is a reference number.

WILLIAMS   And the No. 209 shows the sequence of this telegram?

GOUZENKO   Yes, it is the serial number of the outgoing telegram.

WILLIAMS   Was the practice to commence to number the telegrams at the beginning of the year and carry the numbering through consecutively, or to number them through a month?

GOUZENKO Through all the year.

WILLIAMS So the first telegram sent out in 1945 would be No. 1, and the second No. 2, and so on?

GOUZENKO Yes.

WILLIAMS Right through to the end of the year?

GOUZENKO Yes.

WILLIAMS The reference to "Sam" is to Sam Carr?

GOUZENKO Yes.

WILLIAMS Then what is the reference to the corporators?

GOUZENKO That is the nickname of Communist parties abroad, outside of Russia. . . .

WILLIAMS So that this word "corporators" here means — ?

GOUZENKO A member.

WILLIAMS Members of the Communist party?

GOUZENKO Yes. . . .

MR. COMMISSIONER KELLOCK Then just so that I am perfectly clear, when a man is called a corporator, as in this document, does that mean that he is a member of the Canadian Communist party?

GOUZENKO "Corporant" means —

KELLOCK No; "corporator."

GOUZENKO "Corporator" means a member of any Communist party abroad, outside of Russia.

KELLOCK Then do I understand that "Comintern" means a federation of all these Communist parties abroad and the Communist party in Russia?

GOUZENKO Yes.

KELLOCK So that a corporator, by virtue of being a member, we will say, of the Communist party in Canada, is also a member of the Comintern?

GOUZENKO The Communist International, the Comintern, is the staff headquarters which directs the activities of the Communist parties all over the world. . . .

MR. WILLIAMS The document Exhibit 14 is a genuine document from the files of the Russian embassy in Ottawa?

GOUZENKO That is right.

WILLIAMS And the signature "Grant" is the cover signature or nickname of Colonel Zabotin?

GOUZENKO That is right.

WILLIAMS The document is in his handwriting, with the exception of the date put on at the top?

GOUZENKO Yes.

WILLIAMS Is that in your handwriting?

GOUZENKO That is mine.

WILLIAMS That is 12/7/45; and it is written by yourself?

GOUZENKO That is right.

WILLIAMS And is the date upon which you coded this telegram into the code and handed it to be sent off?

GOUZENKO That is right.

MR. COMMISSIONER KELLOCK   I just want to come back to that last subject for a moment, to make it perfectly clear to myself. I am looking at Exhibit 19, the first sheet, which is headed "Registration card" dealing with Sam Carr. The last two lines read, "Detailed biographical information." Apparently that is the form before it was filled in; after that it says: "the Comintern. Knows Russian perfectly. Finished the Lenin school in Moscow." If the Comintern means the staff in Moscow which runs the Communist party, as I understand it, in Russia and abroad, does that reference on Carr's registration card mean that he is a member of that staff?

GOUZENKO   No.

KELLOCK   All right; then what is the explanation?

GOUZENKO   On every Communist there is a file at the Comintern at Moscow; for every Communist in the whole world there is a file at the Comintern at Moscow. More detailed information is on the files at the Comintern.

KELLOCK   So this reference on the registration card means that if anybody is looking at this registration card and wants more information on Carr than it contains, there is more information on file at Moscow?

GOUZENKO   That is right.

MR. WILLIAMS   And am I correct in understanding that the word "Comintern" is also used in Russia to refer to the secretariat in Moscow of the foreign Communist parties? Is that correct?

GOUZENKO   No. The Comintern or Communist International is like a headquarters that directs the activities of the Communist parties in the whole world.

WILLIAMS   That is approximately what I said; a headquarters staff?

GOUZENKO   Yes. . . .

WILLIAMS   Then we come to Exhibit 20-A, and if you will follow that I will read the translation to you and ask you if it is correct. The No. 232 is in the upper right-hand corner. "To the director." "1. We have agreed with Sam about the transfer of connections to us."?

GOUZENKO   "With Promety."

WILLIAMS   "We have agreed with Sam about the transfer of connections to us with Promety." I thought, Mr. Commissioners, that when we got the translation agreed upon in each case I would ask the meaning of the words and various things, instead of taking them up singly. "The latter is at present in Florida."?

GOUZENKO   Yes.

WILLIAMS   "The transfer will take place in the town of Sam on his return from Florida."?

GOUZENKO   Yes.

WILLIAMS   "I consider it expedient to give Brent the connection with Promety."

GOUZENKO   That is right. . . .

WILLIAMS   "2. Sam promises to give us several officers from — and what is that blank space?

GOUZENKO   "From central headquarters of active forces."

WILLIAMS   "At the present time it is fairly difficult to do this, that is, in the staffs is taking place change of service by the officers returning from overseas."

GOUZENKO   That is right.

WILLIAMS   "3. We have received from Gray the whole correspondence on the question of the theory of the deformation of the shell in the channel of the barrel.''

GOUZENKO   That is right.

WILLIAMS   "Altogether about 150 pages. We shall send them in rote.''?

GOUZENKO   That is right.

WILLIAMS   Signed "Grant,'' and the date at the bottom is 2/8/45?

GOUZENKO   Yes.

WILLIAMS   First of all, this does not appear to be an answer to a telegram?

GOUZENKO   That was on his initiative.

WILLIAMS   So it did not need a number up here?

GOUZENKO   No.

WILLIAMS   And why was no date filled in at the bottom?

GOUZENKO   I forgot to put it.

WILLIAMS   And the Sam referred to in this telegram is Sam Carr?

GOUZENKO   That is right. . . .

WILLIAMS   And Brent was the cover name for Rogov?

GOUZENKO   That is right.

WILLIAMS   Now what is the significance of this giving Brent the connection with Prometheus?

GOUZENKO   Colonel Zabotin is proposing to hand over the contact with Prometheus through Brent, and Brent would contact Prometheus.

WILLIAMS   Up to this time Prometheus was contacting direct?

GOUZENKO   Through Sam Carr.

WILLIAMS   And now they were going to change that, and he would contact through Rogov?

GOUZENKO   That is right; direct.

WILLIAMS   Then in the third sentence "Gray" is the code name for Gerson?

GOUZENKO   Yes.

WILLIAMS   That is from Gerson?

GOUZENKO   Yes.

WILLIAMS   And this Exhibit 20-A is an original and genuine document from the offices of the Russian embassy in Ottawa?

GOUZENKO   That is right.

WILLIAMS   Written by Colonel Zabotin in his own handwriting, and signed by his cover name or nickname, Grant?

GOUZENKO   Yes.

WILLIAMS   And the director is the same director that we have already referred to. . . .

GOUZENKO   That is right. . . .

WILLIAMS   Now I come to Exhibit 20-B. The number is 233, and it is addressed to the director: "My son Vladimir has finished his tenth year successfully. He has declined to enter the Institute of International Relations and is about to enter the First Moscow Artillery School in the name of Krasin, which I finished in 1924. In order to send my son off I ask to leave for a very short time. It appears to me that the time has come for me to be at the centre to discuss the question of our work.''?

GOUZENKO   "Serious questions.''

WILLIAMS   '' — to discuss serious questions''?

GOUZENKO   Yes, "of our work."

WILLIAMS   "If it is indeed impossible for me to leave, I ask that my wife be sent with my son."

GOUZENKO   That is right.

WILLIAMS   "I ask for co-operation in the entry of my son in the artillery school, and to advise me of the time of departure."

GOUZENKO   Yes.

WILLIAMS   "My wife cannot fly in an aeroplane."

GOUZENKO   That is right.

WILLIAMS   And that has been signed "Grant" first, and "Grant" has been struck out and he was signed "N. Zabotin."?

GOUZENKO   Yes. This is why I picked this, only because it is Grant and Zabotin. This is why I took it, because Grant is struck out and Zabotin signs his name; otherwise the document is no good.

WILLIAMS   Was Exhibit 20-B codified by you; was it sent in code?

GOUZENKO   Yes.

WILLIAMS   There is a reference in it, however, to the "centre"?

GOUZENKO   Yes.

WILLIAMS   What is "the centre"?

GOUZENKO   That is Moscow, or more accurately the general intelligence headquarters.

WILLIAMS   That is referred to as the centre?

GOUZENKO   Yes. That is the usual expression in Soviet circles referring to the headquarters of the respective departments.

MR. COMMISSIONER TASCHEREAU   You said that the only importance of that Exhibit 20-B, signed by Zabotin, is that he struck out "Grant" and wrote "Zabotin"?

GOUZENKO   Yes.

TASCHEREAU   So it proves that Grant is Zabotin?

GOUZENKO   Yes.

TASCHEREAU   And that is Zabotin's handwriting?

GOUZENKO   That is right. . . .

TASCHEREAU   When it is signed "Grant"?

GOUZENKO   That is right.

MR. WILLIAMS   Then Exhibit 20-C. This is No. 234. It is addressed to the director: "Gray has obtained a copy of a letter of the deputy minister of Munitions and Supplies, G.K. Sheils, to all government companies, to government companies which are under private management, and to the principal directors of production branches, May, 1945. I report the contents of the letter."

GOUZENKO   That is right.

WILLIAMS

All the three branches of the armed forces of the Department of National Defence decided to review all the facts available from the point of view of selection and definition of the necessary arms and munitions which they will need. However, they (the army, navy and air force) still have not got a list of the necessary supplies which we are producing. We would like the production branches and government companies to take part in filling up forms of the production being turned out for handing them over to the corresponding branch of the armed forces indicating for whom the designated arms and munitions were produced (for the needs of Canada or for orderers). Naturally, each branch of the armed forces will need different lists corresponding to their requirements. The preparation and distribution of these lists must be completed 31st of May of this year. On receipt of the completed forms all three services will indicate the category of the materials of arms and equipment in which they are more interested. The council of post-war arsenals which is interested in preserving such technical information, has been contracted on the following dislocation of supplies material:

(1) Guns, set-ups, etc. Dominion Engineering Works, Longueuil, Quebec.

GOUZENKO   That should be "mountings."

WILLIAMS

"Guns, mountings, etc. Dominion Engineering Works, Limited, Longueuil, Quebec. (2) Shells for guns, Lindsay Arsenal, Lindsay, Ontario. (3) Infantry arms and machine guns — Small Arms Limited, Long Branch, Ontario. (4) Ammunitions for infantry arms — Dominion Arsenal, Quebec. (5) Equipping (in the sense of shell filling, etc.) plant — Defence Industries Limited, Cherier, Quebec. (6) Explosive materials and chemicals, not decided. (7) Optical appliances, instruments for radio locator — Research Enterprises, Limited." Then there is the second sheet: "(8) Automobiles and tanks — Orleans Proving Grounds, Montreal. (9) Radio and other means of communication — Signal Workshop, Eastview. (10) Shell cases — not decided. (11) Appliances for chemic. defence — Respiration Assembly Plant, Ottawa, Ontario. Deputy Minister (signature) Grant 2.8.45."

GOUZENKO   Yes.
WILLIAMS   That translation is correct?
GOUZENKO   Yes.
WILLIAMS   Gray is Gerson?
GOUZENKO   Yes. . . .
WILLIAMS   The next telegram which is No. 241 will be Exhibit No. 20-D . . .   (To the witness)   This reads: "To the Director, the facts given by Alec: (1) The experiments with the atomic bomb were conducted in New Mexico (with "49", "94-239")."
GOUZENKO   That is right.
WILLIAMS   "The bomb thrown on Japan was made of uranium 235. It is known that the release of uranium 235 is produced to the amount of 400 grams daily at the magnetic separation plant in Clinton."
GOUZENKO   That is right.

WILLIAMS   "The release of "49" is likely two times greater (some graphite units composed on 250 moda matta)."

GOUZENKO   That is megawatts; it is in English.

WILLIAMS   It is 250 mega?

GOUZENKO   Watts.

WILLIAMS   "Megawatts. That is, i.e., 250 grams a day. The scientific research work in this field is scheduled to be published, but without the technical details. The Americans already have a printed book on this subject. (2) Alec handed over to us a platinum with 162 micrograms of uranium 233 in the form of acid, contained in a thin lamina. We had no news about the mail. Grant. 9.8.45." This is correct?

GOUZENKO   Yes. . . .

WILLIAMS   Each one of these telegrams in Exhibit 20, all of the Exhibit 20 telegrams were coded by yourself?

GOUZENKO   That is right.

MR. COMMISSIONER KELLOCK   And received by the witness from Zabotin?

GOUZENKO   Yes.

MR. WILLIAMS   They were all in his handwriting, all in this exhibit?

GOUZENKO   That is right.

WILLIAMS   Do you know who Alec is?

GOUZENKO   It is a nickname of a scientist.

WILLIAMS   Do you know the real name of the scientist?

GOUZENKO   Yes.

WILLIAMS   What is it?

GOUZENKO   Alan Nunn May.

WILLIAMS   How did you learn that?

GOUZENKO   Moscow sent a telegram and it said that it is imperative to establish contact with Alan Nunn May who is a very valuable source. For certain reasons we had to stop contacting him. It was a very delicate business, therefore, to establish contact with him and must be done with the greatest care. He works in a scientific laboratory in Montreal. He is a member of the English corporation.

MR. COMMISSIONER TASCHEREAU   Does he actually work in Montreal or did he work before in Montreal?

GOUZENKO   In the telegram it said that he works in Montreal and he arrived from England.

MR. WILLIAMS   You said that he is a member of the British corporation? Do you mean that he is a member of the British Communist party?

GOUZENKO   That is right.

TASCHEREAU   The witness said that there were certain reasons, and he used the pronoun "we" had to stop contacting him. Will he explain what he means by that?

GOUZENKO   For some unknown reasons which Zabotin did not tell me, Zabotin did not know; he was told that Moscow had good reasons for stopping to make contact with him in England, but now when he was in Canada they wanted to renew the contact.

TASCHEREAU   He is back in England now?

MR. COMMISSIONER KELLOCK   That was before. What the witness was telling us before was really the contents of this telegram from Moscow to Canada and in that telegram, as I understand it, it was said that they — we will say the Russians — for certain reasons had had to stop contacting May in England. (*To the witness*) Is that right?

GOUZENKO   No. He did not say in England; he said for certain reasons we had to stop contacting him temporarily.

KELLOCK   Then they went on to say that they wanted the Ottawa embassy, the Canadian embassy in Ottawa, to contact him?

GOUZENKO   That is right. . . .

February 14, 1946.

MR. WILLIAMS   Among the documents which you brought with you was one which I show you now and which is written in Russian on ruled paper and which looks as though it had been taken out of or torn out of a notebook?

GOUZENKO   That is right.

WILLIAMS   And is it all written in the same handwriting?

GOUZENKO   That is right.

WILLIAMS   Whose handwriting is it?

GOUZENKO   Colonel Zabotin's. . . .

WILLIAMS   Obviously this has been torn into three pieces at one time?

GOUZENKO   That is right.

WILLIAMS   Who did that?

GOUZENKO   Colonel Zabotin.

WILLIAMS   Did he do it in your presence?

GOUZENKO   That is right.

WILLIAMS   When did he do it, and where?

GOUZENKO   In Room 12.

WILLIAMS   Room 12. That has already been referred to. What did he do with the pieces?

GOUZENKO   He give them to me to burn. . . .

WILLIAMS   When you came to the police for protection you brought with you the three pieces?

GOUZENKO   That is right.

WILLIAMS   Which have now been pasted together?

GOUZENKO   That is right.

WILLIAMS   I ask you to follow it while I read a translation and I ask you to say whether or not the translation is correct. . . . Do you remember just when it was that this document Exhibit No. 22 was torn and given to you to burn?

GOUZENKO   Middle of August, 1945.

WILLIAMS   The exhibit has been torn out of something; do you know what it was torn out of?

GOUZENKO   A notebook. There were empty pages; he left the empty pages. He tore out the ones that had been written on.

WILLIAMS   As a matter of fact you brought other sheets with you out of the same notebook?

GOUZENKO   That is right.

WILLIAMS   This is one of them?

GOUZENKO   Yes.

WILLIAMS   And you saw him tear this out of the notebook?

GOUZENKO   Yes, that is right.

WILLIAMS   So there was nothing left in the notebook but blank sheets?

GOUZENKO   That is right.

WILLIAMS   This is headed, "Second Group (Ottawa-Toronto). Sam (Frank). Jew. Organizer. Studied with us in 1924-26 in Soviet school. Speaks Russian. Leon became acquainted with Frank at a meeting in October, 1942."

GOUZENKO   That is right.

WILLIAMS   "He proposed Foster."

GOUZENKO   That is right.

WILLIAMS   "He proposed Foster — Englishman. . . . Assistant to the superintendent of distribution of war production with the Ministry of Munitions and Supply."

GOUZENKO   That is right.

WILLIAMS   "Gave material about war material?"

GOUZENKO   That is right.

WILLIAMS   "Guns and other kinds of supplies"?

GOUZENKO   That is right.

WILLIAMS   "Obtaining other work with promotion"?

GOUZENKO   That is right.

WILLIAMS   "Can give better materials"?

GOUZENKO   That is right.

WILLIAMS   How do you translate the next line?

GOUZENKO   "He is contacting with Martin."

WILLIAMS   Would "tied up" be a good translation or is "contacting" better?

GOUZENKO   "Contacting."

WILLIAMS   The next word is "our." Then "too Ernst — Jew. Works in the United" — is that correct as far as it goes?

GOUZENKO   "The United Committee of Military Production."

WILLIAMS   Part of the exhibit seems to be torn off but all the words are left.

WILLIAMS   We can reestablish it. It is United Committee of Military Production (United States and Canada) (coordination)*.

WILLIAMS   That is all on the one side. Will you turn over and I will read you the translation of what appears on the reverse side of Exhibit No. 22. "He gives detailed information about all kinds of industries, plans for the future."

GOUZENKO   That is right.

WILLIAMS   "Supplies detailed accounts of sessions"?

GOUZENKO   That is right.

WILLIAMS   Then what follows?

GOUZENKO   "He gives daily materials and works well" — a good worker.

WILLIAMS   Would the translation be that "he gives materials daily"?

GOUZENKO   Yes.

WILLIAMS   "A good worker," and the next?

---

*Joint War Production Committee

GOUZENKO	"He is connected with Foster."
WILLIAMS	"Both live in Ottawa."
GOUZENKO	That is right. "Taken to work at the end of January."
WILLIAMS	This line should be struck out?
GOUZENKO	That is right.
WILLIAMS	Then three?
GOUZENKO	"Polland" [Poland].
WILLIAMS	It is "H" but it should be a "P". "Polland. Ministry of Aviation."
GOUZENKO	Yes.
WILLIAMS	"Works in Toronto in the Intelligence Branch"?
GOUZENKO	That is right.
WILLIAMS	At the moment is being transferred to Ottawa"?
GOUZENKO	That is right.
WILLIAMS	"He gave a map" — is map or plan a better translation?
GOUZENKO	"Map."
WILLIAMS	"He gave a map of the instructional schools"?
GOUZENKO	"Training schools."
WILLIAMS	"Up to the present is not working."
GOUZENKO	That is right.
WILLIAMS	There is a note on the side opposite Poland which reads, "New names not introduced."
GOUZENKO	That is right.
WILLIAMS	Then there is 4. What is that word?
GOUZENKO	"Surensen."
WILLIAMS	What is next?
GOUZENKO	"He works in the naval ministry. He works in Intelligence."
WILLIAMS	Gave materials about?
GOUZENKO	It is hard to read in Russian because it is badly written, but I think it is "construction of ships. He went overseas."
WILLIAMS	Is "left for overseas" a good translation? . . .
GOUZENKO	Yes.
WILLIAMS	"Both worked up to April"?
GOUZENKO	That is right.
WILLIAMS	Looking at Exhibit No. 22, we have already dealt with the same Sam. You have said that is Sam Carr?
GOUZENKO	That is right.
WILLIAMS	And he also had the cover name or nickname of Frank?
GOUZENKO	That is right.
WILLIAMS	And Leon was Milsky, was he not?
GOUZENKO	No, Leon was Koudriadtzev.
WILLIAMS	Then Foster was the cover or nickname for Benning?
GOUZENKO	That is right.
WILLIAMS	Martin is the cover name for Zheveinov. . . . Then the next is Ernst, which you have identified as the cover name or nickname of Eric Adams?
GOUZENKO	That is right.
WILLIAMS	Then we come to Poland. Is that a real name or a cover name?
GOUZENKO	I do not know.
WILLIAMS	Do you know Surensen?

GOUZENKO   This is the only time I saw it.

WILLIAMS   That is the only time you saw that name?

GOUZENKO   Yes, in this exhibit.

WILLIAMS   You do not know whether it is a real name or a cover or nickname?

GOUZENKO   No.

WILLIAMS   Had you heard of Poland other than what you saw in that document? Had you heard his name mentioned?

GOUZENKO   That is right.

WILLIAMS   What did you hear about him?

GOUZENKO   I saw it in a telegram which was sent by Zabotin to Moscow in 1943 concerning Poland and he suggested to give Poland to the N.K.V.D.

WILLIAMS   Just explain, will you please, what you mean by giving Poland to the N.K.V.D.

GOUZENKO   Poland was described as a clever man and Colonel Zabotin proposed to Moscow in a telegram to hand him over to Neighbors, which is the N.K.V.D. Neighbors is the nickname for the N.K.V.D. Moscow replied that it was not worth while, to wait a while so that he might develop into a good worker. I still do not know his real name or nickname. That was the only other time I saw the name Poland and still I do not know whether it was his real name or his nickname.

WILLIAMS   Did you have any knowledge apart from Exhibit No. 22 of what Poland was doing?

GOUZENKO   The telegrams that were sent on this subject made no detailed mention of his activities.

WILLIAMS   I think perhaps at this stage, Messrs. Commissioners, I should make the application which we have in mind. Counsel request the commissioners to authorize them to make a communication to the Right Honourable Minister of Justice reading in this way:

> By reason of the nature of the evidence already submitted to the Royal Commission, the undersigned Counsel to the Commission have recommended to the Commissioners that you should be requested to exercise the powers conferred upon you by P.C. 6444, 6th October, 1945, and to issue Orders for interrogation and, for that purpose, detention of the following persons:

ISIDORE HALPERIN	RAYMOND BOYER
DAVID SHUGAR	JAMES SCOTLAND BENNING
M.S. NIGHTINGALE	H.S. GERSON
F.W. POLAND	ERIC ADAMS
NED MAZERALL	EMMA WOIKIN
DURNFORD SMITH	GORDON LUNAN.

MR. COMMISSIONER TASCHEREAU   I understand that all the names that you have just mentioned are the names of persons who were mentioned yesterday in the evidence.

WILLIAMS   Yesterday and this morning, yes.

TASCHEREAU   As to Poland; the witness mentioned Polland, with two "l's" but

70

he did not identify that cover name of Poland as being the person mentioned in your application.

WILLIAMS   That is so, but evidence will be placed before you to show that a man named F.W. Poland occupied the position indicated in the note of Colonel Zabotin at the time.

TASCHEREAU   That he works in Toronto in the Intelligence Branch.

WILLIAMS   Yes.

MR. COMMISSIONER KELLOCK   You say, "at that time." What time?

WILLIAMS   At the time the witness has referred to, and in fact during the whole period of 1943 and he was subsequently transferred to Ottawa.

TASCHEREAU   He would be F.W. Poland?

WILLIAMS   Yes.

KELLOCK   You say you will have other evidence with regard to him and identifying him as the person holding the qualifications mentioned in Exhibit No. 22?

WILLIAMS   And further evidence that he resided with Lunan.

TASCHEREAU   It is your desire and the desire of the other counsel that a letter be sent to the Right Honourable Mr. St. Laurent?

WILLIAMS   Yes.

TASCHEREAU   To detain these persons for interrogation by the Mounted Police?

WILLIAMS   Yes.

TASCHEREAU   Mr. Commissioner Kellock and myself have come to the conclusion that we should accept your advice and that such a request should be sent to the minister of justice. The reasons which impel us to accept your advice are the extremely serious nature of the disclosures so far made and indicated by the evidence and also the fact that cover names of persons who have not so far been identified also appear in the evidence and indicate that the full extent of the ramifications of the disloyal practices and the persons engaged therein may be even greater than is already known and may be continuing. The matter appears to be so serious from the national standpoint that Mr. Commissioner Kellock and myself believe that the course you advise should be pursued in these exceptional circumstances.

WILLIAMS   Thank you, sir.

KELLOCK   I agree with my brother Taschereau. We had an intimation yesterday that such an application would be made and we have both had an opportunity of giving it very careful consideration.

WILLIAMS   I suggest that I resume the consideration of the documents forming part of Exhibit No. 20. The next one will be Exhibit No. 20-E, and it deals with telegram No. 242.   (*To the witness*)   I now show you a blue sheet of paper upon which is written a telegram in the handwriting of Colonel Zabotin?

GOUZENKO   That is right.

WILLIAMS   I shall read the translation and ask you to say whether it is correct. It is to the Director. "Alek has reported brief data on our task about the electronic shells. In particular these shells are being adapted against the Japanese suicide aviators by the American navy. In the shell there is a small radio transmitter with one electronic lamp." Is that "lamp" or "bulb"?

GOUZENKO   "Lamp". . . .

WILLIAMS   The literal translation of the Russian word would be "lamp", but it means bulb?

GOUZENKO   Yes.

WILLIAMS   "And is fed by dry batteries. The body of the shell is the antenna."

GOUZENKO   That is right.

WILLIAMS   "The bomb explodes in the proximity of an aeroplane from the action of the reflecting waves of the plane of the transmitter. The main difficulties were found to be the manufacture of a bulb and battery that would withstand the discharge." Is there anything in brackets following that?

GOUZENKO   No.

WILLIAMS   "And in determining the rotary speed of the shell."

GOUZENKO   That is right.

WILLIAMS   "Which would not require special adaptation during preparation of the shell. The Americans have attained this result but apparently have not handed this over to the English. The Americans have adapted a plastic covering for the battery which resists the force of pressure during the motion of the shell."

GOUZENKO   That is right.

WILLIAMS   That is signed "Grant", and the date is 9.7.45.

GOUZENKO   That is right. . . .

WILLIAMS   The Alek referred to in Exhibit No. 22-E has already been identified as Professor Alan Nunn May?

GOUZENKO   This is the first time I heard him being called a professor. I did not know he was a professor. I knew his name Alan Nunn May.

WILLIAMS   Alec is the cover name or nickname for Alan Nunn May?

GOUZENKO   That is right. . . .

WILLIAMS   Then I show you original telegram No. 243, which is in the handwriting of Colonel Zabotin?

GOUZENKO   That is right. . . .

WILLIAMS   I would ask you if the translation is a correct translation? "To the director. Alec reported to us that he met Norman Veal (he was at his home)" —

GOUZENKO   Yes.

WILLIAMS   "Veal works in the laboratory of the Montreal branch of the Scientific Research Council, where he is responsible for making apparatus and other glass work."

GOUZENKO   That is right.

WILLIAMS   "He arrived from England in 1943, where he was a member of the party for several years."

GOUZENKO   That is right.

WILLIAMS   "He worked on meteorology in the British B.B.C."

GOUZENKO   That is the air force; the British R.A.F.

WILLIAMS   "In the British R.A.F."?

GOUZENKO   Yes.

WILLIAMS

"He takes part in the Canadian Association of Scientific Workers, and works there as foreign correspondent. In this connection he visited our embassy and spoke with one of our press attachés who is in charge of the press distribution of journals, etc. He asked the opinion of Alec, would it be worth his while —'' and after the word "his" the word "Veal" is in brackets — "worth Veal's while to hand over information about the atomic bomb.'' Then on the reverse side it continues: "Alec expressed himself in the negative. Alec reported that Veal occupies a fairly low position and knows very little. He is inclined to be careless, and he began this conversation in the presence of his wife. He is pretty well known in the laboratory as a Red. His age is about twenty-five years. He is married and has one child. His address is Van Horne, 2870, apartment 5; telephone Atlantic 2084. We gave Alec no tasks about Veal. The possibility is not excepted that he may have already tied up with the neighbour. I consider it necessary to warn the neighbour. Please correct.''

And that is signed "Grant"?
GOUZENKO   That is correct.
WILLIAMS   We have already identified Alec, and we have already had a reference to Veal, whose name was spelled Veale in one of the other exhibits?
GOUZENKO   That is right.
WILLIAMS   I would ask you about this sentence: "He arrived from England in 1943, where he was a member of the party for several years.'' What party is referred to there?
GOUZENKO   The Communist party.
WILLIAMS   Then in a later sentence: "He takes part in the Canadian Association of Scientific Workers and works there as foreign correspondent.'' Foreign correspondent for whom; do you know?
GOUZENKO   I would understand that to be that he was the Canadian correspondent, the English correspondent in Canada.
WILLIAMS   For what?
GOUZENKO   I understand that he was the English correspondent for Canada.
WILLIAMS   But for what?
GOUZENKO   For England.
WILLIAMS   But for the Communist party, or for journals or publications?
GOUZENKO   In Russian "correspondent" means "journalist". . . .
MR. COMMISSIONER TASCHEREAU   "Veal" is not a cover name?
MR. WILLIAMS   No; "Veal" is a real name.   (To the witness)   Then in the next sentence there is a reference to "our embassy." That is the Russian embassy?
GOUZENKO   That is right.
WILLIAMS   Then on the reverse side, in the third last sentence: "The possibility is not excepted that he may have already tied up with the neighbour." The words "the neighbour" are an expression referring to what?
GOUZENKO   It is the nickname of N.K.V.D.
WILLIAMS   And the next sentence: "I consider it necessary to warn the neighbour," means to warn N.K.V.D.?
GOUZENKO   Yes. Personally it would be Pavlov.
WILLIAMS   That is the warning to the N.K.V.D. would go to Pavlov?
GOUZENKO   That is right.
MR. COMMISSIONER KELLOCK   Pavlov is in Ottawa here, is he?
GOUZENKO   Yes.

MR. WILLIAMS   Pavlov is shown on Exhibit 15 as secretary and consul under the ambassador, Zaroubin?

GOUZENKO   That is right. . . .

WILLIAMS   I now show you an original telegram, No. 244, which is Exhibit 20-G. That is in the handwriting of Colonel Zabotin?

GOUZENKO   Yes. . . .

WILLIAMS   I will now read a translation to you and ask you to say whether it is a correct translation: "To the director. We have worked out the appearance with Alec in London."

GOUZENKO   I do not know exactly the translation in English. . . .

WILLIAMS   I think that could be accepted: "We have worked out the conditions for a meeting with Alec in London."?

GOUZENKO   That is right.

WILLIAMS   So the first sentence reads in the translation: "We have worked out the conditions for a meeting with Alec in London. Alec will work in King's College, Strand. He may be found there through the telephone book."?

GOUZENKO   That is right.

WILLIAMS   "Meetings: October 7/17/27. On the street in front of the British museum. The time, 11 o'clock in the evening. Identification sign: 'Best regards from Mikel'."

GOUZENKO   Just a moment. "The paper under his left arm."

WILLIAMS   "Identification sign." Is that right?

GOUZENKO   Yes.

WILLIAMS   Then there is something omitted in this translation. "A paper under his arm." Is that it?

GOUZENKO   "A newspaper under the left armpit.". . .

WILLIAMS   Then what follows?

GOUZENKO   "Password: 'Best regards from Mikel'."

WILLIAMS   That is spelled "Mikel"?

GOUZENKO   Yes.

WILLIAMS   And then in brackets how is it spelled?

GOUZENKO   "Maikl."

WILLIAMS   "He cannot remain in Canada. In the beginning of September he must fly to London."

GOUZENKO   That is right.

WILLIAMS   "Before his departure he will go to the uranium plant in the Petawawa district, where he will be about two weeks."

GOUZENKO   That is right.

WILLIAMS   "If possible he promises to meet us before his departure."

GOUZENKO   That is right.

WILLIAMS   "He said he will come next year for a month in Canada."

GOUZENKO   That is right.

WILLIAMS   "We handed over $500 to him." And the signature is "Grant"?

GOUZENKO   That is right.

WILLIAMS   Alec is Alan Nunn May?

GOUZENKO   That is right. . . .

WILLIAMS   I now show you telegram No. 247, in Colonel Zabotin's handwriting, a telegram which you coded and which is an original document from the Russian embassy?

GOUZENKO   That is right.

WILLIAMS   I will read the translation to you and ask you if it is a correct translation: "To the director. Although you send us operational sums of money through Metro we must nevertheless get them through the bank. Thus nothing is gained with the conspiracy."

GOUZENKO   That is right.

WILLIAMS   "Can you send us Canadian dollars by mail?"

GOUZENKO   That is right.

WILLIAMS   "The latter will ensure full conspiracy for the requested sums."

GOUZENKO   "For the operative sums."

MR. COMMISSIONER KELLOCK   Would that word "conspiracy" be better translated "secrecy"?

GOUZENKO   "Conspiracy" would be more correct. . . .

KELLOCK   Could that not mean "nothing is gained from the standpoint of secrecy"?

GOUZENKO   In Russian "conspiracy" and "secrecy" are very close together, practically one and the same thing.

MR. COMMISSIONER TASCHEREAU   It must be "secrecy" then?

GOUZENKO   Yes. . . .

TASCHEREAU   What is the meaning of the word "Metro"?

GOUZENKO   That is the nickname or pseudonym for the embassy in Ottawa.

MR. WILLIAMS   And in the sentence "The latter will ensure full secrecy for the operative sums."?

GOUZENKO   Yes, that is right.

WILLIAMS   "At present the sums sent by you should not attract attention, as we are carrying out repairs, receipt of machines, arrival of people, etc."

GOUZENKO   That is right.

WILLIAMS   "In the future this will be noticeable."

GOUZENKO   That is right.

MR. COMMISSIONER KELLOCK   I notice this exhibit appears to be dated September 11. The witness had left before September 11. Is there any explanation of that?

WILLIAMS   Mr. Commissioner Kellock pointed out that this is dated September 11, but you had left the embassy before that date?

GOUZENKO   That was a mistake on the part of Colonel Zabotin. He very frequently made mistakes. . . .

WILLIAMS   This exhibit is all in his handwriting?

GOUZENKO   Yes, sir.

WILLIAMS   And is signed by Colonel Zabotin as "Grant"?

GOUZENKO   Yes.

MR. COMMISSIONER TASCHEREAU   The following telegram, which is numbered 248, is dated August, so this one should be August?

GOUZENKO   Yes; that is proof of it.

MR. WILLIAMS   So the date at the bottom of Exhibit 20-H should be 11/8/45?

GOUZENKO   That is right. . . .

WILLIAMS   I now show you telegram No. 248, in Colonel Zabotin's handwriting;

an original telegram coded by yourself and an original document from the Russian embassy?

GOUZENKO   That is right.

WILLIAMS   I will now read you a translation and ask you to say whether it is a correct translation: "To the director. I was scolded for some kind of material which apparently became known to Metro."

GOUZENKO   That is right.

WILLIAMS   "I ask you to advise me about what material is concerned."

GOUZENKO   That is right.

WILLIAMS   "I informed the master of Metro on political, economic and military questions in accordance with instructions given to me by the chief director and Comrade Malenkoff."

GOUZENKO   That is right.

WILLIAMS   "The sources were never reported by me."

GOUZENKO   That is right.

WILLIAMS   "Please instruct for the future. Am I to inform the ambassador about questions concerning Canada and received from my sources?"

GOUZENKO   That is right.

WILLIAMS   "From afar it seems to me that Metro should be one of the most informed persons."

GOUZENKO   That should be "the master of Metro."

WILLIAMS   There is a reference in Exhibit 20-I to the chief director. Is that the director of intelligence appearing on Exhibit 15, or is it some person else?

GOUZENKO   That is the nickname of the chief of the general intelligence headquarters of the Red Army.

WILLIAMS   And then it goes on to say, "and Comrade Malenkoff." Is "Malenkoff" a real name or a nickname or cover name?

GOUZENKO   It is a real name.

WILLIAMS   And who is Malenkoff?

GOUZENKO   He is a member of the politburo of the central committee of the Communist party of Russia. . . .

WILLIAMS   Then who is described as the master of Metro?

GOUZENKO   That is the nickname of the ambassador. . . .

WILLIAMS   I now show you Exhibit 20-J, an original telegram in the handwriting of Colonel Zabotin and one of those coded by yourself, an original document from the Russian embassy?

GOUZENKO   That is right.

WILLIAMS   And I read you a translation and ask you to say whether it is a correct translation: "To the director —" what is the next word?

GOUZENKO   "To the director, in answer to number so and so."

WILLIAMS   "— in answer to No. 11295. 1. The tasks will be detailed to Gray, Bacon and the Professor through Debouz."

GOUZENKO   That is right.

WILLIAMS   "The Professor is still on command."

GOUZENKO   That means that he is away somewhere on a detailed trip. . . .

WILLIAMS   And in English that signifies that he is on a job away from home?

GOUZENKO   That is right.

WILLIAMS   "Debouz will meet at the end of the month."

GOUZENKO   That is right.

WILLIAMS   "2. Martin received reply from Dekanosov with permission to return home. As a result of Martin's work at the San Francisco conference and his sickness about a month the latter was unable to write all his reports on your task. The question of the current situation in Canada after the elections and the interruption of the class forces in the country he will write at our place."

GOUZENKO   Yes.

WILLIAMS   "And we will send them to you by courier, while the remaining questions of the task he will write at the centre."

GOUZENKO   That is right.

WILLIAMS   Then the signature is "Grant."

GOUZENKO   That is right.

WILLIAMS   And the date is 14/8/45?

GOUZENKO   That is right.

WILLIAMS   We have already identified Gray as the cover name or nickname of Gerson?

GOUZENKO   That is right.

WILLIAMS   Bacon is the cover or nickname of Halperin. The Professor is the cover or nickname of Professor Boyer, and Debouz is the cover or nickname for Fred Rose?

GOUZENKO   That is right.

WILLIAMS   Then Martin has been identified as the cover name for Zheveinov of Tass?

GOUZENKO   Yes.

WILLIAMS   And Dekanosov is a real name?

GOUZENKO   Yes.

WILLIAMS   And he is whom?

GOUZENKO   He is the assistant of Molotov in Moscow.

WILLIAMS   And who is Molotov?

GOUZENKO   He is People's Commissar of foreign affairs. . . .

WILLIAMS   And, "the centre" referred to — ?

GOUZENKO   Moscow. . . .

WILLIAMS   Exhibit No. 20-K will be telegram No. 252, which is in the handwriting of Colonel Zabotin and was codified by you?

GOUZENKO   The former telegram and this telegram were coded by Koulakov. He has a different system of marking his words.

WILLIAMS   You can tell by the checks that Koulakov had coded this. You were present?

GOUZENKO   Yes.

WILLIAMS   And he was working with you?

GOUZENKO   That is right. . . .

WILLIAMS   I will ask you to follow the original while I read the translation to you. It is addressed to the director. "At the end of August will be leaving Martin and his family."

GOUZENKO   That is right.

WILLIAMS   "I am sending with him Klark with his family and my son. In connection with the departure of my son I beg you to allow me the sum of $300 to $400 in advance, to be repaid in three-four months. If it were possible,

I would beg you to register my son in the First Artillery school of candidates."
That is signed "Grant" and the date is 16.8.45.

GOUZENKO   That is right.

WILLIAMS   We have already identified Martin. Who is Klark?

GOUZENKO   It is my nickname.

WILLIAMS   That is your nickname?

GOUZENKO   That is right. . . .

WILLIAMS   The next exhibit will be Exhibit No. 20-L. That is in the handwriting of Colonel Zabotin and is a telegram coded by you?

GOUZENKO   That is right.

WILLIAMS   This is an original document from the Russian embassy?

GOUZENKO   On the occasion when I got this telegram Colonel Zabotin said it was not necessary and he took it because he changed his mind and tore it up.

WILLIAMS   And you brought the pieces with you?

GOUZENKO   That is right.

WILLIAMS   Did he give the pieces to you to be destroyed?

GOUZENKO   That is right.

WILLIAMS   And instead of destroying them you kept them and brought the pieces with you when you came to the police for protection and it has since been pasted together?

GOUZENKO   That is right.

WILLIAMS   I will ask you to follow the translation and tell me if it is an accurate translation. "To the Director. 1. In my brief account on two years of work the beginning of the second point on the nine page was not coded by me. It should read: "Commander of aviation Mak Kell. 2. In your letter is indicated that No. 1 — superintendent of operational branch Colonel Jenkins, but the characteristics are taken from the matter of Dick. Colonel Jenkins did not appear discharge." Is that correct?

GOUZENKO   "Colonel Jenkins is not a candidate for development."

WILLIAMS   "With Jenkins there have been established good business cooperative relations."

GOUZENKO   That is right.

WILLIAMS   "From him I got fairly valuable materials."

GOUZENKO   That is right.

WILLIAMS   "As for example, recently I received from him a series of materials on the tasks mentioned in your telegram No. 109221."

GOUZENKO   That is right.

WILLIAMS   "I have never planned to develop the latter as he is a reserve officer and must soon retire."

GOUZENKO   That is right.

WILLIAMS   "His retirement is not in our interest as it is hardly likely that his future replacement will be as good a man as he."

GOUZENKO   That is right.

WILLIAMS   "Up to the present there has not been an occasion when Jenkins has refused us anything whatsoever."*

---

*Col. Jenkins' job involved dealing with military attachés and his transactions with the Russians were entirely proper.

GOUZENKO   That is right.

WILLIAMS   "I consider that the subject of your letter referred to Dick?"

GOUZENKO   That is right.

WILLIAMS   Two, will you translate that?

GOUZENKO   That is all.

WILLIAMS   That is the end of it. The other is evidently a translator's note and we will eliminate that. It is signed "Grant" and is dated 23.8.45.

GOUZENKO   That is right.

WILLIAMS   Do you know whether Mak Kell is a real name or cover name or anything about it?

GOUZENKO   It is a real name.

WILLIAMS   Do you know who he is or what he does?

GOUZENKO   He is assistant to the chief of the personnel department, Ministry of Aviation.

MR. COMMISSIONER KELLOCK   Canada?

GOUZENKO   Canada. . . .

MR. WILLIAMS   And the words "Mak" and "Kell" would be the way a Russian-speaking person would write a name that sounded like Makell?

GOUZENKO   Yes.

WILLIAMS   Then we come to the name Colonel Jenkins. Is that a real name or a cover or nickname?

GOUZENKO   It is a real name.

WILLIAMS   How do you know that?

GOUZENKO   He is well known and he works in the operative branch. There were very many conversations about him between Colonel Zabotin and Lieutenant-Colonel Motinov and Rogov.

WILLIAMS   Did you hear those conversations?

GOUZENKO   Oh, yes.

MR. COMMISSIONER KELLOCK   What operational branch is referred to?

GOUZENKO   General staff; operative branch, general staff.

KELLOCK   The Canadian General Staff?

GOUZENKO   Yes. It says in the telegram he is chief of the operative division.

MR. WILLIAMS   The translation already in is superintendent of operational branch.

GOUZENKO   I do not know what is best, chief of operative division, I think is better. . . .

WILLIAMS   Then we have the name Dick. Is that a real name or a nickname or cover name?

GOUZENKO   It is a cover name.

WILLIAMS   Do you know who it is the cover name for?

GOUZENKO   Lieutenant-Colonel Letson.*

WILLIAMS   How do you know that?

GOUZENKO   From documents I have read.

WILLIAMS   What documents are those?

GOUZENKO   He was frequently mentioned in telegrams in connection with his development in this work.

---

*Col. Letson had no improper relations with the Russian embassy.

WILLIAMS   When you say "his development," what do you mean by that?

GOUZENKO   They were developing plans for drawing him into the agency network. . . .

WILLIAMS   I show you now Exhibit 20-M, telegram No. 263, and ask you whether the translation which I am going to read you is a correct translation: "To the director. Gray was earlier given the task of taking all necessary measures for staying on his old job. At the last contact the latter stated that in the near future great reductions will begin." Is that reduction in staff or just "great reductions"?

GOUZENKO   "Reductions" is the word used.

WILLIAMS   "Great reductions will begin" but it means in staff?

GOUZENKO   Yes.

WILLIAMS

> In the event that it will be impossible to remain on the old job, Gray proposes to form a geological engineering consultative office in Ottawa. Gray is a geological engineer by profession, and therefore can head this office. The expenses for organizing the office are as follows: Rent of premises, $600 a year; wages for one clerk, $1,200 a year; office equipment, $1,000; payment to Gray as director, $4,200 a year. Altogether it needs $7,000 a year. Gray said that Canada is entering a boom period in the mining industry.

Then is that repeated, "in the mining industry"?

GOUZENKO   No.

WILLIAMS   "And it is therefore very likely that within two years the office will be in a position to support itself. The initial expenditure on its operation will be returned in the future. Gray thinks that it is necessary to begin establishing the office gradually, that is prior to his completion of the work at the old place. I beg to get your decision." And that is signed "Grant" and dated 25/8/45?

GOUZENKO   That is right.

WILLIAMS   And Gray has been identified as the undercover name or nickname for Gerson?

GOUZENKO   Yes. . . .

WILLIAMS   I now show you Exhibit 20-O, telegram No. 265, and ask you if what I am going to read you is a correct translation: "To the director. 1. In the change of plans of the output of war materials sent to you in Gray's materials 16th of August, there was issued an announcement of the British university of supply."

GOUZENKO   That should be "ministry of supply."

WILLIAMS   "— on the production of the following war materials. Shells, 25 pounds, cannon, 350,000." Is that right?

GOUZENKO   "Shells for 25 pound cannon."

WILLIAMS   "350,000"; is that right?

GOUZENKO   Yes.

WILLIAMS   Then what comes next?

GOUZENKO   "The same, but only "smoke shells, 170,000."

WILLIAMS   "Cases for the same, cannons, 1,050,000"?

GOUZENKO   That is right.
WILLIAMS   "Six pound shells, 30,000"?
GOUZENKO   That is right.
WILLIAMS   "5.5 inch shells, 180,000"?
GOUZENKO   That is right.
WILLIAMS   "Grenades, Mk. II, 221,000"?
GOUZENKO   That is right.
WILLIAMS   "Grenades of the make WP, 240,000"?
GOUZENKO   That is right.
WILLIAMS   "Mines for Piat" —
GOUZENKO   That would be "grenades" or "mines". . . .
WILLIAMS   Do you know what the Piat is?
GOUZENKO   Yes. It is a grenade thrower.
WILLIAMS   Anti-tank?
GOUZENKO   Yes, that is right.
WILLIAMS   "450,000. 2. On the 14th August an urgent announcement on
    production was made by the general staff. Twenty-five pound shells, 850,000.
    Smoke, 150,000. Cases for them, 1,000,000. Seventeen pound shells, 90,000.
    Two-inch smoke mines, 250,000. Three-inch mines, 350,000. For Piat, 150,000,
    and three-inch smoke mines, 31,440.''?
GOUZENKO   That is right.
WILLIAMS   And that is signed "Grant" and the date is 25/8/45?
GOUZENKO   Yes.
WILLIAMS   And Gray has been identified as the cover name for Gerson?
GOUZENKO   That is right. . . .
WILLIAMS   I now show you Exhibit 20-P, a telegram No. 266, and ask you if
    this translation which I will read to you is a correct translation: "To the director.
    We have received from Badeau seventeen absolutely secret and secret documents
    (British, American and Canadian)"?
GOUZENKO   That is right.
WILLIAMS

    — on the question of magnet-, radio-locators for field artillery, three
    secret scientific-research journals of 1945, altogether about 700 pages.
    In the course of the day we were able to photograph all the documents
    . . . with the help of the Leica and the photofilter. In the next few days
    we will receive almost the same amount of documents for three to five
    hours and with one ribbon or film we will not be able to do it.

GOUZENKO   That is right.
WILLIAMS   "I consider it necessary to examine the whole of the library of the
    scientific research council.
    "Your silence on my No. 256 may interrupt our work on photographing
    the materials. All materials have been sent by mail in turn." That is signed
    "Grant" and dated 27/8/45?
GOUZENKO   That is right.
WILLIAMS   And Badeau is the nickname or cover name for whom?
GOUZENKO   Durnford Smith. . . .

WILLIAMS   I now show you Exhibit No. 20-Q, telegram No. 267, and ask you if the translation which I will read to you is a correct translation: "To the director, on No. 11295." Could that be read, "To the director in answer to No. 11295"?

GOUZENKO   That is right.

WILLIAMS   "1. Your task on —" and what is the next word?

GOUZENKO   "Explosive materials."

WILLIAMS   Is it "V.V."?

GOUZENKO   Yes.

WILLIAMS   "— we have begun to fulfil. From Gray we received materials on —" and what is the next word?

GOUZENKO   "Torpex."

WILLIAMS   And then next in brackets; is that "V.V." again?

GOUZENKO   Yes.

WILLIAMS   "— (V.V. for depth bombs.) With the mail of 24th August were sent lamina from the above mentioned materials."

GOUZENKO   Yes.

WILLIAMS   What does "lamina" mean?

GOUZENKO   In Russia it means film. . . .

WILLIAMS   Then the translation continues: "In addition to this I sent you correspondence on the use of the double shell (17 pound and 6 pound — for cannon)" . . . Then it continues: "As the Canadians have told (us) — that this shell was very effective in Europe. 2. All the materials are in laminae."

GOUZENKO   That is film. . . .

WILLIAMS   And the signature is "Grant" and the date is 28/8/45?

GOUZENKO   Yes.

WILLIAMS   And Gray is Gerson?

GOUZENKO   That is right. . . .

WILLIAMS   I now show you Exhibit No. 20-T, telegram No. 270, and ask you about the correctness of the translation which I will now read to you: "To the director, re No. 12293." Is that "re" or is it "in answer to"?

GOUZENKO   It is "in answer to."

WILLIAMS   "In answer to No. 12293. 1. The ambassador has agreed to help us by giving us an amount of money from the embassy, and he proposed that the money be returned in small amounts, sent to him and to the commercial counsellor. Small sums may also be added to the expenditure of the representation, until it is completed." Is "representation" a good word there?

GOUZENKO   That is expenses connected with the representative staff, expenses connected with putting on lunches, cocktail parties, and so forth.

WILLIAMS   "Could the representative send a part of the money with the diplomatic mail, for as is known to you, we had to spend in the last two months much, in view of the great expenses, and there was nothing left in the treasury for the month of August."

GOUZENKO   That is right.

WILLIAMS   "For the diplomatic mail alone (July, August) it was necessary to pay $2,500."

GOUZENKO   That is right.

WILLIAMS   "I therefore beg you to send out urgently money for the operations."

GOUZENKO   That is right.

WILLIAMS   And that is signed "Grant" and is dated the 29th of August, 1945?

GOUZENKO   That is right.

WILLIAMS   The reference in that to the ambassador is to the Russian ambassador to Canada, living in Ottawa?

GOUZENKO   That is right.

WILLIAMS   And the commercial counsellor is the commercial counsellor living in Ottawa, who at that time was Krotov?

GOUZENKO   That is right. . . .

WILLIAMS   The reference here to sums of money being sent — in the documents which have already been put in here before the Commission there are references to the payment of moneys to various agents. You have seen those, have you not?

GOUZENKO   That is right.

WILLIAMS   And that only deals with payments of which we have a record in the documents here. Were other payments being made to agents from time to time?

GOUZENKO   Yes, of course.

WILLIAMS   And did you at any time see the records of those payments?

GOUZENKO   I coded telegrams in which accounts of those payments were made.

WILLIAMS   Did you yourself ever have anything to do with making payments to any agents?

GOUZENKO   No.

MR. COMMISSIONER TASCHEREAU   That went through Grant? All those payments were made through Grant?

GOUZENKO   Grant had charge of the operative funds, which he handed to Motinov for payment. Motinov was responsible for the agency work.

TASCHEREAU   So that on certain telegrams that we have seen up to now we see that certain payments have been made to certain agents; but it is to your knowledge that other payments have been made?

GOUZENKO   That is right.

WILLIAMS   To persons already mentioned?

GOUZENKO   It is hard to remember. Each agent received money from the contact man who met him.

TASCHEREAU   So do you mean to say they were all paid?

GOUZENKO   As far as I know they would all receive money, with the exception of such a man as the Professor, who was very rich and did not need money.

TASCHEREAU   That was Professor Boyer of Montreal?

GOUZENKO   That is right. . . .

MR. WILLIAMS   I now show you Exhibit No. 20-V, telegram No. 275, and ask you if what I am about to read to you is a correct translation: "To the director. I ask you to advise to what degree do the materials of Alex on the question of uranium (his reports on production, etc.) satisfy you and our scientific workers."

GOUZENKO   That is right.

WILLIAMS   "It is imperative for us to know in order that we may place the tasks on this question to our clients." Would "agents" be a better word there?

GOUZENKO   Sometimes instead of "agents" they use "clients". . . .

WILLIAMS   "Have you received all NN —"

GOUZENKO   That means numbers.

WILLIAMS "— mail up to July of this year?" And it is signed "Grant", and the date is 31/8/45?

GOUZENKO That is right.

WILLIAMS And that brings us to the end of Exhibit No. 20; and all of the telegrams in this exhibit are in the handwriting of Grant?

GOUZENKO Yes, sir.

WILLIAMS That is Colonel Zabotin. They were coded by you or by Koulakov in your presence?

GOUZENKO That is right. . . .

WILLIAMS I now show you five pages written in a handwriting which you have identified as that of Colonel Rogov, and ask you to tell us what these five pages are. You said they were not telegrams?

GOUZENKO They are notes written by Lieutenant-Colonel Rogov.

WILLIAMS You say these are notes written by Colonel Rogov, and you brought these five sheets with you together with the other documents when you came to the police for protection?

GOUZENKO That is right.

WILLIAMS Where did you get them.

GOUZENKO They were in the brief case of Lieutenant-Colonel Rogov and were kept in the safe of room No. 12.

WILLIAMS So that when you left you took them out of Colonel Rogov's brief case which was in the safe to which you had access, and brought them with you?

GOUZENKO That is right.

WILLIAMS I would ask you to follow the original while I read the translation, and tell me whether the translation is a correct one: "Results of the last meeting of Back's group (research). 1. Bacon categorically refused to give any kind of written information and also any kind of documents to be photographed."

GOUZENKO That is right. . . .

WILLIAMS "A possibility exists, but he is afraid. He gives only oral information, and this does not answer our purpose since Back is a writer and not a scientific worker."

GOUZENKO That is right.

WILLIAMS "In an oral conversation he told that Canada and the United States produced special electric —" and what is the next word?

GOUZENKO "Shells." . . .

WILLIAMS "— special electric shells, thanks to which —"?

GOUZENKO "Thanks to which the object for destruction is automatically fixed accurately."

WILLIAMS "Thanks to which the object for destruction is automatically fixed accurately."

GOUZENKO "Based on the principle of reflection of radio waves.". . .

MR. COMMISSIONER TASCHEREAU Would you tell us why it was that Rogov sent these telegrams instead of Zabotin?

WILLIAMS These are not telegrams. The witness wishes to state why he took this particular document.

GOUZENKO On one page of this document the name of Fred Rose appears together with his nickname. . . .

WILLIAMS This is the translation of page 2 of these notes now marked Exhibit

No. 21. "Electronic shells are called 'V bombs'. It consists of a small high frequency centre which manufactures the waves which rebound from the target."

GOUZENKO   That is right.

WILLIAMS   "These shells are already used on the front and there exists special instructions which he did not absolutely consent to bring."

GOUZENKO   "Which he did not promise to bring."

WILLIAMS   Should the word "absolutely" be in?

GOUZENKO   "Which he did not firmly promise to bring."

WILLIAMS   "2. Badeau wants to work. Gave written information about research in the fields of radio technique optics and various apparatus, material is very technical."

GOUZENKO   There should be a period.

WILLIAMS   That would read, "Gave written information about research in the fields of radio technique, optics and various apparatus." Then it goes on, "Material is very technical and is hard to make it out on the place."

GOUZENKO   Yes, "to develop it."

MR. COMMISSIONER KELLOCK   "On the spot."

GOUZENKO   "On the spot," that is right.

WILLIAMS   "Sent out by mail."

GOUZENKO   That is right.

WILLIAMS   "It is necessary to have concrete questions for him."

GOUZENKO   That is right.

WILLIAMS   According to facts given by him the organization of the National Research Council from the top down is as follows — the Committee of the Secret Council for Research Problems, Chairman, O.A. MacKennon."

GOUZENKO   That is right.

WILLIAMS

Under him is — then we go to the next page — C.G. MacKenzie. There are three floors, two divisions on each floor. On the first floor is the Division of Plans and Publications and the Division of the Chief Assistant S.P. Eagleson. On the second floor there is the Division of Assistant Research. Here also is the combined committee of scientists. The division (apparently) of statistics and stenographers with A.F. Gill as chief. On the third floor the Division of Applied Biology, chief, W.H. Cook, the division of Chemistry and the Division of Mechanical Engineering, chief, J.H. Parcen, and the Division of Physics and Electricity, Chief, R.W. Bedeau.

GOUZENKO   "Boyle."

WILLIAMS   "He asks —"

GOUZENKO   "Bedeau [Badeau] asks."

WILLIAMS   "Bedeau [Badeau] asks a decision about changing over for the work on uranium. There is a possibility that he could enter either by invitation or by suggesting it himself, but he must be warned that they are very careful about selecting workers and keep them under strict observation."

GOUZENKO   That is right.

WILLIAMS   Then page 4. "3. Bagley. So far no contact has been made. The reason is that he lives so far out from the city and his wife's influence who does not want him to galavant [sic] around at night."

GOUZENKO   "The influence of his wife who does wish that he should meet with corporators."

WILLIAMS   "Does not want him to meet corporators. To Back's suggestion for a meeting he answers that he is working and will continue."

GOUZENKO   "On the invitation of Back to meet he replies that he is engaged, that he is busy and lives far away from town, but at the same time he invites him to his house."

WILLIAMS   This translation is substantially correct. "To Back's suggestion for a meeting he answers that he is working and lives too far away"?

GOUZENKO   "He is busy and lives far away but at the same time he invites" —

WILLIAMS   "He is busy and lives far away but at the same time he invites him to his house."

GOUZENKO   Does not say whom he invites.

WILLIAMS   "Back communicated that he would have a meeting during the period of 5-20 and 6-5?"

GOUZENKO   That is right.

WILLIAMS   What does the "5-20" and the "6-5" mean? . . .

GOUZENKO   May 20th and June 5th.

WILLIAMS   There has been a sentence struck out and the translation of the sentence that is struck out is, "He added that Bagley knows nothing about his immediate work since Debouz" — Fred has been written in — "talked with him and he talked to him and generally he recommended to him for Back to get acquainted and only after that for him to start working with him."

GOUZENKO   "He recommended him to study Back carefully."

WILLIAMS   "And only after that for him to start working with him"?

GOUZENKO   That is right. . . .

MR. COMMISSIONER KELLOCK   "Since Debouz talked with him and he talked to him and generally —"

GOUZENKO   That is right.

KELLOCK   "He recommended to him." What does that mean?

GOUZENKO   Let us translate from the beginning. "He further added that Bagley knows nothing about his immediate work because Debouz spoke with him in a general way and he recommended to him to study Back carefully."

KELLOCK   As I understand the meaning, it is that Debouz talked to Bagley and recommended to Bagley that he study Back?

GOUZENKO   That is right, and only after this to begin working with him.

KELLOCK   This paragraph 3 is headed "Bagley." "So far no contact has been made. The reason is that he lives so far from the city." That is Bagley lives so far from the city. "And his wife's influence who does not want him to meet corporators. To Back's suggestion for a meeting" — that is, to Back's suggestion to Bagley — "he answers" — that is Bagley — "that he is busy" but to come out to his house. Then Back stated that he would have a meeting at Bagley's house between May 20 and June 5. Then it says "He added." That must be that Back added that Bagley knows nothing about his immediate work. That must be Back's immediate work. "Since Debouz talked with him." Debouz talked with whom, Back or Bagley?

GOUZENKO   Back.

KELLOCK   "And in a general way he recommended this meeting to Back"?

GOUZENKO   That is right.

KELLOCK   Debouz recommended to Back to get acquainted with Bagley and only after that to start working with him?

GOUZENKO   That is it.

KELLOCK   (*To Mr. Williams*)   That is not what he said.

MR. WILLIAMS   Mr. Commissioner, you will remember that that fits in with the set-up that is given in the file on Back which is in as an exhibit. There was a diagram. . . .   (*To the witness*)   Before I go on with the balance of the translations I want to draw your attention to the portion that has been struck out and the name "Fred" which was written in by Rogov?

GOUZENKO   That is right.

WILLIAMS   That is Fred talked with him?

GOUZENKO   That is right.

WILLIAMS   Then above the word "Fred" there is written in in handwriting, "Debouz"?

GOUZENKO   That is right.

WILLIAMS   In whose handwriting is that word "Debouz"?

GOUZENKO   Colonel Zabotin. . . .

WILLIAMS   And Debouz is the cover name or nickname for certain purposes for Fred Rose?

GOUZENKO   That is right.

WILLIAMS   Let us continue with the translation of page 4. "As to Back himself the possibility does not exist to use him as a contact"?

GOUZENKO   Back himself has not the possibilities. He is being used as a contact.

WILLIAMS   What does that mean?

GOUZENKO   It means he has not the possibility of giving information.

WILLIAMS   Then how does the next part read?

GOUZENKO   "He is being used as a contact."

WILLIAMS   "At the last meeting he said that a baby will be born to him the end of June"?

GOUZENKO   That is right.

WILLIAMS   Then page 5. "He hinted about money. So far $200 have been given him at various times."

GOUZENKO   That is right.

WILLIAMS   "Conclusions drawn: 1. Tell Back to continue to draw Bacon into our work gradually and to take dictation from Bacon some time and also to make drawings by hand"?

GOUZENKO   That is right.

WILLIAMS   "2. It is not recommended that Badeau should transfer into the uranium industry but is to do broader work in the research in the future"? Is that right?

GOUZENKO   "To develop work in research more broadly."

WILLIAMS   How does that go on?

GOUZENKO   That is all, period.

WILLIAMS   Then how does the next read?

GOUZENKO   "In the future with the object of more concrete direction it is expedient to detach him from the group Back."

MR. COMMISSIONER KELLOCK   Instead of "more concrete"?

GOUZENKO   "More efficient."

MR. WILLIAMS   "More efficient direction, it is expedient to detach him from Back's group"?

GOUZENKO   "Transfer him on independent contacting."

WILLIAMS   "3. To recommend that Back have one meeting (for contact) at Bagley's apartment and that they there agree upon future meetings"?

GOUZENKO   That is right. . . .

WILLIAMS   I understand that the practice was that outgoing telegrams would be written on blue sheets?

GOUZENKO   That is right.

WILLIAMS   Those are the ones we have been dealing with?

GOUZENKO   That is right.

WILLIAMS   Incoming telegrams would be written on pink sheets?

GOUZENKO   That is right.

WILLIAMS   And when you came to the police for protection you brought with you a number of pink sheets upon which were recorded incoming telegrams?

GOUZENKO   That is right. . . .

WILLIAMS   And when you brought these pink ones had you made the selection of them in advance?

GOUZENKO   In the same way as I had made the selection of the blue ones.

WILLIAMS   And do the incoming telegrams come in in code?

GOUZENKO   That is right.

WILLIAMS   And then they would be decoded by yourself?

GOUZENKO   Yes, by myself or by Koulakov.

WILLIAMS   And any work that Koulakov did, he did while you were present?

GOUZENKO   Yes.

WILLIAMS   That is when he was getting ready to take over from you on your return to Moscow?

GOUZENKO   Yes, to practise.

WILLIAMS   In whose handwriting are these pink documents, eleven in number, that I am now putting before you?

GOUZENKO   Koulakov. . . .

WILLIAMS   Is each one of them certified or signed by Grant?

GOUZENKO   It must be; I do not know exactly. Each one should be signed by Grant but sometimes he did not sign them. . . .

WILLIAMS   Each one of these documents which have now been marked as Exhibit No. 23 is an original document brought by you from the Russian embassy?

GOUZENKO   That is right.

WILLIAMS   The first one has the number "10458" in the upper right-hand corner, and the date is 30.7.45?

GOUZENKO   That is right.

WILLIAMS   I will read you a translation and ask you if it is correct. It is headed "To Grant. In reply to No. 218."

GOUZENKO   That is right. . . .

WILLIAMS   "Work out and wire the instructions and watchword of Alec to our man in London"?

GOUZENKO   That is right.

WILLIAMS   "Try to get from him before departure the detailed information on the progress of the work of uranium"?

GOUZENKO   That is right.

WILLIAMS   "Talk it over with him: does he think expedient for our undertaking to stay on the spot"?

GOUZENKO   That is right.

WILLIAMS   "Will he be able to do it, or it is more useful for him and more urgent to depart for London"?

GOUZENKO   That is right.

WILLIAMS   It is signed "Director."

GOUZENKO   "Director."

WILLIAMS   And who is that director?

GOUZENKO   The chief of the first intelligence headquarters.

WILLIAMS   And his name is?

GOUZENKO   At that time Major-General Bolshakov.

WILLIAMS   At that time?

GOUZENKO   Yes.

WILLIAMS   Then there is a date opposite the word "Director."

GOUZENKO   "28.7.45."

WILLIAMS   Then in the left-hand corner there is the signature "Grant."

GOUZENKO   That is right.

WILLIAMS   And the date 31.7.45?

GOUZENKO   That is right. . . .

WILLIAMS   The next telegram, which will be Exhibit No. 23-B is No. 11273. That is correct, is it not?

GOUZENKO   That is correct.

WILLIAMS   The date is 11.8.45. Will you tell me if the translation which I am about to read is correct? "To Grant. It is very important for us to receive information on the following matters: (a) to confirm the official facts about the transfer of the American troops from Europe to the U.S.A. and to the Pacific, also the army headquarters of the 9th Army, 3, 5, 7, 13 Armoured Corps, 18 Armoured Division, 2, 4, 8, 28, 30, 44, 45, 104th divisions and 13th"?

GOUZENKO   Infantry.

WILLIAMS   104th Infantry Division?

GOUZENKO   "And 13th Tank Division."

WILLIAMS   "Find out and establish also the dates of their moves"?

GOUZENKO   That is right.

WILLIAMS   "(b) The disbandment of the army headquarters"?

GOUZENKO   "Dislocation."

WILLIAMS   Would not disbandment be the word?

GOUZENKO   It means the place where they are, in Berlin, Paris. . . .

WILLIAMS   "The location of the army headquarters of the 8, 16 Armoured Corps, 29 (75) 89th divisions"?

GOUZENKO   "Infantry divisions."

WILLIAMS   "10th, 13th and 17th"?

GOUZENKO   "10th Tank Division."

WILLIAMS   13th and 17th. Is there anything following that?

GOUZENKO   Yes, an abbreviation "Agg."

WILLIAMS   That is a Russian word and you do not know what it signifies; it is an abbreviation?

GOUZENKO   Abbreviation of some kind of division.

WILLIAMS   "Also all about the location of the Brazilian division"?

GOUZENKO   "Brazilian infantry division". . . .

WILLIAMS   "Are there in Europe the 6th and 12th army groups, what is their composition and location"?

GOUZENKO   That is right.

WILLIAMS   "Then where are they going to move"?

GOUZENKO   "The dates and direction of the movements". . . .

WILLIAMS   "(d) Was there organized a chief of army headquarters by the American troops in Germany, and if so, give the place where it is located and the name of the officers commanding."

GOUZENKO   "Is there organized a staff of American occupation troops in Germany, its location, who is appointed in command". . . .

WILLIAMS   "The location of the first air defence army." You mean the parachute troops?

GOUZENKO   That is right.

WILLIAMS   What is the rest of it?

GOUZENKO   "The plans for its future use. Urgent."

WILLIAMS   That is signed "The Director" and then there is "8.8." Is that a date?

GOUZENKO   "8.8," that is all.

WILLIAMS   It is No. 8.8. The signature is "The Director" and in the lower left-hand corner it is signed "Grant" and the date 11.8.45 and "To make known to Brent." Brent is?

GOUZENKO   Rogov. . . .

MR. COMMISSIONER TASCHEREAU   To your knowledge was there an answer given to that telegram?

GOUZENKO   While I was there, no.

TASCHEREAU   You do not know who had the task of obtaining this information?

GOUZENKO   Colonel Rogov expected to be able to get the information through conversations with members of the armed forces.

TASCHEREAU   Canadian armed forces?

GOUZENKO   Yes. . . .

MR. WILLIAMS   The next telegram, which will be marked Exhibit No. 23-C, is No. 11295 with the date 14.8.45. Will you check this translation? "To Grant. In the mail of 23.8.1944, were received from you Gray's two materials."

GOUZENKO   That is right.

WILLIAMS   "The monthly reports on the research of separate technological questions in the field of production of war materials"?

GOUZENKO   "Munitions" is better.

WILLIAMS   "Production of munitions. On the basis of short and unrelated data it is impossible to judge the method of work of the Canadian and English and production of munitions, powders and chemical materials.''

GOUZENKO   That is right.

WILLIAMS   "It is therefore desirable to obtain the following information:''

GOUZENKO   That is right.

WILLIAMS   "1. The method and technological processes of the production of BB and the powders.'' Is that "BB" or "VV"?

GOUZENKO   There is a word meaning "processes of production of munitions, explosives and powders.''

WILLIAMS   First of all, it is "VV," is it?

GOUZENKO   Yes. . . .

WILLIAMS   "2. The composition and process of the plastic VV.'' Is that right?

GOUZENKO   In Russian that means "the formula for the plastic explosives''. . . .

WILLIAMS   "— the production of TH and HS, their purpose —''

GOUZENKO   "Their composition, purpose and specific qualities.'' That is all in brackets.

WILLIAMS   "Their composition, purpose and specific qualities''?

GOUZENKO   Yes.

WILLIAMS   What is "TH," do you know?

GOUZENKO   I don't know.

WILLIAMS   Do you know what "HS" is?

GOUZENKO   I don't know.

WILLIAMS   "3. The application of —'' what is that word?

GOUZENKO   "Picrite.'' That is the Russian spelling.

WILLIAMS   That would be Picric, as we call it, I suppose; then what is the next word? Will you spell it in Russian?

GOUZENKO   "Nitro-gushchedina.'' Then it reads, "I repeat —''

WILLIAMS   And then it repeats the Picrite and nitro-gushchedina?

GOUZENKO   Yes.

WILLIAMS   Then it continues: "4. The technique of producing the capsules of detonators and igniting capsules. Wire to whom do you consider it possible to give the said task. If Bacon still keeps on working in the artillery committee, this task should be handed over to him.''

GOUZENKO   That is right.

WILLIAMS   And it is dated 9/8/45 and signed by the director?

GOUZENKO   That is right.

WILLIAMS   And it is signed by "Grant" and dated 14/8/45?

GOUZENKO   Yes.

MR. COMMISSIONER TASCHEREAU   Do you know if the task has been given to Bacon?

GOUZENKO   In my presence Colonel Zabotin handed this task over to Davy or Sokolov for the purpose of giving it to an agent.

TASCHEREAU   Without giving any names?

GOUZENKO   No, he did not give any name.

TASCHEREAU   And do you know if Sokolov gave it to somebody?

GOUZENKO   I don't know; but in my presence he re-wrote the data for the task from the telegram.

TASCHEREAU   To be given to the agent?

GOUZENKO   Yes.

WILLIAMS   And while you were in the embassy was there any telegram sent back in connection with this task that had been given to Sokolov?

GOUZENKO   No. I do not think he had enough time to hand it over to an agent for completion. . . .

MR. WILLIAMS   Now, exhibit 23-D is telegram No. 11436, dated August 14, 1945; and I would ask you to tell me whether the translation which I am going to read is a correct one, and I would ask you first of all to translate to me the words at the top of the telegram?

GOUZENKO   "Implement to telegram No. 11438."

WILLIAMS   Could we get a better word than "implement"? Does it mean something that is following up No. 11438, or additional instructions?

GOUZENKO   Not additional instructions. It is an expression when you send a different telegram instead of one telegram.

WILLIAMS   An addition; to add to it?

GOUZENKO   It means that if the cipher clerk made two telegrams in one telegram, this second part would be the "abzatz" part of the first telegram.

MR. COMMISSIONER KELLOCK   And what does the "abzatz" part mean?

MR. WILLIAMS   (To the witness)   Would not "continuation" be a good translation?

GOUZENKO   Suppose this director wrote two telegrams and gave them to the same code division. The cipher clerk might get one telegram as one telegram, so the second would be as an "abzatz" to the first telegram.

WILLIAMS   It is in addition to, or may be a part of?

GOUZENKO   May be an appendix. Perhaps that would be it. . . .

WILLIAMS   It is rather interesting that the other telegram — this is No. 11436 we are dealing with, and we will also have 11438, to which this is the "abzatz," and perhaps that will show exactly what it means. For the present we will use the word "appendix." I continue the translation.   (To the witness)   "To Grant. Re No. 227." That is better translated is it not, "in answer to" or "in reply to"?

GOUZENKO   That is right.

WILLIAMS   "1. Further delay in the matter of the passport is no longer possible. Therefore the signature on the new questionnaire should be made by Frank's man himself."

GOUZENKO   That might be "form"; that would be better than "questionnaire."

WILLIAMS   "Should be made by Frank's man himself"?

GOUZENKO   Yes.

WILLIAMS   "2. Prepare for the next regular mail to be sent with it a short report on the technical procedure of receiving and delivering of passports, and a second one containing all the particulars about it for the use of our own purposes, indicating clearly who of Frank's men will be in charge of it."

GOUZENKO   That is, "the delivering of passports and other documentation."

WILLIAMS   Then how should this read?

GOUZENKO   "The delivering of passports and other documentation for our purposes."

WILLIAMS   Then we should strike out "a second one"?

GOUZENKO   Yes.

WILLIAMS "The delivering of passports for documentation for our purposes"?

GOUZENKO Yes.

WILLIAMS "Indicating clearly"?

GOUZENKO Yes, "who is actually from Frank's side who would be engaged with this business, or with this matter."

WILLIAMS Then this translation, while a little free, indicates the whole thing, "indicating clearly who of Frank's men will be in charge of it"?

GOUZENKO They ask who personally or concretely on the side of Frank would be in charge of this business.

WILLIAMS That is, which one of Frank's operators or agents?

GOUZENKO Yes; that is quite right.

WILLIAMS Then we have again the word "abzatz" which we have translated "appendix" and it goes on: "The pseudonym 'Sam' has long ago been changed to 'Frank'. In the future use the latter."

GOUZENKO Yes.

WILLIAMS And the date, 10/8, and signed by the director?

GOUZENKO Yes, sir.

WILLIAMS Then on the left-hand corner, Grant has signed and the date, 14/8/45?

GOUZENKO That is correct.

MR. COMMISSIONER KELLOCK That rather indicates that "abzatz" means postscript, does it not?

GOUZENKO Yes. That is a better term in this case. . . .

MR. WILLIAMS Now I come to Exhibit 23-E, which is telegram No. 11437 of August 14, 1945. Will you follow that while I read the translation and tell me if the translation is accurate: "To Grant. Your telegram No. 232. 1. In my telegram of 19.7 I have advised that until the information re material —" Is that "material" or is it "munitions"?

GOUZENKO "Before receiving information on the materials from Promety.". . .

WILLIAMS Then would this be a good reading of it: "I have advised that until the information is received from Prometheus, and until his possibilities in the navy department are established, contact with him should be maintained through Frank"?

GOUZENKO Yes, that is right.

WILLIAMS That is the way it should read: "Until the information is received from Prometheus, and until his possibilities in the navy department are established, contact with him should be maintained through Frank. Should it prove that Prometheus is a truly valuable man to us, direct contact may then be established with him."

GOUZENKO That is right.

WILLIAMS "However, it is not desirable to entrust Brent with making the contact. If you find no objection, it is better to let Chester make this contact."

GOUZENKO That is right.

WILLIAMS "Have in mind that we have here almost no other information on Prometheus except his family name and his place of employment."

GOUZENKO That is right.

WILLIAMS "Wire in full his name and family name, his position in the navy department, and the address of his residence."

GOUZENKO   That is right.

WILLIAMS   "Collect the remaining data and send by mail."

GOUZENKO   That is right.

WILLIAMS   "2. As for obtaining persons from the said departmental services, we are definitely interested."

GOUZENKO   No. "We are interested in obtaining people from the given departments."

WILLIAMS   That is the full sentence?

GOUZENKO   Yes. . . .

WILLIAMS   "Let Frank, after the staffs have been set up —"?

GOUZENKO   Yes, that is the best expression.

WILLIAMS   "— recommend one or two candidates for our study"?

GOUZENKO   That is right.

WILLIAMS   We have identified Prometheus, Frank and Brent. We have not identified Chester, have we? Is that a nickname or a cover name?

GOUZENKO   Yes.

WILLIAMS   And it is the cover name or nickname of whom?

GOUZENKO   Of Driver Gorshkov.

MR. COMMISSIONER TASCHEREAU   He is the chauffeur for the military attaché?

GOUZENKO   Yes. . . .

February 15, 1946

MR. WILLIAMS   I now place before you Exhibit No. 23-G, which is telegram No. 11924, and ask you if the translation which I am now about to read to you is the correct translation. It is dated 22/8/45. "To Grant. 1. Your 243. We have no compromising data against Veale, nevertheless the fact that he has in his hands a letter of recommendation from a corporant who was arrested in England (which he did not trouble to destroy) compels us to refuse to have any contact with him whatsoever, the more so as many people already call him 'Red'."

GOUZENKO   That is right.

WILLIAMS

> Our neighbour must surely know of him. If not, inform him of the break as in my instructions. Warn Alec that he must have no conversation with him about our work.
> 2. Your mail of 27/7 has been received. From data received from you previously, Bedeau [Badeau] is the physicist Dornfort [Durnford Smith] and Bagley is the radio-engineer Mazeral [Mazerall]. In your latest communication you indicate that the radio-engineer is Badeau and Bagley an electrical engineer. Your communication in telegram No. 198 that Badeau works as the assistant of the chief of the Scientific Research Council is apparently —

Will you read from there on? There is some question about this translation.

GOUZENKO   "— is apparently erroneous."

WILLIAMS   Then what follows?

GOUZENKO   "Advise us of his family name, pseudonym, profession and employment or duties."

WILLIAMS   "Advise us of his family name, pseudonym, profession and employment"?

GOUZENKO   Yes.

WILLIAMS   Then what follows?

GOUZENKO   Apparently it was not possible to decipher this very well, but from the sense it is evident that the information is erroneous.

WILLIAMS   Then what follows after that, following No. 4? How do we translate that?

GOUZENKO   "Why was the mail of the 27/7 with the materials of Badeau about which you advised us in your No. 210, not sent?"

WILLIAMS   Would this be a fair translation: "Why did you not send the materials of Badeau about which you informed in your No. 210 by mail of 27/7"?

GOUZENKO   Correct.

WILLIAMS   Then there is the date, 18/8, and it is signed "Director"?

GOUZENKO   That is right.

WILLIAMS   And Grant has signed on the right-hand side under the word "Director" and the date there is 22/8/45?

GOUZENKO   Yes.

WILLIAMS   And you have already identified the various nicknames or cover names used in this letter and have told us that "neighbour" refers to the N.K.V.D.?

GOUZENKO   Yes. . . .

WILLIAMS   I now place before you Exhibit No. 23-H, and ask you if the translation which I will read to you is a correct translation. It is headed up: "Abzatz to No. 11923," and the telegram itself is No. 11931. The date is 22/8/45: "To Grant. Take measures to organize the obtaining of documentary materials of the atomic bomb:"?

GOUZENKO   That is right.

WILLIAMS   "The technological process, drawings, calculations."

GOUZENKO   That is right.

WILLIAMS   That is signed "Director" and Colonel Zabotin has signed his cover name, Grant, on the left-hand side and put the name in his own writing, 22/8/45. That is correct?

GOUZENKO   That is correct.

MR. COMMISSIONER TASCHEREAU   (*To Mr. Williams*)   Do you know if there is any evidence to show that there was an answer given to this telegram, which is now Exhibit 23-H?

WILLIAMS   Only as it can be covered through the other documents. It will appear that certain information was given.

TASCHEREAU   But apart from those other documents, does the witness know anything about other answers that might have been sent to Moscow on this particular subject?

GOUZENKO   Colonel Zabotin did not reply to this telegram, because the telegram said that he had to take measures, and later there was a telegram sent outlining the tasks for the whole of 1945.

MR. COMMISSIONER KELLOCK   Sent from where?

GOUZENKO   From Moscow to Zabotin, wherein the main task was to obtain information about the atomic bomb before the end of 1945.

MR. COMMISSIONER TASCHEREAU   And did he obtain a copy of that telegram in room 12?

GOUZENKO   This is not a copy.

TASCHEREAU   No, I mean the telegram giving the various tasks for 1945, the telegram of which you spoke there?

GOUZENKO   No. I can explain that because that telegram was not sent by Grant.

TASCHEREAU   But do you know to whom that particular task was given, to obtain the information about the atomic bomb?

GOUZENKO   That task was given to Colonel Zabotin from Moscow, and he was to take all measures through his agents to fulfil it, to use every agent who had any connection with this thing.

TASCHEREAU   But do you know to whom Zabotin gave the task here in Canada?

GOUZENKO   He had no time to take the measures to fulfil the task, as my step interrupted this process.

MR. COMMISSIONER KELLOCK   By your "step" you mean your leaving?

GOUZENKO   Yes, my action in leaving.

MR. COMMISSIONER TASCHEREAU   But I understand you have some other evidence concerning this particular task about the atomic bomb?

MR. WILLIAMS   Nothing later than the date that the witness left the embassy. There was the cut-off as of September 5.

TASCHEREAU   But I read somewhere that something had been done in connection with the atomic bomb.

WILLIAMS   Yes. The exhibits will show what has been done down to their dates.

TASCHEREAU   Before the witness left the embassy?

WILLIAMS   Yes.

TASCHEREAU   But personally the witness knows nothing about it?

WILLIAMS   Not since September 5, and before that only from the documents which are already in and those still to go in . . .   (*To the witness*)   I now place before you Exhibit 23-I, telegram No. 11955, and I would first of all point out to you that there have been certain alterations or corrections made in a red pencil. Were those made in the document at the time you brought it from the embassy?

GOUZENKO   That is right.

WILLIAMS   This document and all of the other documents are in exactly the same condition in which you brought them from the embassy?

GOUZENKO   That is right.

WILLIAMS   And you did not make any changes in them in any way?

GOUZENKO   No. . . .

WILLIAMS   Would these red marks be made by Koulakov?

GOUZENKO   That is right.

WILLIAMS   Now would you listen to this translation and tell me if it is correct. The date is 22/8/45; the number of 11955, and it starts off, "To Grant." Will you read the next? Is it "In answer to No. 244" or "re"?

GOUZENKO   "In answer."

WILLIAMS   "In answer to No. 244. The instructions have not been worked out satisfactorily."

GOUZENKO   No.

WILLIAMS   Just read the first sentence, then.

GOUZENKO   "The conditions of the meeting have not been worked out satisfactorily.". . .

WILLIAMS   I continue the translation: "I am issuing new ones. 1. Place: In front of the British museum in London, on Great Russell Street, at the opposite side of the street, about Museum Street, from the side of Tottenham Court Road, repeat: Tottenham Court Road. Alec will go from Tottenham Court Road, the contact man from the opposite side, Southampton Row."

GOUZENKO   That is right.

WILLIAMS   "2. Date: As indicated in yours —"

GOUZENKO   That should be "Time."

WILLIAMS   I will read it again, then: "Time: As indicated in yours. However, it would be expedient to carry out the meeting at twenty o'clock, if it should be convenient to Alec, as at twenty-three o'clock it is too dark."

GOUZENKO   That is right.

WILLIAMS   Then on the reverse: "As for the time, it has to be agreed upon with Alec and the decision communicated to me. In case the meeting should not take place in October, the time and day shall then be fixed likewise the next month."

GOUZENKO   That is right.

WILLIAMS   "3. Identification signs. Alec shall have under his left arm the newspaper 'Times' —"?

GOUZENKO   Yes.

WILLIAMS   "— the contact man will have in his left hand the magazine 'Picture Post'."

GOUZENKO   That is right.

WILLIAMS   "4. The watchword:" I think you suggested once that "password" would be a better translation. "Password" or "watchword" would be equally good?

GOUZENKO   "Password" I think.

WILLIAMS   I will read this again, then. "4. The password: The contact man saying: 'What is the shortest way to the Strand?' Alec: 'Well, come along. I am going that way.' In the beginning of the conversation —"

GOUZENKO   That should be "in the beginning of the business conversation."

WILLIAMS   "In the beginning of the business conversation Alec says: 'Best regards from Mikel.'* The handing over of the conditions to Alec must be reported."

GOUZENKO   That is right.

WILLIAMS   What does "conditions" mean?

GOUZENKO   That means conditions of meeting.

---

*Alec — Nunn May — was allowed to return to England in September 1945 in the hope that this meeting would be kept and provide leads to the British espionage rings. The meeting did not take place, however.

WILLIAMS   Then there is the date, 18/8, and there is an abbreviation. What would you say that indicated?

GOUZENKO   "Director."

WILLIAMS   Then Colonel Zabotin has signed his name in the lower right-hand corner and has written in the date, 22/8/45?

GOUZENKO   Yes. . . .

WILLIAMS   I now place before you Exhibit 23-J, telegram No. 12200, dated 24/8/45, and ask you if the translation which I am about to read is a correct one? "To Grant. In answer to No. 248. 1. In telegram No. 8267 of 20th June you were instructed as to the inadmissibility of disclosing to the ambassador our agency network."

GOUZENKO   That is right.

WILLIAMS   "The handing over to the ambassador of Wilgress' report of 3/11/44 about the financial credits for assuring trade between the U.S.S.R. and Great Britain after the war, in the same form as it was received, has uncovered the identity of our source on the objective Elli." What should those words be?

GOUZENKO   "On the object of Elli." . . .

WILLIAMS   Does that mean the purpose?

GOUZENKO   That means that the ambassador will be able to surmise that where Elli works, the Soviet government has an agent.

MR. COMMISSIONER KELLOCK   That is, that the Soviet government has a secret agent in England going under the name of Elli?

GOUZENKO   Not in England; in Canada.

MR. WILLIAMS   And you have identified Elli as Kay Willsher, who works in the office of the High Commissioner in Ottawa?

GOUZENKO   That is right. In other words, it means that the ambassador can realize that in the office of the High Commissioner there is a secret agent.

MR. COMMISSIONER TASCHEREAU   He was not supposed to know that?

GOUZENKO   No.

MR. COMMISSIONER KELLOCK   I suppose it might read, "has uncovered the existence of our secret agent Elli?"

GOUZENKO   No, that is not correct. He does not know about Elli. By this document he will understand that in the office of the High Commissioner there is somebody who can give this document of Wilgress to Zabotin.

MR. COMMISSIONER TASCHEREAU   And the ambassador will know that?

GOUZENKO   After Zabotin gives him that document.

MR. COMMISSIONER KELLOCK   I suppose it means, "has disclosed the fact that Zabotin has an agent or a person acting as an agent in the office of the High Commissioner in Ottawa"?

GOUZENKO   That is right.

KELLOCK   And while the ambassador does not know the name or the cover name of that agent, in fact it is Elli?

GOUZENKO   That is right.

MR. WILLIAMS   Do you know whether Elli was used as a nickname or cover name for any person other than Miss Willsher?

GOUZENKO   Yes. There is some agent under the same name in Great Britain.

WILLIAMS   Do you know who it is?

GOUZENKO   No.

WILLIAMS   Then I continue with the translation of the exhibit: "Furthermore, the translator of the embassy was made acquainted with that document, in so far as the document was in the local language."

GOUZENKO   That is right.

WILLIAMS   "2. With regard to urgent political and economic questions affecting the mutual relations of Canada and Great Britain with the U.S.S.R., you should inform the embassy, but indicating only the authenticity of the source and are not to reveal to the ambassador either the source itself or the place from which the information was received."

GOUZENKO   That is right.

WILLIAMS   "3. The information should be handed over after it has been prepared to this effect, excising any passage which may disclose the secrecy of the source."

GOUZENKO   That is right.

WILLIAMS   "4. In all questions of which you will inform the ambassador, you must refer to me in your information as the source for it and inform me thereof."

GOUZENKO   That is right.

WILLIAMS   That is signed the director, and the date is 21/8?

GOUZENKO   Yes.

WILLIAMS   And Colonel Zabotin has signed his cover name or nickname, Grant, in his own handwriting, and has also put on the date, 25/8/45?

GOUZENKO   That is right. . . .

MR. COMMISSIONER KELLOCK   I should like to ask you this, Mr. Gouzenko. I suppose that the last telegram is pretty plain. I take from it that there was a pretty clear understanding that Zabotin had his instructions that his activities in connection with the operation of this agency network in Canada were not to be disclosed to the ambassador, Zaroubin. Is that right?

GOUZENKO   That means that although the ambassador knows of the existence of the system, he must not know the details of its workings. That is why I took this telegram. The ambassador knew of the existence of the system, but he must not know the details of the system. It is plain in this telegram.

KELLOCK   In other words he knew what Mr. Zabotin was doing, but he was not given the information that Mr. Zabotin was obtaining or who the agents were?

GOUZENKO   That is right.

MR. COMMISSIONER TASCHEREAU   He knew that Zabotin was the chief of that organization here?

GOUZENKO   That is right.

MR. WILLIAMS   You referred a little earlier in your evidence to a journal in which entries were made of the incoming and outgoing correspondence?

GOUZENKO   That is right.

WILLIAMS   Was a similar journal used to make entries of the incoming and outgoing telegrams?

GOUZENKO   That is right.

WILLIAMS   And who would keep that journal?

GOUZENKO   I.

WILLIAMS   You would keep that?

GOUZENKO   Yes.

WILLIAMS   And where would that be kept; in the safe in Room 12?

GOUZENKO   That must be kept in the same pouch or sack where the code and the telegrams were kept. It was an ordinary notebook.

WILLIAMS   And it was a separate journal entirely from the journal in which the correspondence records were kept, the letters?

GOUZENKO   You mean the mail?

WILLIAMS   Yes. I understood you to say that there was a journal of the letters kept some place, a record of the letters in a journal, as well as in the lists?

GOUZENKO   What letters do you refer to?

WILLIAMS   I understood you to say that besides the lists, Exhibit 16, which was a record of the letters mailed, there was some kind of a ledger or journal or book in which a record of the letters was kept as well. Was I right or wrong?

GOUZENKO   You are right. I only want to explain that it may be more clear. I kept in this pouch actually two journals. In the first journal I kept the numbers of the outgoing and the incoming telegrams. In the second journal I registered the numbers of the outgoing and incoming packages of mail.

WILLIAMS   We have here now five sheets of notepaper, all apparently written in the same handwriting and written in English. You brought these five sheets with you when you came to the police for protection?

GOUZENKO   That is right.

WILLIAMS   Do you know in whose handwriting they are?

GOUZENKO   I understand that that is the handwriting of Nora.

WILLIAMS   What makes you think it is the handwriting of Nora?

GOUZENKO   Because when Colonel Zabotin translated the letter into Russian on the telegrams he said, "material given by Nora."

WILLIAMS   And you knew that Nora was the cover name or nickname for whom?

GOUZENKO   Emma Woikin. . . .

WILLIAMS   These five sheets . . . found by you where, when you took them?

GOUZENKO   During the day of the 5th September, Colonel Zabotin came to room 12, where I was, and after he had finished writing the translation for the telegram. . . .

WILLIAMS   Colonel Zabotin translated the five sheets of Exhibit 24 into Russian?

GOUZENKO   That is right.

WILLIAMS   Did he then transmit them by telegram?

GOUZENKO   He sent the translation by telegram. . . .

WILLIAMS   And did you turn the Russian translation into code?

GOUZENKO   I hadn't time to do them all, because the same evening I cut off my relations with them. . . .

MR. COMMISSIONER TASCHEREAU   When you have coded a document, do you not make a little mark at each word?

GOUZENKO   I make a mark only in the Russian. I considered it was more important to bring the original in Nora's handwriting than bring the Russian translation by Colonel Zabotin, of which we have already several. Actually Colonel Zabotin translated all the sheets of Exhibit 24. I had time only to send one part. Apparently Koulakov sent the balance. It is quite difficult to remember what I sent and what I did not.

MR. WILLIAMS   We will take this one first. Supposing we take them in this order.

The first part of Exhibit 24 which you think you codified from the Russian translation is headed: "From: The Secretary of State for Dominion Affairs, London. To: The Secretary of State for External Affairs, Ottawa. London, August 24, 1945. His Majesty's ambassador Belgrade has heard from a number of sources that fairly serious fighting between Yugoslav armies and —" and the next word is Cetnika, "— is going on to the east of —" Is the next word Banyaluka?

GOUZENKO   Yes.

WILLIAMS   "He suggests that General Mihailovic may be there." From memory you think this telegram is one which you coded from the Russian translation?

GOUZENKO   That is right. . . .

WILLIAMS   Then I will read the next one, which is also dated August 24, 1945:

> From: The Secretary of State for Dominion Affairs, London.
> To: The Secretary of State for External Affairs, Ottawa.
> London, August 24, 1945.
> The problem of Bulgaria, Yugoslavia, Hungary and Roumania has been brought up and discussed in a piecemeal fashion time and time, but as a whole (as it really is the same problem) Russia has never agreed to discuss it. They are all under the influence and supervision of Russia. Elections are being planned in all these countries, but they will only result in a totalitarian system and again under the supervision of the Russians.
> We have to gain the confidence and attention of these countries and have to show what we have to offer in ways of economics and culture.

Does your memory tell you whether or not you coded that from the Russian translation?

GOUZENKO   I coded this. . . .

WILLIAMS   (*To the Commission*)   That was all of the 24th; there are two pages under date of the 28th, which will be Exhibit 24-C:

> From: The Secretary of State for Dominion Affairs, London. To: The Secretary of State for External Affairs, Ottawa. London, August 28, 1945.
> *Spain*
> Gousev pointed out to the Minister for Foreign Affairs, Mr. Bevin, that Britain was carrying out the agreements of the Potsdam Conference, especially in regard to Spain. Gousev said, from Bevin's speech of August 20th, Franco could well see that no action was intended against him.
> Bevin said that Britain would welcome a change of government in Spain, but would not countenance any action that would bring on civil war. He also added that Britain carrying out the agreements of Potsdam Conference — and then on the back of the sheet, — and asked, "was not the Soviet Union asking them to overstep them?" To this Gousev made no reply.

The second sheet reads: "The present continual differences in regard to these countries will endanger our relations with Soviet Union." (*To the witness*)   You think this belongs to the other one, do you?

GOUZENKO   I do. The first sheet is separate, and I think the second one belongs to it.

WILLIAMS   Then we will have to add the second sheet to Exhibit 24-B?

GOUZENKO   Yes. . . .

WILLIAMS   (*To the Commission*)   Then the second sheet of Exhibit 24-B reads:

The present continual differences in regard to these countries will endanger our relations with Soviet Union.

There is not much hope for Yugoslavia having a Democratic government. Tito is evidently breaking all agreements of Subasic-Tito agreement, but we feel it is too early to step in.

Austria has a better chance of forming a democracy than any of the other countries because three-quarters of it is occupied by United Kingdom, United States, and France, and yet in case of forming a government, it will be the Russians imported from Moscow that will be in the lead.

These differences will eventually bring out different opinions between us and United States, and above all we have to try to prevent that.

That completes Exhibit No. 24-B. . . .

Now we come to Exhibit 24-D, which is dated August 31, 1945:

From: The Secretary of State for Dominion Affairs, London.

To: The Secretary of State for External Affairs, Ottawa.

London, August 31, 1945.

Hungary.

British political representative advises that municipal elections in Hungary are to be held October 7th. General Miklos says the Russians are hurrying up the elections, but he is afraid to oppose too strenuously as he may be forced to resign and may be replaced by the extreme Leftists.

British political representative thinks that these elections are to be held as a test. If the outcome will be favourable to the Leftists, they and the Russians will rush a general election soon after.

(*To the witness*)   Do you remember whether you coded that?

GOUZENKO   Yes. . . .

WILLIAMS   Yesterday morning we put in as Exhibit 22 a page torn out of Colonel Zabotin's notebook?

GOUZENKO   That is right.

WILLIAMS   And in addition to that page you brought with you when you came to the police for protection several other pages torn out of Colonel Zabotin's notebook?

GOUZENKO   That is right.

WILLIAMS   Were all of those pages torn out at the same time?

GOUZENKO   That is right. They were torn out by Colonel Zabotin.

WILLIAMS   In your presence?

GOUZENKO   Yes.

WILLIAMS   And handed to you?

GOUZENKO   To destroy.

WILLIAMS   He had already partly destroyed them. He had torn them, had he not?

GOUZENKO   That is right; but they were to be burned.

WILLIAMS   Now I show you another one of those pages, which will be Exhibit 25. This is one of the pages torn out by Colonel Zabotin and partly destroyed, and handed to you for final destruction?

GOUZENKO   That is right.

WILLIAMS   I put before you the original page, Exhibit 25, and ask you if the translation as I am going to read it to you is a correct translation: "3. *Professor*. Frenchman. Well known chemist, about forty years. Works in McGill University."

GOUZENKO   "Montreal."

WILLIAMS   Is "Montreal" in there?

GOUZENKO   Yes.

WILLIAMS   "Works in the McGill University, Montreal. Is one of the best specialists on —"?

GOUZENKO   "Explosives." . . .

WILLIAMS   "The best specialist on explosives on the American continent."?

GOUZENKO   Yes. . . .

WILLIAMS   "Gives full information about explosives and chemical plants. Very rich. He is afraid to work."

GOUZENKO   That is right.

WILLIAMS   Then in brackets "(Gave the formula RDX up to present there is no valuation from the master.)"

GOUZENKO   Yes.

WILLIAMS   Then what is the next line?

GOUZENKO   "Gave materials on poison gas."

WILLIAMS   And that poison gas is represented by two initials?

GOUZENKO   Yes; "OV."

WILLIAMS   Then below that on the right-hand side: "*Auxiliary Group*. 1. Gini (Jew)"?

GOUZENKO   That is right.

WILLIAMS   "Owner of a chemistry store"?

GOUZENKO   That is a "drug store" or "pharmacy."

WILLIAMS   "Owner of a pharmacy or drug store"?

GOUZENKO   It is better "pharmacy."

WILLIAMS   "Owner of a pharmacy. He supplied a place for photography. Has a photo laboratory." Then how would you translate the next?

GOUZENKO   Just, "He has a photo laboratory." Then, "With him works —"

WILLIAMS   Oh, I see. The next sentence starts, "With him works A:" and then what is next?

GOUZENKO   "Gol."

WILLIAMS   Then that reads, "With him works, A: Gol. A young artist. Works on photography."

GOUZENKO   That is right.

WILLIAMS   That is all on the front of this page, which is to be Exhibit 25?

GOUZENKO   Yes, sir.

WILLIAMS   Then on the back of the exhibit the first word is "Contact." It goes on: "1. Freda. Jewess. Works as a co-worker in the international Bureau of Labour."

GOUZENKO   That is right. . . .

WILLIAMS   (*To the Commission*)   I intend to ask the witness about this. Freda is unidentified at the present time.   (*To the witness*)   Then it continues: "A lady friend of the professor."

GOUZENKO   Yes.

WILLIAMS   "2. Galya. Housewife. Neighbouring apartment to Davie. Husband works as a salesman. Contact is established with Fred. After the reorganization contact with Gray."

GOUZENKO   That is right.

WILLIAMS   Then below that, "Nobody in the group knows Leon."

GOUZENKO   That is right.

WILLIAMS   "Davie's wife was the contact between Leon and Davie. Galya was sometimes contact with her."

GOUZENKO   That is right.

WILLIAMS   You have already told us that the Professor is the cover or nickname for Professor Boyer?

GOUZENKO   That is right.

WILLIAMS   Do you know who Gini is?

GOUZENKO   No. . . .

WILLIAMS   And you cannot identify Gol?

GOUZENKO   No.

WILLIAMS   Then on the reverse we have the name Freda. Are you able to identify Freda?

GOUZENKO   From telegrams, and from this document.

WILLIAMS   That is, you have seen the name Freda in telegrams?

GOUZENKO   Yes. . . .

WILLIAMS   But do you know whether Freda is a real name or a cover name?

GOUZENKO   No.

WILLIAMS   You don't know anything about Freda?

GOUZENKO   Yes. I can guess that it is a cover name. . . .

WILLIAMS   Then Galya. Do you know anything about Galya?

GOUZENKO   The same as the others; it can be a real name or it can be a cover name. I don't know. . . .

WILLIAMS   Then it says, "Neighbouring apartment to Davie," and you have already identified Davie as Major Sokolov?

GOUZENKO   That is right.

WILLIAMS   Then Fred has been identified as the cover name or nickname, or rather as the name of Fred Rose?

GOUZENKO   Yes.

WILLIAMS   Whose cover name or nickname is Debouz?

GOUZENKO   That is right.
WILLIAMS   And Gray has been identified as Gerson?
GOUZENKO   Yes.
WILLIAMS   Then Leon has been identified as Koudriadtzev?
GOUZENKO   That is right. . . .
WILLIAMS   Then you have before you another page of Colonel Zabotin's notebook, obtained at the same time and in the same way, showing that it has been torn and it has been pasted together?
GOUZENKO   That is right. . . .
WILLIAMS   I will read you the translation and ask you if it is a correct translation; this will be Exhibit 25-B. The heading is, "Before reorganization. Director Davie."
GOUZENKO   No; that should be, "Directed by Davie."
WILLIAMS   "1. Fred — director of the corporation."
GOUZENKO   Yes, sir.
WILLIAMS   "Previously he worked with the neighbour, up to 1924."
GOUZENKO   That is right. . . .
WILLIAMS   And "Fred" is Fred Rose?
GOUZENKO   That is right.
WILLIAMS   "In May-June, 1942, came to Davy with a proposal to join."
GOUZENKO   "With a proposal to help."
WILLIAMS   "Davy checked up on Fred through New York."
GOUZENKO   That is right.
WILLIAMS   And what is the next word?
GOUZENKO   "Molier."
WILLIAMS   That is in brackets?
GOUZENKO   Yes.
WILLIAMS   "The neighbour proposed to use Fred. After this in 1942 September Fred contacted Davy on instructions from Molier. Molier was sent to work in Ottawa —" now translate the next part for me.
GOUZENKO   "For organizational work."
WILLIAMS   That would be "to organize the work." That is a good translation?
GOUZENKO   Yes, "to organize the work."
WILLIAMS   And what is the next?
GOUZENKO   "At the present time in the list of parliamentary candidates in Quebec." . . .
WILLIAMS   Then it goes on: "Fred's work. The group in Montreal active." Then what is next?
GOUZENKO   "Gray."
WILLIAMS   And then following that?
GOUZENKO   "Jew."
WILLIAMS   Go on. . . .
GOUZENKO   "The chief of the branch of the directorate for securing or procuring war materials for the allies."
WILLIAMS   And what is the next sentence?
GOUZENKO   "Taken to work on 1/9/42."
WILLIAMS   What is next?
GOUZENKO   "Works well. Gives materials on shells and cannon in films."

WILLIAMS   Then on the reverse side: "2. Green. Works in the administration of the tank plant 'Locomotive' in Montreal."*

GOUZENKO   That is right.

WILLIAMS   And that means in the administration of the tank plant?

GOUZENKO   Yes.

WILLIAMS   Assistant to the superintendent of the department of contracts"?

GOUZENKO   That is right.

WILLIAMS   "Gives information about —"?

GOUZENKO   "About the numbers of tanks delivered or despatched only."

WILLIAMS   We have identified Davy who is referred to here, and Fred, who is Fred Rose. Who is Molier?

GOUZENKO   That is the nickname of the first secretary in New York, the counsellor, Mikhailov.

WILLIAMS   That is in the Russian service?

GOUZENKO   That is right.

WILLIAMS   Is he the Russian consul, or the first secretary in the consulate?

GOUZENKO   I think he is first consul, as far as I know.

WILLIAMS   Then you have identified Gray as Gerson?

GOUZENKO   Yes.

WILLIAMS   Do you know anything about Green? Who is Green?

GOUZENKO   I only know what is written here.

WILLIAMS   You do not know whether it is a nickname or a real name?

GOUZENKO   No, but I think it is a nickname. . . .

WILLIAMS   Then you have here another sheet from Colonel Zabotin's notebook, obtained at the same time and in the same way. It had also been torn and was in pieces when you brought it with you when you came to the police?

GOUZENKO   That is right.

WILLIAMS   I put this translation to you, and ask you whether it is a correct translation: "Did not work for us directly but for Sam's organization."

GOUZENKO   That is right.

WILLIAMS   This is a continuation of another page. Would it be the continuation of the last page we read?

GOUZENKO   That is right. I would like to look over the previous pages.

WILLIAMS   I show you Exhibits 22, 25-A and 25-B, and ask you whether the page which you are now holding is a continuation of any of those?

GOUZENKO   I think this is it. . . .

WILLIAMS   The first two lines of Exhibit 25-C you say translated are, "Did not work for us directly but for Sam's organization"?

GOUZENKO   That is right.

WILLIAMS   And that is referring to who?

GOUZENKO   I understand Surensen and Poland. . . .

WILLIAMS   Then it goes on: "1. Davie — worked well. 2. Martin — (with Ernst and Foster). Main task — information about the army and to look for new people."

GOUZENKO   That is right.

WILLIAMS   "Submitted three reports — about aviation, the fleet and the army."

*Montreal Locomotive Works

GOUZENKO   That is right.

WILLIAMS   "3. Economist — has not been working since the month of October."

GOUZENKO   That is right.

WILLIAMS   And we have identified Davie, Martin, Ernst, Foster and the Economist?

GOUZENKO   That is right. . . .

WILLIAMS   Amongst the documents which you had with you when you came to the police for protection was a photostat of three sheets written in English and containing certain drawings?

GOUZENKO   That is right.

WILLIAMS   We will mark this document Exhibit 26, and I ask you where you obtained it?

GOUZENKO   They were lying in the brief case of Lieutenant-Colonel Rogov, beside the blue sheets of notes which have already been submitted.

WILLIAMS   And this is in exactly the same state and condition as when you took it out of Lieutenant-Colonel Rogov's brief case?

GOUZENKO   I brought them as they are here.

WILLIAMS   It was a photostat?

GOUZENKO   Yes. . . .

WILLIAMS   (*To the Commission*)   This is very hard to read. I have a translation of it here, or at least someone has typed it out. This document is all written in English.   (*To the witness*)   Is that so?

GOUZENKO   All in English.

WILLIAMS   Do you happen to know whose handwriting it is?

GOUZENKO   No. It must be in the handwriting of one of the group of agents in the Research Council.

WILLIAMS   Why do you say that; because of the contents?

GOUZENKO   Because of its contents and the drawings, and because it is marked Badeau and Bacon.

WILLIAMS   We will establish the handwriting by other evidence.

MR. COMMISSIONER TASCHEREAU   Do you know where these photostats were made? Were they made by the Russians or by those who gave them to Zabotin or Rogov?

GOUZENKO   They may have been done either in the house of the military attaché or by one of the agents.

TASCHEREAU   But at the house of the military attaché did they have the necessary appliances to make photostats?

GOUZENKO   They have a photo laboratory in the house of the military attaché. . . .

MR. WILLIAMS   I think you told me that Exhibit No. 27 was also in Colonel Rogov's brief case?

GOUZENKO   In Colonel Rogov's brief case.

WILLIAMS   In the vault in Room 12?

GOUZENKO   That is right.

WILLIAMS   The exhibit seems to be divided into one-third and two-thirds, the one part written one way on the page and the other the other way. Possibly it may be two sheets that have been photostated at the same time. The lower part reads as follows:

> Badeau continues to be agreeable to our arrangement but is extremely cautious and takes a long time to commit himself to any course of action. I hope you can understand the enclosed scientific explanation of his work, which is beyond my limited knowledge of the subject. He encloses a biography and a photograph.
>
> The most important thing about Badeau is that he is willing to apply for a position in the new nuclear —

Then we turn the page the other way and it continues:

> — physics set-up located at McGill University, Montreal. It's considered quite natural that he should apply for this work, as he is qualified in this branch of science. He knows nothing about how it is organized, but says that it is of the highest secrecy. A very careful check-up of the personnel is involved. I have encouraged him to apply but have also advised him to be extremely careful of his associations during the period of check-up. I do not think it advisable that I see him for several weeks after he makes application.

Then it continues:

> Bacon. He has become very difficult to work with especially after my request for Ur 235. He said it was absolutely impossible to obtain it so far as he knew. In fact, he claimed that it probably did not exist in any appreciable —

That is where it breaks off.   (*To the Commission*)   We believe and think we will be able to establish that Exhibit No. 27 is in the handwriting of Lunan. We have already identified Badeau as the nickname or cover name for Durnford Smith and Bacon is the cover name for Halperin.

MR. COMMISSIONER TASCHEREAU   There is a K. Willsher, who is known under the cover name of Elli. She is secretary to the High Commissioner here in Ottawa.

GOUZENKO   That is right.

TASCHEREAU   And there is also a cover name Elli, and I understand that he or she, I do not know which, has been identified as an agent in England?

GOUZENKO   That is right.

TASCHEREAU   Would that be the same person?

GOUZENKO   No.

TASCHEREAU   You are sure of that?

GOUZENKO   As far as I know.

TASCHEREAU   Did Miss Willsher come from England or is she Canadian born? . . .

MR. WILLIAMS   (*To the Commission*)   I can answer that. Miss Willsher has been in this country for fifteen years, although she did come from England.

TASCHEREAU   She has been here for the last fifteen years?

WILLIAMS   Yes.   (*To the witness*)   Another document that you brought with you is one in English on sheets of ruled paper, written on both sides. That is now before you and I want to ask you where this particular document, which will be Exhibit No. 28, was when you got it to bring with you.

GOUZENKO   In the safe in Room 12.

WILLIAMS   And do you know whose handwriting it is in?

GOUZENKO   I think this is the handwriting of Gray or his wife.

WILLIAMS   What makes you think that?

GOUZENKO   I took it from the sheets of material which was the material given by Gray and which was put by Colonel Zabotin in the safe with a note to put in the mail to deliver to Moscow.

WILLIAMS   Did Colonel Zabotin indicate to you that this sheet came from Gray?

GOUZENKO   It was obviously from him because of the conversations he had with Major Sokolov.

WILLIAMS   Do I understand that you were present at that conversation?

GOUZENKO   That is right. . . .

WILLIAMS   And Gray is the cover name for Gerson?

GOUZENKO   Gerson.

WILLIAMS   This evidently comes from a folder or file because you will notice there are holes on the left-hand side. Was it in a book or loose?

GOUZENKO   Loose.

MR. COMMISSIONER TASCHEREAU   (*To Mr. Williams*)   Did he say where he found it?

WILLIAMS   (*To the Commission*)   In the safe in Room 12. Then I will not read it all into the record at this stage, but it starts in this way: "The gun being slightly elevated, some liquid RDX1 TNT flowed back along the grooves into the chamber. The shell were rammed by hand, no great force being necessary. Results was normal." Then follow records of what are called firing 1(c), 1(d) and a record of the observations . . .   (*To the witness*)   Another document which you brought with you is one written in Russian on one side of a sheet of ruled or lined paper. From where did you get that document?

GOUZENKO   I tore it from the general notebook that was in the safe.

WILLIAMS   In whose handwriting is this document which will be Exhibit No. 29?

GOUZENKO   Lieutenant-Colonel Motinov.

WILLIAMS   Was that notebook kept by Lieutenant-Colonel Motinov or by him and others?

GOUZENKO   By him and others and was in the safe of the military attaché.

WILLIAMS   By him and others. Would that be others of the staff of the military attaché?

GOUZENKO   In this book can write only Colonel Zabotin.

WILLIAMS   Just the two?

GOUZENKO   Yes.

WILLIAMS   Colonel Zabotin and Lieutenant-Colonel Motinov?

GOUZENKO   That is all. It is written with Motinov's remarks for the business.

WILLIAMS   By that you mean the particular branch of the work he was doing?

GOUZENKO   Yes.

WILLIAMS   If you will follow that I will read the translation to you and ask you if it is correct. "Squadron Leader Mat Nantingale." That would be the way in which a Russian would write the word "Nightingale"?

GOUZENKO   That is right.

WILLIAMS   "155 O'Connor Street, Apt. 1, telephone 2.45.34. Sam is known to him as Walter. The first meeting took place 19.12.44 at 21 o'clock at the house"?

GOUZENKO   That is right.

WILLIAMS   "Possibilites: 1. Network of aerodromes in the country (both coasts). 2. Map of the coast. He has been detached from the corporants." Detached is the literal translation?

GOUZENKO   That is correct.

WILLIAMS   "He has been detached from the corporants." . . . "That is he is reserved for the future."

GOUZENKO   That is right.

WILLIAMS   "He does not work in the corporation"?

GOUZENKO   "For the corporation."

WILLIAMS   "The contact is merely of a control nature twice a year"?

GOUZENKO   That is right.

WILLIAMS   "He is married to an Englishwoman, is getting a divorce."

GOUZENKO   That is right.

WILLIAMS   "She is going to England to her mother. Reason — she does not like Canada."

GOUZENKO   That is right.

WILLIAMS   "Prior to the war he worked with the Bell Telephone Co."

GOUZENKO   That is right.

WILLIAMS   "On 25.1.45 he advised Brent about his demobilization"?

GOUZENKO   That is right.

WILLIAMS   "He is going to the Bell Company. Next contact on 24.2.45 at 20:30 at the corner of Elgin-Macleod streets. At the contact on 24.2.45 he gave the address Mair."?

GOUZENKO   I think that is Montreal. It may be short for Montreal.

WILLIAMS   You think it is Montreal abbreviated?

GOUZENKO   Yes.

WILLIAMS   "1671 Sherbrooke 57(51)."

GOUZENKO   It is in Russian karty.

WILLIAMS   You are not sure what that word means in English?

GOUZENKO   It may be maps.

WILLIAMS   But it may be maps. "Telephone 1.16.84. Next contact 24.3.45 at 20.30 Metcalfe-Somerset. He will give the coast (R.A.F.) and listening-in on the telephone"?

GOUZENKO   That is right.

WILLIAMS   "Task — (1. recruiting) (2. Materials of the company)"?

GOUZENKO   That is right.

WILLIAMS   "(3. Dubox)"?

GOUZENKO   "Dubok." That is a nickname for any hiding place for documents or things to be handed over.

WILLIAMS   That is followed by "Gini" and that is followed by "how."

GOUZENKO   Yes. . . .

WILLIAMS You have already identified Nightingale who was known by the cover name of Leader?

GOUZENKO That is right.

WILLIAMS Sam is the next referred to. That is the one whom you have identified as Sam Carr?

GOUZENKO That is right.

WILLIAMS But Sam Carr is known to Nightingale as Walter?

GOUZENKO That is what is said here.

WILLIAMS The cover name for Sam Carr with Nightingale is Walter. Then you have identified Brent as?

GOUZENKO Lieutenant-Colonel Rogov. . . .

WILLIAMS We have already had reference to Gini or Hini, and I understood you to say you do not know who Gini was?

GOUZENKO Whether it is a code or real name, no. . . .

WILLIAMS Then the word "how" at the end; what does that signify?

GOUZENKO I cannot explain.

WILLIAMS This task was the task that was given to Nightingale?

GOUZENKO That is right.

WILLIAMS Another document you brought with you is a double sheet of ruled paper, evidently also taken out of a notebook. It is written on the front and on the third sheet in Russian. Where did this document, which will be Exhibit No. 30, come from?

GOUZENKO From the same notebook which was taken with the previous documents.

WILLIAMS The same notebook as the previous documents. It was torn out of the notebook by yourself?

GOUZENKO By myself.

WILLIAMS And that notebook was the one that was kept in the safe in Room 12?

GOUZENKO That is right.

WILLIAMS And whose handwriting is on the front of the document?

GOUZENKO Lieutenant-Colonel Motinov.

WILLIAMS That is the handwriting of Lieutenant-Colonel Motinov, including the part written in pencil?

GOUZENKO Yes.

WILLIAMS And the part which is in the lined oblong?

GOUZENKO This I have some doubt about.

WILLIAMS You have some doubt about the part within the lines?

GOUZENKO That is right.

WILLIAMS I will read the translation to you and ask you to follow the original and tell me if it is correct. This is headed "Alek." "1. Sample-Uran. N235." . . . Uranium is abbreviated to "uran." and then there is a number 235 which follows?

GOUZENKO Yes.

WILLIAMS "2. Characteristics of the work of the laboratory and the people"?

GOUZENKO That is right.

WILLIAMS And then what follows that in pencil?

GOUZENKO "Friend Henry Ferns."

WILLIAMS I am not sure where this belongs and I will have you say which line it belongs to, this part in pencil "Friend Henry Ferns." Then it continues: "3. Report about the work for 1st July"?

GOUZENKO   That is right.

WILLIAMS   "4. Routine-10.5 money, whisky."

GOUZENKO   That is right.

WILLIAMS   "5. Where is the plant U.S.A. atomic bomb?"

GOUZENKO   That is right.

WILLIAMS   "6. How about his friend-Henry Ferns." Is that right?

GOUZENKO   Yes.

WILLIAMS   "Possibility of proposing development."

GOUZENKO   That is right.

WILLIAMS   "Is it possible to photograph"?

GOUZENKO   That is right.

WILLIAMS   "7. Letter."

GOUZENKO   That is right.

WILLIAMS   "8. To think about development."

GOUZENKO   That is right.

WILLIAMS   Then there has been written under that and struck out, what?

GOUZENKO   "Fred Rose."

WILLIAMS   Then what is that after that?

GOUZENKO   "Henry F."

WILLIAMS   Then below that has been written something that has been struck out?

GOUZENKO   "Boyer."

WILLIAMS   Then still in the same handwriting, "The plant is in Grande-Mère, Quebec N13551."

GOUZENKO   That is right.

WILLIAMS   The pencilled words you have translated as "friend Henry Ferns" have been written opposite items 2 and 3?

GOUZENKO   Yes.

WILLIAMS   In pencil. Then in the insert marked around with a line, "200 dollars Alek."

GOUZENKO   That is right.

WILLIAMS   What is that word?

GOUZENKO   "And two bottles whisky."

WILLIAMS   "Handed over 12.4.45."

GOUZENKO   That is right.

WILLIAMS   And the signature is?

GOUZENKO   "Baxter."

WILLIAMS   Who is Baxter?

GOUZENKO   Angelov.

WILLIAMS   Would this part within the lines be Angelov's writing?

GOUZENKO   It can be, but it is very likely Lieutenant-Colonel Motinov himself; he just signed.

WILLIAMS   The signature Baxter is in Angelov's writing?

GOUZENKO   That is right.

WILLIAMS   But you think the other is also Motinov's writing?

GOUZENKO   Right. . . .

WILLIAMS (*To the Commission*) As this is all one document it will probably be marked as the one exhibit. I will give the translation of the part inside, on what would be the third page. (*To the witness*) There is something written in Russian. Whose handwriting is that?

GOUZENKO Lieutenant-Colonel Motinov.

WILLIAMS It is headed "Leader." "1." What is that word?

GOUZENKO "Biography."

WILLIAMS There is a blank in the translation. "Biography, photo."

GOUZENKO That is right.

WILLIAMS "2. Possibilities."

GOUZENKO That is right.

WILLIAMS "3. Contacts — letter."

GOUZENKO That is right.

WILLIAMS "4. Call up."

GOUZENKO "Recruiting."

WILLIAMS "5. Money."

GOUZENKO That is right. . . .

WILLIAMS From your knowledge of the way in which these operations are carried on would you say that these memos in Exhibit No. 30 are Motinov's ideas of what should be done in respect to the work that Alek was doing and the work that Leader was doing?

GOUZENKO That is right.

WILLIAMS And the way he should continue to work with them?

GOUZENKO Yes.

WILLIAMS Alek we have identified as being Alan Nunn May?

GOUZENKO That is right.

MR. COMMISSIONER TASCHEREAU (*To Mr. Williams*) In whose handwriting is this part on the inside sheet?

WILLIAMS He said Motinov's.

TASCHEREAU You did not ask him anything about Henry Ferns.

WILLIAMS I am sorry, I had intended to do that. (*To the witness*) On the front there there is a reference to Henry Ferns. Does that mean anything to you?

GOUZENKO Yes, I know him.

WILLIAMS You know him?

GOUZENKO I know what the subject is that is being spoken of. Moscow sent a telegram to the effect that we know that in the research laboratory in Montreal there is a friend of Alan Nunn May, one Henry Ferns, and that contact should be made through Alan Nunn May.*

WILLIAMS There was another document you had with you when you came to the police for protection. This is a document written in Russian on a page such as is put in loose leaf binders. This will be marked as Exhibit No. 31. Where did this particular document come from?

GOUZENKO From the same place as the photographs which we were discussing.

WILLIAMS That is from Lieutenant-Colonel Rogov's brief case?

GOUZENKO That is right.

---

*There was an officer employed in the Department of External Affairs until the end of 1944 by the name of Henry Ferns, but never in the Montreal laboratory. The reference remains incomprehensible.

WILLIAMS   The document reads, "Characteristics for (blanks. application forms)."

GOUZENKO   That is right.

WILLIAMS   "Smith-Durnford. Degrees. B.Sc. Excellent mathematics and Physics, McGill University '34. M. Sc. Physics — McGill University '36. Research Work — M. Sc. Dissertation Geiger — Muller indicators for exciting radio-activity."

GOUZENKO   That is right.

WILLIAMS   "Work — Building the indicators G-M for detection of weak sources of B plus. Bulbs and stimulator feeding the indicator."

GOUZENKO   That is right.

WILLIAMS   That "B" is written something like the character Beta, the Greek letter?

GOUZENKO   Yes.

WILLIAMS   And then, "To Gouseev."

GOUZENKO   This must be separate.

WILLIAMS   Down to "To Gouseev"?

GOUZENKO   This must be separate.

WILLIAMS   Down to "To Gouseev" has been written by Lieutenant-Colonel Rogov, but not the rest?

GOUZENKO   Yes.

WILLIAMS   He has written in the words "To Gouseev" and he put in the arrow?

GOUZENKO   Yes.

WILLIAMS   That indicates a task that has been turned over to Govseev to do?

GOUZENKO   Yes.

WILLIAMS   And then in brackets "(Bell Telephone) — Telephone." The words in brackets "Bell Telephone" are in English while the word "telephone" is in Russian?

GOUZENKO   Yes.

WILLIAMS   "The indicator working up to 300 counts per minute, which was established by the study of factual interval distribution (counts — blows, number) from the theory of probability. Preparation of" and the next word is what?

GOUZENKO   "Alpha partub."

WILLIAMS   That alpha is the Greek alpha?

GOUZENKO   Yes.

WILLIAMS   There is just the one letter. Could you translate what "partub" means?

GOUZENKO   I do not know.

WILLIAMS   It is written in, "preparation of alpha partub sources. R a C sources are prepared from used rod on bulbs from the hospitals. The lamps were smashed in the inside of a small vessel making possible R to spread in the space covered by a very thin mica pane. After R a C forms about the pane, the sources were used for activizing AC in the reaction."

GOUZENKO   That is right. I think it is "L"; AL and not AC.

WILLIAMS   In the next line it is "alpha plus AL minus P^x plus n." Is that right?

GOUZENKO   Yes.

WILLIAMS   "The counted period of action B plus was 2.7 minutes. (Work under

114

the direction of Dr. D.A. Keys.)" Those words are underlined. "Ph.D. work. All Ph.D. trials finish with the dissertation work, which must be done on research of spectrums Beta by means of the magnetic spectrograph, were actually partly of the pre-war cyclotron program of McGill University, and the spectrograph although it had been projected had not been built." On the reverse side there is the heading "(Work under the direction of Dr. I.S. Foster). To Gouseev (During the time spent on Beta spectrograph he worked during the day time as radio engineer in the Canadian Bell Telephone Co. 1937-42. Since that time he works on the microwave radio for National Research (Scientific Research Laboratory.)"

GOUZENKO   I think it is Gouseev's writing because Gouseev finished the military radio institute and is an engineer by profession although he is a doorman by specialty. . . .

WILLIAMS   Among the documents which you brought with you when you came to the police for protection were two sheets, also on ruled paper of the kind usually supplied for loose leaf books, with three holes on the left-hand side, written in Russian. These will be marked as Exhibit No. 32. In whose writing are those two sheets?

GOUZENKO   I am a little in doubt but I think it is Levin's.

WILLIAMS   It is all the same writing on the two sheets?

GOUZENKO   Yes. This is a translation.

WILLIAMS   Where did those two sheets come from?

GOUZENKO   They were in the same brief case of Lieutenant-Colonel Rogov, where the others came from. . . .

WILLIAMS   At the top of the first sheet there is written something in red pencil; is that also in the same handwriting as the rest of it?

GOUZENKO   I think it is Lieutenant-Colonel Rogov.

WILLIAMS   And it reads, the part in red, "Back's Group" or "Group of Back."

GOUZENKO   That is right.

WILLIAMS   Then "Mat No. 1." That is apparently an abbreviation for Material No. 1. I will read the translation to you and ask you to tell me if it is correct. "It has become very difficult to work with him, especially after my request about Ur 235 (Uran 235). He said that it is absolutely impossible to get it, as far as he knows. Thus for example, he advised that probably there is not any appreciable quantity. Bacon explained to me the theory of atomic energy, which is probably known to you." Is that right? . . . "He refuses to write anything and does not wish to give a photograph or information about himself. I think that at present he appreciates the gist of my requests more fully and he does not like them very much."

GOUZENKO   That is right.

WILLIAMS   "With that kind of thoughts which he has, it is impossible to get anything from him, excepting oral descriptions, and I am not in a position to understand everything fully where this touches technical details."

GOUZENKO   That is right.

WILLIAMS   "I asked him what is involved in the building of a very large plant (Chalk River near Petawawa, Ontario) in general opinion, the principle of which is based on the physical characteristics of the atom, in connection with his expressed opinion that Uran 235 was impossible to obtain. He replied that he does not know. He thought that the project was still in the experimental stage."

GOUZENKO   That is right.

WILLIAMS   The second sheet reads:

> Then he described to me the general principles of the electron shell and the bomb detonator, which are being produced in the plants in the U.S.A. and Canada, which is the reason for the accurate fire of destruction of rocket bombs (V-bombs). It has the form of a small transmitter of high frequency, the ray of which is reflected from the target. When the power of the reflected wave in opposition to the rayed frequency reaches a definite strength the battle (destructive) charge is exploded electrically. I asked him if it would be possible to obtain instructions for it, he replied that that would be possible. I was not able to extract anything in other ways. In conclusion, Bacon (took the position) announced that he will talk with me but he will not write anything whatsoever, and I do not think that he is ready to begin to work more deeply, as for example — to obtain samples (specimens). He says that he does not know anything but what is already known to you.

GOUZENKO   Yes. . . .

WILLIAMS   (*To the Commission*)   This fits in with the file on Lunan. Some of the material that is there we will tie in for you later on. It is interesting to note how so much of this can be pieced together.   (*To the witness*)   Another of the documents which you brought with you from the embassy is typewritten in Russian. There are two sheets of this. Where did this document, which will be Exhibit No. 33, come from?

GOUZENKO   From the safe in Room 12.

WILLIAMS   And was it from any particular file or was it lying loose?

GOUZENKO   Lying loose with other papers of the same nature.

WILLIAMS   There is something written in Russian in handwriting at the top, certain words; whose handwriting is that?

GOUZENKO   Colonel Zabotin's.

WILLIAMS   Is that his signature, Grant?

GOUZENKO   That is right.

WILLIAMS   And the other words are "I confirm: Grant. 5.11.44."

GOUZENKO   That is right.

WILLIAMS   I will read the translation of the typed part to you and ask you if it is a correct translation. "Questions requiring explanation by Lamont and Brent about Jack and Dick."

GOUZENKO   That is right.

WILLIAMS   "1. For both. (1) To explain the principal service data: (a) Present occupation, where did he work previously; (b) Prospects of remaining in the service after the war and where; (c) From what year in the army, does he like the service." . . . It means what year he entered the service and how he likes the service. "(d) Relations with his immediate superior."

GOUZENKO   That is right.

WILLIAMS   "(2) To explain brief biological data: (a) (Age), parents; (b) Education, principal pre-war specialization; (c) Party affiliation, attitude towards the politics of King; (d) Financial status; trends re establishing his family welfare."

GOUZENKO   That is right.

WILLIAMS

(Intentions to engage in business, to own a car, his own home and what impedes the fulfillment of this plan); (e) Attitude towards our country and her policies; (f) Wherein does he see the development of Canada (in friendship with America or in retaining English influence). (3) Personal dependability and negative sides. (a) Inclination for drinking, good family man; (b) Lover of good times, inclination for solitude and quietness; (c) Influence of his wife on his actions, independence in making decisions; (d) circle of friends and their brief characteristics.

GOUZENKO   Yes.

WILLIAMS   I suppose that means their characteristics in brief. "(4) Platform for the future: (ideological of materialistic require establishing)."

GOUZENKO   That is right.

WILLIAMS   Is that ideology?

GOUZENKO   "Ideological."

WILLIAMS

(5) Especially: (1) The first — Frenchman and all the family are French; (2) The second — Englishman (Anglo-Saxon), but his wife is a French woman. Their views on some points are different but he, knowing the strictness of the Catholic religion, endeavours not to offend his wife in which connection he occasionally refuses to discuss questions which concern the religion of his wife. Both the first as well as the second work in responsible jobs, therefore they gave their signatures not to divulge military secrets. Therefore the character of the work must be usual — personal generality with conversation on various themes, beginning with themselves, with their biography, occupation and life, at times asking them as if for comparison with this or that situation, etc.

The signature is "Lamont."

GOUZENKO   That is right.

WILLIAMS   Who is Lamont?

GOUZENKO   Lieutenant-Colonel Motinov.

WILLIAMS   At the beginning we have, "Questions requiring explanation by Lamont and Brent." Lamont is Motinov and Brent is?

GOUZENKO   Rogov.

WILLIAMS   "About Jack and Dick."

GOUZENKO   That is right.

WILLIAMS   Do you know who Jack is?

GOUZENKO   Colonel LeBlanc.

MR. COMMISSIONER TASCHEREAU   Is it LeBlanc?

GOUZENKO   Sub-adjutant to the chief of the Canadian army staff, the chief of the general staff. . . .

MR. WILLIAMS   From where did you learn that Jack was supposed to represent Colonel LeBlanc; from whom did you learn that?

GOUZENKO   From telegrams which were sent and in which was mentioned both his real name and his cover name.

WILLIAMS   And did you hear Zabotin or Rogov or any others speak about him or did your information come solely from the telegrams?

GOUZENKO   From the telegrams.

WILLIAMS   From the telegrams only?

GOUZENKO   That is right.

WILLIAMS   I think you have already identified Dick?

GOUZENKO   Lieutenant-Colonel Letson.

WILLIAMS   Then there is reference here to the "attitude towards the politics of King." To whom does that refer?

GOUZENKO   Prime Minister King of Canada.

MR. COMMISSIONER TASCHEREAU   Are you sure about that Colonel LeBlanc?

GOUZENKO   It is the only time I have seen the name. I think there is some additional material from which he can be identified through family connections.

MR. WILLIAMS   (*To the Commission*)   I may say that up to the present time we have been unable to identify Colonel LeBlanc. . . .   (*To the witness*)   You also brought with you from the embassy when you came to the police for protection two sheets written in Russian, on ruled pages evidently torn out of a notebook. These will be marked as Exhibit No. 34. Where did you get those two sheets?

GOUZENKO   These were in a separate notebook wherein Lieutenant-Colonel Motinov prepared telegrams which Colonel Zabotin later would send away, rewrite and send away.

WILLIAMS   So that this is a draft telegram prepared by Lieutenant-Colonel Motinov to be submitted to Colonel Zabotin?

GOUZENKO   That is right.

WILLIAMS   Do you know whether this telegram was ever actually sent?

GOUZENKO   Yes, it was sent. . . .

WILLIAMS   I will place that before you and read the translation and ask you if it is correct. "To the Director. Debouz advised that the Minister of Fisheries Bertrand told him that the war will end in a month, that is about 1st of September of this year."

GOUZENKO   That is right.

WILLIAMS   "Three days before the uprising, the attempt on Hitler the same Bertrand told Debouz that very shortly there would be events of tremendous import in Europe which no one suspected."

GOUZENKO   That is right.

WILLIAMS   "Jean Louis Gagnon told Debouz that the head of the French Telegraph Agency in Washington, Saint Jean, told Jean Louis that the Washington government knows and is convinced that the German generals did everything possible to ensure the landings of Anglo-American troops in Normandy."

GOUZENKO   That is right.

WILLIAMS   "Jean Louis Gagnon also told Debouz that De Gaulle had told him during his presence in Quebec City. De Gaulle — 'I am extremely surprised at the extraordinary slow advance of the Anglo-American troops in France.' "

GOUZENKO   That is right.

WILLIAMS   That is signed "Grant."

GOUZENKO   Yes, by the hand of Motinov.

WILLIAMS   Then it continues . . .

> To the director. Gray's wife has relatives in Bukovina and Bucharest.
> Apart from relatives she has many acquaintances among doctors and
> other specialists. Recently Gray handed Davie a reply of the Canadian
> Red Cross of March 1942 wherein it is announced that the relatives of
> Gray's wife are in their . . . own places, that is in Roumania. Gray's
> wife through Gray asks advice as to whether it is possible to send them
> money or other things. Davie replied that this was a complicated and
> difficult question, and that he could not promise anything. He suggested
> he be furnished with addresses and letters from Gray's wife for these
> acquaintances. In the letters it could be proposed (that is through Gray's
> wife — he will agree to that) that they contact the man who will deliver
> the letter. If you agree to such an idea — we shall receive the addresses
> and letters from the wife of Gray.

And what is the next word?

GOUZENKO   "Roofs of the doctor."

WILLIAMS   What does that mean?

GOUZENKO   "Roof" means cover for secret activities. It means open cover for
secret activities.

WILLIAMS   That is what it means in this case?

GOUZENKO   Yes. This case is cover to maybe send secret letters to official
doctors, to doctors and other specialists.

MR. COMMISSIONER KELLOCK   I do not get that. Would you explain that again?

GOUZENKO   "Roofs" means a cover for secret activities. I cannot explain
exactly. The official military attaché here is the roof for the illegal work carried
on by the members of the staff.

MR. WILLIAMS   Does this mean, then, that communications which are to be kept
secret should be sent to the addresses of doctors and other specialists?

GOUZENKO   That is right, as I understand it.

WILLIAMS   (To the Commissioner)   Does that answer the question?

KELLOCK   Yes. I did not get the answer before. I understand the answer, but
I am not sure I understand the full significance of it. I had better clear that
up.   (To the witness)   Moscow was not sending, as far as we have heard
here, any communications to doctors or specialists. They were sending their
communications direct to the Russian embassy, so I do not know what you
mean or rather I do not know the significance of the translation of this part of it.

GOUZENKO   The roof or cover means that it would be the official title of some
business firm or, as in this case, a doctor that would be used for covering up
the actual activities of the individual. In this case at that time Roumania had
not been out of the war, and was not occupied, and therefore the cover was
necessary to send parcels and things in an illegal way, evidently, to relatives
of Gray's wife. . . .

MR. WILLIAMS   And it continues, "Letters from —" and what is the name?

GOUZENKO   "Lesovia." That is a nickname for Canada; it means land of forests."

WILLIAMS   "Letters from Lesovia," and how does the rest of it read?

GOUZENKO   "There are no suspicions against us."

WILLIAMS   And that is signed "Grant," by Lieutenant-Colonel Motinov, and the date is put on in blue pencil, 28/4/44, but it was not sent?

GOUZENKO   No.

WILLIAMS   Then it continues with the following: "To the director, on N —" and there is no number; the number is missing?

GOUZENKO   That is right.

WILLIAMS   "I advise your appearance for Berman in London."

GOUZENKO   That is right.

WILLIAMS

The meeting will take place two weeks after Berman's departure from Montreal. The first Sunday after his departure is to be counted as the date of his departure, even if he should have left on a Wednesday. The meeting will take place at fifteen hours Sunday in front of the office of the High Commissioner for Canada, London, S.W.1 (Canada House, Trafalgar Square). If the first Sunday it does not take place, it will be transferred to the next Sunday at the same hours etc. until contact is established. Berman will be in civilian clothes — brown suit (tweed), a raincoat without a hat, with a newspaper in his right hand. Password: "How's Elsie?" Berman will reply: "She's fine." Thereupon our man will give him a letter signed "Frank".

If the meeting at the designated place appears impossible, or inconvenient for us, Berman will send his address to his wife, the latter will give it to Debouz, and the latter to us and it may be possible to undertake the contact at the address of his living quarters. When you advise us that the contact will be more convenient at the apartment, then we will tell Debouz, and he (will tell) Berman's wife. Berman's wife will write him a letter with the following phrase: "Ben has not been feeling too well." After that he will await contact at his apartment.

Supplementary data. He entered the party in 1938. Worked as an insurance agent. His wife entered the party in 1939. During the illegal period he worked in the central apparatus of the party on organizational work.

GOUZENKO   That is right. . . .

WILLIAMS   Do you know anything about Berman other than what is in this document?

GOUZENKO   This was the first time I saw him, in this document.

WILLIAMS   The first time you ever saw the name Berman was in this document, Exhibit 34?

GOUZENKO   Yes.

WILLIAMS   Did you hear anything about him, in addition to what you saw in the document?

GOUZENKO   Oh, yes. Colonel Zabotin sent a telegram to Moscow that there was sent to Moscow with Tunkin the biography and photograph of Berman. . . .

MR. FAUTEUX   I am told that it is a Jewish name.

GOUZENKO   Yes.

WILLIAMS   Or it could be an English or a German name; it is a Teutonic name as well.

MR. COMMISSIONER TASCHEREAU   Because the code name might be Berman and the right name Burman.

WILLIAMS   Yes. We have some further information about Berman.   (*To the witness*)   And the Debouz referred to in the first part of Exhibit 34 is the cover name of Fred Rose?

GOUZENKO   That is right. . . .

WILLIAMS   Another of the documents which you brought with you is also written on a sheet torn out of a notebook, on lined paper, and it will be marked Exhibit 35. From where did this document, Exhibit 35, come from?

GOUZENKO   From the same notebook which the previous documents came from. . . .

WILLIAMS   And you tore this sheet out of the notebook, the way you did the other sheets?

GOUZENKO   The other previous sheets.

WILLIAMS   And this document is in the handwriting of Lieutenant-Colonel Motinov?

GOUZENKO   Yes.

WILLIAMS   Although the signature at the bottom is Grant, that is written by Motinov?

GOUZENKO   That is right.

WILLIAMS   And this is the draft of a telegram prepared by Motinov to be submitted to Colonel Zabotin, whose cover name is Grant?

GOUZENKO   That is right.

WILLIAMS   I will read the translation to you and ask you to tell me if it is correct:

To the director. The Professor advised that the director of the National Chemical Research Committee Steacie told him about the new plant under construction: Pilot plant at Grand-Mère, in the Province of Quebec. This plant will produce "uranium." The engineering personnel is being obtained from McGill University and is already moving into the district of the new plant. As a result of experiments carried out with uranium it has been found that uranium may be used for filling bombs, which is already being done in a practical way. The Americans have undertaken wide research work, having invested 660 million dollars in this business.

The signature is "Grant," written by Motinov, at the bottom?

GOUZENKO   That is right.

WILLIAMS   Was that telegram ever sent?

GOUZENKO   I think not. It is hard to say.

WILLIAMS   You do not recollect having received it on a blue sheet from Colonel Zabotin for coding? . . .

GOUZENKO   I do not recall. I cannot say. Zabotin sometimes did not send the telegrams which Motinov would write.

WILLIAMS   On the back of Exhibit 35 something is written, and then it has been crossed out; and that writing is also the writing of Lieutenant-Colonel Motinov?

GOUZENKO   Yes, sir.

WILLIAMS   I will read the translation to you and ask you to tell me if it is correct: "To the director on N." Then no number is there.

> To-day we received through Debouz: a photograph of Berman and a letter signed by Debouz for Berman. Below is given appearance worked out by Debouz for Berman. Berman will know one thing, that the letter will be given him by Debouz's man. The latter is known to him as Frank. The contact must take place two weeks after the departure of B. from Montreal counting Sunday, in front of the building (office) of the High Commissioner of Canada Sunday at fifteen hours. If it does not take place — it will be carried over to the following Sunday at the same time etc. until the meeting takes place.

GOUZENKO   That is right.

WILLIAMS   There is a sentence there, or two sentences I will read again: "Berman will know one thing, that the letter will be given him by Debouz's man. The latter is known to him as Frank." Does that refer to Debouz or to Debouz's man?

GOUZENKO   To Debouz's man; the man of Debouz.

WILLIAMS   And will the man of Debouz be known as Frank in this case, or will Debouz be known as Frank?

GOUZENKO   This man of Debouz is known to Berman as Frank. . . .

WILLIAMS   Then you brought with you from the embassy another document, written on lined paper, and which we will mark as Exhibit 36. This is written on a sheet evidently torn out of a notebook. Did it come from the same notebook that the previous exhibit came from?

GOUZENKO   That is right. Just a moment. This came from the other notebook, wherein were notes, among others the note that had the signature of Baxter. You remember the first notebook I mentioned? This is from the first notebook. This sheet came from the first notebook that was mentioned, the notebook that contained notes by Lieutenant-Colonel Motinov; not the second notebook, where Lieutenant-Colonel Motinov composed drafts of telegrams. . . .

WILLIAMS   This is from the notebook in which the notes of telegrams were made?

GOUZENKO   No.

WILLIAMS   You tore this out of the notebook in question?

GOUZENKO   Yes.

WILLIAMS   I will read the translation to you, and get you to say if it is correct.

> To Debouz. Stenberg — 'Berger' 4133.
> Debouz to tie up with Berger and depending on the circumstances make a proposal that he work for us or for the corporation. Contact in Washington with Debouz man. To work out the method of contact and to telegraph. To give out 600 dollars. If Debouz is unable to go to U.S.A. then a letter from Debouz to Berger containing a request to assist the man delivering the letter to Berger.
> 12.5.45   2200   St. Patrick & Cumberland.

122

GOUZENKO   That is right.

WILLIAMS   Who is Stenberg, do you know?

GOUZENKO   That is a scientist in the United States.

WILLIAMS   How did you learn that?

GOUZENKO   In previous telegrams.

WILLIAMS   Is it the real name of the man or is it a cover name?

GOUZENKO   It is the real name.

WILLIAMS   Do you know anything more about him than that?

GOUZENKO   Yes; there were further telegrams about him.

WILLIAMS   Did you ever hear him discussed by Zabotin or Motinov or any of the others in the embassy?

GOUZENKO   There were telegrams which were written by Colonel Zabotin.

WILLIAMS   So of your own knowledge, it all comes from telegrams?

GOUZENKO   Yes.

MR. COMMISSIONER KELLOCK   "Berger" then is a cover name for Stenberg?

GOUZENKO   That is right. . . .

MR. COMMISSIONER TASCHEREAU   Do you know in what city in the United States Stenberg lives?

GOUZENKO   No.

TASCHEREAU   Is he connected with the atomic bomb, when you say he is a scientist?

GOUZENKO   In the telegrams which Colonel Zabotin sent to Moscow he described him as a scientist who was a friend of Debouz and was very well acquainted with the development of the atomic bomb.

TASCHEREAU   Do you know if Debouz went to Washington, or was it his friend who made the contact with Stenberg?

GOUZENKO   In later telegrams that were sent it was pointed out that Debouz's man had handed over Stenberg to the military intelligence in Washington.

MR. WILLIAMS   That is the Russian military intelligence in Washington?

GOUZENKO   Yes.

WILLIAMS   And the contact was to be made in Washington?

GOUZENKO   Yes, sir.

WILLIAMS   Through the officials of the Russian service?

GOUZENKO   Yes.

MR. COMMISSIONER TASCHEREAU   So Debouz did not go himself; it was his man who made the contact in Washington?

GOUZENKO   This telegram to which I refer was sent much later, and it was not indicated whether Debouz had made the contact, but the contact was established.

MR. WILLIAMS   Do you know the name or the cover name of Debouz's man in Washington?

GOUZENKO   No, but in the telegram that reported the handing over of Berger, it mentioned that it was done through Freda. It was not a contact; it was handing over.

WILLIAMS   And you have not been able to identify Freda?

GOUZENKO   No.

WILLIAMS   Another document you brought with you, also written on a piece of notebook paper, came from where?

GOUZENKO   From the same pages as the last one, the same notebook.

WILLIAMS   And whose handwriting is it in?

GOUZENKO   Lieutenant-Colonel Motinov.

WILLIAMS   This will be Exhibit No. 37, and I will read you a translation and ask you to say if it is correct. "Professor. Research Council — report on the organization and work. Freda to the Professor through Grierson."

GOUZENKO   That is right.

WILLIAMS   Who is Grierson?

GOUZENKO   From the documents which I have read I have assumed that that is Grierson of the Canadian Film Board, chairman of the National Film Board. . . .*

MR. COMMISSIONER TASCHEREAU   What is the meaning of that: "Freda to the Professor through Grierson"?

GOUZENKO   I understand it means that they wished to appoint Freda to work with the Professor, through Grierson. I want to explain.

TASCHEREAU   Yes, I would like to you to explain that.

GOUZENKO   The work that Freda was doing in the film board was not satisfactory to Moscow. Therefore they asked Colonel Zabotin to place her in some more important department. Therefore it looks as if Colonel Zabotin was to place Freda to work with the Professor, using Grierson's influence to get her into the position.

MR. WILLIAMS   So Freda, who has not been identified yet, is a person who lived in Ottawa?

GOUZENKO   I understand yes.

WILLIAMS   And had worked for the National Film Board?

GOUZENKO   The last time; yes.

WILLIAMS   But do you know if she changed her position?

GOUZENKO   From telegrams, I understand yes, she changed.

WILLIAMS   And she went to work, after she left the Film Board, where?

GOUZENKO   At first I understand from telegrams she was working in the International Labour in Montreal, and then in the National Film Board.

MR. COMMISSIONER TASCHEREAU   But Colonel Zabotin was not satisfied with her work at the National Film Board, and he could obtain nothing, so he suggested that she should work somewhere else?

GOUZENKO   Yes, in scientific work.

TASCHEREAU   And that she would be helped to get that new postition by Grierson?

GOUZENKO   I understand so from this.

TASCHEREAU   And do you know if she got this new job?

GOUZENKO   No, I don't know. . . .

February 16, 1945

MR. WILLIAMS   You came to the Mounted Police on September 7, 1945, to get protection from them?

GOUZENKO   That is right.

---

*John Grierson's testimony is found below on p. 341

WILLIAMS   And you have received that protection since?
GOUZENKO   That is right.
WILLIAMS   From September 7, 1945?
GOUZENKO   That is right.
WILLIAMS   And on October 10, 1945, you wrote out in your own handwriting a summary of your reasons for taking the steps that you did and that you have described?
GOUZENKO   Yes; all of which I had said orally on September 7.
WILLIAMS   So this statement on October 10 was in written form what you had already said to the Mounted Police on September 7, 1945?
GOUZENKO   That is right. . . .
WILLIAMS   I will read a translation of the statement and ask you to tell me whether you approve of the translation:

> Statement.
> I, Igor Gouzenko, wish to make the following statement of my own will:
> Having arrived in Canada two years ago I was surprised during the first days by the complete freedom of the individual which exists in Canada but does not exist in Russia. The false representations about the democratic countries which are increasingly propagated in Russia, were dissipated daily, as no lying propaganda can stand up against facts.
> During two years of life in Canada I saw the evidence of what a free people can do. What the Canadian people have accomplished and are accomplishing here under conditions of complete freedom, the Russian people, under the conditions of the Soviet regime of violence and suppression of all freedom, cannot accomplish even at the cost of tremendous sacrifices, blood and tears.
> The last elections which took place recently in Canada especially surprised me. In comparison with them the system of elections in Russia appear as a mockery of the conception of free elections. For example, the fact that in elections in the Soviet Union one candidate is put forward, so that the possibilities of choice are eliminated, speaks for itself.
> While creating a false picture of the conditions of life in these countries, the Soviet government at the same time is taking all measures to prevent the peoples of democratic countries from knowing about the condition of life in Russia. The facts about the brutal suppression of the freedom of speech, the mockery of the real religious feelings of the people, cannot penetrate into the democratic countries.
> Having imposed its Communist regime on the people, the government of the Soviet Union asserts that the Russian people have, as it were, their own particular understanding of freeedom and democracy, different from that which prevails among the peoples of the western democracies. *This is a lie.* The Russian people have the same understanding of freedom as all the peoples of the world. However, the Russian people cannot realize their dream of freedom and a democratic government on account of cruel terror and persecution.
> Holding forth at international conferences with voluble statements

about peace and security, the Soviet government is simultaneously preparing secretly for the third world war. To meet this war the Soviet government is creating in democratic countries, including Canada, a fifth column, in the organization of which even diplomatic representatives of the Soviet government take part.

The announcement of the dissolution of the Comintern was, probably, the greatest farce of the Communists in recent years. Only the name was liquidated, with the object of reassuring public opinion in the democratic countries. Actually, the Comintern exists and continues its work, because the Soviet leaders have never relinquished the idea of establishing a Communist dictatorship throughout the world.

Taking into account least of all that this adventurous idea will cost millions of Russian lives, the Communists are engendering hatred in the Russian people towards everything foreign.

To many Soviet people here abroad it is clear that the Communist party in democratic countries has changed long ago from a political party into an agency net of the Soviet government, into a fifth column in these countries to meet a war, into an instrument in the hands of the Soviet government for creating artificial unrest, provocation, etc., etc.

Through numerous party agitators the Soviet government stirs up the Russian people in every possible way against the people of the democratic countries, preparing the ground for the third world war.

During my residence in Canada I have seen how the Canadian people and their government, sincerely wishing to help the Soviet people, sent supplies to the Soviet Union, collected money for the welfare of the Russian people, sacrificing the lives of their sons in the delivery of these supplies across the ocean — and instead of gratitude for the help rendered, the Soviet government is developing espionage activity in Canada, preparing to deliver a stab in the back to Canada — all this without the knowledge of the Russian people.

Convinced that such double-faced politics of the Soviet government towards the democratic countries do not conform with the interests of the Russian people and endanger the security of civilization, I decided to break away from the Soviet regime and to announce my decision openly.

I am glad that I found the strength within myself to take this step and to warn Canada and the other democratic countries of the danger which hangs over them.

That is signed, "Gouzenko." That translation which I have read to you, you have already read over yourself and have stated: "I have read the foregoing translation, which was made from my original statement in Russian, and have found it to be correct," and that is your signature?

GOUZENKO   That is right.

WILLIAMS   And that is dated October 10, 1945?

GOUZENKO   Yes, sir. . . .

WILLIAMS   And you finally made your decision to take the step indicated on September 5, did you not?

GOUZENKO   That is right.

WILLIAMS   And you had been considering taking that step for how long before September 5?

GOUZENKO   I think it is maybe about half a year.

WILLIAMS   I want to ask you some questions, because you understand that other reasons may be given by other people for why you did it, and that is the reason I am going to ask you these questions.

GOUZENKO   Yes.

WILLIAMS   You got your first warning that you would be recalled to Moscow when?

GOUZENKO   In September of 1944.

WILLIAMS   And it was not then that you had in mind taking the step that you eventually took?

GOUZENKO   By that time I had already been influenced by my impressions of life in Canada.

WILLIAMS   But as I understand it, you did not begin to form the opinion that you would do what you have now done until the spring of 1945? You did not begin to think about it?

GOUZENKO   Yes.

WILLIAMS   Had anything happened between the time that you got the first warning that you would be going back to Moscow and the time you began to think about doing what you did, that caused you to come to think about it?

GOUZENKO   As I told, there were elections in Canada which impressed me very much, and that was one of the main reasons which influenced me, together with others, to take this step; because for the first time in my life I saw how a free people elects its own government.

MR. COMMISSIONER KELLOCK   I have heard it said that Russian people in this country, seeing what you say you saw, form the idea that elections here were not genuine at all, that they were just something on the surface; in other words, that the Russian people did not believe that our elections, which appeared to be free, actually were free. What do you say about that? . . .

GOUZENKO   Officially, a man like Goussarov at the embassy naturally says that this is all lies and false, but there are very few members at the embassy who believe Goussarov's version. If it was in Russia it would be false, but not in Canada.

MR. WILLIAMS   When it was first suggested that you were going to be recalled to Moscow, did it come to you as a surprise?

GOUZENKO   Yes, it was a surprise in a way.

WILLIAMS   When you were sent to the embassy at Ottawa was anything said about how long you would remain in Ottawa?

GOUZENKO   They said two or three years. . . .

WILLIAMS   Long before the two or three years were up you got word that you were going back to Moscow, and you were somewhat surprised?

GOUZENKO   Yes.

WILLIAMS   At the time that it was first suggested to you that you were going back to Moscow, was any reason given why you were being taken back?

GOUZENKO   No.

WILLIAMS   Was any reason given to you at any time as to why you were being taken back to Moscow?

GOUZENKO   They told me that I was being called back for work at the centre, but that is a usual phrase which does not mean anything.

WILLIAMS   Did your superior, Colonel Zabotin, or any other person in authority at the embassy tell you that your behaviour had been improper?

GOUZENKO   No, nobody ever mentioned that. Colonel Zabotin told me officially that my work was very good, and very satisfactory.

WILLIAMS   Did you ever receive any criticism of your work there from any of your superiors?

GOUZENKO   No.

MR. COMMISSIONER TASCHEREAU   But as a matter of fact when Colonel Zabotin got that order, in August 1944, to send you back to Russia, he insisted that you should stay here?

GOUZENKO   That is right.

TASCHEREAU   And you had read some telegrams exchanged between Moscow and Ottawa concerning that particular matter?

GOUZENKO   That is right; but he suggested to transfer me as an interpreter, which is regarded as higher than a cipher clerk's position.

MR. WILLIAMS   That would have been a promotion?

GOUZENKO   Yes; but it would also cut me away from the secret work, from my knowledge of secrets.

MR. COMMISSIONER KELLOCK   This suggestion of transferring you to the position of an interpreter — would that still be in the embassy at Ottawa?

GOUZENKO   Yes. He suggested that I should be the interpreter with the military attaché at Ottawa. . . .

MR. WILLIAMS   But if you had been appointed interpreter, that would have been a promotion?

GOUZENKO   Yes.

WILLIAMS   Would it have meant higher pay?

GOUZENKO   No.

WILLIAMS   When you first came to Ottawa what was your rate of pay as cipher clerk?

GOUZENKO   1000 roubles, which amounts to a little more than $200. . . .

WILLIAMS   Did you get a special bonus on account of the secrecy of your work?

GOUZENKO   Yes.

WILLIAMS   Was that in addition to the 1000 roubles?

GOUZENKO   Yes.

WILLIAMS   How much did that special bonus amount to?

GOUZENKO   For two years of secret work abroad, 10 per cent; for three years, 20 per cent.

WILLIAMS   And was your pay as cipher clerk increased between the time you first came to Ottawa and September 5, 1945?

GOUZENKO   That is right.

WILLIAMS   How much was it increased?

GOUZENKO   I actually received at the end, $275 a month. . . .

WILLIAMS   Did anybody in the embassy at any time charge you with failure to carry out your duties properly?

GOUZENKO   No, there was no charge.

WILLIAMS   Let us get right down to it. Was there any suggestion of any kind, even if it was a minor one we want to know everything about it.

GOUZENKO   Well, there were some minor things, but actually everybody had the same failures.

WILLIAMS   Will you just tell the Commission what those little things you speak of were; what was the kind of thing that they spoke to you about?

GOUZENKO   I came late for work on several occasions and Colonel Zabotin drew my attention to that.

WILLIAMS   I suppose there were others in the Russian embassy who did that?

GOUZENKO   Yes, so this was not serious.

WILLIAMS   Was there anything else for which he at any time reprimanded you or spoke to you about?

GOUZENKO   I was very cautious in my conversations and never told my feelings about the country or anything so nobody had any chance to accuse me of any political weakness which is considered a grievous crime and for which anyone can be called back to Moscow immediately.

WILLIAMS   During the whole time you were here did you live in the same apartment up to September 5?

GOUZENKO   First I lived only for a few days in the Chateau Laurier and then after that I lived in an apartment at 511 Somerset.

WILLIAMS   Outside of the few days that you lived at the Chateau you lived in the same apartment the whole time you were in Ottawa until September 7, 1945?

GOUZENKO   That is right.

WILLIAMS   Was it suggested to you by anybody in authority that you were talking too much outside of office hours?

GOUZENKO   Nobody accused me of this.

WILLIAMS   I should explain that the reason we are asking you these questions is that at a later date reasons may be given by other people for what you did and we want to know anything that might be said about you.

GOUZENKO   I expect everything.

WILLIAMS   That is the reason we are asking the questions so that we can deal with any such suggestions. Was it ever charged against you that you had taken moneys of the embassy?

GOUZENKO   No.

WILLIAMS   Would it have been possible for you to get your hands on money of the embassy? Was it kept where you could get at it?

GOUZENKO   No, I never kept money.

WILLIAMS   Supposing, for instance, it is said that you stole money from the Russian embassy? Supposing somebody comes along and says that, was there any way in which you could have got Russian embassy funds?

GOUZENKO   Only by official channels. I can ask and if they find it necessary to give me some advance, they can give it.

WILLIAMS   You did not have access to any place where the funds of the Russian embassy were kept?

GOUZENKO   No.

WILLIAMS   Outside of these documents which you took away with you and which you have put before the Commission, did you ever take away from the embassy any property of the embassy?

GOUZENKO   No, they took my property.

WILLIAMS   I am going to deal with that in a few minutes. I want to discuss with you any possible charge that might be made against you by anybody. That is the reason we are asking these questions.

GOUZENKO   I understand.

WILLIAMS   So that you say that you never took any property of the Russian embassy with the exception of these documents you brought with you when you came to the police on September 7?

GOUZENKO   That is right.

WILLIAMS   So that if anybody says you took money that would not be true?

GOUZENKO   That is right. . . .

WILLIAMS   You were not in the embassy on September 5?

GOUZENKO   I was.

WILLIAMS   For how long?

GOUZENKO   Until eight o'clock in the evening.

WILLIAMS   So at eight o'clock on the evening of the 5th of September, 1945, you left the embassy and never went back.

GOUZENKO   That is right.

WILLIAMS   And if they say that some time on the 5th or before the 5th you took money belonging to the embassy that did not belong to you, that would be wrong?

GOUZENKO   That would be wrong.

WILLIAMS   If they say that you took any other belongings of the embassy except the documents which you brought with you, that would be wrong.

GOUZENKO   That would be wrong?

WILLIAMS   Can you think of any other suggestion that might be made by any person about any wrongdoing on your part while you were there up to eight o'clock on the night of the 5th of September?

GOUZENKO   The suggestions can be unlimited because the imaginations of Pavlov and Gousarov are very rich.

WILLIAMS   On what day did you come to your final conclusion to do what you did; on what day did you make up your mind to do that? Was that on the 5th at eight o'clock that you finally decided to do that?

GOUZENKO   I wanted to choose a moment so that my object in warning Canada would not be spoiled through somebody accidentally catching me with the documents.

WILLIAMS   You realized that it was a very serious step that you were taking?

GOUZENKO   Very serious.

WILLIAMS   And that you were carrying away with you official documents of the Russian embassy?

GOUZENKO   That is right. . . .

WILLIAMS   Secret official documents. You realized further that by leaving you were giving up your whole career in the service of the Russian government?

GOUZENKO   That is right.

WILLIAMS   And your purpose in bringing the documents was what?

GOUZENKO   To confirm what I had said in my statement. . . .

WILLIAMS   In this statement which you wrote on the 10th of October and which was a summary of what you had told the police on the 7th September, you said this: "Convinced that such double-faced politics of the soviet government towards the democratic countries do not conform with the interests of the Russian people and endanger the security of civilization, I decided to break away from the Soviet regime and to announce my decision openly."

GOUZENKO   Yes.

WILLIAMS   You did as a matter of fact go to the two daily newspapers published in Ottawa with that intention?

GOUZENKO   To one.

WILLIAMS   Which one was it?

GOUZENKO   The Ottawa *Journal*.

WILLIAMS   You went to the Ottawa *Journal* with the intention of announcing it openly?

GOUZENKO   That is right.

WILLIAMS   And you had with you when you went to the office of that newspaper the documents which you have placed before the Commission?

GOUZENKO   I went directly from the embassy to the Ottawa *Journal*.

WILLIAMS   With those documents on your person?

GOUZENKO   That is right.

WILLIAMS   And you were prepared to announce it in the press?

GOUZENKO   That is right.

WILLIAMS   And to take whatever consequences came as a result of it?

GOUZENKO   That is right.

WILLIAMS   Nothing came of your visit to the newspaper?

GOUZENKO   That is right, they suggested —

WILLIAMS   They made certain suggestions to you?

GOUZENKO   Yes.

WILLIAMS   But they did not take your documents or publish your story?

GOUZENKO   No, they did not.

WILLIAMS   And you were accompanied, were you, on that trip that night by your wife, or were you alone on that occasion?

GOUZENKO   I was alone on that occasion.

WILLIAMS   On the night of the 5th after you had been to the Ottawa *Journal*, you returned to your home?

GOUZENKO   That is right. There is a description of my steps.

WILLIAMS   I do not think it is necessary to go into it in too great detail unless you want to, but I do want to get the substance of it. You got home to your apartment on the night of the 5th of September at what time?

GOUZENKO   It was already nine o'clock.

WILLIAMS   And you remained at home that night?

GOUZENKO   That is right.

WILLIAMS   And left your apartment again the next morning?

GOUZENKO   Together with my wife and child.

WILLIAMS   Accompanied by your wife and child?

GOUZENKO   Yes.

WILLIAMS   You remained away from your apartment how long that day?

GOUZENKO   From the apartment almost all day until about six or seven o'clock.

WILLIAMS   In the evening of the 6th?

GOUZENKO   Yes. . . .

WILLIAMS   Accompanied by your wife and child, that is the little boy of whom you have spoken?

GOUZENKO   That is right.

WILLIAMS   You left your apartment on the morning of the 6th about what time?

GOUZENKO   To reach the place I was going at nine o'clock.

WILLIAMS   You remained away all day, you and your wife and boy, until six or seven o'clock in the evening?

GOUZENKO   That is right. . . .

WILLIAMS   Just tell us in order where you went to, not what happened but where you went to?

GOUZENKO   To the Minister of Justice, Mr. St. Laurent; the office of the minister of justice. I did not see the minister.

WILLIAMS   Next?

GOUZENKO   Back to the Ottawa *Journal* and then to the Naturalization Bureau of the Mounted Police.

WILLIAMS   In what building was that?

GOUZENKO   In this building.

WILLIAMS   In the Justice Building?

GOUZENKO   Yes.

WILLIAMS   Then where?

GOUZENKO   To Nicholas Street, to the magistrate's office. Then I came to the apartment of a neighbour who we was acquainted with because we already was afraid to go back in our apartment expecting somebody would be there. . . .

WILLIAMS   You arrived at your neighbour's apartment about seven o'clock, between six and seven o'clock in the evening?

GOUZENKO   That is right.

WILLIAMS   Tell the Commission what happened from then on?

GOUZENKO   In the apartment of the neighbour where the little boy was she noticed the boy had wakened up and my wife went to the back door of our apartment to see if everything was in order and there was nobody around. I remained in the apartment with the boy. My wife returned and said there was nobody there and we could go.

I and my wife with the boy went to the back door into our apartment. I was very tired by this time and lay down on the bed. In about fifteen minutes I got up and looked out of the window and saw that there were two men standing on the opposite boulevard looking up at the apartment, sitting on a bench looking into the windows of my apartment. I told my wife and she agreed that it would be dangerous to remain in the apartment with the child. A little later a knock came to the door of the apartment. The person knocking continued to knock for about ten or fifteen minutes and one time only he called my name, Gouzenko. I did not answer. But my child ran across the room in the apartment and he naturally knew that there was somebody in the apartment.

WILLIAMS   Did you recognize the voice of the person who called you?

GOUZENKO   Yes, I recognized it; that was the driver, Lovrentyev. My wife and I decided to go to a neighbour and ask if we could leave the child with them overnight. I went to one of my neighbours and he readily agreed to keep the child.

132

WILLIAMS   Was that the same neighbour with whom you had left the child earlier in the evening or afternoon?

GOUZENKO   No.

WILLIAMS   Was there another neighbour?

GOUZENKO   The first neighbour was in a house.

WILLIAMS   The first neighbour was in a house?

GOUZENKO   Yes, it was a woman.

WILLIAMS   And this other neighbour was a neighbour living in the same apartment block?

GOUZENKO   He is a military man, Canadian aviation.

WILLIAMS   What is his name?

GOUZENKO   I do not know his name.

MR. COMMISSIONER TASCHEREAU   How could you come through if the men were still at the door?

GOUZENKO   I understood the men had already left, but in any case I went to my neighbour's across the balcony. He had a balcony the same as mine, the back door. He agreed to take the boy. I had just time to take the boy into the neighbour's apartment when I looked out and saw a man dressed in a dark blue suit walking around the back of the house and looking up at my apartment. I should explain that the apartment is on the second floor. The military man, who was a neighbour, also saw this man because he was on his own balcony.

MR. WILLIAMS   That was your neighbour standing on his own balcony?

GOUZENKO   That is right.

WILLIAMS   And he saw the man?

GOUZENKO   That is right. When he saw this he said that there was something unpleasant going on and he got on to his bicycle and went to call the police. At this time another neighbour, a lady who lived opposite on the corridor, said that her husband was in the country for a day or two and that she would with pleasure, not only take the child but also the whole family.

In this way all three of us went to her and she made a bed for us and the child went to bed. A policeman came back with the neighbour, the military man. The policeman asked what was the matter and it was explained to him that we were expecting something not very nice. The military man explained this to the policeman and I also explained in short what was going on.

The policeman said, "All right, we will keep a watch in the park and if anything happens you can put on the light in the bathroom," which looked out towards the park. After a little while we went to bed. About twelve o'clock we could hear a noise of an arriving automobile and the noise of steps coming up the stairs. Then I heard knocking at my door, the door of my apartment. We all got up and the lady of the apartment put the light on in the bathroom.

With the door a little ajar I looked over toward my apartment, and I saw Rogov, from the military attaché's office, and Pavlov, first secretary of the embassy, and two others: Farofontzov, the cipher clerk of the N.K.V.D., and Angelov, the secretary of the military attaché. Looking from behind the curtain in the window I looked down the street and saw another tall man standing beside the car. When they did not get a reply to the knocking at the door, they began to try the lock; and looking one way and another up and down the corridor. Then they unlocked the door and put on the light.

WILLIAMS   How did they unlock the door?

GOUZENKO   I understand they broke the lock, because the policeman told us later that he found traces of breaking in.

WILLIAMS   Did they have in their possession a key to your apartment?

GOUZENKO   No.

WILLIAMS   You had never given them one?

GOUZENKO   No. We saw from our own position through the window and through the door that after they had been in the apartment for a little while they put out the light. At this moment the police came; and as the policeman told me later, when the police put on the light they all crawled out from under the bed and behind the chesterfield and from hiding places.

WILLIAMS   Which police was it that came at that time?

GOUZENKO   The city police. . . .

WILLIAMS   Go ahead, please.

GOUZENKO   They were very much afraid when they saw the police, and the police said later that Farofontzov, who got out from behind the chesterfield, actually had to sit down.

   The policeman asked for their documents. Two of them showed their diplomatic passports. After this the policeman said, very undecidedly, "I am not sure what I should do about this." Pavlov said simply, "Well, what is there to do? Let us go; that is all." The policeman showed him that the lock had been tampered with, had been broken in, but Pavlov insisted that that had been done before. At this they went downstairs, got into the car and departed.

MR. COMMISSIONER KELLOCK   Did the policeman take their names?

GOUZENKO   Yes, and also this man who was standing beside the car; the policeman said was a Canadian.

   After this we went to bed. The police remain in the apartment to keep watch with us. About four o'clock in the morning we heard new steps. The policeman went out and asked who was there. That was Driver Gorshkov, who is the driver for the military attaché. The policeman looked at his document and let him go.

   About ten o'clock in the morning a car from the police came and took us away to the Royal Canadian Mounted Police, where we made our statement.

MR. WILLIAMS   You and your wife and son were taken to the office of the police together, were you?

GOUZENKO   No, only I alone went, and the policeman remained with my wife and with the child.

WILLIAMS   And when you came to the office of the Mounted Police you were received by Superintendent Rivett-Carnac?

GOUZENKO   Inspector Leopold and Inspector Williams.

WILLIAMS   And you said to them that you desired to make a statement and to have the protection of the police?

GOUZENKO   That is right.

WILLIAMS   I understand you made a statement to the police, and since that time you have been under their protection?

GOUZENKO   That is right.

WILLIAMS   Did you have the documents which you have produced before the Commission with you when you came to the Mounted Police on September 7?

GOUZENKO   Yes, I had them.

WILLIAMS   And you delivered them to the Mounted Police at the time you made your statement?

GOUZENKO   That is right.

WILLIAMS   Why did you feel that you needed protection?

GOUZENKO   You mean on the 6th or on the 7th?

WILLIAMS   At any time. When did you first feel that you needed protection?

GOUZENKO   In the Naturalization Bureau they told me it would be best to go to Nicholas Street to get protection. I asked them to give me protection. . . .

WILLIAMS   What did you want protection from?

GOUZENKO   I was sure that by that time it was possible that they had discovered the fact that there were documents missing and that I had disappeared, and that they would try to find me and they would not hesitate in this case to kill me even on the street in daylight.

WILLIAMS   You say "they." Whom do you mean by "they"?

GOUZENKO   I mean some of the men from the N.K.V.D. system, some of Pavlov's men.

WILLIAMS   Have you knowledge of action of that kind taken by the N.K.V.D. in other cases?

GOUZENKO   I heard about this.

WILLIAMS   And were you afraid of the N.K.V.D. and what action they would take?

GOUZENKO   I was afraid that all my efforts would be lost in this case.

WILLIAMS   Did you have any real fear that you yourself might be injured or killed?

GOUZENKO   At this moment I did not feel for my person, I assure you.

WILLIAMS   You mean at the time you asked for protection?

GOUZENKO   Yes.

MR. COMMISSIONER KELLOCK   I do not quite understand that. I thought he said that he did fear he would be killed day or night.

WILLIAMS   That is what he said at first, but he said that at the very moment he asked for protection he was thinking, as I understand it, that he did not want his documents to be lost or to be prevented from doing what he wanted to do. (*To the witness*)   But subsequently you did fear for your own safety?

GOUZENKO   I never separated my own safety from these other efforts to help Canada. If I would be killed it would mean that Canada would not get the facts.

MR. COMMISSIONER KELLOCK   What you mean is that you were willing to accept any risk there was involved?

GOUZENKO   That is right.

KELLOCK   But you did feel there was a risk involved, that you might be killed?

GOUZENKO   Yes.

KELLOCK   That is what you mean?

GOUZENKO   Yes. I said before —

KELLOCK   That is what you meant in what you said?

GOUZENKO   Yes, in the same way I know that I might lose my life.

MR. WILLIAMS   Your wife and child were subsequently given protection, at your request?

GOUZENKO   That is right.

WILLIAMS   And they are receiving protection at the present time in the same way you are?

GOUZENKO   That is right.

WILLIAMS   There are two or three other questions I want to ask you. How does the size of the organization in Ottawa, particularly the numbers, compare with the size of the organizations in other places? . . .

GOUZENKO   I do not know the number of employees at the Russian embassy at Washington, but compared to the Washington number, the number employed in Ottawa would be very small. Perhaps not very small, but smaller, anyway.

WILLIAMS   There are a large number of persons employed in the Russian embassy at Ottawa?

GOUZENKO   Yes, it is large.

WILLIAMS   In one department alone there are some 97; is that not right?

GOUZENKO   What is that?

WILLIAMS   In the commercial attaché's branch I believe there are some 97 employees?

GOUZENKO   Recently there was talk that they intended to increase the number of workers in the commercial attaché's department to 97, in a very short time.

WILLIAMS   And from information that you got by telegrams which you have coded and decoded you know that the Russian embassy at Washington is very much larger than the one here?

GOUZENKO   Not from telegrams; just from general conversation about the number of employees at Washington. It is very large; it runs into thousands, I think.

WILLIAMS   You have brought documents here and have told us about the espionage activities which are carried on in Canada from the headquarters of the Russian embassy?

GOUZENKO   That is right.

WILLIAMS   Do you know whether the same thing is being done in the United States and in the United Kingdom?

GOUZENKO   I know that in the United States and the United Kingdom the same is done.

WILLIAMS   And does the N.K.V.D. operate in those countries as well as in Canada?

GOUZENKO   I am sure it does, but I have no proof.

WILLIAMS   No documents showing that?

GOUZENKO   No. It is an apparent fact to every Russian who comes here.

WILLIAMS   Is it something that would get you into difficulty with the N.K.V.D. if you were heard to express your views that you thought Canada was a good country to live in, a pretty well-governed country?

GOUZENKO   If I would express it in such a way, I would be sent away immediately; so I never expressed it.

WILLIAMS   You kept that to yourself?

GOUZENKO   Yes.

WILLIAMS   Is it a fair way to put it to say that the other employees of the Russian embassy at Ottawa and elsewhere are in terror of the N.K.V.D. all the time?

GOUZENKO   It is absolutely correct.

WILLIAMS   (*To the Commission*)   I think that completes the evidence of Mr. Gouzenko.

MR. COMMISSIONER TASCHEREAU   You have mentioned quite a number of cover names during your evidence, and practically all those cover names were mentioned in telegrams that were sent to Moscow?

GOUZENKO   Yes.

TASCHEREAU   Do you know of any other cover name or any other person covered by a name who had dealings with the Russian organization here in Ottawa, which was not mentioned in the telegrams?

GOUZENKO   Oh, yes, I know.

TASCHEREAU   You know some others?

GOUZENKO   Yes, I do.

TASCHEREAU   Would you name them, please?

GOUZENKO   I mentioned all those in my report; I cannot repeat it here. Cover name Jan. It is a captain, I think maybe now a major; Sozansky, secretary of the Czechoslovakia military mission.

TASCHEREAU   But he is not in Canada here?

GOUZENKO   He was in Canada, and then he left for London, but I understand he came back.

TASCHEREAU   He was the military attaché of the Czechoslovak legation here?

GOUZENKO   Yes.

TASCHEREAU   And he was one of your agents?

GOUZENKO   He was an agent of the Soviet military attaché in Canada.

TASCHEREAU   Was he working for Russia also?

GOUZENKO   Yes.

TASCHEREAU   Under the cover name of Jan?

GOUZENKO   Yes.

TASCHEREAU   And you say he is not here now, but he is coming back?

GOUZENKO   I understand he is here now, because he received a promotion after he left.

TASCHEREAU   Do you know of any others?

GOUZENKO   I know names, but not cover names. There was mentioned in the report Emmie Rutherford. She was kept in reserve.

TASCHEREAU   Where is she from?

GOUZENKO   I understand she is a member of the Communist party in Canada.

TASCHEREAU   In Ottawa?

GOUZENKO   I don't know very well. She was kept in reserve.

TASCHEREAU   Is she a Canadian?

GOUZENKO   Yes, she is a Canadian. Then also in reserve, the fiancée of Sozansky.

TASCHEREAU   What do you mean by "in reserve"?

GOUZENKO   That means she doesn't work now as an agent, but in case she is needed she will work.

TASCHEREAU   Did you give us the name of the military attaché working for Czechoslovakia?

GOUZENKO   It is Ambrous. He was in very good relations with Colonel Zabotin, but I do not think he was an agent.

TASCHEREAU   Do you know of any others?

GOUZENKO   Then it was mentioned in one telegram, Ballantyne; only one time, I think, in the autumn of 1944.

TASCHEREAU   What Ballantyne is that? What is the first name?

GOUZENKO   I understand that is a real name.

TASCHEREAU   But what is his first name?

GOUZENKO   Oh, I don't know.

TASCHEREAU   And is he in Montreal?

GOUZENKO   He is in the Labour Organization in Montreal.

MR. COMMISSIONER KELLOCK   Do you mean the International Labour Organization?

GOUZENKO   Yes. . . .

MR. COMMISSIONER TASCHEREAU   Do you know of any others?

GOUZENKO   There was also mentioned the name, as I mentioned in my report, of Norman Freed.

TASCHEREAU   Where is he from?

GOUZENKO   From Toronto, I think. That is the end of 1944. Moscow had asked Colonel Zabotin if he knew one Norman. He replied that he didn't know him. Later on, in one of the issues of a Russian newspaper here in Canada, *Vestnik (News)* a photograph of Norman Freed appeared, urging the people to vote for him in the municipal elections.

TASCHEREAU   He was running in the municipal elections in Toronto?

GOUZENKO   Yes. Lieutenant-Colonel Motinov asked Colonel Zabotin whether that was not possibly the Norman about whom Moscow had asked previously. Colonel Zabotin instructed Lieutenant-Colonel Motinov to go to Pavlov and ask him if it was possible that this was one of his men. Pavlov said, "He is ours. Don't touch him." All this information was sent to Moscow, and no reply was received from them after that . . .

MR. WILLIAMS   Besides the N.K.V.D., do you know of any other group in the Russian embassy that worked on espionage?

GOUZENKO   As a rule there are N.K.V.D. systems, the military intelligence systems and the naval intelligence.

MR. COMMISSIONER TASCHEREAU   All independent one from the other?

GOUZENKO   Yes, absolutely independent.

MR. WILLIAMS   And does the N.K.V.D. carry on its espionage system apart entirely from Colonel Zabotin?

GOUZENKO   Yes, absolutely entirely.

WILLIAMS   And would you say the N.K.V.D. system is bigger or smaller than Colonel Zabotin's?

GOUZENKO   There is grounds for believing that the N.K.V.D. system in Canada is much larger than the system of the military attaché. In the first place the military intelligence was organized actually only in 1942, after it took over from Koudriadtzev, or when Koudriadtzev and Molier organized it. From the notes that are in evidence it is clear that the N.K.V.D. system existed before 1924, at least 1924.

MR. COMMISSIONER TASCHEREAU   In Russia?

GOUZENKO   No, in Canada. There are some small notes of Colonel Zabotin. Another proof is that Farofontzov, who is the cipher clerk for the N.K.V.D., works more than I do, so actually it was proof that he had more material to transfer.

MR. WILLIAMS   Then let me ask you this. If the N.K.V.D. has been operating in Canada since 1924, for a long period during that time there was no Russian embassy here. Where were they getting their operators?

GOUZENKO   There was a Communist party in Canada; there was correspondents, journalists and such men, and actually there were some trade representatives, not official but they were here. So it is no reason to believe there was not an N.K.V.D., because actually in some countries there were no diplomatic relations but the system still existed.

WILLIAMS   So the N.K.V.D. system started at least as early as 1924, has been operating continuously here, and is operating at the present time apart from Zabotin?

GOUZENKO   Yes.

WILLIAMS   And you think the N.K.V.D. system is much larger than Zabotin's?

GOUZENKO   Yes.

MR. COMMISSIONER TASCHEREAU   And both are working actually?

GOUZENKO   Yes.

TASCHEREAU   And is there a navy system of intelligence also?

GOUZENKO   I think they are in Vancouver or Halifax. I suspect they were going to organize in Ottawa also, because Captain, First Rank Pantzerney —

TASCHEREAU   But of course you know nothing about the organization of those systems personally?

GOUZENKO   No; but about N.K.V.D. there were more grounds to believe that they are working very actively. There were some rumours inside, and you know how the rumours are, so that actually everybody knows they are working; but from the documents it will be much more evident and much more firmly established that it does exist.

MR. WILLIAMS   And would you say there was any relation between the N.K.V.D. and the Communist party in Canada?

GOUZENKO   Not only between the N.K.V.D. and the Communist party, but also the military intelligence and the Communist party. The Communist party is the base from which these agents work, the base for their activities.

MR. COMMISSIONER TASCHEREAU   And nearly all the agents are chosen from among the members of the Communist party?

GOUZENKO   If you go over all these names of these agents you will see that the most important ones are members of the Communist party, and the largest number will be members of the Communist party. All the most important ones are members of the Communist party.

MR. WILLIAMS   I think, Messrs. Commissioners, that you would wish me to thank the witness for coming here to assist the Commission, and advise him that while we will discontinue his interrogation at the present time he may be asked to come again and to help us further; and I take it that in the meantime the Commission will adjourn? . . .

IGOR GOUZENKO, *recalled*

MR. WILLIAMS   You say that it was Rogov's idea to make up files on the different people who were working?

GOUZENKO   Yes.

WILLIAMS   And he started files like Exhibit 19?

GOUZENKO   That is right.

WILLIAMS   They had not kept files like that before?

GOUZENKO   No, they had not.

WILLIAMS   He began that in 1945?

GOUZENKO   That is right, March or April, 1945.

WILLIAMS   It might be a little bit earlier?

GOUZENKO   Then some of the material they had before on Sam Carr he put on there?

WILLIAMS   That is, other material that they had was taken out of notebooks?

GOUZENKO   And put in this file.

WILLIAMS   And pasted in Exhibit 19?

GOUZENKO   To make a complete file.

WILLIAMS   This first sheet in Exhibit 19-A was not typed out until early in 1945, but it contains a reference to the Comintern, does it not?

GOUZENKO   Yes.

WILLIAMS   The Comintern was supposed to have been abolished before 1945?

GOUZENKO   Supposed to be abolished in 1943, but it is not so.

WILLIAMS   It is not abolished?

GOUZENKO   That is right.

WILLIAMS   In 1945 Rogov typed or had typed the statement that they had Comintern records still available to refer to?

GOUZENKO   He knew very well the Comintern existed in Moscow.

WILLIAMS   Rogov knew the Comintern had not been abolished and that all the records were complete there?

GOUZENKO   That is right.

MR. COMMISSIONER KELLOCK   It would have been possible — I am not saying it is so — for the Comintern to have been abolished as an organization and all the records still kept?

GOUZENKO   That is right, and all the personnel is still kept in Moscow; it is just the name that is abolished.

KELLOCK   Where were you when the statement was made that the Comintern had been disbanded or abolished, were you in Canada or Russia?

GOUZENKO   I think I was in Russia. I remember this statement in the papers; yes, I think so. I think it was in the spring of 1943.

KELLOCK   Was it believed in Russia, that it had been abolished?

GOUZENKO   Well, the men who know, know that it is not abolished in Russia, but that is not our business, that is a matter of government. There was an ironical attitude about it, that it was going to be abolished.

KELLOCK   When you came here to Canada in July, 1943, was there any conversation in the embassy about the abolition of the Comintern? Did they talk about it? Did they laugh about it? Did they make any jokes about it?

GOUZENKO   It is a dangerous thing to make jokes on that, so they did not make any jokes. There was never any exchanges of conversation about this matter. We knew that the Comintern existed, that is, all the people knew.

KELLOCK   You say that you knew it existed. How did you know it existed if you did not talk about it?

GOUZENKO   Obviously, when the party in Canada is taking the very same line as the party in the United States, and they both change that line on the one day we know that that cannot be done without some contact with headquarters. We know the headquarters are in Moscow. There was no conversation about this because officially it is abolished. Everybody knew that it was the policy of the government to establish the Communist system by force, by the use of all means necessary.

KELLOCK   What did you say was the policy?

GOUZENKO   It is the principle to establish communism in all the world. That is the idea of the leaders of the Communist party in Russia, and the leaders of the Communist party in Russia are the leaders of the Comintern. It is just the same thing actually. That principle is never forgotten and never abolished. Even during wartime they were stressing it to the people in Russia that there would be communism in all the world. They are working for that. There might be temporarily what they called a retreat, but they never forget that principle.

KELLOCK   While we are on that subject, I would like to ask you this: You made some reference when you were here before about the possibilities of another war?

GOUZENKO   That is right.

KELLOCK   Why do you say that?

GOUZENKO   I say that because it is sure that Russia is preparing for war, even now. It may be that Mr. Zaroubin would know, but then he might only suspect. He would not be able to confirm that because actually he was not so close to the inner policy of the Soviet government. But I was close to those secret documents and from those documents I saw that the Soviet government are interested in war.

For example, they were trying to establish a fifth column in Canada. What transpired is only a modest or small part of all that is really here. You may have discovered fifteen men but it still leaves in Canada this dangerous situation because there are other societies and other people working under every embassy, under every consul in each place where there is a consulate.

It is just like a number of small circles. There are parallel systems of spies or potential agents. The last telegrams showed that they are going to encourage the work of a fifth column which would be a real danger to Canada and which would be a real help for Russia in case of invasion or something like that.

KELLOCK   Was that language used in the telegrams which you refer to?

GOUZENKO   No, they cannot use this language. The last telegram asked about the mobilization of resources in Canada. They wanted to know everything possible about everything concerned in Canada. They wanted to know the natural resources that Canada could mobilize in case of war, her coal, oil, rare metals and so on. They wanted the general picture, not so many details.

Then the case of the atomic bomb was important. Then take the situation in Russia. There is a preparation for war there. They are educating the people.

They are telling the people that everything that is outside the borders of Russia is an enemy. Even during the most dangerous moments during the last war they told the people that even though the Allies were fighting at their side, they might still be enemies.

There was one last conversation that Colonel Zabotin had with us. This was before the 5th of September. He gathered us in this room at 14 Range Road and said, "Yesterday they were Allies, to-day they are neighbours, tomorrow they will be our enemies." In Russia there is a great deal of propaganda carried on by conversation of the propagandists and sometimes even in the press. It is all done to train the people to think that they must fight another war, that maybe it will be our final war.

In *Pravda* they are more or less careful because that newspaper is read by foreigners who think that that is the attitude of the government. But by means of the conversation of hundreds of agitators and in all these meetings of the Communist party, in all the meetings of these other interests, the principle of communism by force is always stressed, that we must prepare for war, that we must fight in this war, that we must be strongest in this war.

Decoding these telegrams I involuntarily know these facts of the secret side of the policy of the Soviet government. The Russian people, thanks to the enforcement of the Soviet government, is isolated from life in the democratic countries. They do not know the reality beyond the bounds of the Soviet Union border. They are imbued with the idea that the people in democratic countries live in some kind of chaos. Prior to the war the word "democracy" even had a bad meaning. If you were to call a man in Russia a democrat he will be offended.

The Russian people are being brought up in the single-minded idea that the system existing in Russia is the only system having a future; the systems of the democratic countries, in accordance with this teaching, are doomed to defeat and will be destroyed by force and replaced by communism. . . .

MR. WILLIAMS   Let me ask you this. In the event of a war with Russia on one side and Canada, we will say, on the other side, is any training being given to the members of the fifth column in sabotage, for instance? Do you know of anything like that?

GOUZENKO   I understand that the fifth column is not necessarily work of small sabotage. It is political sabotage. It is more serious than to blow up some bridge.

WILLIAMS   I am talking now if a state of war came, if there was war, has there been any training along the lines of working through them against Canada by sabotage or by strikes or by labour troubles? Are they being trained in that at all?

GOUZENKO   I am sure in this there is no question about it.

WILLIAMS   For instance, in these documents that you have brought, the names of a large number of agents have been mentioned, and persons who were being worked with. We realize that you have only been able to bring a very small portion of the documents that were there because you had to take them all at once.

GOUZENKO   Yes.

WILLIAMS   In the documents that are there which you were not able to bring are there names of more agents that we have not seen here?

GOUZENKO   There is no new names of the military intelligence in the other documents except such documents as I did not see. Maybe there are, but I do not think there is a big possibility. All the documents kept in this safe their names are here.

WILLIAMS   So far as you know these documents you have brought show the names of all the agents down to the time you left?

GOUZENKO   Yes, military intelligence. I could not take it from N.K.V.D. because it is another man, another room, another safe.

WILLIAMS   You were one of five sections?

GOUZENKO   That is right.

WILLIAMS   You can only tell about what was going on in your section?

GOUZENKO   That is right.

WILLIAMS   N.K.V.D. might have a whole lot of other agents that you do not know about?

GOUZENKO   Yes, and I suspect there are more than here.

WILLIAMS   You suspect there are more in the N.K.V.D. than in Zabotin's organization?

GOUZENKO   That is right.

WILLIAMS   Then there would be some in the commercial counsellor's organization? We have seen that Sokolov —

GOUZENKO   Oh, no, Sokolov is in the military intelligence system. The counsellor has nothing secret in his work; as commercial counsellor, persons on the staff work as contact men in the military intelligence system or along the line of the Comintern.

WILLIAMS   You remember, Mr. Gouzenko, the telegram that referred to the Economist having come back from his trip to Moscow?

GOUZENKO   That is right.

WILLIAMS   And telling Colonel Zabotin he was going to have 97 people in his organization?

GOUZENKO   That is right.

WILLIAMS   Then it went on to say, as I remember it, that Davey was going to stay with the Economist?

GOUZENKO   That is right.

WILLIAMS   That was Sokolov?

GOUZENKO   And the Economist was correct.

WILLIAMS   Was Sokolov in the commercial attaché's office?

GOUZENKO   That is right.

WILLIAMS   But he was working with Zabotin?

GOUZENKO   And the same as the Economist, the commercial counsellor, but he is working as an agent in the military intelligence system, the head of which is Zabotin.

WILLIAMS   My point is this, that besides Sokolov there might have been others in the commercial counsellor's office who were working with the N.K.V.D., we will say?

GOUZENKO   That is right, and the same with the Tass agency, Zheveinov, the head of the Tass agency, was working in the military intelligence system, the system of Colonel Zabotin, and under him was Afanasyev. He is contact man, the same work as Zheveinov, under Pavlov.

MR. COMMISSIONER KELLOCK   How did Tass, Zheveinov, send his despatches to Moscow, through what agency, through what clerk?

GOUZENKO   His despatches concern his Tass work. His work is cutting articles in Canadian newspapers and sending them through official channels without any code. If it is something like intelligence work, he sends through diplomatic channels, but when he met Eric Adams he would give all of this information which he received from him to Colonel Zabotin directly. . . .

MR. WILLIAMS   Would you tell the Commission a little more about the N.K.V.D. organization here in the embassy?

GOUZENKO   When I was working in Moscow as a cipher clerk at that time, that is the first time I saw this expression "Neighbour." I worked there about a year and from the telegrams I saw and from conversation I understood that that was the cover name for another system, a parallel system, an independent system. The N.K.V.D. system is under the Minister of Internal Affairs — there is no commissar now. This system exists as a parallel. When I arrived in Canada, some days later I understood that Pavlov is the N.K.V.D., the second secretary; he is the head of the N.K.V.D. The first telegrams, the first case was Agent Poland. Sam Carr said that he had not good characteristics; he called him a careless man and he suggested to get rid of him. So Zabotin sent a telegram to Moscow and said, "I think it is better to get rid of him, or to give him to the neighbour." Moscow said, "No, maybe he will be good."

In 1945 the question of Poland was raised again. This time Moscow said, "All right, discuss it with the neighbour.". . . Then there was another case when two members of the commercial counsellor's office went to the Canadian Patent Office and asked for information about the secret invention of radar. They spoke bad English and the Canadian authorities thought that they were German agents and called the police. They were held and they were checked up and then released.

WILLIAMS   Who went to the Canadian Patent Office?

GOUZENKO   Two employees of the commercial counsellor's office.

WILLIAMS   What purpose did they go there for?

GOUZENKO   They asked about the invention of radar, and because what they asked for was secret they were under suspicion. They were arrested but were released immediately. Of course this was mentioned to Sokolov and Sokolov immediately told it to Zabotin. Zabotin became very angry and he wrote a big telegram to Moscow. He said that the Neighbour should not work with such hooligan methods. He described what had happened and he said that these were Neighbour's people, Pavlov's people. It was Matrenichev and Zhukov.

WILLIAMS   I see that Matrenichev is mentioned on Exhibit 15, but I do not see Zhukov.

GOUZENKO   I do not think I mentioned Zhukov.

MR. COMMISSIONER TASCHEREAU   You mentioned him but he is not on Exhibit 15.

GOUZENKO   No, because this is the commercial attaché's office, and there are fifty or more people. I could not mention all of them. I just mentioned several of them. They said that such careless work would attract the attention of the Canadian authorities to the military attaché, but they would not suspect Pavlov or anybody else. So he suggested that Pavlov must stop using such methods.

He called them hooligan methods. Moscow answered and asked more details about Zhukov. Then according to conversations between Sokolov and Zabotin I think they suspected that there existed a parallel military intelligence, another military intelligence system parallel to Zabotin's. The same thing was true in the United States, according to a telegram I saw. The chief of the technical bureau is head of one parallel system; military intelligence has another system.

MR. COMMISSIONER KELLOCK   As I understand you, from this conversation between Sokolov and Zabotin they came to the conclusion that in addition to the N.K.V.D. system there was another military intelligence system?

GOUZENKO   Yes, because from what Moscow said obviously they knew this Zhukov. Then a telegram came from Moscow from the N.K.V.D. and the chief of military intelligence saying that all disputes must be settled, that there should be no more quarrels between them. Not only in Canada, but in other countries there were quarrels over agents like this. . . .

May 17, 1946

IGOR GOUZENKO, *recalled*

MR. WILLIAMS   Mr. Gouzenko, you are still under the same oath you took quite a long time ago here?

GOUZENKO   Yes.

WILLIAMS   There are a few more matters we just want to go into in a little detail with you. The first was in connection with the delivery of the supply of uranium to Angelov by May. You know how that supply of uranium got to Moscow, don't you?

GOUZENKO   Yes, I know.

WILLIAMS   How did it go; how was it taken?

GOUZENKO   From May to Angelov; through Angelov to Lieutenant-Colonel Motinov or Zabotin — it was the same thing — and Motinov was at that time called to Moscow, because Moscow at that time decided to send him to Washington on the same job, as assistant military attaché. So before sending him to Washington they called him to Moscow, where they said in a telegram they wanted to give him new instructions. At the same time he received this uranium, and so on, and Colonel Zabotin wrote a telegram to Moscow, where he said that Motinov personally would take the uranium with him and would deliver it by plane.

MR. COMMISSIONER TASCHEREAU   How do you know that May gave it to Angelov?

GOUZENKO   On account of this meeting and the results of this meeting, which were in a telegram; and this small tube was during this time, before Lieutenant-Colonel Motinov took it, kept in the safe.

TASCHEREAU   In Room 12?

GOUZENKO   That is correct. Then on this tube were obviously typed the words, at least this word, "Enriched," and then the figure, the number. I remembered it, but now I forget this figure. It said, "Enriched two and a half times" or something like this. It said it was enriched so many times, so Colonel Zabotin wrote a telegram that he would take this label from the tube and send this label by telegraph, so you must put on this tube in Moscow this word "Enriched" so and so, so that in case something happened to Lieutenant-Colonel Motinov those words on the tube would not be disclosed.

TASCHEREAU   The words were not on the tube?

GOUZENKO   No.

TASCHEREAU   They would not be on the tube if anything happened to Motinov?

GOUZENKO   That is right. It would look like innocent maybe aspirin tablets, or something.

TASCHEREAU   But you say there was a meeting. I heard you say a moment ago that there was a meeting?

GOUZENKO   With Alan May, with Angelov. Angelov and May.

TASCHEREAU   Where did they meet?

GOUZENKO   The first time, as I told before, Moscow suggested that Sam Carr might meet Alan Nunn May, but Zabotin said that he did not want to give this work to Sam Carr, so he proposed Angelov. Moscow agreed. After this Angelov found by the telephone book the address of Dr. May.

TASCHEREAU   In Montreal?

GOUZENKO   Yes, and came directly to this apartment. In his account he described this Alan May, how he looked, and told the conversation he had with Alan May in the first meeting. Later, however, at the next meeting, they had it outside the apartment on the street, because at the first meeting they made arrangements when to meet, but not in the apartment.

TASCHEREAU   Then in Montreal Dr. May gave that tube of uranium to Angelov?

GOUZENKO   That is right.

WILLIAMS   Angelov came to Ottawa with it?

GOUZENKO   Yes, sir.

TASCHEREAU   And here it was deposited in the safe?

GOUZENKO   Yes, sir.

TASCHEREAU   And was it a long time in the safe before Motinov flew to Moscow with it?

GOUZENKO   It don't think it is a long time. I don't think it is more than two weeks.

TASCHEREAU   Had you seen it in the safe?

GOUZENKO   Yes, I saw that.

TASCHEREAU   Do you know who put it in the safe?

GOUZENKO   Several times Lieutenant-Colonel Motinov — the first actual time, when Angelov brought this, Motinov brought it to the room.

TASCHEREAU   Motinov brought it to your room?

GOUZENKO   Yes, and Colonel Zabotin looked at it. They were together and looked at the thing, and Colonel Zabotin wrote the telegram about this "Enriched" so and so, and said that Lieutenant-Colonel Motinov would bring this himself personally. . . .

TASCHEREAU   What was Pavlov's official position?

GOUZENKO   Second secretary.

TASCHEREAU   At the embassy?

GOUZENKO   Yes.

TASCHEREAU   And he always remained second secretary; he never changed?

GOUZENKO   No, he was always second secretary.

TASCHEREAU   How old is Pavlov?

GOUZENKO   He is quite a young looking man; about 35 years, I think. Looking at his picture, he is young looking.

TASCHEREAU   And how long was he chief of the N.K.V.D. in Ottawa here?

GOUZENKO   I think from the beginning he was sent as chief or head of the N.K.V.D.

TASCHEREAU   And in what year did he arrive?

GOUZENKO   The whole embassy was established in 1942, and he arrived together with the staff of the embassy.

TASCHEREAU   So from 1942 up to now, or up to the time when you left, he was always second secretary?

GOUZENKO   He was always second secretary; that is right.

TASCHEREAU   Is that normal, to remain second secretary as long as that? If he had not been in the N.K.V.D. would he have had a better position than second secretary?

GOUZENKO   A second secretary actually is a high position in the diplomatic branch. First is the ambassador; the next man is the first secretary, and then the second secretary; and besides, he is not only second secretary. He is consul.

TASCHEREAU   He is consul at the embassy?

GOUZENKO   Yes, he is consul. He was the consul for the Ontario region. It is all divided. So actually his position is high, and I think it is quite natural that he is always there.

TASCHEREAU   So he is the man who gives the visas for the passports, and those things?

GOUZENKO   That is right. He dealt with that.

TASCHEREAU   Did you ever hear anything or see anything that would lead you to think that Pavlov was also expanding his organization?

GOUZENKO   Yes, I think I heard such evidence. First of all, his obvious desire to have as small as possible agents, and this is actually what led to this clash of interests. They approached one time Sam Carr and his work . . . There was his eagerness to take this Poland, also.

TASCHEREAU   We have seen that Zabotin was using both Sam Carr and Fred Rose, who were the two leading men in the Communist party in Canada?

GOUZENKO   That is right.

TASCHEREAU   Would Pavlov be working other leading men in the Communist party in Canada?

GOUZENKO   Oh, we can only guess about this. However, don't forget that, in my opinion, the N.K.V.D. system is old, so maybe during this time they have also very prominent people, maybe not necessarily Communist leaders, who were able to develop other people, so these prominent people may be working as recruiting agents for the N.K.V.D., maybe not necessarily members of the Communist party. Don't forget that this is an old system, older than the military attaché system.

TASCHEREAU   But supposing there were in Canada ten leading members of the Communist party. Zabotin, we will say, would take two, in the form of Rose and Carr?

GOUZENKO   Yes, sir.

TASCHEREAU   Would the practice be to divide the others up between other agencies, or would that depend entirely upon circumstances?

GOUZENKO   Quite possibly, because actually Pavlov, if he is looking for people, if he is looking for men, naturally in the case of Sam Carr, men who know the people in his party, who have influence, who can say to the people and they will obey his orders, and probably like Zabotin they would try to have such a man, and I think it is natural.

TASCHEREAU   Tim Buck is mentioned, and it is known that he is a prominent member of the Communist party. Did you ever hear of any of the other departments, say Pavlov or Krotov, going after Tim Buck or using Tim Buck?

GOUZENKO   No, I never heard about this, and I think in this case, in the case of Tim Buck, I suppose with Colonel Zabotin — I would imagine how it would work in that case. If Colonel Zabotin wrote a telegram to Moscow and said, "I approached Tim Buck and talked with him, and he agreed, and he can be a good recruiting agent," I am sure Moscow would say, "No, don't touch Tim Buck. He is big enough. He is very big, and he is a figure man." Moscow never permitted Zabotin to meet agents, in the same way, because he is the diplomat, and he is the head military attaché. In the same way, they would never permit Tim Buck to do it. He has also important work, more important, maybe more serious, pertaining to the whole Communist party, to conduct the Communist party's activities, in agreement with the instructions from Moscow.

TASCHEREAU   In other words it would be better not to tie him up with any of these particular organizations, but to keep him free from any suspicion of that as leader of the party?

GOUZENKO   That is right. It is obvious, I am sure. . . .

THE TESTIMONY OF LAURENT BEAUDRY

February 21, 1946

MR. FAUTEUX   What is your occupation, Mr. Beaudry?

BEAUDRY   I am a civil servant.

FAUTEUX   And what department are you connected with?

BEAUDRY   Department of External Affairs.

FAUTEUX   And in the Department of External Affairs what division are you working for?

BEAUDRY   I am in the diplomatic division.

FAUTEUX   Am I right in saying that you are chief of that division?

BEAUDRY   I am chief of the division. . . .

FAUTEUX   I notice in the Ottawa morning papers the text of a statement broadcast by the Moscow radio and which purports to have reference to the statement published on the 15th February, 1946, by the Canadian government concerning a leakage of information to persons not entitled to it, among them persons employed by a foreign mission in Ottawa. . . . Did you bring with you a complete file relating to the disappearance of or theft of money from the Soviet embassy by Mr. and Mrs. Gouzenko?

BEAUDRY   I did.

FAUTEUX   It refers to the disappearance or alleged theft of money from the Soviet embassy by Mr. and Mrs. Gouzenko. Would you indicate to the Commission the first note received from the Soviet embassy in regard to this matter?

BEAUDRY   The first note received from the Soviet embassy bears the number "35" and is dated 7th September, 1945.

FAUTEUX   In what language is it?

BEAUDRY   It is in Russian.

FAUTEUX   You have a translation?

BEAUDRY   There is a translation attached to it.

MR. COMMISSIONER KELLOCK   Who signed it?

BEAUDRY   The translation?

KELLOCK   The original?

BEAUDRY   It is in the third person form. It begins, "The Embassy of the U.S.S.R. in Canada presents its compliments.". . .

FAUTEUX   Would you be good enough to read the translation?

BEAUDRY   (*Reads*)

Translation of Note No. 35 of
Sept. 7th from the Embassy of
the U.S.S.R.

The embassy of the U.S.S.R. in Canada presents its compliments and has the honour to inform the Department of External Affairs of the following:

A colleague of the Embassy, Igor Sergeievitch Gusenko living at 511 Somerset St., failed to report for work at the proper time on the 6th September.

In connection with this and for the purpose of clarifying the reasons for the failure of I. Gusenko's reporting for work, Consul V.G. Pavloff and two other colleagues of the Embassy visited the apartment of I. Gusenko at 11:40 on the 6th Sept.

When Mr. Pavloff knocked at the door of Gusenko's apartment no one answered. After this the apartment was opened by the above-mentioned colleagues of the Embassy with Gusenko's duplicate key, when it was discovered that neither Gusenko, nor his wife Svetliana Borisovna Gusenko nor their son Andrei, were in the apartment.

It was later established that I. Gusenko robbed some money belonging to the Embassy and had hidden himself together with his family.

At the time when Consul Pavloff and the two other colleagues of the Embassy were in Gusenko's apartment, i.e. about 11:30 p.m., Constable Walsh of the Ottawa City Police appeared together with another policeman and tried with a rude manner to detain the diplomatic colleagues of the Embassy, in spite of explanations given by Consul Pavloff and the showing of diplomatic cards.

As a result of the protest expressed by Mr. Pavloff, Walsh called Inspector of the City Police Macdonald, who appeared at the Gusenko apartment in fifteen minutes, and also in a rude manner demanded that Consul F.G. Pavloff and the other diplomatic colleagues of the Embassy go with him to the Police Station, refusing to recognize the diplomatic card shown by Consul Pavloff.

Upon the refusal of Mr. V.G. Pavloff to go to the Police Station, Mr. Macdonald went away, leaving a policeman in the Gusenko apartment with the colleagues of the Embassy, for the alleged purpose of finding out who it was who had notified the police of the "forced entry" (lit. "breaking the door") into the Gusenko apartment.

Consul V.G. Pavloff and the other two colleagues of the Embassy, after waiting for Mr. Macdonald to return for 15 minutes, left, having locked the Gusenko apartment.

The Embassy of the U.S.S.R. asks the Dept. of External Affairs to take urgent measures to seek and arrest I. Gusenko and to hand him over for deportation, as a capital criminal, who has stolen money belonging to the Embassy.

In addition the Embassy brings to the attention of the Department of External Affairs the rude treatment accorded to the diplomatic colleagues of the Embassy by Constable Walsh and Inspector of the City Police Macdonald, and expresses its confidence that the Department will investigate this incident and will make those guilty answerable for their actions.

The Embassy asks the Department that it should be informed of action taken in relation to the above.

OTTAWA, 7th. Sept. 1945. . . .

MR. COMMISSIONER KELLOCK   Are you in a position to tell us when it was received?

BEAUDRY   It was received on 8th September, 1945.

MR. FAUTEUX   At 9:11 a.m.?

BEAUDRY   9:11 a.m., yes. . . .

MR. COMMISSIONER KELLOCK   Following the receipt of that first communication from the Soviet embassy is there anything else in your file in regard to a telephone communication?

BEAUDRY   Yes, there is a memorandum on the file dated 9th September, 1945, bearing the typewritten initials "N.A.R."

KELLOCK   That is?

BEAUDRY   The initials are those of Mr. Norman A. Robertson, Under-Secretary of State for External Affairs, and the memorandum indicates that Mr. Pavlov had telephoned. . . .

MR. FAUTEUX   Will you kindly read that memorandum?

BEAUDRY   (*Reads*):

Mr. Pavlov of the Soviet Embassy telephoned about six o'clock this afternoon to inquire if we had received his note about the disappearance of Mr. Gusenko. I told him that it had been translated and referred to the Police, whom we had asked to make enquiries. It would be very helpful if we could be furnished with full particulars and descriptions of the missing persons, as the information we had about them from Certificates of Exemption from Registration was very meagre. He promised to send us this information by mail in the morning.

Mr. Pavlov was concerned about the empty apartment at 511 Somerset Street West, and he would like to have the property guarded. I said we would be glad to ask the municipal police to put a constable there. He wished to have the premises sealed by the Soviet Embassy. I said we would have no objection to the premises being sealed and would get in touch with him tomorrow, so that an officer of the Embassy could go with the Police Department officer to close up the apartment.

The top of the memorandum is marked "Memorandum for the File."

FAUTEUX   After that telephone conversation does the file indicate that anything else came to your department from the Soviet embassy?

BEAUDRY   Yes, there was a note, No. 36, from the Embassy of the U.S.S.R., dated Ottawa, September 11, 1945.

FAUTEUX   And addressed to?

BEAUDRY   It is addressed to the Department of External Affairs, East Block, Ottawa.

FAUTEUX   And it is in English?

BEAUDRY   This is in English.

FAUTEUX   And was received by your department?

BEAUDRY   On September 11, at 5:22 p.m.

FAUTEUX   Will you read that, please?

BEAUDRY   (*Reads*):

No. 36

The Embassy of the Union of Soviet Socialist Republics presents its compliments to the Department of External Affairs and has the honour with reference to the telephone conversation of Mr. V. Pavlov with Mr. Beaudry on September 10th, to enclose herewith the description of Mr. and Mrs. Gouzenko.

1. IGOR GOUZENKO

Born January 13, 1919. Arrived to Canada July 20, 1943.

Height — 5'6"

Weight — 145-150 pounds

Colour of hair — brown

Colour of eyes — gray.

Nose — straight

Sometimes wears spectacles.

2. SVETLANA GOUZENKO

Born December 12, 1919. Arrived to Canada July 20, 1943.

Height — 5'7"

Weight — 140 pounds

Colour of hair — light brown

Colour of eyes — blue

Figure — slender

Nose — straight

Have a son — Andrei, 21 months of age.

Ottawa, September 11, 1945.

Department of External

Affairs,

East Block,

Ottawa. . . .

FAUTEUX Will you proceed to tell us what took place after that?

BEAUDRY I have in my hand a copy of Note No. 30 of September 11, 1945, addressed to His Excellency, the Ambassador of the Union of Soviet Socialist Republics, Embassy of the U.S.S.R., Ottawa, and signed by Mr. N.A. Robertson, for the secretary of state for External Affairs. . . .

FAUTEUX Will you read that please?

BEAUDRY (*Reads*):

No. 30   Ottawa, September 11, 1945.

Excellency —

I have the honour to refer to your note No. 35 of September 7 with regard to the case of Mr. Gusenko.

The Canadian authorities have been asked to make every effort to find Mr. Gusenko and his family with a view to investigating the charges which you have made against him. When Mr. Pavloff of your Embassy discussed this matter by telephone at the beginning of the week, it was suggested that it would be helpful to the Canadian authorities if full particulars could be furnished. It would be important to obtain not merely descriptions of the missing persons, but also complete information as to the money or other items which Mr. Gusenko may have taken from the Embassy, and such evidence as you may have available to establish the charge of theft.

You will, of course, understand that, under the laws in force in Canada, it is impossible to comply in all respects with your request. The Canadian Police have no authority to arrest Mr. Gusenko and hand him over to your Embassy for deportation. If they adopted such a course, they would be open to civil action and the effectiveness of the proceedings could be challenged by *habeas corpus*, involving a complete enquiry into the circumstances and the release of the accused if it were established that the arrest was designed to enable him to be handed over within this country to a foreign authority.

In your note, you have made a complaint with regard to the rude treatment accorded to Mr. Pavloff and his associates by Constable Walsh and the Inspector of City Police, [Macdonald]. It is a matter of very great regret that any Canadian Police authorities should fail in their duty to accord due courtesy to the persons with whom they are dealing, and it is particularly unfortunate that there should be any lack of courtesy in dealing with members of your Embassy. I hope that you will bear in mind the special circumstances, including the lateness of the hour and the fact that the apartment had been entered without the authority of the tenant or a magistrate's warrant. The Police authorities in such circumstances cannot be too severely criticized for questioning the claims to diplomatic status of Mr. Pavloff and his party, and for doubting their credentials.

If an occasion arises in the future when you desire to enter these premises, arrangements will be made to apply for the necessary authority. In the meantime, under arrangements which were discussed by Mr. Pavloff by telephone, the apartment is being closed and sealed.

Accept, Excellency, the renewed assurances of my highest consideration.

> N.A. Robertson
> for the
> Secretary of State
> for External Affairs.

His Excellency,
The Ambassador of the Union of
Soviet Socialist Republics,
Embassy of the U.S.S.R.,
Ottawa.

FAUTEUX   That note is dated 11th September?
BEAUDRY   1945, yes. . . .
FAUTEUX   What is this?
BEAUDRY   I have in my hands a copy of a short personal note.
FAUTEUX   Dated?
BEAUDRY   Dated September 13, 1945.
FAUTEUX   Would you read that, please?

The Department of External Affairs presents its compliments to the
Embassy of the Union of Soviet Socialist Republics and, with reference
to the Embassy's note No. 36 of the 11th September, 1945, giving the
description of Mr. and Mrs. Gusenko, has the honour to advise that the
Royal Canadian Mounted Police has been informed accordingly in order
that it may be in a position to help the Embassy in the search for the
missing persons. Ottawa, September 13th, 1945.

FAUTEUX   Were there any other notes exchanged between the two governments,
after that one?
BEAUDRY   There was received from the Soviet embassy note No. 37. . . .
FAUTEUX   Will you read the translation?
BEAUDRY

Translation of Note No. 37 of September 14th from the Soviet
Embassy, Ottawa.

The Embassy of the U.S.S.R. presents its compliments to the
Department of External Affairs and has the honour to acknowledge the
receipt of the Department's notes Nos. 30 of the 11th September, relating
to the affair of I. Gusenko and the notes of the 14th September,
acknowledging receipt by the Department of the Embassy's note No. 36
of September 11th, containing a description of Gusenko and his wife,
and stating that the Royal Canadian Secret Police had been informed
in order that it might be in a position to render assistance to the Embassy
in the search for the above mentioned persons.

Confirming its communication in the note No. 35 of September 7th
of the fact that Gusenko had robbed public funds, the Embassy, upon
instructions from the government of the U.S.S.R. repeats its request to
the government of Canada to apprehend Gusenko and his wife, and
without trial, to hand them over to the Embassy for deportation to the
Soviet Union.

The Soviet government expresses the hope that the government of
Canada will fulfil its request.
Ottawa, 14th September, 1945. . . .

AFTER Igor Gouzenko had testified, representatives of the Ottawa police
department, neighbours of Gouzenko and members of the Royal Canadian
Mounted Police presented evidence on the events of September 5th through
7th, 1945. Inspector W.H. Williams of the Criminal Investigation Branch, "A"
Division, of the R.C.M.P. received Gouzenko on September 7th and placed
the former cipher clerk and his family in protective custody in a tourist camp
on the outskirts of Ottawa. Superintendent Charles Rivett-Carnac, the director
of Criminal Investigation, conducted the first interrogation of Gouzenko. "In
the course of the conversation," Rivett-Carnac told the Commissioners,
Gouzenko "said that there were many spies in Canada, and that the activities
of these spies worked a detriment to the interests of the Canadian people."

At the Soviet embassy, Gouzenko told the superintendent, "they were continually discussing or speaking about a third world war." Moreover, Gouzenko reported that "when the explosion of the first atom bomb took place, . . . the officials of the Soviet Union were astounded, and that the task of obtaining information in regard to the atom bomb was given No. 1 priority." In describing the ring of Soviet agents, Gouzenko mentioned for the first time Alan Nunn May, Emma Woikin and Kay Willsher.

Inspector John Leopold, who was as close to an expert on communism and the Soviet Union as the R.C.M.P. possessed, testified that he had examined some of Gouzenko's documents on September 7th, and that they "appeared to me genuine and of great interest to us. . . ." Gouzenko himself impressed the inspector, who told the commissioners that there was "no doubt in my mind at the time that there was any ulterior motive behind his actions or underlying his actions." Gouzenko reiterated to Leopold his contention that the Soviet Union was now preparing for a third world war, and that Soviet policies camouflaging that aim were in fact "a farce."

THE TESTIMONY OF EMMA WOIKIN

February 22, 1946

EMMA WOIKIN, *called*

THE SECRETARY   Will you take the Bible in your right hand, please. You understand the oath? What religion are you?

EMMA WOIKIN   I am a Doukhobor.

THE SECRETARY   Do you understand the oath when you are sworn on the holy Bible?

WOIKIN   Yes.

THE SECRETARY   Your full name is Emma Woikin?

WOIKIN   Yes.

EMMA WOIKIN, *sworn*

MR. FAUTEUX   What is your name, please?

WOIKIN   My name is Emma Woikin.

FAUTEUX   And where were you born?

WOIKIN   Blaine Lake, Saskatchewan.

FAUTEUX   What year?

WOIKIN   1921.

FAUTEUX   Speak up, please?

WOIKIN   January 1, 1921.

FAUTEUX   Both of [your parents] I understand, came from Russia?

WOIKIN   Yes.

FAUTEUX   They were born in Russia?

WOIKIN   Yes.

FAUTEUX   And they came to Canada in what year?

WOIKIN   I am not quite sure, but I think it is around 1899.

FAUTEUX   But you were born in Canada?

WOIKIN   Yes.

FAUTEUX   Where did you attend school?

WOIKIN   First of all I attended public school on the farm.

FAUTEUX   And then?

WOIKIN   That was from six to twelve.

FAUTEUX   Where was that?

WOIKIN   In the school near Blaine Lake.

FAUTEUX   Then?

WOIKIN   I attended school in 1942, commercial school, in Marcelin.

FAUTEUX   And after that?

WOIKIN   I have been attending school since October here in Ottawa, Technical [High] School.

FAUTEUX   What languages do you speak?
WOIKIN   English and Russian.
FAUTEUX   And what languages do you write?
WOIKIN   English and Russian.
FAUTEUX   I understand that you are married?
WOIKIN   I am a widow.
FAUTEUX   When did you marry?
WOIKIN   When I was 16; 1937.
FAUTEUX   And when did your husband die?
WOIKIN   1942.
FAUTEUX   What was the first employment you had?
WOIKIN   I worked on the farm all the time, and in 1942 — no; I am sorry. It was in 1943, after I finished my commercial class, I worked in a hospital; St. Paul's.
FAUTEUX   At what place?
WOIKIN   Saskatoon.

After writing a civil service examination in Saskatoon, Woikin secured a job in the Passport Office of the Department of External Affairs in Ottawa at a monthly salary of $52. She remained in that post for six months, from September 1943 until the spring of 1944, when she transferred to External Affairs' Cipher Division.

FAUTEUX   Would you tell us what were your particular duties in the cipher division; if you would kindly explain to the Commission what your duties were?
WOIKIN   I worked on typex machines and codes and ciphers.
FAUTEUX   What is the last?
WOIKIN   The codes and ciphers, incoming and outgoing.
MR. COMMISSIONER KELLOCK   What is a typex machine?
WOIKIN   It is a ciphering machine. . . .
KELLOCK   So was it part of your duties to decipher messages that were coming into the department?
WOIKIN   Yes.
KELLOCK   And was it also part of your duties to cipher messages that were going out?
WOIKIN   Yes.
KELLOCK   And was it also part of your duties to type these incoming or outgoing messages?
WOIKIN   On rare occasions when there were not enough typists. . . .
MR. FAUTEUX   Now I refer you to Exhibit 24-A. Will you say whether this is in your handwriting, too?
WOIKIN   Yes.
FAUTEUX   I refer you to Exhibit 24-B. Is it in your handwriting also?
WOIKIN   Yes.
FAUTEUX   I refer you to Exhibit 24-C, which is also in your handwriting?
WOIKIN   Yes.
FAUTEUX   And finally to Exhibit 24-D. This one is also in your handwriting?
WOIKIN   Yes.

FAUTEUX   All these exhibits to which I have just referred you, that is Exhibit
    24-A, Exhibit 24-B, Exhibit 24-C, and Exhibit 24-D, purport to be messages
    from the Secretary of State for Dominion Affairs, London, to the Secretary
    of State for External Affairs, Ottawa. Is that true?

WOIKIN   Yes.

FAUTEUX   Tell me when you wrote these exhibits? Tell the commissioners when
    you wrote them?

WOIKIN   I cannot remember what date I wrote them.

FAUTEUX   Where did you take the information that appears on these
    documents? Will you tell the Commission?

WOIKIN   At work. . . .

MR. COMMISSIONER KELLOCK   You have four documents in front of you in your
    handwriting?

WOIKIN   Yes.

KELLOCK   And you say you wrote them from memory?

WOIKIN   Yes.

KELLOCK   How soon after in each case did you write each one of those
    documents after the time that you had decoded the message?

WOIKIN   Well, probably a few days; I cannot remember exactly how many days
    it would be.

KELLOCK   Where were you when you wrote out those documents?

WOIKIN   Well, in my room.

KELLOCK   In your room where you live?

WOIKIN   Yes.

KELLOCK   So that you did not make out those documents when you were at
    work?

WOIKIN   No. . . .

KELLOCK   Well then, what you must have done is that as you were decoding the
    message you committed it to memory word for word?

WOIKIN   Yes, I remembered it.

KELLOCK   Yes, but you made an effort to remember it?

WOIKIN   Well, yes.

KELLOCK   That is to say, to put it in ordinary language, Mrs. Woikin, as you
    decoded the message you memorized it with the intention of writing it out later
    on?

WOIKIN   Yes. . . .

MR. FAUTEUX   Will you tell the Commission what is the purpose of marking
    these documents "Top Secret" or "Secret"?

WOIKIN   The word explains it.

FAUTEUX   Pardon me?

WOIKIN   The word itself explains it.

FAUTEUX   I would like to have your interpretation of it. I am quite satisfied with
    what it means, that the documents so marked contain information which it
    would be against the interest of the state to communicate with another foreign
    power?

WOIKIN   Correct. . . .

FAUTEUX   Will you tell the Commissioners how you reached the decision which
    undoubtedly was a serious one to take copies of these documents, of these

telegrams? Let me put it another way. You have looked at Exhibit Nos. 24-A, 24-B, 24-C and 24-D which are in your handwriting. You evidently did not take that information for yourself?

WOIKIN   Yes.

FAUTEUX   You did not take the information for yourself?

WOIKIN   No, I did not.

FAUTEUX   Because you could always have got it in the files in the department if you had access to those files. Why did you copy these telegrams and to whom did you give the copies that you made?

WOIKIN   Do you want to know the name of the person?

MR. COMMISSIONER KELLOCK   Yes.

WOIKIN   Well, has that got any bearing on it?

KELLOCK   Yes. You must answer the question put to you.

WOIKIN   The name of the person or the name of the —

KELLOCK   The name of the person. What did you do with these documents?

MR. COMMISSIONER TASCHEREAU   The first person to whom you gave them?

WOIKIN   I would not like to say the name of the person.

KELLOCK   You have to.

TASCHEREAU   You have to.

KELLOCK   Just answer the question.

WOIKIN   The foreign power is —

KELLOCK   That will not do — the person.

WOIKIN   Whoever it is it is not a Canadian.

KELLOCK   That does not matter. Will you please answer the question?

WOIKIN   His name is Sokolov.

KELLOCK   Who is Sokolov?

WOIKIN   Major Sokolov is from the Soviet embassy here.

MR. FAUTEUX   When did you meet Sokolov for the first time?

WOIKIN   In 1944, I think it was, at a public gathering.

FAUTEUX   In 1944. What was the balance of the answer?

WOIKIN   At a public gathering.

FAUTEUX   Where was that gathering?

WOIKIN   That was at a dinner before a concert at the Capitol Theatre.

Woikin testified that she had first met Major Sokolov at a concert given by the Glinka Choir from Montreal.

FAUTEUX   Did you about that time express a wish to go to work in Russia?

WOIKIN   About that time?

FAUTEUX   About March, 1944?

WOIKIN   Do you mean at work?

FAUTEUX   Yes. Did you express a wish to work in Russia at that time, in the spring or around the month of March, 1944?

WOIKIN   I had at one time mentioned it at the office. I spoke to some of the employees about it. I cannot remember now when it was when I was speaking.

MR. COMMISSIONER KELLOCK   What prompted that?

WOIKIN   I do not know; there was not any one thing that prompted it, but I always wanted to — there were many foreign openings and I thought I had a better chance to get that position than any other one because I had the language. . . .

MR. FAUTEUX   Will you tell me at what time you discussed with Major Sokolov the conveyance of information from where you were working for the benefit of the Soviet Union?

WOIKIN   In the early summer, 1945.

FAUTEUX   Where did you discuss that? . . .

WOIKIN   His residence.

MR. COMMISSIONER KELLOCK   Where?

WOIKIN   King Edward Street [Avenue].

KELLOCK   In the city of Ottawa?

WOIKIN   Yes.

MR. FAUTEUX   Who was present besides you?

WOIKIN   His wife.

FAUTEUX   And who else?

WOIKIN   Nobody else.

FAUTEUX   No one else?

WOIKIN   His wife was not in the room at the time.

FAUTEUX   His wife was not in the room at that time. Tell us what took place at that meeting.

WOIKIN   Well —

MR. COMMISSIONER KELLOCK   Would you speak up?

WOIKIN   I do not know what exactly you want to know by what took place.

KELLOCK   We want to know the substance of it. You are not expected to remember the very words, but what took place, what was the conversation?

MR. COMMISSIONER TASCHEREAU   Give us a summary.

WOIKIN   Well, the conversation consisted of asking my willingness —

TASCHEREAU   Pardon?

WOIKIN   Asking whether I would be willing to do that.

TASCHEREAU   To do what?

WOIKIN   Convey the information that would be of interest.

TASCHEREAU   That is, Sokolov asked you if you would be willing to do that; is that so?

WOIKIN   Yes.

TASCHEREAU   That is, he asked you if you would be willing to give him information which you could get from the Department of External Affairs where you worked?

WOIKIN   Yes.

TASCHEREAU   What kind of information?

WOIKIN   Which would be of interest, does not matter.

TASCHEREAU   Well, it would be messages coming in or going out of that department?

WOIKIN   No matter whichever would be, whatever would be of interest; that is all.

TASCHEREAU   He said either messages coming in or going out that you thought would be of interest to him, whether you would be willing to get them for him?

WOIKIN   Yes.

TASCHEREAU   What did you say?

WOIKIN   Well, I did.

TASCHEREAU   Pardon?

WOIKIN   I did.

TASCHEREAU   Not what you did, what did you say?

WOIKIN   I said I would help him.

MR. FAUTEUX   He asked you whether you were willing to give him information which would be of interest. Of interest to whom?

WOIKIN   He said the Soviet Union.

FAUTEUX   And you accepted that?

WOIKIN   Yes.

FAUTEUX   The information he was requiring was not necessarily limited, I understand from your answer, to information that you could gather from incoming or outgoing telegrams, but any information you could obtain, wherever you could obtain it?

WOIKIN   No.

FAUTEUX   Or any information that you could obtain in the course of your work?

WOIKIN   Well, I think that was the only way I could have had a chance.

FAUTEUX   That was understood by him and by you?

WOIKIN   I think so.

FAUTEUX   And that took place you said in the early summer of 1945?

WOIKIN   Yes.

MR. COMMISSIONER KELLOCK   Do you remember the month?

WOIKIN   No, I am afraid I do not.

KELLOCK   It must have been as early as May?

WOIKIN   As I said, along in May, the first days of June.

KELLOCK   When Mr. Sokolov asked you that, was that question a surprise to you?

WOIKIN   Well, in a way it was, yes.

KELLOCK   And in what way was it not?

WOIKIN   Just, I do not know, really; I could not answer that.

KELLOCK   In other words, his proposition to you was not entirely unexpected?

WOIKIN   I had no reason to expect it, no. . . .

KELLOCK   So that when Major Sokolov made that proposition to you, you say that was a complete surprise to you?

WOIKIN   Yes.

KELLOCK   But you agreed to it right away, is that what you say?

WOIKIN   I agreed to it.

KELLOCK   Right away?

WOIKIN   No.

KELLOCK   Well, what occurred?

WOIKIN   I asked to be given — I did not give any answer then.

KELLOCK   When did you give your answer?

WOIKIN   A few days later.

KELLOCK   You are sure of that?

WOIKIN   Yes.

KELLOCK   You did not say that a minute ago; you did not say that a few minutes ago when you were answering the question. You said that you were asked what occurred on that occasion when Major Sokolov made you that proposition, and you said you agreed.

WOIKIN   I agreed, yes, but I did not give him an answer right then.

KELLOCK   It was a few days later?

WOIKIN   Yes.

MR. COMMISSIONER TASCHEREAU   How long after you had agreed did you furnish the first information to him?

WOIKIN   I cannot exactly remember; a few weeks, maybe some time during the summer.

TASCHEREAU   You agreed approximately during the middle of May, 1945, and you started to give information during the last days of May or approximately that time?

WOIKIN   Approximately, yes.

MR. FAUTEUX   When you gave him your answer that you were ready to do what he was asking you to do, where did you give him this answer? Did you meet him again?

WOIKIN   I did.

FAUTEUX   At what place did you meet him on the second occasion when you gave him your answer?

WOIKIN   I made it by phone.

FAUTEUX   Where did you meet him to give him your answer that you were willing to do what he was asking you to do? Do you understand the question?

WOIKIN   Yes, I do.

MR. COMMISSIONER KELLOCK   What is the answer?

WOIKIN   I spoke to him on the phone.

MR. COMMISSIONER TASCHEREAU   Why do you take so long to tell us that you spoke to him over the phone?

MR. FAUTEUX   What was the conversation over the phone?

WOIKIN   I cannot remember.

FAUTEUX   Did you just tell him you were ready to carry out the scheme that he was proposing to you?

WOIKIN   Yes.

MR. COMMISSIONER KELLOCK   Did he call you or did you call him on the phone?

WOIKIN   I called him.

MR. FAUTEUX   When that proposition was discussed I imagine you must have discussed the means of conveying the information. Did you say you would transmit the information to him?

WOIKIN   Yes.

FAUTEUX   Tell us what was the arrangement as far as the transmission of information was concerned. How were you to do it?

WOIKIN   I met his wife.

FAUTEUX   You met his wife, where?

WOIKIN   Anywhere in town.

MR. COMMISSIONER KELLOCK   The arrangement was that you were to hand over the information to Mrs. Sokolov for transmission to Major Sokolov?

WOIKIN   Right.

MR. FAUTEUX   And was that arrangement carried out afterward?

WOIKIN   Yes.

FAUTEUX   How often after that did you meet Mrs. Sokolov for that purpose?

WOIKIN   Three times, about.

FAUTEUX   Three times. Do you remember those three times? You remember quite well the three times?

WOIKIN   Yes.

FAUTEUX   Where did you meet her the first time?

WOIKIN   The first time was on her way to the theatre.

FAUTEUX   On the street?

WOIKIN   Yes.

FAUTEUX   And you gave the information on the street?

WOIKIN   No.

FAUTEUX   Where did you give the information the first time?

WOIKIN   In the theatre. . . .

FAUTEUX   How long did you carry on the transmission of information? You said you started in the spring of 1945, or the early summer?

WOIKIN   The last days of August, sometime.

FAUTEUX   And when did you stop?

MR. COMMISSIONER KELLOCK   No, you didn't start in the last days of August?

WOIKIN   I am sorry; I stopped.

KELLOCK   In the last days of August?

WOIKIN   Yes. . . .

MR. FAUTEUX   Well, then did you decide that yourself or did you have instructions to do so?

WOIKIN   I had instructions; yes.

FAUTEUX   By whom?

WOIKIN   Mrs. Sokolov.

FAUTEUX   And what reason did she give for that?

WOIKIN   When I met her she didn't have very much time to give me any reason; she just told me —

FAUTEUX   She may not have had much time to say very much, but she must have given a reason for this discontinuance?

WOIKIN   Well, from what I gathered there was a little bit of trouble, that is all. . . .

FAUTEUX   And what did she say?

WOIKIN   She said, "We are not meeting any more," and that was all. . . .

FAUTEUX   Did you ever receive any money from Sokolov for the work you were doing for him?

WOIKIN   No, I didn't get money for it.

FAUTEUX   Pardon?

WOIKIN   I didn't get money for it.

MR. COMMISSIONER KELLOCK   Did you get money?

FAUTEUX   I am asking you whether you received money from Sokolov?

WOIKIN   I received a gift one time; $50.

FAUTEUX   And that gift was in the nature of what?

WOIKIN   It was money.

MR. COMMISSIONER KELLOCK   It was $50, you say?

WOIKIN   Yes.

MR. FAUTEUX   Where were you when Sokolov gave you that $50?

WOIKIN   His wife gave it to me. . . .

FAUTEUX   Miss Woikin, when you had the proposition put up to you the first time by Mr. Sokolov, and you say in a few days you agreed, why did you agree?

WOIKIN   Well, that is a feeling one can't quite express.

FAUTEUX   What is that?

WOIKIN   That is a feeling that you cannot quite express.

FAUTEUX   I do not understand that. You were born in this country?

WOIKIN   Yes.

FAUTEUX   Your parents have been here since before 1900?

WOIKIN   Yes.

FAUTEUX   Then would you explain why you were willing to do what Sokolov asked you to do?

WOIKIN   Perhaps it is because I have a feeling of love for that country. Perhaps it is because we think that there is — we may be wrong or we may be right, but there is hope for the poor or something.

FAUTEUX   Yes?

WOIKIN   I don't know why I had that, but I did.

FAUTEUX   If I understand what you mean, it is that you were sympathetic with the Soviet Union?

WOIKIN   Yes.

FAUTEUX   And not so sympathetic with your native country?

WOIKIN   I couldn't exactly say that. . . .

FAUTEUX   He offered you money when he made the proposition to you, but you did not agree to that?

WOIKIN   Not when he made the proposition. Later.

FAUTEUX   Later he said there would be money in it for you?

WOIKIN   Yes.

FAUTEUX   But you say you did not agree to that; it that right?

WOIKIN   Yes.

FAUTEUX   I am putting it correctly to you, am I?

WOIKIN   Yes.

FAUTEUX   But it was after that Mrs. Sokolov handed you this money?

WOIKIN   Yes.

FAUTEUX   Did you apply to have Soviet citizenship?

WOIKIN   Yes.

FAUTEUX   At what time?

WOIKIN   About a month ago.

FAUTEUX   Where?

WOIKIN   At the embassy.

FAUTEUX   Who did you see there?

WOIKIN   Mr. Pavlov and Mrs. Voronina. . . .

FAUTEUX   So you were introduced to Mr. Pavlov in his office at the embassy?

WOIKIN   Yes.

FAUTEUX   What took place there?

WOIKIN   I asked whether I could apply for citizenship; that was all.

FAUTEUX   There must have been a little more than that; you must have told him who you were?

WOIKIN   No, I didn't. There was very little in that interview.

FAUTEUX   He didn't ask you who you were?

WOIKIN   Yes, my name. . . .

FAUTEUX   You seriously wanted to have Soviet citizenship?

WOIKIN   Yes.

FAUTEUX   You were eager to have it?

WOIKIN   I have applied for it, yes.

MR. COMMISSIONER KELLOCK   Does that mean you wanted to go to Russia to live?

WOIKIN   Yes. . . .

KELLOCK   Did you think perhaps it would be just as well for you to get out of the country?

WOIKIN   No, I didn't do it for that.

KELLOCK   I didn't ask you if you did it on that account; I asked if that occurred to you?

WOIKIN   No, it didn't occur to me. . . .

MR. FAUTEUX   Are you a member of the Communist party?

WOIKIN   No.

FAUTEUX   Were you ever a member of the Communist party?

WOIKIN   No.

FAUTEUX   You are not?

WOIKIN   No.

FAUTEUX   Did you ever apply to be a member of the Communist party?

WOIKIN   No.

FAUTEUX   What?

WOIKIN   No.

FAUTEUX   Did you ever have any dealings with the Communist party?

WOIKIN   No.

FAUTEUX   Pardon me?

WOIKIN   No, I have not.

FAUTEUX   Did you ever have any connections with them?

WOIKIN   No, I do not know of one actually.

FAUTEUX   Pardon me?

WOIKIN   I do not know of one actually in Canada.

FAUTEUX   Do you know anyone anywhere?

WOIKIN   There is a Communist party in the Soviet Union, that is all I know.

FAUTEUX   All right, did you have any connection with that party?

WOIKIN   No, not as a member, no.

FAUTEUX   How did you have connections with it if not as a member? Will you explain to the Commissioners, please?

WOIKIN   It was only what I read before. I have know of them, that is all, and the people who were Soviet citizens. . . .

FAUTEUX   I refer now to Exhibit No. 83 which is an application for national registration. One question is, "Nationality or country of allegiance: — British subject (a) by birth?" And you answered, "No." Then, "If not British subject, to what country do you owe allegiance?" And you answered, "Owe allegiance to no country." Why did you at a later stage want to owe allegiance to the Soviet Union when you asked to become a citizen of the Soviet Union? Why did you want to owe allegiance to that country?

WOIKIN   When I answered that that was what my husband wished me to do and I did it. Now I would like to be a Soviet citizen.

FAUTEUX   Now you would like to be a Soviet citizen?

WOIKIN   Yes.

FAUTEUX   Why?

WOIKIN   I cannot answer that, I do not know how to answer it.

FAUTEUX   Take your time and tell us what you believe and what you think?

WOIKIN   Maybe it was from the kind of life I had, maybe — just that I look to that country for security and I would like to live there.

FAUTEUX   Who told you that there was security in that country? How do you know that?

WOIKIN   Well —

FAUTEUX   How did you reach that conclusion?

WOIKIN   I do not know how I reached that conclusion.

FAUTEUX   You must have had some reason?

WOIKIN   Well, maybe it was from what I read — what I read, really that is what I mean.

FAUTEUX   What do you mean by security?

WOIKIN   Well, there was a time when I was quite poor, I guess, and my baby died because we had no medical care and nobody seemed to care. My husband was sick and to such a stage where nobody seemed to intervene at all.

MR. COMMISSIONER KELLOCK   There was no public health service out where you were living?

WOIKIN   No, there was not. . . .

MR. FAUTEUX   Did you not try in 1944 to obtain some work at the Soviet embassy?

WOIKIN   Yes, I did. . . . I wrote a letter and then I was referred to see Pavlov, but I never heard about it any more.

MR. COMMISSIONER KELLOCK   How were you referred to see Pavlov?

WOIKIN   After I wrote the letter I phoned and asked whether they received my letter and whether they considered it and they told me, yes, they would give me an appointment with Pavlov. So I did see him but I never heard anything about it.

KELLOCK   You saw Pavlov on that occasion?

WOIKIN   Yes, but I never heard about it later.

MR. COMMISSIONER TASCHEREAU   Who told you to write to Krotov?

WOIKIN   There was a girl that worked there and I asked her whether it would be possible for me to work there.

TASCHEREAU   You knew that girl before?

WOIKIN   I had met her here in Ottawa.

TASCHEREAU   She was Russian?

WOIKIN   Yes, she was from Saskatchewan.

TASCHEREAU   Did you know her before coming here?

WOIKIN   No, I had met her here. . . .

MR. FAUTEUX   Before we conclude this examination I should like to know what excuse or justification you may wish to offer for conveying secret information to a foreign power. If you wish to offer any excuse or justification you are free to do so.

WOIKIN   There is not much I can say. . . .

February 28, 1946.

EMMA WOIKIN, *recalled*

MR. COMMISSIONER TASCHEREAU   Mrs. Woikin, you have been heard already as a witness?

WOIKIN   Yes.

TASCHEREAU   As Royal Commissioners we have been conducting an inquiry into what officials and other persons in positions of trust or otherwise may have communicated, directly or indirectly, secret and confidential information, the disclosure of which might be inimical to the safety and interests of Canada, to the agents of a foreign power, and the facts relating to and the circumstances surrounding such communication.*

One of the authorities under which we were appointed is the Inquiries Act, a Canadian Statute. By Section 12 of this Statute, it is provided that any person against whom any charge is made in the course of an investigation such as this shall be allowed to be represented by counsel. By Section 13 of the same Statute, no report shall be made against any person until reasonable notice shall have been given to him of any charge of misconduct alleged against him and he shall have been allowed full opportunity to be heard in person or by counsel.

We are of the opinion that the evidence produced before us will require us to report that you, a person in a position of trust or otherwise, have communicated directly or indirectly secret and confidential information, the disclosure of which might be inimical to the safety and interests of Canada, to the agents of a foreign power.

We are, therefore, proposing to report to the Governor in Council our findings, and should the proper authorities see fit you may be charged in the courts, where you will have the opportunity to be represented by counsel.

Before this Commission you have already been heard as a witness and been invited to make any statements you wished. We now further advise you that if you wish to say anything else, or to adduce further evidence, or if you wish to have counsel appear before us on your behalf, you are so entitled.

You understand what I have just said to you?

WOIKIN   I think so.

TASCHEREAU   Have you anything to say or anything else to add to the evidence that you have already given?

WOIKIN   No.

TASCHEREAU   Before we make our recommendation to the Governor in Council do you wish to be represented by counsel?

WOIKIN   By that you mean I should have an attorney?

TASCHEREAU   This Commission is not a criminal court, we just report to the government.

WOIKIN   Yes.

TASCHEREAU   But before we make that report we want to tell you that you are entitled to have counsel appear before us.

WOIKIN   No.

TASCHEREAU   You do not wish to have counsel appear before us?

WOIKIN   No.

TASCHEREAU   That will be all, thank you. . . .

*A similar statement was made to others who were to testify before the Commission.

167

THE TESTIMONY OF KATHLEEN WILLSHER

February 25, 1946.

KATHLEEN MARY WILLSHER, *sworn*

MR. FAUTEUX   Miss Willsher, where were you born?

WILLSHER   London, England.

FAUTEUX   What year.

WILLSHER   1905.

FAUTEUX   What school did you attend?

WILLSHER   James Allan's Girls' School.

FAUTEUX   And then?

WILLSHER   The London School of Economics.

FAUTEUX   Are you a graduate of that school?

WILLSHER   Yes.

FAUTEUX   In what year?

WILLSHER   1926.

FAUTEUX   Do I understand that you speak German?

WILLSHER   Yes.

FAUTEUX   You read German, too?

WILLSHER   Yes.

FAUTEUX   What other language do you speak?

WILLSHER   French.

FAUTEUX   You read and speak French?

WILLSHER   Yes.

FAUTEUX   And Russian?

WILLSHER   Very little.

FAUTEUX   When did you start to learn Russian?

WILLSHER   I haven't done any for some years now. I don't know very much. . . .

FAUTEUX   Will you tell the commissioners in what your duties consisted as assistant registrar? [at the U.K. High Commission in Ottawa]

WILLSHER   Registration of letters and despatches and telegrams; filing; all that deals with registration; incoming and outgoing mail. That is the general description. Card indexing, I suppose.

FAUTEUX   In your capacity would you have access to all incoming and outgoing messages?

WILLSHER   I suppose so, unless they were highly secret, in which case they are not registered.

FAUTEUX   But the majority of them, either secret or top secret, you would have access to?

WILLSHER   Yes. I didn't at first —

FAUTEUX   And you would have access to the files —

MR. COMMISSIONER KELLOCK   Will you complete your answer, please?

WILLSHER   When I was deputy assistant I did not do as much work as I have done afterwards.

KELLOCK   But as assistant registrar you would have access to all these documents, except those which were highly secret?

WILLSHER   Yes.

KELLOCK   Will you look at this photograph and say whether you recognize the person represented there?

WILLSHER   Yes.

MR. COMMISSIONER TASCHEREAU   Whose picture is that?

MR. FAUTEUX   Eric Adams.   (*To the witness*)   When did you meet him?

WILLSHER   At a private meeting; I don't know whether it was his or somebody else's.

FAUTEUX   When was that?

WILLSHER   I think it is 1942. I don't know, to be exact.

FAUTEUX   In what circumstances?

WILLSHER   In a study group.

FAUTEUX   Who was present?

WILLSHER   Miss Chapman.

FAUTEUX   Who is Miss Chapman?

WILLSHER   She works in the Bank of Canada, or in the Bureau of Statistics. . . .

FAUTEUX   And who was present the night you met Adams?

WILLSHER   Somebody Benning, I think.

FAUTEUX   What is his first name?

WILLSHER   I have forgotten.

FAUTEUX   How old is he, about?

WILLSHER   About 30.

FAUTEUX   I suggest that his name was James Scotland Benning?

WILLSHER   Scott; that's right.

FAUTEUX   And where was he employed at the time?

WILLSHER   I think it is the Department of Munitions and Supply.

FAUTEUX   Who else was there?

WILLSHER   I don't know. It was very small. I think there was only one other person.

FAUTEUX   How many persons were present?

WILLSHER   I couldn't say; I think four or five.

FAUTEUX   There was yourself; there was Adams, Chapman, Benning and who else?

WILLSHER   I am trying to remember the name. It was Luxton. . . .

FAUTEUX   And what was his position or occupation.

WILLSHER   I think he was in the Bank of Canada.

FAUTEUX   Was he working with Adams?

WILLSHER   I couldn't tell you.

FAUTEUX   What was the nature of that meeting?

WILLSHER   It was a study group; economics.

FAUTEUX   When was that formed?

WILLSHER   At that moment. It might have been operating before I joined it, I don't know; I didn't ask, and nobody told me.

FAUTEUX   And what took place that night?

WILLSHER   Well, we discussed socialist literature, Marxist literature, I suppose you would call it.

FAUTEUX   I wasn't there, and you were; you know. You say you suppose?

WILLSHER   It was a study group for that; that is all I remember. I don't know what particular chapter, or what.

FAUTEUX   Who was in charge of that; who took the initiative in that study group?

WILLSHER   I don't know.

FAUTEUX   Who appeared to be in charge when you were there?

WILLSHER   Mr. Adams, I think.

FAUTEUX   And how long did the meeting last?

WILLSHER   About an hour and a half.

FAUTEUX   And what was decided?

WILLSHER   To have further ones.

FAUTEUX   Where?

WILLSHER   At the houses of the people in the group.

FAUTEUX   When?

WILLSHER   Well, within three weeks; two weeks. It varied; it was not regular.

FAUTEUX   How often?

WILLSHER   About every three weeks; but then when Christmas came you would have a longer time.

FAUTEUX   Was that understanding carried out?

WILLSHER   I think so.

FAUTEUX   For how long?

WILLSHER   I think until Mr. Adams probably left here.

FAUTEUX   Until Mr. Adams left for where?

WILLSHER   Montreal.

FAUTEUX   When was that?

WILLSHER   The end of 1944.

FAUTEUX   So it started in what year?

WILLSHER   I think it was during 1942. I don't know the date.

FAUTEUX   And it lasted until the time Mr. Adams left for Montreal, or until 1944?

WILLSHER   Yes. . . .

MR. COMMISSIONER KELLOCK   Was employment in the government service a qualification for membership in this group?

WILLSHER   Not that I know of.

KELLOCK   What was the qualification?

WILLSHER   Interest in the same kind of study.

KELLOCK   Interest in communistic writings and teachings?

WILLSHER   Yes.

KELLOCK   How long have you had such an interest, Miss Willsher?

WILLSHER   Oh, quite a number of years. About ten years. It is a sort of socialistic — it began as an interest in the Labour party in Britain, and in socialistic interest here, and then I gradually read more, and it became communistic.

KELLOCK   Could you fix it, when your interest became communistic, approximately?

WILLSHER   Yes; about 1936.

MR. FAUTEUX   That is the time you joined the party?

170

WILLSHER   Yes.

KELLOCK   And do you know at what time the others joined the party?

WILLSHER   I don't know anything about them.

MR. COMMISSIONER KELLOCK   What party is this?

WILLSHER   The Labour-Progressive party, now. . . .

MR. COMMISSIONER TASCHEREAU   How did you make your application to join the Communist party?

WILLSHER   I didn't write it, or make it; I was just asked if I was interested in giving a regular donation. There was no form or anything.

TASCHEREAU   To whom did you pay those dues every month?

WILLSHER   To whoever was treasurer in the group I studied with. I don't know who was treasurer. People changed, and apparently the funds were handed over, and I know nothing more about them as far as that goes.

MR. COMMISSIONER KELLOCK   It was a monthly fee, was it?

WILLSHER   Yes.

KELLOCK   How much?

WILLSHER   It depends on the income.

KELLOCK   How much in your case?

WILLSHER $1. I don't remember quite now. . . .

KELLOCK   There is something I would like to get clear. You spoke of this study group which started in 1942?

WILLSHER   Yes.

KELLOCK   You are now speaking about another group, are you, which started in 1936, when you became a member of the Communist party?

WILLSHER   Yes.

KELLOCK   You paid a monthly due ever since 1936?

WILLSHER   No; it stopped. From 1939 to 1942 I did not pay. There was nothing to pay; we had no groups, as far as I know. I mean I wasn't in any group.

KELLOCK   Then was this study group a revival of your original Communist party organization?

WILLSHER   The same type of organization; not the same people.

KELLOCK   The same type of organization?

WILLSHER   Yes. . . .

MR. FAUTEUX   I show you this photograph, which has been filed as Exhibit 60. Do you recognize that person?

WILLSHER   Yes.

FAUTEUX   Who is he?

WILLSHER   Mr. Rose.

FAUTEUX   What is his first name?

WILLSHER   Fred.

FAUTEUX   What is his occupation?

WILLSHER   Member of Parliament.

FAUTEUX   And besides that?

WILLSHER   Member of the Communist party.

FAUTEUX   And in the Communist party what is he doing?

WILLSHER   I don't know. I suppose he is on the national executive.

FAUTEUX   When did you meet Fred Rose for the first time?

WILLSHER   At Mrs. Turner's.

FAUTEUX   In what year?

WILLSHER   1935.

FAUTEUX   1935?

WILLSHER   Yes, when I went there sometimes.

FAUTEUX   Is he the first one who suggested you could contribute to the promotion of the Soviet government by giving him in general terms information of value which passed through your hands in the office, the High Commissioner's office?

WILLSHER   He didn't say "Soviet government." He said the Canadian party, the Canadian Communist party.

MR. COMMISSIONER KELLOCK   Just what did he say to you?

WILLSHER   That the party would be very glad to have some information sometimes in order that their policy — to affect public opinion — the sort of facts they could have. That is all I know.

KELLOCK   Do I understand you, Miss Willsher, to say that Mr. Rose in 1935 suggested to you that you should furnish, from your sources of information in the High Commissioner's office, information to him?

WILLSHER   He just said any general ideas I might have about things. Nothing was ever suggested about giving him data. He said it would be of value to the Party in formulating its program.

KELLOCK   That is not what I understood you to say a few moments ago. Just tell us, please, what Mr. Rose did suggest to you?

WILLSHER   That I could give him some general ideas of what was going on.

KELLOCK   What do you mean by "general ideas of what was going on"?

WILLSHER   They were pursuing a policy of a united front.

KELLOCK   Who were?

WILLSHER   The Communist party was — and that facts pointing towards that, it would help to know if there was likely to be one or not.

KELLOCK   What facts, now?

WILLSHER   I don't know.

KELLOCK   And you were quite clear on what he said to you at the time?

WILLSHER   Yes.

KELLOCK   That was 1935?

WILLSHER   Yes.

KELLOCK   Do you want us to understand that Mr. Rose was asking you for your own original ideas, or information that you might obtain?

WILLSHER   Well, a general view of the information; not specific details at all.

KELLOCK   That is information to which you would have access at your employment?

WILLSHER   Yes.

KELLOCK   So then, to be quite clear about it, you understood Mr. Rose quite clearly at the time to suggest to you that he or his party would be glad to have from you information which you might obtain from the High Commissioner's office in the course of your employment?

WILLSHER   Yes. . . .

KELLOCK   Miss Willsher, you recognized, I suppose, when Mr. Rose made that suggestion to you, that he was suggesting an improper thing for you to do?

WILLSHER   Well, I did, but I felt that I should contrive to contribute something towards the helping of this policy, because I was very interested in it. I found it very difficult, and yet I felt I should try to help.

KELLOCK   Then you appreciated that from the standpoint of your relationship to your employer it was an improper suggestion. That is right?

WILLSHER   Yes. I also felt that I had something I should contribute.

KELLOCK   Would it be right to put it this way; that you felt that there was a higher law, owing to your, let me say, political convictions?

WILLSHER   Yes. It was a struggle; it always is a struggle.

KELLOCK   You cannot serve two masters without a struggle; but what I want to put to you, Miss Willsher, is this. You said this group where this suggestion was first made to you was a broad group. If you recognized Mr. Rose's suggestion as an improper suggestion, and this was a broad group, Mr. Rose would not be making his suggestion to you in a loud voice so that all the members of this broad group could hear?

WILLSHER   No. As I say, it would be addressed to me. It would not be addressed to anyone else.

KELLOCK   A little private conversation with you?

WILLSHER   Yes. As I say, when a meeting breaks up —

KELLOCK   There is an opportunity for such private conversation?

WILLSHER   Yes, there is an opportunity when you go to a house to do that, I suppose.

KELLOCK   So that as early as 1935 —

WILLSHER   It was probably just before 1936 when I actually — I mean I must have been feeling pretty strongly on the subject. . . .

MR. FAUTEUX   Did you gave your answer immediately to Mr. Rose, when he made that request to you?

WILLSHER   No; I gave it some consideration.

FAUTEUX   And when did you give him your answer?

WILLSHER   I couldn't exactly say.

FAUTEUX   How long after, about? At the next meeting?

WILLSHER   That I don't know. It would not be a great deal of time; perhaps a month.

FAUTEUX   And you gave him an affirmative answer. You accepted?

WILLSHER   Yes. I found it very difficult, and yet I felt that I was trying to —

FAUTEUX   And from then on you conveyed to him whatever information you thought he wanted to obtain from the department in which you were employed?

WILLSHER   Yes. There was not a great deal, as a matter of fact.

FAUTEUX   How would you convey that information to him?

WILLSHER   Just telling him. . . .

MR. COMMISSIONER KELLOCK   Did you arrange to meet him regularly?

WILLSHER   No; just occasionally I saw him. There was not any regular arrangement. I suppose I was invited to a place and he would be there, but it wasn't very often. There was a great deal of time in between. It didn't seem that I was of very great importance.

KELLOCK   Were you going to places where you would meet Mr. Rose periodically, or would expect to meet him periodically?

WILLSHER   No. I mean he must have known when he wanted to meet me, and I suppose it was arranged, but I was not aware of any regularity or any setting of a future date. There was nothing like that at all.

KELLOCK   But you did in fact meet him from time to time?

WILLSHER   A few times. It wasn't very many times.

MR. FAUTEUX   For how long?

WILLSHER   I suppose till about sometime in 1939, after which I haven't seen him since.

FAUTEUX   You have not seen him since 1939?

WILLSHER   No, not myself. . . .

FAUTEUX   Who else asked you to get information from the same source for the benefit of the Party or the Soviet Union?

WILLSHER   Mr. Adams.

FAUTEUX   When did he ask you? That is the same person whom you have already identified?

WILLSHER   Yes. . . .

FAUTEUX   When was the first meeting you had with Adams?

WILLSHER   I do not know whether it was the first or second; I was not aware there was ever a specific point made that he had to meet me.

FAUTEUX   For how long did you continue to give information to Adams?

WILLSHER   Until about last September, the last time I saw him.

FAUTEUX   From 1942 to last —

WILLSHER   1945.

FAUTEUX   September of 1945?

WILLSHER   Yes.

MR. COMMISSIONER KELLOCK   What happened then?

WILLSHER   I do not know, I just have not seen him since, that is all.

MR. FAUTEUX   He was not in Ottawa during all that period of time, was he?

WILLSHER   No, he was in Montreal.

FAUTEUX   While in Ottawa how would you convey information to him?

WILLSHER   I might see him at the study group.

FAUTEUX   That is where you would give it to him?

WILLSHER   Before or after the meeting.

FAUTEUX   And then —

WILLSHER   I did not see him very often.

FAUTEUX   Did you ever have occasion to drive with him?

WILLSHER   No, not until he had gone to Montreal.

FAUTEUX   That is when he had gone?

WILLSHER   Because he drove to Ottawa and had his car.

FAUTEUX   So while he was in Ottawa you would convey information at these meetings?

WILLSHER   Yes.

FAUTEUX   Did you ever telephone to him?

WILLSHER   No.

FAUTEUX   Why?

WILLSHER   I did not telephone to him; I have never been asked to telephone to him; I do not take the initiative.

FAUTEUX   Why?

WILLSHER   I do not know; I never have taken the initiative.

FAUTEUX   Why would not you take the initiative?

WILLSHER   Unless I was asked, I did not go out and direct the thing. If he wanted something he could ask, but I did not know or say anything.

FAUTEUX   Where did he ask?

WILLSHER   As I say, at the meetings.

FAUTEUX   And any information he was asking for you would try to obtain that in the course of your employment?

WILLSHER   Yes, but he generally just asked me a question or two and I answered them then. I did not have to go and do anything about it. It was just anything I happened to remember.

FAUTEUX   Will you tell us what Adams said the first time he asked you to give confidential information; how did he ask you?

WILLSHER   Well, he said that they wanted — I was given to believe that the policy of the Party was that they wanted the war to be — the Soviet Union was in the war and they wanted —

MR. COMMISSIONER TASCHEREAU   They wanted what?

WILLSHER   The war to go ahead and for there to be a second front and did I know anything about that sort of thing because they said that the policy in Canada — there might be a change in public opinion — that we must make the war effort go ahead and —

MR. FAUTEUX   In what way did he ask you that?

WILLSHER   Well, for any sort of —

FAUTEUX   That is not an ordinary question to ask a person. You explained the occasion when Rose was asking for information, that you had to go through certain difficulties before you made up your mind?

WILLSHER   Yes.

FAUTEUX   Did you have the same difficulties when the request came from Adams?

WILLSHER   Yes.

MR. COMMISSIONER KELLOCK   Why?

WILLSHER   Because it always is difficult for me yet I feel it is expected of me that I should do something. It is not easy to explain.

KELLOCK   Well, I would like to understand it a little more clearly. Do you mean, Miss Willsher, that by becoming a member of the Communist party you are expected to do what you are asked to do regardless of any obligation you may have in any other direction; is that what you mean?

WILLSHER   That is the sort of thing, yes.

KELLOCK   And what Mr. Adams asked you in 1942, whatever it was, it was that he wanted you to supply him with information you could get from your office of employment?

WILLSHER   Which I felt was relevant to any question he might ask regarding the war effort. That was, as I say, the interest of the Party at that time; it was to —

KELLOCK   To get it in as simple language as possible, the interest of the Party at that time was whatever would be in the interests of the Soviet Union, was it not?

WILLSHER   Well, to make plain the unity of the Allies.

KELLOCK   I want you to answer my question. I am asking you as to whether what was in the interest of the Party was whatever would be in the interest of the Soviet Union. Is that a fair way of putting it?

WILLSHER   Well, I suppose they would want them to have the same interests at that time.

KELLOCK   That is the way you understood it, in any event?

WILLSHER   Yes.

KELLOCK   What Mr. Adams asked you to obtain from the office of your employers would be information you thought would be of interest to the Soviet Union?

WILLSHER   He did not put it like that. He said the Party policy is to do this, and they would like information, but he never mentioned the Soviet Union.

KELLOCK   I see.

WILLSHER   It was always as a member of the Party, it was the Party's policy to support the maintenance of allied unity which included the Soviet Union.

KELLOCK   And therefore he was satisfied to leave the support of the Allies to the Allies themselves, he wanted you to get some special information from your office? That is right? He was asking you to get information from your office?

WILLSHER   We were Allies.

KELLOCK   Mr. Adams was asking you to try to get information from your office of employment?

WILLSHER   Yes.

KELLOCK   To give to him?

WILLSHER   Yes.

KELLOCK   And do I understand that the information you would get from your office would be such information as you thought would be of interest or of value to the Soviet Union?

WILLSHER   I did not think of the Soviet Union; I thought of the Canadian party.

KELLOCK   You thought of the Canadian Communist party?

WILLSHER   The Party's policy.

KELLOCK   What plan or what idea did you have in mind in selecting this information or that information to pass on to Mr. Adams?

WILLSHER   He asked questions. That was the basis on which he asked me.

KELLOCK   I am asking you. How would you determine in your mind what information was of interest to the Party? I am asking you, would it be information which you thought would be of interest to the Soviet Union?

WILLSHER   No, I did not think of it in that way.

KELLOCK   How did you cull out the information, on what principle did you work?

WILLSHER   I did not think about it a great deal. If he asked me a question, I tried to answer it.

KELLOCK   If he asked you a question, if he said to you, "I want you to get this particular information," you would try to get it, of course?

WILLSHER   Yes.

KELLOCK   That would be easy; you would know what you were looking for?

WILLSHER   Yes.

KELLOCK   Well, did it always arise in that way, that Mr. Adams asked you to get particular information?

WILLSHER   Yes, usually; yes, it was particular, not in the sense of detail, but a particular subject, I suppose.

KELLOCK   For instance, if somebody was visiting in this country, he might ask you to get what information you could on that subject?

WILLSHER   Yes. I cannot think of any case where that happened, though. It always seemed to me quite logical the things he asked.

KELLOCK   What I am trying to understand for my own part is what things he did ask. I am asking you if he asked you to get information on particular subjects?

WILLSHER   There was the financial angle.

KELLOCK   That was one particular subject that he asked you to get information about?

WILLSHER   Yes.

KELLOCK   I suppose there were other particular subjects, were there?

WILLSHER   Yes, he asked if I thought — he asked once or twice if I thought the second front would start some time, if I thought all our efforts were being made and it was likely to come soon. That was in a general way. Actually when it did come he had not asked me for some time.

KELLOCK   Not what you thought, but what information you could obtain in the commissioner's office?

WILLSHER   Yes.

KELLOCK   In addition to these particular subject matters did you have a sort of roving commission to get any information that you thought might interest Mr. Adams?

WILLSHER   No, not particularly.

KELLOCK   You never obtained any information except what Mr. Adams specifically asked you for?

WILLSHER   Yes.

KELLOCK   It was always that he gave you —

WILLSHER   Along the lines.

KELLOCK   Just a minute. He gave you jobs to do, did he?

WILLSHER   More or less, yes.

KELLOCK   Suppose, for instance, that Mr. Adams asked you for information on a particular subject. Would you just try to look up the documents in your office on that subject and pass on the information to Mr. Adams? Is that the way it worked?

WILLSHER   He would ask me and usually it was answered at the time. I do not think there was any looking through a particular file; it was just anything I might be aware of in answering the questions he put.

KELLOCK   In any event you gave him such information from time to time?

WILLSHER   Yes.

MR. FAUTEUX   May I suggest that, for instance, he asked you for information regarding the friendship between the United States of America and the United Kingdom?

WILLSHER   Yes.

FAUTEUX   That was discussed?

WILLSHER   Yes.

FAUTEUX   He asked you to supply information in that regard?

WILLSHER   Yes, and I did not know —

FAUTEUX   What?

WILLSHER   I did not get any.

FAUTEUX   You tried to supply some?

WILLSHER   I think of various things but I can think of no information on that line. Very often I had no answer because I did not know.

FAUTEUX   Did he question you on the office organization, the staff and the various functions of the people working in the High Commissioner's office?

WILLSHER   Yes, in a general sense. It was how big it was and the sort of subjects it would deal with, and I gathered he was getting information of that sort on embassies and consulates. I do not know why, but I think —

FAUTEUX   You have been a member of the Party a long time, have you not?

WILLSHER   Yes, but I mean I do not have any close contacts.

FAUTEUX   You must have some idea as to the inspiration of the theory of that Party, where it comes from?

WILLSHER   Well, there are similar parties in all countries.

FAUTEUX   From where would you say that those parties receive their instructions?

WILLSHER   I do not know that they receive instructions; I think they exist —

FAUTEUX   Do you know whether they are federated?

WILLSHER   I do not know that there is any federation.

FAUTEUX   You do not know that there is?

WILLSHER   No.

FAUTEUX   Or put it another way: What would be the interest of the Soviet Union in those parties?

WILLSHER   Because they were similar to the Party itself in its own country.

FAUTEUX   Because they were similar to what?

WILLSHER   Its own party. I mean, it is natural they would not be antagonistic. I think each country carries out its own policy as far as possible. Naturally they would support each other's policies to a certain extent. I mean, I mean I believe, as I have read in *The Tribune*, the executive are Canadians and they have a policy.

FAUTEUX   But who directs?

WILLSHER   They naturally would be friendly.

FAUTEUX   Who directs that policy?

WILLSHER   I do not know; I am not on the executive.

FAUTEUX   You have read many books?

WILLSHER   Yes. I would not say that their policy was dictated; I would say that they made their policy because conditions vary in different parts of the world and you cannot —

FAUTEUX   You remember speaking about the various subjects on which information was given by you to Adams. You remember a visit by Lord Keynes in Ottawa at the end of the year 1944?

WILLSHER   It has been brought to my attention.

FAUTEUX   There was some information required from you by Adams on that particular subject?

WILLSHER   He wanted to know if the proposals, I think, had gone forward to the parties, but on the details he was in position to see himself, I think, because he did finance work.

FAUTEUX   Where, in his office in the Bank of Canada?

WILLSHER   I suppose so.

FAUTEUX   I suppose he was getting information at both ends, at the Bank of Canada as far as the Canadian government was concerned and from the High Commissioner's office as far as England was concerned?

WILLSHER   He would see those proposals because they would be put to the Government of Canada.

MR. COMMISSIONER KELLOCK   Cannot you just tell us what you did, what you arranged with Adams?

WILLSHER   He asked, I think, if the proposals had come and if they were going forward and there may have been a general idea of what they were, but I do not believe now that they were.

KELLOCK   What did you say when you got that request?

WILLSHER   I think they had come; I said they had come.

KELLOCK   What did you expect that Mr. Adams was going to do with the information you gave him?

WILLSHER   I do not know.

KELLOCK   I asked you what you expected?

WILLSHER   I do not know; I did not think of what he was going to do with it.

KELLOCK   Did you expect that Mr. Adams would pass that information on to the Soviet Union?

WILLSHER   No, certainly not.

KELLOCK   What did you expect he would do with it?

WILLSHER   I do not know. I suppose he might tell the national executive. It was the only thing I ever knew him, that I expected him to do with it.

KELLOCK   The national executive of the Communist party in Canada?

WILLSHER   Yes.

KELLOCK   What would be the interest of that body in that information?

WILLSHER   I do not know. I did not think of what the interest would be.

KELLOCK   You mean to say you did not —

WILLSHER   No, I mean I did not know what its interest would be, if there was any particular interest. He was interested in financial matters, therefore when he asked me financial questions I was not surprised, but why he asked them I do not know.

KELLOCK   If he had any interest in financial matters he could satisfy that interest in the Bank of Canada where he was employed, could he not?

WILLSHER   I would have felt so.

KELLOCK   Why did you think that he was going around asking you to give him information? You are not being very frank, Miss Willsher. I would like you to be frank.

WILLSHER   I did not ask him.

KELLOCK   I did not ask you that; I asked you what you expected — we will come back to that.

WILLSHER   I think he wanted to know a little ahead perhaps when they were discussed. That is the only possible reason.

MR. COMMISSIONER TASCHEREAU   Mr. Adams was a member of the Party?

WILLSHER   Was what?

TASCHEREAU   He was a member of the Party?

WILLSHER   I suppose so.

TASCHEREAU   He attended those meetings?

WILLSHER   Yes.

TASCHEREAU   So he was a member of the Party?

WILLSHER   Yes.

TASCHEREAU   And he had asked you to give him information?

WILLSHER   Yes.

TASCHEREAU   So you knew perfectly well he would deliver that to the Party, everything you told him?

WILLSHER   Yes, I suppose he would. . . .

February 26, 1946.

MR. FAUTEUX   Miss Willsher, I will continue your examination now under the same oath that you took yesterday.

WILLSHER   Yes.

FAUTEUX   You told us that Adams left Ottawa for Montreal around 1944?

WILLSHER   Yes.

FAUTEUX   How did you meet him thereafter?

WILLSHER   He came to Ottawa sometimes.

FAUTEUX   How often?

WILLSHER   About three or four times, as far as I can remember.

FAUTEUX   Four or five times?

WILLSHER   No, I think three or four. I don't remember.

FAUTEUX   And how would you get in touch with him then?

WILLSHER   Miss Chapman told me that he was coming.

FAUTEUX   Every time?

WILLSHER   Yes.

FAUTEUX   She would phone you?

WILLSHER   Yes, or if I happened to see her anywhere.

FAUTEUX   Or if you would meet her?

WILLSHER   Yes.

FAUTEUX   Tell us exactly what procedure was followed?

WILLSHER   She would telephone, or tell me if she happened to see me somewhere.

FAUTEUX   Miss Chapman would telephone you and tell you she had to see you somewhere?

WILLSHER   No. She might telephone me and tell me that he was coming, or she might meet me somewhere in the normal course of events and tell me.

FAUTEUX   That Adams was coming?

WILLSHER   Yes.

FAUTEUX   And then?

WILLSHER   I would arrange to meet him.

FAUTEUX   How would you arrange to meet him?

WILLSHER   He usually was driving, and he would just pick me up.

FAUTEUX   That is the way the meeting would take place, but how did you arrange to meet him; through whom? How would you contact him?

180

WILLSHER I didn't contact him; Miss Chapman just told me he was coming, and she apparently did the contacting.

MR. COMMISSIONER KELLOCK She told you he would be in his car at a certain place at a certain time?

WILLSHER Yes.

KELLOCK And you were to be there?

WILLSHER Yes.

MR. FAUTEUX And what time of the day would these meetings take place?

WILLSHER After work. I think the early evening, as far as I can remember.

FAUTEUX And where would they take place? Any corner? Any place on the street?

WILLSHER I remember at the corner of Lisgar and Bank, at the street car stop. I don't remember any other place, just there or somewhere like that.

FAUTEUX And any time you were notified that he would be at any particular place, you would meet him?

WILLSHER I would try to; yes.

FAUTEUX You did, as a matter of fact?

WILLSHER Yes.

FAUTEUX Any time?

WILLSHER Yes, any time.

FAUTEUX And what would take place from then on?

WILLSHER Just go for a short drive and talk. . . .

FAUTEUX And would he drive you home afterwards, or leave you on the street?

WILLSHER Just drop me wherever we happened to be.

FAUTEUX When the conversation was over?

WILLSHER Yes.

FAUTEUX And when the information was transmitted to him?

WILLSHER Yes.

FAUTEUX And how long would that last?

WILLSHER Ten minutes or a quarter of an hour.

FAUTEUX Why would you not meet him at your place?

WILLSHER Well, he didn't suggest it. He said he had the car, he would meet me at a certain place.

FAUTEUX Why did you not meet him at Miss Chapman's place?

WILLSHER If he suggested it, I would. I had met him at her place when he was in Ottawa.

FAUTEUX What reason could you give us why you would have to meet him in that extraordinary way?

WILLSHER I don't know.

FAUTEUX You have no idea?

WILLSHER No. . . .

FAUTEUX I am asking you this question. Have you taken any documents from the High Commissioner's office?

WILLSHER No.

FAUTEUX You are sure of that?

WILLSHER I am sure.

FAUTEUX Or did you take any memos?

WILLSHER No.

FAUTEUX   Memorandums?

WILLSHER   No.

FAUTEUX   Photos?

WILLSHER   No.

FAUTEUX   You took nothing away from your work?

WILLSHER   No.

FAUTEUX   All the information you conveyed you memorized it and gave it to Adams afterward?

WILLSHER   Yes.

FAUTEUX   But you never took any documents?

WILLSHER   No.

FAUTEUX   Why did you discuss the Wilgress report with Adams?

WILLSHER   Because it mentioned credits.

FAUTEUX   You discussed those reports with Adams?

WILLSHER   That one — I do not remember the other one.

FAUTEUX   I take it that you saw the red boxes at the office?

WILLSHER   Yes.

FAUTEUX   You have also a blue box there?

WILLSHER   Yes.

FAUTEUX   What is the blue box for?

WILLSHER   For the atomic bomb.

FAUTEUX   How did you know that?

WILLSHER   We all knew that.

FAUTEUX   Will you tell the commissioners what information or what discussion you had with Adams in relation to that subject?

WILLSHER   It would be sort of casual when I was there last September about the future control, the question of whether it would be within the group of three countries or under international control. It seemed that in order to have world peace we should have international control. We were just discussing the subject generally.

FAUTEUX   You discussed that in September?

WILLSHER   Yes.

FAUTEUX   1945?

WILLSHER   Yes.

FAUTEUX   Where?

WILLSHER   Montreal.

FAUTEUX   Montreal?

WILLSHER   Yes, just casually. Naturally we talked about a few things when I was there, and this was one of them.

FAUTEUX   You were alone with him at the time?

WILLSHER   Yes, driving.

FAUTEUX   What was his reaction on the subject?

WILLSHER   He did not say very much.

FAUTEUX   He said something; perhaps not much but what did he say? What were his views and your views on it?

WILLSHER   I gather he agreed.

FAUTEUX   What?

WILLSHER   He agreed. I do not remember anything, but he thought international control was better.

FAUTEUX   International control by whom?

WILLSHER   I suppose the United Nations.

FAUTEUX   It would be controlled by what country?

WILLSHER   All countries, members of the United Nations combination.

FAUTEUX   Is that the first time that he spoke to you about that subject or had there been previous conversations?

WILLSHER   No.

FAUTEUX   While he was in Ottawa?

WILLSHER   No.

FAUTEUX   Or after, while he was coming from Montreal?

WILLSHER   No, he never asked me anything about it.

FAUTEUX   There was never any question about it?

WILLSHER   No. . . .

MR. COMMISSIONER KELLOCK   Is that why you did not tell anybody, either in your employer's office or elsewhere, outside of these people who were already in the Communist party, that you were a member of the Party?

WILLSHER   Yes, that is understood.

MR. FAUTEUX   You did not want it known?

WILLSHER   Not any more than they would.

MR. COMMISSIONER KELLOCK   You did not want it known?

WILLSHER   No.

KELLOCK   By anybody else except these select few?

WILLSHER   Yes.

KELLOCK   Why not?

WILLSHER   Well, because it is not considered — it is not a popular thing to have ideas like that.

KELLOCK   You think that if the fact had been known to your employers it might not have been as easy for you to get the information you were getting?

WILLSHER   I suppose not — I did not ever think — I mean one does not just go around saying — I mean there are other people you have to think of as well as other people who are members of the group. It is not a thing — people do not talk about that.

KELLOCK   That is the recognized practice, is it, in the Communist party?

WILLSHER   Yes, unless people are working on a newspaper or on the national executive or —

MR. FAUTEUX   Did you tell anybody about your meetings with Rose?

WILLSHER   No.

FAUTEUX   Did you tell anybody about your meetings with Adams, I mean besides the people who were immediately concerned?

WILLSHER   No.

MR. COMMISSIONER KELLOCK   Did you tell Miss Chapman; of course, Miss Chapman —

WILLSHER   She knew because she arranged it.

KELLOCK   You did not tell anybody else in this group?

WILLSHER   No.

MR. FAUTEUX   Did you tell anybody or did you consult anybody about the trouble you had with your conscience when Rose asked you to supply information for the benefit of others?

WILLSHER   No.

FAUTEUX   Did you consult anybody about the trouble that you had with your conscience?

WILLSHER   No.

FAUTEUX   I have not finished putting my question. Did you consult anybody about the trouble you had with your conscience when you arrived at the decision to meet with Adams, when he asked you to give him information from your work which was secret and confidential, and so on?

WILLSHER   No.

FAUTEUX   You made that decision by yourself?

WILLSHER   Yes.

FAUTEUX   You did not want anyone to know that?

WILLSHER   No.

FAUTEUX   And you never spoke to anyone about the meetings you had with him?

WILLSHER   No.

FAUTEUX   I am going to put this question to you, but before I do so I should like to read to you an answer that you gave during your interrogation. This question was asked:

> Q   At approximately what stage or what year did Fred Rose suggest to you that you could contribute to the promotion of the United front and the Soviet Government by giving him in general terms any information of value which passed through your hands in the office of the High Commissioner for Canada?
> A   I think about 1937.

WILLSHER   It should have been 1935.

MR. COMMISSIONER KELLOCK   (*To Fauteux*)   Did you ask the witness whether she had been asked those questions?

MR. FAUTEUX   Were you asked that question?

WILLSHER   Yes.

FAUTEUX   And you answered, "I think about 1937," but it should have been 1935?

WILLSHER   Yes.

FAUTEUX   As you told us yesterday?

WILLSHER   Yes.

FAUTEUX   The next question was:

> Q   You are sure it was not in 1938 or the latter part of 1937?
> A   Up until 1938 no person other than Fred Rose made any suggestion to me that I might assist the Soviet Government by transmitting information.

Do you remember if that is the answer you gave?

WILLSHER   Yes. Nobody asked me —

FAUTEUX   So you knew then, Miss Willsher —

WILLSHER   But it does not say —

FAUTEUX   Just a minute —

WILLSHER   You have —

MR. COMMISSIONER KELLOCK   (*To the witness*)   Just a minute, please. Wait for the question to be put.

FAUTEUX   The answers you gave at that time were the truth?

WILLSHER   That was not about the Soviet Government.

FAUTEUX   Why did you say that?

WILLSHER   I do not know, it was put to me quickly.

KELLOCK   (*To the witness*)   Will you keep your voice up, please?

WILLSHER   As far as I knew it was the Canadian party. . . .

FAUTEUX   You told us yesterday that when you were asked by Fred Rose to betray your employer and pass on information that it created in your mind and in your heart and in your conscience considerable trouble?

WILLSHER   Yes, because it should not occur to anybody.

FAUTEUX   And that you gave thought to it at that time?

WILLSHER   Yes.

FAUTEUX   And that being called upon to make a decision as between your master and the country you were working for, on the one hand, and the Communist party, on the other hand, you told us that you decided in favour of the Communist party?

WILLSHER   Yes.

FAUTEUX   Because you felt that you owed loyalty to the Communist party first?

WILLSHER   Yes.

FAUTEUX   Whom do you think the Communist party held loyalty to?

WILLSHER   As I say, I think they are in their own country, they are all connected, because they all have the same aims in view.

FAUTEUX   What is the Comintern?

WILLSHER   It does not exist.

FAUTEUX   Since when?

WILLSHER   I do not know; from a few years ago.

FAUTEUX   What was it when it existed?

WILLSHER   It was a union of the Soviet parties. I do not think of it in the sense of one country versus another; it was part of all countries.

FAUTEUX   I do not think it was one country against another either. But the Comintern was what?

WILLSHER   It was a union of all Communist parties in the world.

FAUTEUX   And the Communist party of Canada was a section of it?

WILLSHER   Yes. . . .

FAUTEUX   And when you made your decision you were fully aware, not only of the ordinary loyalty that you owed to the country for which you were working, but also of the provisions of the Official Secrets Act?

WILLSHER   Yes.

FAUTEUX   Which you had read. You knew the penalties which were involved?

WILLSHER   Yes.

FAUTEUX   Notwithstanding all that, you decided to give priority to the duties which were imposed on you by the Communist party?

WILLSHER   Yes. I signed that in 1939 so I did not sign it before this; in the second period it would —

FAUTEUX   Would it have made a difference, anyway?

WILLSHER   I suppose I had got to the point where I would not — I was already —

FAUTEUX   You were ready —

WILLSHER   Enthusiastic over it.

FAUTEUX   You were ready to do anything the Party asked you to?

WILLSHER   Yes.

MR. COMMISSIONER KELLOCK   I suppose even in 1935 you knew it was an improper thing to do?

WILLSHER   Yes.

KELLOCK   That is what caused this struggle in your mind?

WILLSHER   Yes. I know I can be shot quite easily, if necessary.

KELLOCK   You know you can be what?

WILLSHER   Shot, if necessary.

KELLOCK   Where?

WILLSHER   The provisions are very strict.

KELLOCK   What are you speaking about now?

WILLSHER   I just mentioned that.

KELLOCK   What are you speaking about, what are you referring to?

WILLSHER   The Official Secrets Act — do not they execute people?

KELLOCK   I had not heard of that myself in this country. . . . What about the effect if the information that you passed on to Mr. Adams was passed on to Russia; what about that?

WILLSHER   That is very unfortunate.

KELLOCK   Pardon?

WILLSHER   That would be a great misfortune. I did not think that was going to occur.

KELLOCK   You never dreamed of that?

WILLSHER   No.

MR. COMMISSIONER TASCHEREAU   What did you think would happen to the information you gave him?

WILLSHER   I did not think of it for Russia. I think the Communist party has done itself a great deal of harm. I do not think that it has — there would be an effect on public opinion which would be very strong over this kind of thing. . . .

THE TESTIMONY OF EDWARD WILFRED MAZERALL

February 27, 1946

EDWARD WILFRED MAZERALL, *sworn*

MR. FAUTEUX   Mr. Mazerall, where were you born?

MAZERALL   Fredericton, New Brunswick.

FAUTEUX   What year?

MAZERALL   1916. . . . When I left the university I went to the Canadian Westinghouse Company for a year.

FAUTEUX   In what city?

MAZERALL   Hamilton

FAUTEUX   You were there for a year?

MAZERALL   Just almost exactly a year.

FAUTEUX   What year would that be?

MAZERALL   That was 1938-1939. Then from 1939 I was with the Canadian Broadcasting Corporation in Ottawa at C.B.O. until I think it was January, 1942, when I went to the National Research Council. . . .

FAUTEUX   Mr. Mazerall, will you tell us when you first met Fred Rose; tell the commissioners when you first met Fred Rose?

MAZERALL   I really cannot give you any date. It was shortly after he was elected the first time, if I remember correctly.

FAUTEUX   Shortly after he was elected where?

MAZERALL   To the House of Commons.

FAUTEUX   And where did you meet him?

MAZERALL   I believe it was at the home of Miss Agatha Chapman.

FAUTEUX   In Ottawa?

MAZERALL   That is correct.

FAUTEUX   On what street?

MAZERALL   Somerset Street, I believe; yes, Somerset Street.

FAUTEUX   And how did you come to go there?

MAZERALL   It was a meeting of representatives from various study groups who were sympathetic to the Labour-Progressive party. . . .

FAUTEUX   And who else was present?

MAZERALL   There was Miss Chapman, and I believe Robert Edmonds; Mrs. Nielsen, Mrs. Dorise Neilsen; there was a nurse, but I cannot recall her name, and possibly one or two others, whom I cannot recall. . . .

FAUTEUX   What was the occasion of the meeting?

MAZERALL   It was to hear Fred Rose give an analysis of the difference in the stand taken by the Labour-Progressive party and the C.C.F.

FAUTEUX   And that is the first occasion when you met Fred Rose?

MAZERALL   To the best of my knowledge it is.

FAUTEUX   But it was not the first occasion that you had assisted at these meetings?

MAZERALL   No. . . .

FAUTEUX   When did you start these meetings?

MAZERALL   I can't say definitely; about the year 1941.

FAUTEUX   And who asked you to join these meetings?

MAZERALL   Robert Edmonds.

FAUTEUX   What is his occupation?

MAZERALL   At that time he was an announcer on C.B.O. Subsequently he went to the Film Board, I think as producer, and later still he went to Hamilton, I think. I don't know what he is doing there, or if he is still there.

FAUTEUX   And the first meeting at which you assisted, what was decided? Would you explain the nature of those meetings to the commissioners, Mr. Mazerall?

MAZERALL   Mainly the study of Marxist philosophy. . . .

FAUTEUX   To cut it down to the shortest possible description, you considered that was a cell of the Communist party?

MAZERALL   You might consider it so.

FAUTEUX   I want to have your views on that, your honest views, Mr. Mazerall.

MAZERALL   I really never did consider that I belonged to the Communist party.

FAUTEUX   I am not speaking of you; I am speaking of the organization, the study group there.

MAZERALL   Yes, it might have been.

FAUTEUX   I want a better answer than that, if it is possible. You say it might; I want to have your views on it.

MAZERALL   Yes. Well, I think it was; yes. . . .

FAUTEUX   And how long did you continue these activities in that group, or assist at those meetings? For what period?

MAZERALL   Fairly regularly up to a year ago, and then very sporadically up to about four or five months ago.

FAUTEUX   And how often would these meetings be held?

MAZERALL   Once every two weeks or so.

FAUTEUX   Where would they be held?

MAZERALL   At the homes of various people concerned.

FAUTEUX   At the homes of the various people who were attending them?

MAZERALL   Correct.

FAUTEUX   And how many of those people would you say there were?

MAZERALL   Sometimes as little as three; sometimes as many as five or six.

FAUTEUX   What would be the number of persons who, throughout the period of your assistance, would have attended the meetings?

MAZERALL   Well, I had occasion to go to another — to two different groups, and in all that time I imagine I met some fifteen and twenty people.

FAUTEUX   In the two groups?

MAZERALL   In three.

FAUTEUX   There were three groups?

MAZERALL   Yes.

FAUTEUX   Would you kindly explain those various groups to the commissioners?

MAZERALL   The groups were made up of people who had similar pursuits; that is, they tried to keep people together who had things in common.

FAUTEUX   What job?

MAZERALL   Whatever they were working at.

FAUTEUX   And then?

MAZERALL   Then I moved from one group to another, and still to another.

(Mazerall testified about the groups he attended, which consisted largely of individuals working for the National Film Board. He was then questioned about "the third group.")

MAZERALL   Subsequent to the forming of that (the third) group at that time, Durnford Smith joined; then David Shugar, and still later this chap Gordon Lunan.

MR. COMMISSIONER KELLOCK   Would you give us the approximate times when these three groups existed; the periods. Take the first group?

MAZERALL   The first group would have been from about 1941 to possibly the end of 1941. The next one, through part of 1942 — no, all of 1942, and possibly 1943, and the third one from 1943, I think.

KELLOCK   The third one in 1943 until —

MAZERALL   No; the first one might have gone into 1942, and the second one on into 1943.

MR. COMMISSIONER TASCHEREAU   And when you met Fred Rose for the first time it was at a meeting of what group?

MAZERALL   That was at a meeting of the representatives from each of the other groups.

MR. COMMISSIONER KELLOCK   A number of groups?

MAZERALL   Yes. . . .

MR. COMMISSIONER TASCHEREAU   So how many groups were represented when you met Fred Rose for the first time?

MAZERALL   Four, and possibly five.

TASCHEREAU   Were they all groups from Ottawa?

MAZERALL   Yes.

MR. COMMISSIONER KELLOCK   There is one answer I do not understand. You said you never considered yourself a Communist, although you had been attending these group meetings twice a month since 1941 until sometime in 1945, when it became more irregular. You say you never did become a member of the Party?

MAZERALL   No. Well, it was a sort of tacit consent, you might say, but there was no official party, and no official membership.

KELLOCK   There was no formal act of your becoming a member?

MAZERALL   No.

KELLOCK   But did you consider yourself a member?

MAZERALL   Actually I did not.

KELLOCK   You were still unconvinced, with all this education you were receiving?

MAZERALL   I don't think I received very much, frankly. It was primarily — the meetings were primarily to study various books by Karl Marx.

MR. COMMISSIONER TASCHEREAU   Did you pay a monthly fee?

MAZERALL   Yes, we did subscribe subsequently to the Labour-Progressive party.

TASCHEREAU   How much did you pay?

FAUTEUX   When you say "things in common" you mean the same ideas as far as communism is concerned?

MAZERALL   No, as far as jobs are concerned.

MAZERALL   I think it was around a dollar or so.

TASCHEREAU   A dollar a month or a dollar a meeting?

MAZERALL   No, a dollar a month.

MR. FAUTEUX   To whom did you pay that?

MAZERALL   To the person who was the secretary of the meeting.

FAUTEUX   And did you change secretaries at each meeting, or was there a permanent secretary?

MAZERALL   No, they didn't change at each meeting. It was a more or less permanent secretary. . . .

FAUTEUX   And to whom did you send that money?

MAZERALL   It was given in at the meeting of representatives from the groups.

FAUTEUX   To Mr. Rose?

MAZERALL   No. Mr. Rose was there only on one occasion.

MR. COMMISSIONER KELLOCK   You mean in addition to this group, or these group meetings, the secretaries had their own group meetings?

MAZERALL   That is right.

KELLOCK   And you turned in the money then to whom?

MAZERALL   To the chairman of that group.

KELLOCK   Who was — ?

MAZERALL   I believe that was Miss Chapman.

MR. COMMISSIONER TASCHEREAU   Miss Chapman?

MAZERALL   I think so. . . .

MR. FAUTEUX   Were you paying them when you belonged to the first group?

MAZERALL   Yes, I think we were.

FAUTEUX   That was the first group that you belonged to, in what year?

MR. COMMISSIONER KELLOCK   That would be somewhere between 1941 and 1942?

MAZERALL   Yes.

MR. FAUTEUX   And you say that money went to the Labour-Progressive party?

MAZERALL   Well, there was no Labour-Progressive party then.

FAUTEUX   Well, where did it go?

MAZERALL   Well, actually I don't know. I surmise that it went to Tim Buck, to keep him living.

FAUTEUX   When you paid your dollar you must have known where it was going?

MAZERALL   No, really I didn't.

FAUTEUX   What did you understand about it?

MAZERALL   I can't tell you what I understood then.

MR. COMMISSIONER KELLOCK   You mean you paid your dollar without knowing where it was going, or anything about it?

MAZERALL   Organization fee, was the term. . . .

KELLOCK   And I think you did say, Mr. Mazerall — and you will correct me if I am wrong — that this money did go to the Labour-Progressive party?

MAZERALL   Later on it did.

KELLOCK   Later on?

MAZERALL   Yes.

KELLOCK   Then when you were paying a dollar a month to the Labour-

Progressive party, did you not consider yourself a member or supporter at least of it?

MAZERALL   Oh, a supporter; yes.

KELLOCK   But not a formal member?

MAZERALL   No.

KELLOCK   Is that a fair way of putting it?

MAZERALL   I would say so, yes.

KELLOCK   Then what information or knowledge did you have about the ancestors of the Labour-Progressive party?

MAZERALL   At that time there was really no communication between the groups in Ottawa and elsewhere; to the best of my knowledge there was not.

KELLOCK   What I had in mind and what I will ask you, is this. My own recollection, not from anything I have heard here but my own recollection is that the Labour-Progressive party changed its name at some time which I do not remember, and before that it called itself the Communist party. Is that your recollection?

MAZERALL   Yes.

KELLOCK   Then would you say that the Labour-Progressive party, to which you paid your dollar, was the Communist party under a change of name?

MAZERALL   That would be reasonable. . . .

MR. FAUTEUX   One of the persons you identified here is Lunan. Will you tell me when you met Lunan first?

MAZERALL   That would be just about a year ago, a little less than a year ago.

FAUTEUX   Less than a year ago?

MAZERALL   Yes.

FAUTEUX   At some of these meetings?

MAZERALL   Yes, sir.

FAUTEUX   And do you know how he was invited there?

MAZERALL   No. He was known to some of the others.

FAUTEUX   He was known to whom, as far as you can recollect?

MAZERALL   Oh, I'm not sure. . . .

FAUTEUX   You never spoke of your connection with these groups to anybody else but those who belonged to them?

MAZERALL   That is right.

FAUTEUX   And I can summarize the whole situation by saying they were secret?

MAZERALL   Yes.

FAUTEUX   You met Lunan at one of these meetings, and would you give me the approximate date when you met him?

MAZERALL   Well, it was last winter. It was a little later in the year than this, I think.

FAUTEUX   Last winter; the winter of 1945? How early? Would it be around March or February?

MAZERALL   Well, it might have been in February.

FAUTEUX   And how often did you meet Lunan at these meetings?

MAZERALL   Oh, I don't think he came again then or — I couldn't tell you definitely; it seems to me there was quite a long time that he didn't show up. Altogether I think I may have seen him about three times. . . .

FAUTEUX   But I understand you saw him besides that?

MAZERALL   That is right.

FAUTEUX   Where did you meet Lunan outside of these meetings?

MAZERALL   At the Chateau.

FAUTEUX   That is the Chateau Laurier?

MAZERALL   Yes.

FAUTEUX   At approximately what date?

MAZERALL   The first one would have been early in June, I believe.

FAUTEUX   Referring to Exhibit 111, I notice that on the page dated June 4, 1945, you have marked, "Gordon L." That is who?

MAZERALL   I believe that is Gordon Lunan.

FAUTEUX   You are sure of that?

MAZERALL   That is correct.

FAUTEUX   And the telephone number, 9-7621, which is the telephone number of — ?

MAZERALL   It must have been his office.

FAUTEUX   His office at the time?

MAZERALL   Yes.

FAUTEUX   And that is in your handwriting?

MAZERALL   That is right.

FAUTEUX   And I see in the lower part of the page your initials?

MAZERALL   Yes, that is right.

FAUTEUX   Which you marked, not on June 4?

MAZERALL   No.

FAUTEUX   But when you examined these various pages since you have been detained?

MAZERALL   Yes.

FAUTEUX   Now will you carry on from there and tell us what Lunan asked you during the course of that telephone conversation, and what took place after that? . . .

MAZERALL   We went for a drive in the car, and after some preliminary discussion he asked me if I would supply him with information.

FAUTEUX   For whom?

MAZERALL   For the Soviet Union.

FAUTEUX   And then?

MAZERALL   Well, I didn't say anything at the time, that I can recall. I think I must have told him I would think it over.

FAUTEUX   You mentioned that you drove in a car. Was it your car or his car?

MAZERALL   It was my car.

FAUTEUX   And then?

MAZERALL   Then I dropped him off and went home, and I was to have called him to let him know what my answer was, and I didn't. Subsequently, he called me.

FAUTEUX   How long after?

MAZERALL   Well, now, I couldn't tell you definitely.

FAUTEUX   How many days after, about?

MAZERALL   I couldn't tell you that, either. There is a notation on the page there, but whether that was the date — it would be approximately that date.

FAUTEUX   You have on the page dated Sunday, June 10, 1945, made a reference

192

there — you inscribed there, on that page in lead pencil, "Gordon L.," which is Gordon Lunan; 9-7621?

MAZERALL   Yes; and this number, I think, is his home number.

FAUTEUX   You think the number 5-7120 would be his phone number at home. What occurred on that day, when you inscribed these notes on the calendar pad in your office?

MAZERALL   That was just about a week after the first phone call, and may have been the actual day I first saw him; I am not sure. Evidently on or about this date he did call me again. . . .

MR. COMMISSIONER TASCHEREAU   To get your answer?

MAZERALL   Either to get my answer or to make a definite luncheon appointment.

MR. FAUTEUX   Yes?

MAZERALL   So in any event I didn't see him at all for a month, and I note that I have a luncheon appointment marked on Tuesday, July 24.

FAUTEUX   You note that on the calendar pad; Tuesday, July 24: "Gordon," which is Gordon Lunan, and, "Lunch. 12 o'clock. Chateau."?

MAZERALL   Right.

FAUTEUX   And what took place then?

MAZERALL   On that occasion I had lunch with him and gave him two reports.

FAUTEUX   You gave him two reports. What reports did you give him?

MAZERALL   One was a long term proposal by Dr. McKinley for future civil aids to air navigation. One was a report I had prepared for Dr. McKinley on a distance indicator for civil aids to navigation, short range navigation. Both of these reports had been prepared so that Dr. McKinley might present them at the Commonwealth and Empire Radio and Civil Aviation Conference in London.

FAUTEUX   Which was to be held — ?

MAZERALL   In August.

FAUTEUX   I will come to these reports later, but between the time he asked you to supply information for the Soviet Union and the time you brought these two reports, I would imagine that you must have had occasion to give him an answer to his proposal, which you had delayed on the first occasion?

MAZERALL   I believe the answer came on the same day that I saw him.

FAUTEUX   That is what you recall now?

MAZERALL   Yes; I mean the last time I saw him here. . . .

FAUTEUX   So it would be around the 4th — at the beginning of June, 1945, that Lunan asked you to give some information, the source of which would be in the course of your employment?

MAZERALL   Yes.

FAUTEUX   For the benefit of the Soviet Union?

MAZERALL   Yes.

FAUTEUX   The first information, as far as you can remember, that you brought to him was in written form; or was it in written form?

MAZERALL   It was in published form.

FAUTEUX   And it was these two reports of which you have been speaking?

MAZERALL   That is correct.

FAUTEUX   And on which you had worked yourself, personally?

MAZERALL   Yes.

FAUTEUX   And which eventually, at a later date, were published at the London conference?

MAZERALL   That is right. . . .

FAUTEUX   Did you ask for their return yourself?

MAZERALL   Yes.

FAUTEUX   Why?

MAZERALL   Well, I wanted them.

FAUTEUX   Because you wanted them back. Why?

MAZERALL   They were my own copies of both reports.

FAUTEUX   And what was Lunan to do with these reports while they were in his possession?

MAZERALL   Turn them over to the representatives of the Soviet Union.

FAUTEUX   To the representatives of the Soviet Union?

MAZERALL   Yes.

FAUTEUX   Turn them over to whom, in particular there?

MAZERALL   I beg pardon?

FAUTEUX   Turn them over to what person?

MAZERALL   I don't know.

FAUTEUX   He did not tell you?

MAZERALL   No. . . .

FAUTEUX   Were you ever given a cover name?

MAZERALL   Yes.

FAUTEUX   By whom?

MAZERALL   By Lunan.

FAUTEUX   When?

MAZERALL   On this second occasion, the 24th of July.

FAUTEUX   You say that on the 24th of July Lunan gave you a cover name?

MAZERALL   Yes.

FAUTEUX   What was said about that?

MAZERALL   He merely said that in referring to me to anybody else he would use the name of Bagley.

FAUTEUX   And what did you say to that?

MAZERALL   I don't know that I said anything. . . .

FAUTEUX   I am exhibiting to you a file which comes from the Soviet embassy, and in that file you will notice your name on the first page.

MAZERALL   That is right.

FAUTEUX   "Bagley", your nickname or cover name, and Lunan's name?

MAZERALL   Yes.

FAUTEUX   And his cover name?

MAZERALL   Yes.

FAUTEUX   And Smith, whom you have identified?

MAZERALL   Yes.

FAUTEUX   In a photograph?

MAZERALL   Yes.

FAUTEUX   With the cover name of Badeau. That was known to you also?

MAZERALL   No.

FAUTEUX   You did not know his cover name?

194

MAZERALL   No.

FAUTEUX   You knew Halperin?

MAZERALL   Yes.

FAUTEUX   Did you know his cover name?

MAZERALL   No, I did not.

FAUTEUX   In the same exhibit, if you will read this with me: "I had a very successful meeting with Bagley and he agreed to participate to the furthest of his ability." Is that true?

MAZERALL   I don't think so.

FAUTEUX   You had agreed to what Lunan had asked you?

MAZERALL   I had at that time supplied him with those two reports.

FAUTEUX   You will notice that the report I am showing you in this exhibit is dated July 5, 1945. I continue: "I also received an explanation of what I took to be his early reluctance to meet me. His wife teaches music — " That is true?

MAZERALL   Yes.

FAUTEUX   "— and on the frequent occasions when she has to be away from the house, he has to stay home with the children."

MR. COMMISSIONER KELLOCK   Is that true?

MAZERALL   No.

MR. FAUTEUX   "He is unable to plan his free time very much in advance, hence the difficulty in seeing him." There was no difficulty, I suppose, for you two to meet?

MAZERALL   There actually was no difficulty.

FAUTEUX   There was no difficulty?

MAZERALL   No.

FAUTEUX   And were you carrying on these study group meetings at the time?

MAZERALL   Very sporadically.

FAUTEUX   They were going on just the same?

MAZERALL   Yes.

FAUTEUX   That is before and after the delivery of these two reports?

MAZERALL   Yes.

FAUTEUX   I continue reading: "He is interested in the work and immediately promised to be of assistance. I gave him a full quota of tasks, and he promised reports on his work and on various other aspects of the general work at his place. Since first seeing him, I have been in Montreal, and on the two occasions I tried to get in touch with him for a progress report, he was not available." Were you made aware that he had tried to reach you at some time?

MAZERALL   I am not sure. I actually think he did phone me; in fact I think he got me on that occasion.

FAUTEUX   "He had promised to deliver his work in full in time for this meeting.". . . Is that right?

MAZERALL   I do not recall this.

FAUTEUX   "He had promised to deliver his work in full in time for this meeting. He now informs me, however, that he has not completed the work and will need another ten days." That is the work referred to in this report?

MAZERALL   This had been completed long before.

FAUTEUX   It had been completed long before that?

MAZERALL   I think so; I am not sure.

FAUTEUX   How long before would you say the reports were completed; in what month were they completed?

MAZERALL   They had been completed early in July. . . .

FAUTEUX   If this document we are speaking about, Exhibit No. 107 — as far as that document is concerned, it bears the legend "Confidential." That means that neither you nor any other employee of the Research Council is free to disclose it?

MAZERALL   Yes.

FAUTEUX   Except authorized persons?

MAZERALL   Yes.

FAUTEUX   And Lunan was not an authorized person at any time?

MAZERALL   No.

FAUTEUX   Did not the same thing apply, Mr. Mazerall, to any information that you had about it, apart from what might appear in the formal report, Exhibit No. 107? That is, you were free to disclose the information to authorized persons in the course of your duties, but not to unauthorized persons?

MAZERALL   Yes.

MR. COMMISSIONER TASCHEREAU   You knew perfectly well that you should not give that to Lunan?

MAZERALL   Yes, I did, and as I say I could have given him more important reports which would have been more useful than this to them. While I certainly regret it very much, the fact is that this was the most innocuous report I could have put my hands on.

MR. COMMISSIONER KELLOCK   You had put yourself in a position with Lunan where you had to give him something and you thought this was the least harmful?

MAZERALL   That is what it amounts to. . . .

MR. FAUTEUX   How many meetings did you have with Lunan?

MAZERALL   To the best of my knowledge, three only.

FAUTEUX   On what dates would they be?

MAZERALL   One was early in June, the other was probably this date, the 24th of July, and the third was a couple of days later when he returned the reports.

FAUTEUX   Did he ask you to give him a list of the literature which was used in the Research Council?

MAZERALL   More than possible he did.

FAUTEUX   I would like if possible to get a better answer.

MAZERALL   I cannot say that definitely he did ask me.

FAUTEUX   What, generally speaking, did he ask you?

MAZERALL   He wanted any information he could get, either in the form of reports or knowledge of what reports were available or he would like to have me make a *précis* or synopsis of reports myself and give them to him.

FAUTEUX   What did he say to you when he gave you the reports back?

MAZERALL   I do not recall any conversation.

FAUTEUX   Well, Mr. Mazerall, a proposition is put to you by Lunan?

MAZERALL   Yes.

FAUTEUX   To obtain information for the Soviet Union?

MAZERALL   Yes.

FAUTEUX   Arising out of your work?

MAZERALL   Yes.
FAUTEUX   Which is secret and confidential?
MAZERALL   Yes.
FAUTEUX   And which is covered by three oaths?
MAZERALL   Yes.
FAUTEUX   Beside the loyalty that you owed there?
MAZERALL   Yes.
FAUTEUX   And you asked for some time to think about it?
MAZERALL   Yes.
FAUTEUX   Because you realized how serious it was?
MAZERALL   Yes.
FAUTEUX   And finally you decided to bring some material to him?
MAZERALL   Yes.
FAUTEUX   That material not being verbal, but in writing?
MAZERALL   Yes.
FAUTEUX   And arrangements were made that it would be photostated and then given back to you?
MAZERALL   Yes.
FAUTEUX   You must have realized at that time what you were doing. That was a completion of the proposition that had been made to you. When the documents were given to you were not you curious enough to ask Lunan what the people at the Soviet embassy thought about them?
MAZERALL   No.
FAUTEUX   There was no word said about that?
MAZERALL   Not that I know of.
FAUTEUX   I would ask you to think about that. It was not an ordinary occurrence, was it?
MAZERALL   No, definitely not. The report was given back to me. I drove with them only a few blocks and dropped them off.
FAUTEUX   They were given back to you in the car?
MAZERALL   Yes.
FAUTEUX   And it was Lunan told you to meet him in the car?
MAZERALL   Yes.
FAUTEUX   And subsequent meetings were held in the car?
MAZERALL   No. These were returned to me and subsequently I had no further meeting with Lunan.
FAUTEUX   You say that was the last meeting you had?
MAZERALL   Yes.
FAUTEUX   On the 24th July?
MAZERALL   No, on the 24th of July I gave him the two documents.
FAUTEUX   And the last meeting was when?
MAZERALL   A couple of days later.
FAUTEUX   And you never had any more meetings?
MAZERALL   That is absolutely true.
FAUTEUX   You never met him, for instance, at the study group?
MAZERALL   It is just possible I may have seen him once after that, but I cannot recall it.
FAUTEUX   I think some time previous in your examination you stated that you

continued the meetings of the study group after having given these reports and you admitted that you met Lunan again?

MAZERALL   I may have.

FAUTEUX   You said that, I believe?

MAZERALL   I could not have been definite about it because I cannot remember. It is entirely possible. There would be no reason for my denying it. Certainly I had no personal meeting with him again. I can say that definitely. I may have seen him in the group, but it was not a personal meeting.

FAUTEUX   And when you say that you may have seen him in the group, he would not speak to you about trying to obtain other information for the Soviet Union?

MAZERALL   Oh, no, in the group there would be no reference to it.

FAUTEUX   There would be no reference to it?

MAZERALL   No, indeed.

FAUTEUX   Why do you say "indeed"?

MAZERALL   Because that would mean that he would have to tell the other people in the group.

FAUTEUX   And you wanted that to be kept secret?

MAZERALL   Oh, yes.

MR. COMMISSIONER KELLOCK   Did you form an idea at any time that other members of the group might be doing the same thing for Mr. Lunan or some other agent of the Soviet Union as you were doing?

MAZERALL   Actually subsequently Smith spoke to me and asked me if Lunan had approached me and I told him he had.

KELLOCK   Subsequent to what?

MAZERALL   To my having given Lunan the reports.

KELLOCK   That is after the 24th July?

MAZERALL   Yes.

KELLOCK   And what else took place in that conversation?

MAZERALL   He wanted to know whether we could get together and procure our information, pool it.

KELLOCK   Organize it a little better?

MAZERALL   Yes. I had nothing to do with it.

KELLOCK   Anything else?

MAZERALL   No, this was a very short conversation as we were passing from one building to another.

KELLOCK   What did you say?

MAZERALL   I cannot recall exactly what I said, except that I did not think that I wanted to. . . .

MR. FAUTEUX   Now, Mr. Mazerall, you have told us in the course of the examination that at the request of Lunan you agreed to give information to the Soviet Union, and before doing so, before accepting the proposition, you told us that you gave some consideration to it. Would you tell us what your motives were? You are free to say if there is any explanation that you wish to offer. You must consider that you are free to give it.

MAZERALL   It is very difficult to put in just so many words what my motives could have been, because after all I have been hearing and reading things about the Soviet Union for the last four years, with the result that — well, I would not say I felt kindly towards them; I felt that they stood first and foremost for peace, and that if they had their way there would not be any wars. Not only that, but I must say that I am a socialist, and that there was a government which was a socialist government and if left entirely to themselves could prove socialism would work.

MR. COMMISSIONER KELLOCK   When you use the word "socialist" do you mean that is the same as "Communist"?

MAZERALL   Frankly, I cannot distinguish between them, sir. I know that the so-called socialist parties and Labour and C.C.F. make a distinction, but I have never been able to see it.

KELLOCK   I interrupted you. Just go ahead?

MAZERALL   Well, as I say, it is very difficult.

KELLOCK   You made an answer a little while ago that it is one thing to act because you thought you could do some good, and another thing to be offered money.

MAZERALL   Well, if you like, it was idealism. As I say, I would like to see this country as a socialist country, because I think under those circumstances everyone has a better chance of living and enjoying life. There have been a great many things said about the Soviet Union in the past which have been disproved during the war. The newspapers have printed things in the past which have contradicted those things, and in general we were realizing to some extent that the Soviet Union is not the vicious place it has been painted. Anything that they could do to make their form of government a success would help make people in this country realize that socialism could work here, too.

I would not for a moment suggest that a form of government which would work in Soviet Russia would necessarily work here. It obviously would not. We have a different environment and a different background, but socialism itself — well, we can have Canadian socialism. It is just that the very term itself has been misconstrued.

KELLOCK   You said something this morning, I think in answer to a question of mine, that you gave these two reports to Lunan because you had put yourself in a position to him under which you thought you had to do something. Is that right?

MAZERALL   Yes.

FAUTEUX   What obligation did you feel?

MAZERALL   For some time I had not been happy in the group of which I was a member.

KELLOCK   That is this third group you have described?

MAZERALL   That is correct. At the same time I saw nothing basically wrong with the ideal. I did not exactly want to leave the organization, but at the same time I did not want to carry on. I was in a dilemma.

KELLOCK   What disturbed you?

MAZERALL   The attitude of the people in the group. I would like to have gone to a meeting and felt that everybody was there for a friendly purpose, to read and study the various things that were brought up, that it was in fact a democratic procedure. But there were some of the members who seemed to feel that it was more of a militant organization, and I could not agree to that. In the homes in which we held the meetings there were numerous interesting books around, and I felt on occasion I would like to pick one up to look at it, only to have one of the other members tell me to put the book down and come to order, which I felt a bit high-handed. Well, I didn't like that, and I made as many excuses as I could not to go to meetings, and as a matter of fact I had not been now for some two or three months. But my attitude towards these people's attitude — it didn't change my basic philosophy. That is what made it difficult, you see.

KELLOCK   You mean, then, that you wanted to show Lunan and his higher-ups that your heart was still in the right place, although you were not attending. Is that it?

MAZERALL   No, I wouldn't say that. If I had told Lunan no, by the same token I would have turned around then and left the group; and although in a way I wanted to do that, that is I didn't like the group itself, nevertheless many of the things that they stood for I felt I concurred with.

KELLOCK   But I am still asking you, what was your obligation that you felt to deliver material to Lunan?

MAZERALL   I don't know. . . .

KELLOCK   That is, that you had an intellectual loyalty to the things that the organization to which you belonged stood for? Is that right?

MAZERALL   You can put it that way very well.

KELLOCK   And that you thought that by complying with the request for information from you or your employers you were furthering the interests of that organization?

MAZERALL   That is right. At the same time I did not like the idea of supplying information. It was not put to me so much that I was supplying information to the Soviet government, either. It was more that as scientists we were pooling information, and I actually asked him if we could hope to find this reciprocal.

KELLOCK   Did you ever have that experience?

MAZERALL   I did not; no.

KELLOCK   Have you ever known of any information of any kind being supplied by Russia?

MAZERALL   Very little.

KELLOCK   Any?

MAZERALL   There has been some, but of what importance it has been I do not know.

KELLOCK   Insignificant, you would think?

MAZERALL   I know of one occasion, as a matter of fact, about a year or two ago, at the proceedings of the Institute of Radio Engineers, we published an article from a Russian journal on the magnitron, which was a tube we use in radar. The date of publication of the original Russian article was sometime in 1942, and I know for a fact that at that time, although we considered ourselves very advanced in the use and design of the magnitron, the report described magnitrons which were in advance of ours. That was published by them in 1942, and presumably made available to us.

KELLOCK   That is the only occasion of the kind that you know anything about, the only instance of the kind?

MAZERALL   Well, no. I have heard described a turbine producing liquid gases; rather a vague description, and the fact that they were burning the coal in their mines rather than mining the coal, by partial combustion of the coal or of the gases from the coal, and making use of them at the head of the mine.

KELLOCK   That was, you say, a vague description?

MAZERALL   Yes. It was not a technical description; it was a general description you might put to a layman.

KELLOCK   And even that got into the newspapers, did it not?

MAZERALL   Yes. Well, as a matter of fact Dyson Carter published a pamphlet called, "Soviet Secret Weapons," in which he describes several Soviet scientific advances. It seemed to me only that anything which might be considered a weapon is not described, but things which would be used in peace —

KELLOCK   Well, Mr. Mazerall, I just want to call this to your attention, and perhaps more for your information than anything; I think perhaps you are entitled to it. There is a document which has been filed here dated March 28, 1945; that would be shortly after you had first come into contact with Lunan, would it not?

MAZERALL   Yes, sir.

FAUTEUX   In which Lunan says this about you: "Bagley." This was at a time when you had a tag on you. Did you know you were called Bagley at that time?

MAZERALL   No, sir.

KELLOCK   He says: "I have been unable to see him as yet. He has not been a very regular or enthusiastic supporter for several months, although he is now showing more enthusiasm. He is living in the country, and his wife is antagonistic to his political participation." Is that true?

MAZERALL   Yes, sir.

KELLOCK   "He strikes me as being somewhat naive politically."

MAZERALL   That might be a good description, too.

KELLOCK   I just thought you might like to know the way Mr. Lunan sized you up before he started to use you. I thought you were entitled to that information, and that is why I have given it to you. It might help you in your thinking. . . .

MR. COMMISSIONER TASCHEREAU   Is it a principle of the Communist party that your first loyalty is due to the Party?

MAZERALL   They might consider it so. I should not.

TASCHEREAU   You considered it that way when you gave those documents to Mr. Lunan?

MAZERALL   No, I don't think I had that in mind when I did it.

TASCHEREAU   But is it the teaching of the Communist party that, being an international party, it has priority over your own country?

MAZERALL   I don't think so. I could never subscribe to that. . . .

TASCHEREAU   When you handed those reports over to Mr. Lunan for transmission to the Russians, to be photographed by the Russians, if you had not done that what did you think as to when that information might otherwise get to the Russian government?

MAZERALL   Whenever it was actually given over to the trade magazines.

TASCHEREAU   Which might be when?

MAZERALL   Oh, we had proposed installing a test demonstration line of this equipment for T.C.A. at the earliest possible chance. That is, we had intended to start perhaps last December.

TASCHEREAU   December of 1945?

MAZERALL   Yes.

TASCHEREAU   So you were giving some four or five months' advance information?

MAZERALL   Possibly it would be that. . . .

THE TESTIMONY OF CAPTAIN DAVID LUNAN

February 28, 1946

CAPTAIN DAVID LUNAN, *called and sworn*

MR. FAUTEUX   When did you arrive in Canada?
LUNAN   I arrived in 1938. . . .

   Lunan worked in advertising in Montreal until January 1943, when he joined the army.

FAUTEUX   And did you stay with the army . . . or were you seconded to an organization, the Wartime Information Board?
LUNAN   In November, 1944, I was seconded to the Wartime Information Board.
FAUTEUX   And how long did you stay with the organization?
LUNAN   Up until the present time. That is to say, it changed its name.
FAUTEUX   To what?
LUNAN   To the Canadian Information Service. . . .
FAUTEUX   And Exhibit No. 60-B; what is the name of that person?
LUNAN   I knew him by the name of Jan.
FAUTEUX   That is Colonel Rogov of the Soviet embassy?
LUNAN   I did not know that.
FAUTEUX   You did not know that, but you knew him as Jan?
LUNAN   That is correct. . . .
FAUTEUX   Exhibit No. 60-A?
LUNAN   I have seen this fellow.
FAUTEUX   You know that he is a Russian, too?
LUNAN   Yes.
FAUTEUX   That is Pavlov?
LUNAN   Yes, that is correct. . . .
FAUTEUX   You told us that you met Fred Rose. How long have you known him?
LUNAN   I must have known him for about three years, I would say. . . .
FAUTEUX   How long have you known Jan, that is Rogov?
LUNAN   Since some time early in 1945. . . .
FAUTEUX   How did you meet him?
LUNAN   I met him as a result of receiving a message for an appointment which I kept and which turned out to be him.
FAUTEUX   What was the form of that message?
LUNAN   As I remember it it was a typewritten slip.
FAUTEUX   What was on it?
LUNAN   I cannot recall exactly what was on it, but it contained the place, the rendezvous, and the means of identifying myself to the person I was to meet.
FAUTEUX   And the means of identifying yourself?
LUNAN   Yes.

FAUTEUX   What was the suggestion as far as that is concerned?

LUNAN   It was a sentence of some kind which I would speak on identification.

FAUTEUX   Where did you meet him?

LUNAN   On the street.

FAUTEUX   Where?

LUNAN   I do not remember the place. . . .

MR. COMMISSIONER KELLOCK   How would you know to whom to address those words?

LUNAN   It was at a certain time and a certain place that I would meet somebody.

KELLOCK   Somebody would speak to you?

LUNAN   I do not remember whether I spoke first or whether he spoke first.

KELLOCK   How would you be able to speak first without having some way of identifying the person to speak to?

LUNAN   I did not have any other identification except the coincidence of time and place.

KELLOCK   Was it such an isolated place that there would not likely be any other person there but yourself and this other person?

LUNAN   It so happened that way. . . .

Lunan described a clandestine meeting arranged by Fred Rose.

LUNAN   When I met him I realized almost immediately that he must be a foreigner and subsequently from some of the things that were said, a Russian.

KELLOCK   Was he in civilian attire?

LUNAN   He was in plain clothes.

KELLOCK   What time of day was it?

LUNAN   It was in the evening, probably around nine o'clock I think.

KELLOCK   Will you tell us about the interview?

LUNAN   After we had identified ourselves we started talking. I may say that I found it very difficult to understand him. He had an extremely heavy accent. He asked questions about myself, what the kind of work was along the lines of writing and my particular job. Then I got the idea from his approach that he seemed to want from me some written commentaries on the Canadian political situation and Canadian life in general. Before we parted he gave me an envelope which he asked me to read. . . .

MR. FAUTEUX   There was a document in it. As soon as you reached your place of residence you read it?

LUNAN   That is right.

FAUTEUX   We will come to that document in a moment. Was there any arrangement as to the next meeting that was to follow?

LUNAN   I think there must have been a verbal agreement to meet him again.

FAUTEUX   At what place?

LUNAN   That I do not remember.

FAUTEUX   But with the same secrecy?

LUNAN   Yes.

FAUTEUX   That existed for the first meeting?

LUNAN   Right.

FAUTEUX   Would it be again at the corner of a street?

204

LUNAN   On a street, anyway.

FAUTEUX   How long did it last?

LUNAN   The first meeting?

FAUTEUX   Yes?

LUNAN   Some twenty minutes or even less.

FAUTEUX   Twenty minutes or even less. You went home after that?

LUNAN   Yes. . . .

FAUTEUX   Do you recognize the first document as being the document that was in the envelope?

LUNAN   That was the document.

FAUTEUX   The document reads: "The scheme of your group will be approximate much as it is shown below." Then there is a sketch starting with Jan, which is Rogov. Then there is Back and "G. Lunan," which is your name. It says "(Back-nickname)". Am I right in saying that that was your cover name?

LUNAN   Yes. I never used that.

FAUTEUX   You never used it, but perhaps some other people did.

LUNAN   I suppose so.

FAUTEUX   Then the next is Ned Mazerall, who is the same person as you have identified in the photograph. His cover name was Bagley. That cover name was used to your knowledge?

LUNAN   Yes.

FAUTEUX   Then on the other side is Isidor [Israel] Halperin, the same person whose picture you identified a moment ago. His cover name is Bacon, and that cover name was used?

LUNAN   Correct.

FAUTEUX   Then there is "Doruforth Smith" which should be "Durnford Smith," and his cover name is Badeau?

LUNAN   Right.

FAUTEUX   Which was used?

LUNAN   Correct.

FAUTEUX   Then it goes on:

You only will know me (as Jan) but nobody else. What we would like you to do:

a. To characterize the scales and works carrying out at National Research and also the scheme of this department.

b. To conduct the work of "Bacon," "Badeau," and "Bagley."

It is advisable to put the following tasks to them separately.

Bagley — to give the models of developed radio-sets, its photographs, technical (data) facts and for what purpose it is intended. Once in three months to write the reports in which to characterize the work of radio department, to inform about the forthcoming tasks and what new kinds of the models are going to be developed.

You have found out that that was radar and not the ordinary radio set that you would have in your home?

LUNAN   I did not know at the time.

FAUTEUX   At a later stage you learned that?

LUNAN   Yes.

FAUTEUX   But when you received the letter you did not know?

LUNAN   That is right.

FAUTEUX

Bacon — to give the organization and characters of Valcartier Explosives establishment's direction. To write the report on subject: "What kind of the work is this organization engaged in?" If possible to pass on the prescription (formulas) of explosives and its samples.

Badeau — to write the report: What kind of the work is his department engaged in and what departments it is in contact with (by work).

All the materials and documents to be passed by Bagley, Bacon and Badeau have to be signed by their nicknames as stated above.

If your group have the documents which you will not be able to give us irrevocably, we shall photograph them and return back to you.

I beg you to instruct every man separately about conspiracy in our work.

In order not to keep their materials (documents) at your place, it is advisable that you receive all their materials (documents) the same day you have the meeting with me.

To answer all the above questions we shall have the meeting on March 28th. "J"

After studying burn it.

That is the document that was given to you in the envelope that night?

LUNAN   That is correct. . . .

FAUTEUX   What did you do after reading that document?

LUNAN   I was very disturbed by it and I did not do anything for some weeks. . . .

FAUTEUX   The next document I want to refer to in this exhibit is a letter dated Ottawa, March 28. There is a heading in Russian on it. This will be marked 17-D for reference. I take it that this was typewritten by you and was your answer to the request made in 17-B?

LUNAN   To the best of my recollection, yes.

FAUTEUX   There is no signature except the word "Back"?

LUNAN   Yes.

FAUTEUX   Which is you, and it has reference to the previous document. There is no doubt about that?

LUNAN   That is right.

FAUTEUX   It was an answer to the instructions that this man Rogov had given to you?

LUNAN   That is right. . . .

FAUTEUX   The document is dated Ottawa, March 28. It reads:

Dear Mother and Father:

General approach to work. Your written instructions are understood and some preliminary work has been accomplished on the specific tasks set. It should be understood that neither Bacon —

That is Halperin.

— Bagley —
That is Mazerall.
— nor Badeau —
Which is Smith.
— are well known to me either personally or politically, nor I to them.

The only one that you have stated who was known to you at the time was Smith, and that was from casual meetings?

LUNAN   That is right.

FAUTEUX   What did you mean when you said, "politically"? Would you make that clear for us right away so that we can continue?

LUNAN   Yes, I think I can put it this way. If I might be said to know, let us say, Hitler politically, I might not know him personally. I know nothing about these three people with the possible exception of Smith, and nothing was indicated to me about the political opinions they might have.

FAUTEUX   But you knew the political opinions of Smith, being a member of that Quebec allied organization?

LUNAN   That is something —

FAUTEUX   And also toward the Russian Communist party and so on?

LUNAN   Excuse me, I would not assume that necessarily of a member of that committee.

FAUTEUX   Not necessarily, but that is what you meant by the word "politically"?

LUNAN   That is correct.

MR. COMMISSIONER KELLOCK   For the purposes of the work that you were about to embark on, political opinions were important?

LUNAN   I would say they were, yes, sir.

KELLOCK   That is, one kind of political opinion?

LUNAN   Political motivation, I would say, yes.

KELLOCK   How would you describe that particular political motivation that was an important qualification?

LUNAN   I would say it would have to be people in very close cooperation with Russia.

KELLOCK   And the Communist party?

LUNAN   Not necessarily, but I think it would be an important factor.

KELLOCK   What would be an important factor?

LUNAN   Some sympathy with the Communist party program, anyway.

KELLOCK   Either membership in or sympathy with that party?

LUNAN   I would say that would be a factor in a man's making a decision.

KELLOCK   So that it was really a necessary qualification for any one of these three to become engaged in the work that was wanted?

LUNAN   I think that is a fair enough analysis.

KELLOCK   I want to be fair with you and I want you to be fair with us. Do you think that is accurate?

LUNAN   I do not know whether it is. I can conceive somebody having highly individualistic ideas or principles which might lead him to do something.

KELLOCK   That is, a person might have highly idealistic ideas, but not so as to the Communist program?

LUNAN   Well, I had not at that time either identified myself holus-bolus with the Communist party program.

KELLOCK   Captain Lunan, can we put it this way: What you had in mind, and that is all we are dealing with, in using that language, was that you apparently had no views in connection with those three people but that their political opinions were important in the first place? Is that right?

LUNAN   Yes.

KELLOCK   And that you also had in mind that their political opinions should either be as full members of the Communist party, in the first place, or at least be sympathetic with the purposes of the Communist party? . . .

LUNAN   I would answer it in two ways. One is, if a man were a Fascist, certainly knowing that about his political views, he would be out of the question. The other way is this, that I believe a person could sincerely and with full conviction believe in very close cooperation with the Soviet Union while not necessarily cleaving to Communist party lines.

KELLOCK   As you saw it at that time, the Communist party was the one that was cleaving most closely to the interests of the Soviet Union?

LUNAN   Yes, most closely, but I do not think by any means they were alone.

KELLOCK   Well, shortly, could we put it this way: In the language of Gilbert and Sullivan, you were not looking for a little Liberal or a little Conservative, you were looking for someone sympathetic with the Communist party?

LUNAN   Something like that.

MR. FAUTEUX   You understood the importance of that phrase because there is no reference whatever in the first exhibit, in your instructions, as to the political feelings of the people, what they were to be?

LUNAN   That is right.

FAUTEUX   That is a thought that you had yourself, that in view of the importance of the work, the nature of the work that these people were to be entrusted with, it was necessary for you to ascertain their political beliefs?

LUNAN   That is correct.

FAUTEUX   "Progress has been held up somewhat owing to one or other of them being out of town." Who was out of town?

LUNAN   I think Smith was out of town.

FAUTEUX   "— and by the caution displayed by Badeau —" That is Smith?

LUNAN   Yes.

FAUTEUX   "— (a good thing probably)" — you thought caution was needed to a certain extent?

LUNAN   I cannot deny that. . . .

FAUTEUX   I am continuing to quote from Exhibit 17: "They already feel the need for maintaining a very high degree of security and taking abnormal precautions at their normal meetings (about once in two weeks), since they are definitely not labelled with any political affiliation."

MR. COMMISSIONER KELLOCK   I should like to ask a question there. What did you mean by that, Captain?

LUNAN   As I understood it, one or two of these fellows were getting together for the purpose of political discussion; and owing to the nature of their professional work they would not want publicly to associate themselves with political

208

discussion groups, because it might reflect badly on their professional standards, and integrity.

KELLOCK   You mean Communist political discussion groups?

LUNAN   I had no indication that it was that.

KELLOCK   Why, if I were an engineer, would it be necessary for me, if I got together with somebody else to study the principles of conservatism — that does not make sense to me. Did you really have in mind that these people did not want anybody to know that they had Communist leanings, to put it shortly?

LUNAN   Yes, I think it is fair to deduce that; but here I simply interpret something which was not my reasoning. . . .

KELLOCK   I am asking you if you are not saying there that these people did not want it known that they were meeting with other Communists or people with Communist leanings; they wanted to keep that secret?

LUNAN   Yes.

KELLOCK   That is what you are saying?

LUNAN   Yes.

MR. FAUTEUX   "One or two have even opposed the introduction of new members to our group on the grounds that it would endanger their own security." Who did oppose that?

LUNAN   I don't know. This was an opinion which I had from Smith.

MR. COMMISSIONER KELLOCK   And what do you mean by, "our group"?

LUNAN   I am using the "our" there as far as this fellow Jan was concerned. He knew these people; and using it as simply showing my connection with them.

KELLOCK   You were a member of a little group at that time, were you not?

LUNAN   Not to my knowledge.

KELLOCK   Did you later become a member of a little group?

LUNAN   No.

KELLOCK   We have had some evidence that you were?

LUNAN   I have been thinking about that. I did on two occasions, I think accompany Smith to houses, but there was nothing about what I took to be a social gathering which would indicate that it was a discussion group of any kind. . . .

KELLOCK   There had not been any suggestion, up until this date, March 28, 1945, about new members of the group; and Exhibit 17-B, which sets out this group that you refer to as just Jan, yourself, Mazerall, Halperin and Durnford Smith. There was not any suggestion up to that time, when you wrote this letter of March 28, in answer to the one you got from Jan, about new members of the group. Can that refer to that group? Can it refer to a group which was already in existence before Jan met you?

LUNAN   That is what I assume.

KELLOCK   You are the man who used the language, "our group," and I am asking you what was that group?

LUNAN   Well, I think first of all the language is rather sloppily used. As far as I was concerned, in Jan's eyes I was identified with these people in a group.

KELLOCK   That is, from something said or what took place, you recognized that Jan regarded you and Smith and the others as already belonging to a group with similar ideas?

LUNAN   That is right.

KELLOCK   And would that have been a correct appraisal on his part?

LUNAN   I had been asked, if I remember rightly, by Smith when I first came to Ottawa whether I was interested in joining some discussion group, and told him not. For one thing I was working very busily, and I did not have any particular interest in it or any time.

Looking back, and trying to reconstruct the events, which I must admit became quite foggy to me afterwards, maybe as the result of a psychological reaction, I do not know — I can remember my first meeting with Smith, which was at dinner at his house, afterwards going out for a walk and dropping in, as it seemed to me on the spur of the moment, and joining a group of people, certainly in a house, with all the appearances of a social gathering, in so far as tea and coffee were being served. There was no cohesive discussion or conversation. People were talking in groups. . . .

MR. FAUTEUX   "I therefore believe it wise to approach them carefully and not to advance too great an assignment to them at one time. Also, for the time being, not to characterize the work for what it is, but merely to let it be understood that it is work of a special conspiratorial nature, without mentioning my connection with you." Were you referring there to Halperin, Mazerall and Smith?

LUNAN   That is right.

FAUTEUX   "If I read your instructions correctly —" that is, the instructions that appeared in the document where there is a sketch, the first one exhibited to you?

LUNAN   Yes.

FAUTEUX   "— you assumed that I would discuss the situation frankly with each separately. This I have not done. But I would like to discuss this aspect with you. Another slight resistance to be overcome is the strong sense of security about their work that these men have developed as war scientists." You are always referring to the same men?

LUNAN   Yes.

FAUTEUX   To Smith, Halperin and Mazerall?

LUNAN   Yes.

FAUTEUX   "We have experienced a little difficulty (which we shall, however, overcome, I believe) in making our initial arrangements to meet. There are several reasons for this. Bagley —" That is Mazerall?

LUNAN   Yes.

FAUTEUX   "— lives quite far out of town in the country and is dependent on train schedules. Badeau —" that is Smith, "— lives at the furthest end of Hull and works during the day out of town and out of reach at lunch times and other times convenient to me. My house is out of the question for meeting (and typing) purposes as I have two others living with me. We shall probably solve these difficulties as we gain practice in the work."

Then it goes on: "The following notes describe in detail progress made with each individual on each task set."

MR. COMMISSIONER KELLOCK   (To Mr. Fauteux)   What is that?

FAUTEUX   That is on the back of the page.   (To the witness)

Badeau: Warmed up slowly to my requests and remained non-committal until he had checked independently on my bona fides. Once satisfied, he promised to co-operate. He is preparing the report on his department as requested, *also* a full report on organization and personnel, interlocking departments, etc., of [National Research Council] plus any other information he thinks useful. These reports are promised to me for April 9. I am unable to get them any sooner.

So at that date you had seen Smith?

LUNAN   Yes.

FAUTEUX   And the facts that are mentioned there, as to his state of mind and his willingness, are true, are they?

LUNAN   Yes. I would like to say this, however, that there is considerable discrepancy between the optimism, if you like, of my report here and the actual state of mind of these individuals. In other words, I think it was a natural thing for me to be as optimistic as possible in making the report.

FAUTEUX   Why?

LUNAN   Well, I suppose simply to try and appear to have done better and more than possibly I had done.

FAUTEUX   Why would you want that?

LUNAN   Well, it is hard to say exactly why, except that if I were doing a job I would like to be considered to be doing it well.

MR. COMMISSIONER KELLOCK   And why would you want to misrepresent what you were doing?

LUNAN   Well, everybody tries to put the best possible light on whatever they are doing.

KELLOCK   That is true. . . .

MR. FAUTEUX   "Discussing the work of N.D.C. [N.R.C.] in general, Badeau informs me that most secret work at present is on nuclear physics (bombardment of radio-active substances to produce energy). This is more hush-hush than radar —" "Hush-hush" means more secret, I suppose?

LUNAN   Yes.

FAUTEUX   "— and is being carried on at University of Montreal and at McMaster University at Hamilton. Badeau thinks that government purchase of radium producing plant is connected with this research. In general, he claims to know of no new developments in radar, except in minor improvements in its application." These points you had discussed with Smith at the time?

LUNAN   That is right.

FAUTEUX   And the information you were conveying there to Colonel Rogov you actually had from Durnford Smith?

LUNAN   Correct.

MR. COMMISSIONER KELLOCK   Captain Lunan, in connection with what you said a moment ago about "putting the best face on" your report, you say here, under the heading Badeau: "Once satisfied, he promised to co-operate." Is that true?

LUNAN   I think that would be true.

KELLOCK   Then you go on: "He is preparing a report on his department as requested —" Is that right?

LUNAN   Yes.

KELLOCK   Then you continue, "— also a full report on organization and personnel, interlocking departments, etc., of N.D.C. [N.R.C.] plus any other information he thinks useful.'' Is that right?

LUNAN   Yes, except I don't think he ever did that.

KELLOCK   But it was true when you said it?

LUNAN   It was true when I said it.

KELLOCK   Then you go on: "These reports are promised to me for April 9." Is that right?

LUNAN   Yes; it must have been.

MR. COMMISSIONER TASCHEREAU   But who gave you that information about Badeau in there, because you had not seen Badeau then?

LUNAN   Oh, yes.

MR. FAUTEUX   I intend to come to that.

TASCHEREAU   You told me you had seen only Smith?

LUNAN   That is Badeau.

TASCHEREAU   Oh, yes; I am sorry.

MR. FAUTEUX   When I am through with this letter I intend to come to the first meeting with each one of these, and the circumstances and so on. Then we come now to Bacon, that is Isidor [Israel] Halperin, of whom you identified a photograph?

LUNAN   Correct.

FAUTEUX   You say, "I received an excellent report on Bacon, and approached him more frankly than the others." Who gave you the report on Bacon?

LUNAN   Smith.

FAUTEUX   "He seems anxious to be of help. His attitude is that most of the so-called secret work is a joke, and while it is officially on the secret list, those working on it can see no reason for secrecy. He undertook to provide the information requested on Valcartier." That was the one that was mentioned in the letter of instruction that you had received?

LUNAN   That is right.

FAUTEUX   And it is right to say that Halperin did make that undertaking, to get that information?

LUNAN   Yes. . . .

FAUTEUX   "He suggested that I obtain it direct from his chief in my official capacity —" That is in your capacity or through your connection with the Canadian Information Service?

LUNAN   That is right.

FAUTEUX   "— but I advised him that this was not wise as I do not wish to show any official interest in this field until and unless we decide to do an article on it. He claims there is no particular secrecy about the set-up, but I persuaded him to give me the whole report on the matter." That was about the whole set-up of the National Research Council organization?

LUNAN   No, I think you are mistaken there. Was that not Valcartier?

FAUTEUX   Oh, yes; that is right. (continues) "I did not mention formulae and samples at this meeting, as I don't think Bacon is sufficiently impressed with the conspiratorial nature of the work as yet. But he is definitely keen and will be helpful. I shall see Bacon again on April 2 to hear about his report and to take up our request with him further. He travels a good deal, which complicates our arrangements for meeting.'' All that you say here in relation to Bacon is true, is it not?

LUNAN   Yes. It is definitely true at the time, although my judgment may have changed later. . . .

February 28, 1946.

CAPTAIN DAVID LUNAN, *recalled*

MR. FAUTEUX   The first report that you made is the one dated March 28th and marked 17-D. In that same exhibit there is another document dated April 18, 1945, which will be marked as 17-E. I take it that that was also typewritten by you?

LUNAN   It was.

FAUTEUX   At the same place, in your office and on the same typewriter?

LUNAN   I believe so. . . .

FAUTEUX   "There is relatively little progress to report since last time because of a series of unfavourable circumstances which have made continuous liaison with my people impossible.'' When you say "with my people'' do you refer to the persons mentioned, that is, Mazerall, Smith and Halperin?

LUNAN   I do.

FAUTEUX   And when you refer to "unfavourable circumstances,'' what were those circumstances?

LUNAN   As I recall it, I had a great deal of work on my own part to do and I think also some of those people were themselves either busy or out of town or otherwise not available.

FAUTEUX   "As you will have realized, I was out of town for several days last week and was unable to keep my appointment.'' You had an appointment the week before with him?

LUNAN   No, I did not.

FAUTEUX   Did you have one the week before which you missed?

LUNAN   I must have had one the week before this was written.

FAUTEUX   "Bacon was away from work for several days with a cold. It was inadvisable to see him at his home to discuss matters with him, although I did visit him there once to receive a report from him.'' What report was that? Was it a report dealing with the tasks that had been assigned to him previously?

LUNAN   Yes.

FAUTEUX   And you obtained a report from him?

LUNAN   I believe I did.

FAUTEUX   On those tasks.   (*continues*)   "Badeau also made a trip to Toronto during the one week when I was in town and relatively free to see him, and for the following week he was detained late at the office (laboratory) working on a special rush experiment. The prospect for myself over the next few weeks isn't any brighter, unfortunately. The announcement of the elections, earlier than expected by us —'' You refer to the federal elections?

LUNAN   I do.

FAUTEUX   Which took place in June, 1945? . . . "The announcement of the elections, earlier than expected by us, has involved me in a great deal of rush work which will keep me in Montreal all next week."

LUNAN   That was work in connection with my job.

FAUTEUX

This work, of course, has to be given priority; but it seems that the time available for seeing my people is very severely cut into — especially when they might be busy on those times when I am free.

This is not a very bright picture for the progress of our work. But it is the circumstances in which we find ourselves, and it is only to be hoped that work will ease up soon. Incidentally, I suggest that Jan's call to my office was not strictly necessary, since we already had the arrangement that the meeting would take place three days later if for any reason either party failed to turn up. However, it had this advantage, that it tested out the system of calling on the telephone, which was quite successful.

Will you explain that?

LUNAN   Yes. To the best of my recollection, if I was to receive a telephone call from Jan during which he would ask me questions which I seem to remember had something to do with the publication date of my magazine, that would indicate he wanted to see me.

FAUTEUX   And would it indicate the time and place of meeting?

LUNAN   It must have because I had no definite place of meeting.

FAUTEUX   How could it suggest the place and the hour of meeting just by asking that question?

LUNAN   I think it would be that the next meeting would have been previously arranged and the effect of this telephone call would be to advance it.

FAUTEUX   It would be advanced a week?

LUNAN   It would be advanced to the day following the telephone conversation.

MR. COMMISSIONER KELLOCK   The next day following the telephone conversation?

LUNAN   As I remember it, that was it.

MR. FAUTEUX   At the same time and place?

LUNAN   Yes.

MR. COMMISSIONER KELLOCK   Did you have a regular meeting place?

LUNAN   No, I did not.

MR. FAUTEUX   "Reporting in general on the work done since last meeting: 'Bacon has given considerable thought to my original requests and has given me the material for the attached report. He offers to fill in any details that may be asked for if he can. I have not had the opportunity to ask him about payment'." What is that referring to?

LUNAN   From time to time during my meetings with Jan he was very pressing in the matter of offering money for this work. I certainly did not want to accept money for other people unless they knew about it and I felt I should at least ask them about it.

FAUTEUX   You say there, "Bacon has given considerable thought to my original requests and has given me the material for the attached report." What material did that refer to?

214

LUNAN   Material presumably about the explosives organization.

FAUTEUX   That would be the various formulae of explosives and the samples mentioned in the previous instructions?

LUNAN   No, there were no samples and no formulae.

FAUTEUX   You refer to the attached report. . . . We may as well examine that report. That is headed:

Bacon's Report. Bacon has been personally responsible to a large extent for the preliminary work in connection with organizing C.A.R.D.E. (Canadian Army Research Division, Explosives). This is an organization which is in process of being created. It will have both civilian and military personnel, but will be administered by the Army. It is intended to be integrated with the various arsenals in Canada — at least two of which will probably be maintained permanently after the war.

That was the report you had from Halperin?

LUNAN   That is right.

FAUTEUX   On your request. Then these words follow: "CARDE will contain the following: A. Pilot explosives plant. This is being built by, and controlled by, National Research Council, but with Army funds. The chemical branch of NRC will have very little or nothing to do with it." The "NRC" refers to National Research Council?

LUNAN   Yes.

FAUTEUX   "It will have a large capacity and will be capable of experimental work with new explosives, both HE and propellents." What does "HE" stand for?

LUNAN   High explosive.

FAUTEUX   That is what Bacon told you?

LUNAN   Correct.

FAUTEUX

It is not yet being operated; will be taken over by CARDE when completed. Probable director will be Englishman, Harold J. Poole, who is now Acting Director. He is a permanent civil servant in the explosives field. Said to be slow as an organizer and executive, but a competent technician. Bacon believes that this plant can be of tremendous importance and can improve production methods to meet changing needs. Canadian raw material situation very good.

MR. COMMISSIONER KELLOCK   The words "Englishman, Harold J. Poole" are underlined in ink. Did you do that underlining?

LUNAN   I did not.

KELLOCK   That apparently must have been done by the same hand that wrote the Russian heading on the document?

LUNAN   That is a fair assumption, I would say.

MR. FAUTEUX

(Bacon gave some information on present explosives plants and their capacity. This is probably well known. Can produce information if desired.)

Ballistics laboratory. Under direction of Dr. Laidler. This is the only part of the overall project which is at present in operation. This section is working with the Department of Chemistry at Toronto University in experimenting with a variety of new propellents. They are using a new propellent DINA mixed with RDX as a component in propellents. DINA is intended as an alternative to nitroglycerine. Americans are said to be very interested in one of these new propellents called Albanite. This is a propellent containing DINA and picrite as an alternative to the standard British propellent containing nitroglycerine and picrite.

That information was also given to you by Bacon?

LUNAN   That is correct.

MR. COMMISSIONER KELLOCK   That is, Halperin gave you that information and you wrote it down?

LUNAN   I made notes.

MR. FAUTEUX   What is RDX?

LUNAN   RDX, as far as I know, is an explosive.

FAUTEUX   Can you give any more particulars about it?

LUNAN   No. . . .

FAUTEUX

C. Designs Branch. This will be mostly for designing small ordnance and will include a pilot plant.

D. Field Trials Wing. This will do the work which is now being done at Suffield and Valcartier by the Inspection Board of United Kingdom and Canada. They have a good scientific [team] and do a good job of analysing faults and difficulties of manufacture.

Eventually the organization will consist of A, B, C and D. Dr. Don Chase (an NRC physicist) has already been appointed as Superintendent of CARDE. He will be responsible to the Director of Artillery (Colonel W.E. van Steemberg) who is a biologist and who will in turn be responsible to the Master General of Ordnance. Eventually there will probably be a committee comprising representatives of the three services.

Bacon emphasizes: The importance of CARDE in controlling factory production.

What did he say about that?

LUNAN   That is all.

FAUTEUX   "The laying down of a skeleton armaments research centre which could be taken over by the British in the future if it became necessary. It could take on assignments, and now has some on which to work." That was the report given to you by Halperin as a consequence of a previous request made to him by you, as you had previously yourself been requested by Rogov?

LUNAN   By Jan, yes.

FAUTEUX   Which is Rogov?

LUNAN   Yes, so I understand; you told me.

FAUTEUX   You have identified his picture. I continue with page 1 of 17-E:

Badeau was very disturbed when I brought up the subject of payment. I

216

think he felt that it brought the subject of his work into a different (and more conspiratorial) focus. He was to think it over and let me know, but we have had no opportunity to meet since I was in Montreal in the interim. He is very slow in giving me any information, largely because he actually has no time to sit down and make a report. He offered me the printed report of the Research Council, but I assume that all this information is known or can be readily obtained from a government library. The latest report he could get was also considerably out of date.

When you say that he offered you a printed report, what was the subject of that report?

LUNAN   I think it was the schema of the Research Council organization, the diagram.

FAUTEUX   And he gave you that as a result of a request you made to him?

LUNAN   (No audible answer.)

MR. COMMISSIONER KELLOCK   The witness said that Smith offered it to him, but he did not take it.

LUNAN   I did not take it. . . .

MR. FAUTEUX   "He reported to me in words the general details of his own work. He is in the radio engineering end of things, specializing in radar. Current work, on which there was an emergency rush last week, is in connection with a battleship radar device for use in the Pacific. This is an extremely sensitive detecting device which has been successfully tried out on the east coast." You knew that through Smith?

LUNAN   He told me, yes.

FAUTEUX   "Present work is the designing and construction of a pilot model. Badeau has been largely responsible for this. Possibly there are questions which could be asked about this, as Badeau is a very difficult person to pin down to detail." Whatever information Smith gave you as far as radar was concerned was a result of a previous request from you to him?

LUNAN   A general request.

FAUTEUX   A general request which appeared in the instructions?

LUNAN   Yes.

FAUTEUX   Which were given in the envelope by Rogov to you?

LUNAN   Correct.

FAUTEUX   And which has been referred to as Exhibit No. 17-B. There the reference is to radio, but in fact everybody understood it as meaning radar?

LUNAN   I personally did not understand it until I had spoken to Smith.

FAUTEUX   But Smith understood it?

LUNAN   Presumably; that was his work.

FAUTEUX   That is what he gave you?

LUNAN   That is correct.

FAUTEUX   And what you gave Rogov in turn?

LUNAN   Correct.

FAUTEUX   Was Rogov satisfied with that information when he got it?

LUNAN   Since it was given to him in this form he did not read it in my presence and I do not know.

FAUTEUX   "It has still been impossible to see Bagley and introduce him to his assignment. As I pointed out before, since I know very little of this person, it is my plan to become better acquainted with him and get some idea of his readiness for work of this kind. The time, however, has been quite beyond me as yet. With regard to biographies:'' Those were requested also?

LUNAN   Yes.

FAUTEUX

Both Badeau and Bacon have promised to provide biographical notes. I was to have received these on Monday, but could not keep my appointments, being out of town. Will obtain them for next time. Badeau is married, with two children — about six and six months old. He is about 33 years old and before joining the Research Council worked in the Research Department of the Bell Telephone Company at Montreal. He is a graduate electrical engineer.

Did you know that by him or did you have previous knowledge of that? If you had previous knowledge, did you confirm that?

LUNAN   I had previously known he was working in the Engineering Department of the Bell Telephone Company and he confirmed that to me.

FAUTEUX   "Bacon is a man of about 35, married and with two children and a third on the way. He is a professor of mathematics at Queen's University, Kingston, and intends to go back to that work after the war. He is at present a major in the artillery." All this information you gave to Rogov?

LUNAN   In this form, yes.

MR. COMMISSIONER KELLOCK   This document is the document you typed?

LUNAN   It is the original copy; I would take it to be so.

KELLOCK   You made only one? There is no copy?

LUNAN   That is correct. . . .

KELLOCK   Did you know what you wanted from Bacon? Did you give it to him in written form?

LUNAN   Yes, on several occasions I did.

MR. FAUTEUX   Perhaps if we referred to another page in the same file which will be marked 17-G. That is in Russian. The translation reads:

Assignment No. 1. Given to Back's group (Research).
Given 8-6-45.
Bacon: Give instructions (specifications) for any other kind of material on the electro-projector (the V-bomb).
Write out what new research work is being carried on and what is the latest right now and the question of explosive materials and artillery armament.

Then in the margin it says:

About the points.
1. He promised to obtain it for the next time.
Has no facts whatsoever.

Would that assignment or task be the one referred to in your report of 5th July?

"With regard to the general question on explosive development, he assured me that he has nothing to add to his former report."

Would that be the former report?

LUNAN   That could be.

FAUTEUX   "He is himself curious about the Chalk River plant and the manufacture of uranium." What is the Chalk River plant?

LUNAN   As I now know, it is the atomic fission plant.

MR. COMMISSIONER KELLOCK   What did you know about it at that time?

LUNAN   Simply a plant.

KELLOCK   Who had mentioned it to you, Rogov or Bacon?

LUNAN   I do not think so; I do not remember who had.

MR. FAUTEUX   You evidently discussed the matter because you say, "He is himself curious about the Chalk River plant and the manufacture of uranium." Who else was curious about it at the time?

LUNAN   I presume Jan was.

MR. COMMISSIONER KELLOCK   Do you remember from your dealings with Jan that he was curious about it?

LUNAN   I cannot remember the occasion, but he was curious, yes.

KELLOCK   You remember the fact?

LUNAN   Yes.

KELLOCK   He wanted you to look up that matter?

LUNAN   He must have asked me to, yes.

MR. FAUTEUX

He claims that there is a great deal of talk and speculation on the subject, but that nothing is known outside of the small and carefully guarded group completely in the know. He emphasized that he himself is as remote from this type of information as I am myself. His work is at a virtual standstill; and in any case, his work has been mostly in the field of development (field improvements) on ordnance, and not in the realm of explosives research. He maintains that there is a distinct division between research and development. He expects his work to cease fairly soon, and wants to go back to teaching. This fellow is a mathematician and not a chemist or physicist, which may account for his remoteness from the details of explosives research. I shall continue to see him but he gave me definitely no encouragement last time.

The facts you state about Bacon, they were true?

LUNAN   True, yes. . . .

FAUTEUX   I exhibit to you a photostat of a copy which is Exhibit No. 27. You will recognize your handwriting on that document?

LUNAN   It looks like my writing.

FAUTEUX   If you will look at the typewritten copy of what appears to be a report I will read it to you. Do you recognize that that is a photostat copy of a report that you gave to Rogov?

LUNAN   I do. . . .

FAUTEUX   This reads:

Badeau. Badeau continues to be agreeable to our arrangement but is extremely cautious and takes a long time to commit himself to any course of action. I hope you can understand the enclosed scientific explanation of his work, which is beyond my limited knowledge of the subject. He encloses a biography and a photograph.

The most important thing about Badeau is that he is willing to apply for a position in the new nuclear physics set-up located at McGill University, Montreal. It's considered quite natural that he should apply for this work, as he is qualified in this branch of science. He knows nothing about how it is organized, but says that it is of the highest secrecy. A very careful check-up of personnel is involved. I have encouraged him to apply but have also advised him to be extremely careful of his associations during the period of check-up. I do not think it advisable that I see him for several weeks after he makes application.

When you say there that Badeau encloses a biography and a photograph you are referring to the photograph which you identified this morning and which was filed as Exhibit No. 18?

LUNAN   I take it that was it, yes.

FAUTEUX   And as far as the biography is concerned, if you will look at Exhibit 18, you have there in Russian on the first page, which will be marked for further reference as 18-B, the reference or what purports to be the biography of Badeau, as follows. This is the English translation:

REGISTRATION CARD
1. Last name, given name and patronymic — Daruforth Smith
2. Pseudonym — ''Badeau''
3. Length of time in net —
4. Address
   (a) Business —
   (b) Home — (Ottawa) 3-3870, 145 Ste. Marie (Hull)
5. Place of service and duties — Scientific research, Research Council, Radio Division, Scientific assistant engineer.
6. Material agreement — (financial) — Week. Receives around $300 a month. Needs periodic help.

Detailed biographical information — Is 33 years old. Has two children, one six years, other six months. By profession, radio engineer. Worked in the Scientific Council of the Bell Telephone Company in Montreal. At present time works in the Scientific Research Council in Ottawa. He is member of the ''Labour Progressive Party''. He takes an active part in its work. Very sympathetic to us. Has a great desire to work for us.

That material, I take it, was built up substantially on the biography that Smith had supplied, and to which you referred in this Exhibit No. 27?

LUNAN   I did not read that biography, I can only assume that it contributed to that information now.

FAUTEUX   And the picture is already there?

LUNAN   Yes.

220

FAUTEUX   You also say, in Exhibit 27: "Have encouraged him to apply, but have also advised him to be extremely careful of his associations during the period of check-up." What associations were you referring to, and what advice did you give to Smith in that behalf?

LUNAN   As I recall this whole incident, I was discussing with him, that is with Smith, what his work would be after the war. I was not discussing it at the time in any relation to this business here. He was not a Ph.D., but he was very anxious to earn a Ph.D., and he told me that the branch of science which interested him most and in which he had some knowledge was nuclear physics. It was on the basis of that conversation I had with Smith that I incorporated the details as read in that report.

MR. COMMISSIONER KELLOCK   Was that one of your early conversations with Smith, after your first meeting with Rogov?

LUNAN   Yes, it was one of the early ones.

MR. FAUTEUX   And what particular associations were you referring to?

LUNAN   Political associations.

FAUTEUX   You mean his association with the study groups, and so on?

LUNAN   Yes.

FAUTEUX   Perhaps we would do better to refer to Exhibit 32-A to get a better understanding of that point. It reads as follows. This is the translation of the Russian note there. It is headed, "Back's Group."

Bacon (Translator's note: — The first four lines on this page are translated from the English at the bottom of photostat. There is no English original to conform with the rest of page marked 1). The following is the English translation from the Russian.

It has become very difficult to work with him especially after my request about Ur 235.

Do you remember that you asked Bacon about this?

LUNAN   Yes.

FAUTEUX   About U-235?

LUNAN   Yes.

FAUTEUX   At the request of Rogov?

LUNAN   Yes.

FAUTEUX   "He said that it is absolutely impossible to get it, as far as he knows." Did Halperin say that to you?

LUNAN   He did.

FAUTEUX

Thus for example, he advised that probably there is not any appreciable quantity. Bacon explained to me the theory of atomic energy, which is probably known to you. He refuses to write anything and does not wish to give a photograph or information about himself. I think that at present he appreciates the gist of my requests more fully and he does not like them very much. With that kind of thoughts, which he has, it is impossible to get anything from him, excepting oral descriptions and I am not in a position to understand everything fully where this touches technical details. I asked him what is involved in the building of a very large plant (Chalk River near Petawawa, Ontario) in general opinion, the principle of which is based on the physical characteristics of the atom, in connection with his expressed opinion that Uran 235 was impossible to obtain. He replied that he does not know. He thought that the project was still in the experimental stage.

Then he described to me the general principles of the electron shell and the bomb detonator, which are being produced in the plants in the U.S.A. and Canada, which is the reason for the accurate fire of destruction of rocket bombs (V-bombs).

Did Halperin tell you that?

LUNAN   He did, to the best of my recollection.

FAUTEUX   And you gave that information to Rogov?

LUNAN   Yes.

FAUTEUX   "It has the form of a small transmitter of high frequency, the ray of which is reflected from the target. When the power of the reflected wave in opposition to the rayed frequency reaches a definite strength the battle (destructive) charge is exploded electrically. I asked him if it would be possible to obtain instructions for it, he replied that that would be possible." Is that true?

LUNAN   I don't think so.

FAUTEUX   Did he reply that?

LUNAN   No.

FAUTEUX   "I was not able to extract anything in other ways. In conclusion, Bacon (took the position) announced that he will talk with me but he will not write anything whatsoever — " Is that right?

LUNAN   That is correct.

FAUTEUX   "— and I do not think that he is ready to begin to work more deeply, as for example — to obtain samples (specimens). He says that he does not know anything but what is already known to you." Did he say that to you?

LUNAN   Yes. These words seem strange to me, because I imagine they are a translation; but they are substantially correct.

FAUTEUX   So would you say that the substance of what is related in Exhibit 32-A is right?

LUNAN   The substance is right.

FAUTEUX   So at the request of Rogov you had obtained and given some sort of information from Halperin in regard to the Chalk River plant?

LUNAN   Yes.

FAUTEUX   And U-235?

LUNAN   Yes.

FAUTEUX   And atomic energy and V-bombs?

LUNAN   Yes. Atomic energy was not mentioned as such.

FAUTEUX   How was it mentioned?

LUNAN   It was not mentioned at all. The only mention was of U-235, out of a discussion of which arose mention of atomic energy, and the theory of atomic energy.

FAUTEUX   That came in. You learned that through your discussion with Halperin?

LUNAN   That is correct.

FAUTEUX   And through the requests that were made to you by Rogov?

LUNAN   They led to that. Yes.

FAUTEUX   So the expression was used at that time, at some stage?

LUNAN   At some stage it was.

FAUTEUX   At some stage of the conversation which was carried on at both ends?

LUNAN   Yes.

FAUTEUX   Did Rogov tell you he was very interested in that?

LUNAN   No, he did not.

FAUTEUX   But did you find that he was?

LUNAN   No. He discouraged me from persuading Smith to do anything about it himself.

FAUTEUX   What about Bacon?

LUNAN   And the same for him.

MR. COMMISSIONER KELLOCK   What did you take from that?

LUNAN   I did not know. I simply — I reported that to Smith. However, I think Smith was primarily interested in what he considered to be a good field of science for himself, and I think he retained his own discretion and judgment on that subject.

KELLOCK   But Rogov, previous to discouraging you, had shown an interest in that subject?

LUNAN   Yes, starting with the mention of U-235.

KELLOCK   And as you told us earlier, he asked you to look up that subject?

LUNAN   That is right.

KELLOCK   Through these sub-agents of yours?

LUNAN   That is right.

KELLOCK   And you did so?

LUNAN   And I questioned them about it.

KELLOCK   And at a later stage Rogov discouraged you from proceeding further along that line.

LUNAN   That is right.

KELLOCK   Presumably he had a little better source of information?

LUNAN   I don't know.

KELLOCK   He did not tell you?

LUNAN   He did not tell me.

KELLOCK   And before he discouraged you, you had reported to Rogov that Smith was trying to get himself into this nuclear physics establishment at McGill?

LUNAN   That is right.

MR. FAUTEUX   Now I refer you to Exhibit 17, to the third page, which will be marked 17-H, which is translated "Contents of meeting." I will read this:

Urgent call by telephone.
a. Dial 9-7621 and the question is Lieutenant Lunan.
b. After this, Brent asks "Can you tell me when your next magazine will be published?"
This will mean that the meeting will take place on the following day at 21:00 at the regular meeting place.

Is that the signal to which you have referred previously?

LUNAN   It is.

FAUTEUX   In the course of your evidence?

LUNAN   It is.

FAUTEUX   And dial 9-7621 is your telephone number?

LUNAN   It was at that time.

FAUTEUX   And that was made for urgent calls?

LUNAN   That was the arrangement. . . .

FAUTEUX   Then:

1. A meeting to get acquainted took place on the corner of [King] Edward Avenue and Daly at 21:00. Everything was normal. Regular (meeting) — 28-3-45
Time — 21:00
Place — Corner Driveway and Lewis.

Do you remember that meeting?

LUNAN   Yes, I remember it vaguely.

FAUTEUX   That would be March 20, possibly one of the first meetings you had?

LUNAN   Yes.

FAUTEUX   Then the next one:

2. 28-3-45 Regular (meeting). Everything normal.
Regular (meeting) — 18-4-45
Emergency — 21-4-45
Time — 21:00
Place — Corner Waverley and Macdonald.

Apparently that was an emergency meeting. Do you remember what that was about?

LUNAN   No, I do not. There was only one meeting.

MR. COMMISSIONER KELLOCK   What do you mean, there was only one meeting? You mean one meeting in April?

LUNAN   Yes.

MR. FAUTEUX   At the corner of Waverley and Macdonald?

LUNAN   That is right.

FAUTEUX   Then: "3. 18-4-45 Regular (meeting). Everything normal." Do you remember that meeting?

LUNAN   I think I understand this annotation. If a meeting were not — if neither party turned up to a meeting, it was assumed that three days later that meeting would take place.

MR. COMMISSIONER KELLOCK   Then interpreting that, and talking about the meeting marked "28-3-45" that date was set for the next regular meeting after you had met him the first time?

LUNAN   That is so.

KELLOCK   And then when you met him on the 28th of March, the next regular meeting was set for April 18?

LUNAN   Yes.

KELLOCK   But if for any reason that miscarried, you would understand that you were to meet him on April 21?

LUNAN   That is right.

KELLOCK   The idea was to keep down communication between you and Rogov to a minimum?

LUNAN   I think that was the idea.

MR. FAUTEUX   You are sure?

LUNAN   Yes.

MR. COMMISSIONER KELLOCK   When I say "communication," that is as far as arranging meetings was concerned?

LUNAN   Yes.

KELLOCK   So they would be kept secret?

LUNAN   As secret as possible.

MR. FAUTEUX   Then you had a meeting on April 18. "Regular (meeting) — 5-5-45." Everything normal at that meeting.

MR. COMMISSIONER KELLOCK   That would be, the next meeting that was fixed on April 18 would take place on May 5?

LUNAN   Yes. . . .

MR. COMMISSIONER TASCHEREAU   Did you go to those places in a motor car?

LUNAN   No; on foot.

TASCHEREAU   And was Jan going on foot or in a motor car?

LUNAN   I met him on foot.

MR. COMMISSIONER KELLOCK   Was he always in civilian dress?

LUNAN   Yes, he was.

MR. COMMISSIONER TASCHEREAU   And he always went alone?

LUNAN   When I met him he was alone. . . .

MR. FAUTEUX   Now, if you turn the page, on June 8, 1945, it is headed:

8-6-45 Meeting for an emergency at the appointed place. Everything normal. Regular (meeting) — 5-7-45.
Emergency — 8-7-45.

Then the time and place are indicated. Then it goes on to say: "He is to bring Badeau to the meeting." What arrangement was made there as far as Badeau was concerned? Who suggested that Badeau should be brought to the meeting?

LUNAN   Jan.

FAUTEUX   And what reason did he give for that?

LUNAN   I don't know, except that he wanted to see him.

FAUTEUX   Did you not discuss that with him?

LUNAN   No, I did not.

FAUTEUX   And what arrangements were made?

LUNAN   I subsequently saw Badeau and told him, and eventually I met Badeau and took him to this particular meeting.

FAUTEUX   When you asked Smith, Durnford Smith, to come to that meeting, what was his reaction?

LUNAN   I don't think he was keen to come at first, but in any case he did. . . .

MR. COMMISSIONER TASCHEREAU   Did you ever tell Smith or Badeau that the man he was going to meet was the man to whom you were furnishing the information?

LUNAN   That is correct.

MR. COMMISSIONER KELLOCK   And that he was from the Russian embassy?

LUNAN   I can't remember telling him when I made this appointment, but I certainly assumed that he fully knew that.

MR. FAUTEUX   When did that meeting take place?

LUNAN   The one with Badeau?

FAUTEUX   Yes; Badeau, Rogov and yourself?

LUNAN   It took place in the summer; I imagine it was the next meeting.

FAUTEUX   And that would be what date?

LUNAN   In July.

FAUTEUX   What date in July?

LUNAN   Well, according to this, July 5; but I cannot vouch for the accuracy of that date.

FAUTEUX   At what time?

LUNAN   In the evening.

FAUTEUX   And what hour?

LUNAN   I don't remember the hour.

FAUTEUX   At what corner?

LUNAN   I don't remember that either. . . .

FAUTEUX   Was there any comment from Rogov as to his meeting with Smith?

LUNAN   No. There might have been some comment. Let me see. Certainly no discussion of anything about Smith.

FAUTEUX   Did he say that he was pleased to have met him?

LUNAN   Yes, he did say that.

FAUTEUX   That he was a bright man, a brilliant person?

LUNAN   He said something which was generally complimentary.

FAUTEUX   As to what? Complimentary as to what?

LUNAN   As to his general character and individuality.

FAUTEUX   As being definitely the person for the work that was intended for him?

LUNAN   I doubt very much whether that was the particular connotation of his remarks.

MR. COMMISSIONER KELLOCK   Was Rogov a technical man himself?

LUNAN   I don't know. He certainly must have had some technical information.

KELLOCK   He was able to keep his end up with Smith, as far as you could see?

LUNAN   Well, I didn't hear enough of the conversation to know that.

KELLOCK   But you say it was a technical conversation?

LUNAN   It was a technical conversation, yes. . . .

March 1, 1946

CAPTAIN LUNAN,   (*recalled*)

MR. COMMISSIONER TASCHEREAU   Did Halperin ever get a cent from you?

LUNAN   Certainly not from me.

TASCHEREAU   And Smith?

LUNAN   No.

TASCHEREAU   And Mazerall?

LUNAN   No.

TASCHEREAU   Did you get any?

LUNAN   No, I did not.

TASCHEREAU   From Rogov?

LUNAN   No. It was frequently offered to me but I never took it.

TASCHEREAU   How did he offer you the money?

LUNAN   Well, he would ask me and sometimes actually offer it. That is, I could see it was money. He would try to persuade me to take it. He characterized it as expenses, but I never took it. . . .

MR. COMMISSIONER KELLOCK   Captain Lunan, when you got a request from this fellow Rogov to get information covered by items 5 and 6 on that exhibit, what did you think was behind that request? I would be interested in knowing what you thought about it?

LUNAN   Well, sir, my reaction to these two particular ones since they affected me, was that I would give that information which was generally known or in the nature of rumour or gossip and pass it on as such, but I had no intention of trying to get it in any other way.

KELLOCK   No, you misunderstand me. I am asking you what thought occurred to you as to why these questions were being asked by a Russian officer?

LUNAN   At the time I do not think I gave them enough thought, because everybody, including those of us in the army, were very curious about the rate of discharge, and allocation of troops, and the type of permanent force which we were going to have.

KELLOCK   Why would a Russian officer, just after the conclusion of the war, when there was not going to be any more wars, be interested in that kind of information?

LUNAN   Well, already the whole question of the United Nations Organization was being discussed, and I thought it was in connection with the international commitments.

KELLOCK   Oh, yes; but if Russia wanted to get that information in connection with international commitments, she would not have a spy out here in Canada sneaking around the back door and asking an officer in the Canadian army for it, would she? That is not the way she would go about it?

LUNAN   No, unless they wanted to simply cross-check on other information.

KELLOCK   In any event, you never gave it any thought?

LUNAN   I did not give it enough thought.

KELLOCK   What do you think of it now?

LUNAN   Well, it appears in a totally different light to me now.

KELLOCK   In what light does it appear to you now?

LUNAN   That it would be information which — well, would enable the Russians to devise their own military program accordingly.

KELLOCK   For what purpose?

LUNAN   Well, even now I do not believe for the purpose of making war.

KELLOCK   Well, I just wondered what you thought about it. Thank you.

LUNAN   Well, sir, I did not feel that.

KELLOCK   I suppose you carried out the instructions in the postscript and burned it?

LUNAN   To the best of my recollection. . . .

MR. FAUTEUX   Your wife has been a Communist, to your knowledge, since your marriage?

LUNAN   Yes.

FAUTEUX   Since 1939?

LUNAN   Yes. May I ask a question here? Am I bound to give evidence involving my wife?

MR. COMMISSIONER KELLOCK   You are bound to answer any question that is put to you.

LUNAN   O.K.

KELLOCK   That is, any proper question. If you have a question which you think is improper, you can ask for a ruling.

LUNAN   Yes.

MR. FAUTEUX   You were a member yourself of the artist's branch of section 10 of the Communist party of Canada?

LUNAN   I was a member at one time of an artist's discussion group, but I was not aware that it was a branch of the Communist party.

FAUTEUX   When did you belong to that group?

LUNAN   In 1938, I think, or 1939; perhaps going over the division between the years.

FAUTEUX   And how many times did you meet?

LUNAN   Met quite often; about every two weeks, I think.

FAUTEUX   Where would you meet?

LUNAN   In various houses.

FAUTEUX   Of the members of the group?

LUNAN   That is right.

FAUTEUX   How many members would there be?

LUNAN   Oh, a varying number, from six or so to twelve, maybe.

FAUTEUX   And what would you discuss?

LUNAN   We would discuss mostly politics; current events.

FAUTEUX   You discussed the various theories of the Communist party; communism?

LUNAN   That is right.

FAUTEUX   And these meetings were secret?

LUNAN   Not especially.

FAUTEUX   What I mean is that only those who were members of the group could attend these meetings?

LUNAN   No; there were sometimes visitors.

FAUTEUX   Visitors who were invited because they had possibilities of joining the group?

LUNAN   I think so.

FAUTEUX   That is the fact?

LUNAN   Well, it is hard to say why other people brought visitors, but that would be generally the intention that they would be interested in the discussions of the group.

FAUTEUX   That was the understanding.

LUNAN   Yes.

FAUTEUX   To develop the group?

LUNAN   Yes.

FAUTEUX   To invite visitors — not the police, I imagine — visitors who would eventually become members of the group?

LUNAN   That is right. . . .

FAUTEUX   What about Raymond Boyer? When did you meet him?

LUNAN   Boyer I met originally through my wife. At the time I think Boyer was in the Civil Liberties Union, which was —

FAUTEUX   A political organization?

LUNAN   If you wish.

FAUTEUX   And the word "political" in this instance is being used as "Communist"?

LUNAN   No; I think that would not truly represent the views of all members of the Civil Liberties Union, to call them Communists.

FAUTEUX   What?

LUNAN   It would not truly represent the views of all members of the Civil Liberties Union to call them Communists.

FAUTEUX   What would you call them?

LUNAN   Well, I can think, for instance, of Eugene Forsey, who was a member of that group, who is a functionary of the C.C.F.

FAUTEUX   But you say there were several Communists?

LUNAN   Oh, yes.

FAUTEUX   In other words, if I understand the situation correctly, the Communists have their own secret organization, their own groups, which carry on their operations, and they also join other groups which are operating in the open?

LUNAN   I think they feel free to join any group.

FAUTEUX   Not only free, but they would be interested?

LUNAN   Yes, in special groups.

MR. COMMISSIONER KELLOCK   With the idea of controlling the other organizations, if possible?

LUNAN   Well, with the idea of advancing their own opinions. . . .

FAUTEUX   Captain Lunan, would you care to explain why you agreed to act as agent for Rogov in connection with a number of people who were in positions of trust in Canada? Would you care to give some explanation of that?

LUNAN   Yes, I would like to.

FAUTEUX   I am not asking you to do it, but if you care to do it you are at liberty to do it.

LUNAN   I would like to make some statement, yes. It is difficult in the light of retrospection to analyze one's motivation and try and reconstruct just what did take place. However, I would like to say this, that although I connected up this meeting with Rose I had no preconceived idea of what it was going to be and not until after I had left Rogov at the first meeting and had had an opportunity to look at the document did I begin to understand the nature of it.

Naturally I did not go there with a completely empty head. The conversation

I had with him at the meeting had a lot to do with me as a writer and I was not adverse to writing commentaries which I felt to be a true and fair comment on the Canadian political scene.

I did not go there with any fixed and firm loyalty to the Russians. I went there very much as a Canadian who was acknowledgedly a Communist in sympathy and a well-wisher for the Soviet Union. I had thought often and I still do think that sometimes they show a very superficial knowledge of the Canadian way of life.

MR. COMMISSIONER KELLOCK   Who?

LUNAN   The Russians. My first feelings which of course afterward changed, was that anything I wrote in that connection would help in some little way to improve their appreciation and analysis of Canadian life. Well, of course, I had only to read the typewritten instructions, which appear here as an exhibit, to understand the full nature of this rendezvous.

KELLOCK   That is, Exhibit No. 17-B.

LUNAN   That is right, sir. That is the first time that I fully realized that this was not by any means a casual meeting, that it involved three other people. I felt that I would at least see them and find out what they knew about it and what their attitude was to the thing.

It would be very easy for me to claim very strong and unswerving idealistic motivation, but things did not happen that simply. I began to think very seriously of this position and I reviewed what I had done in the light of my political ideas and my political principles, or if you like, my Communist leanings.

It seemed to me that even before I had been put in the position I found myself, in the position where I had to wrestle with my ideology — I was a member of a committee which tried to help Canadians coming back from Spain who had fought there in the International Brigade. This was, from the prevalent Canadian public opinion, a very unpopular task, but in retrospect it seemed to me that it was a worthwhile thing and that perhaps I and one or two others had been a little ahead of public opinion in seeing the Spanish war in the light of which we did see it and that ultimately nobody would deny that Franco was a fascist tool in Spain and that to close one's eyes to these things would only mean war and loss for Canada.

I followed up this line of reasoning and it seemed to me that much of the time I had been faced with a very difficult decision in which I had to try to turn my principles into action and that I had been right in retrospect. Then I was proud of the position I had taken.

The Quebec Committee for Allied Victory is another example. Many people at the time the Germans attacked Russia felt that Russia would not last. This feeling was compounded of various things, like a lack of knowledge of the Russian people and their resources, and in certain sections I suppose a prejudice in refusing to believe in these people being able to do anything.

Here again I was in a position of being against public opinion. Against any feelings for my own security I joined and took a prominent part in this organization which tried to advocate the necessity of very close cooperation, in the interests, not only of Canada, but of all people, in fighting against the Axis. Here again I think much of the opinion that we voiced very vigorously at that time has since been justified. I felt that I was true to my real convictions and feelings in doing this although because of the branding of this work as communistic I lost my job, for one thing.

While it is true that when I suddenly found myself in the position with this man Rogov it far outweighed any battle with my motives and my convictions that I had. I had to dip down into my assessment of the situation in which we found ourselves and the future —

KELLOCK   What do you mean by "we"?

LUNAN   I mean Canada. War was developing and it had become firmly established, not only in my own mind but I think in many other people's, that the Soviet Union was a very important ally. The beginnings of a much more advanced form of international cooperation were being formed. The Big Three, and sometimes the Big Five were coming together. The whole principle of cooperation by the United Nations was beginning to be put into, as it seemed to me, practice.

Plans for a subsequent organization, the United Nations Organization, had already been laid and I felt that it was both a very necessary part of the need to defeat Hitler and I necessarily felt afterwards in the period of peaceful reconstruction that our friendship and cooperation with Russia was tremendously important.

As I say, it was only after a great struggle on my part, and as a result of that great struggle, that I could bring myself eventually to accept this kind of work as something which would in the long run — I was conscious that it would be in the long run — advance the whole cause of international cooperation.

I certainly did not think of it in terms of cheating Canada out of anything. I felt it was, as I say, that we were perhaps making a very slight contribution or giving a little push to this international cooperation which was the basis of my political ideology.

As the thing went on I do not say and I cannot claim that I unshakingly held to that. After a certain point I was determined to remove myself from this particular work as well as I could, although I think I have vastly underestimated the position I was in and it was not particularly easy for me suddenly to withdraw.

There were two things which tended to keep me in these lines. One was the fact that I believed I would have an opportunity to write, as I said, these commentaries, and in fact I did write one. The other was the question of reciprocity of discussion between people that I was dealing with, that is Smith and the others and the Russians. This was discussed almost right from the beginning, I think, between myself and Rogov and it was one of the first questions that each of the other three people put.

I believe that when Badeau or Smith eventually did meet Rogov there was some reciprocity of information; that is, discussing of things together. I felt Smith was getting some benefit in his work.

Subsequently, when the news of the atom bomb broke I began to see how important some of the questions I had been asked were, and I certainly did not tie up the question of uranium with anything quite so devastating.

There was also in my mind at the time a feeling that scientific subjects were bound to become international and subsequently the discussions of great numbers of scientists all over the world following the atom bomb raid tended to bear out my belief and balanced off to some extent my own misgivings.

I would also like to say that in the light of the discussions at the United Nations Organization in London I found myself still confident that the nations of the world who had fought and beaten Hitler would inevitably draw together within this organization for the peace of the entire world. I feel that Canada's part in the United Nations Organization is a very worthy one. I happened to be in London at the time and I did not feel any sharp contradiction within myself when I viewed the workings of that organization.

I doubt whether I could keep any self-respect at all unless I truly believed in these things and that the very fast pace of world history in this new period in which we find ourselves will catch up to and surpass the results of this thinking on my part and the actions that it led to.

I would also like to say that I had no idea of the scope and extent of this work. I was amazed when it first became clear to me during my interrogation. I never thought of myself as being more than just one person in a small group of five people.

I do not offer this in any sense as an excuse for my work, but I was striving to square myself with my ideals without a full knowledge of the position in which I really found myself.

MR. FAUTEUX   Is that all you wish to say?

LUNAN   That is all I would like to say now. . . .

THE TESTIMONY OF DR. JOHN COCKCROFT

March 1, 1946

DR. JOHN DOUGLAS COCKCROFT, *sworn*

MR. WILLIAMS   Dr. Cockcroft, at the present time you are what is known as a temporary civil servant of the British government?

COCKCROFT   I was until a few days ago; I am now a permanent civil servant.

WILLIAMS   At the present time you hold the position of Director of the Montreal Laboratory of the National Research Council?

COCKCROFT   Yes.

MR. COMMISSIONER TASCHEREAU   Would that be at McGill University?

COCKCROFT   No, the Montreal Laboratory of the National Research Council.

MR. WILLIAMS   It is not at any university?

COCKCROFT   No, but it is in the buildings of the University of Montreal.

MR. COMMISSIONER KELLOCK   As I understand it, Dr. Cockcroft, you are a civil servant of the United Kingdom?

COCKCROFT   Yes.

KELLOCK   But with the National Research Council of Canada?

COCKCROFT   Yes. . . .

MR. WILLIAMS   Do you still hold the Chair of Jacksonian Professor of Natural Philosophy at Cambridge?

COCKCROFT   I hold that until September 30th of this year.

WILLIAMS   And you have held it for how long?

COCKCROFT   Since 1939.

WILLIAMS   In that capacity your particular subject, as I understand it, was nuclear physics?

COCKCROFT   Yes.

WILLIAMS   I believe also you are the first person who split the atom by mechanical means?

COCKCROFT   Yes, that is so.

WILLIAMS   There has been put in in evidence a chart which has been marked as Exhibit No. 102 showing the National Research Council set-up. On one side, working with Dr. Mackenzie, president of the Council, there is the atomic energy project, Montreal and Chalk River, with yourself as director?

COCKCROFT   Yes.

WILLIAMS   You are occupying that position at the present time?

COCKCROFT   That is so.

WILLIAMS   And have occupied it for how long, Dr. Cockcroft?

COCKCROFT   When I first came over here to consider taking up that position, April, 1944, and then I returned to England after two months for a period of one month, so that I took up the position permanently in July, 1944.

WILLIAMS   And you are directly responsible to Dr. C.J. Mackenzie, president of the National Research Council?

COCKCROFT   Yes.

WILLIAMS   Do you know a man named Alan Nunn May?

COCKCROFT   Yes.

WILLIAMS   Was he employed in the National Research Council?

COCKCROFT   Yes.

WILLIAMS   Will you just describe to the commissioners what his position was?

COCKCROFT   He was a British temporary civil servant and would form part of a research group which came over to Canada to start, in collaboration with the Canadian scientists, the Montreal Laboratory of the National Research Council.

WILLIAMS   As I understand it, there are what are described as various levels in the Montreal laboratory with yourself at the top as director. Then immediately below you are a certain number of division heads?

COCKCROFT   Yes.

WILLIAMS   How many of those are there?

COCKCROFT   There are about six.

WILLIAMS   And then below that again there are a certain number of section leaders?

COCKCROFT   Yes.

WILLIAMS   And there are approximately how many section leaders?

COCKCROFT   Between twenty and thirty.

WILLIAMS   And was Mr. May a section leader?

COCKCROFT   He was, yes. . . .

WILLIAMS   I further understand that the knowledge of the work done by the National Research Council at the various levels is as follows: You, as director at the top, would have access to the knowledge of all work being done in the Council by the Council in connection with the atomic energy project?

COCKCROFT   Yes.

WILLIAMS   And the division heads immediately below you would have a certain amount of knowledge but they would not have access to all the information to which you personally would have access.

COCKCROFT   That is so. . . .

WILLIAMS   And the section heads would have access to all the knowledge that the division heads would have and a fortiori to the knowledge that you have?

COCKCROFT   Yes.

WILLIAMS   Reference has been made in the documents before the Commission, Dr. Cockcroft, to uranium. I would be glad if you would tell us in layman's language what ordinary uranium is made up of?

COCKCROFT   Well, uranium is the heaviest element known in nature. It consists of two varieties, a light variety and a heavy variety. The heavy variety is by far the most abundant. It has an atomic weight of 238. The light variety occurs in roughly one part in a hundred and has an atomic weight of 235. Uranium 235 is the important variety for military purposes; it is the more important variety.

WILLIAMS   As I understand it uranium 235 and uranium 238 both occur in nature?

COCKCROFT   Yes.

WILLIAMS   And that in the uranium you would get out of a mine there is slightly under one per cent of uranium 235 in the mixture and the balance is uranium 238?

COCKCROFT   Yes. . . .

WILLIAMS   Then reference has been made to uranium 235 enriched. Would you explain what that means?

COCKCROFT   It is possible to increase the proportion of uranium 235 in natural uranium by the use of special machines which have been erected in the United States. That is to say, instead of having one part in 140, say, of the U-235, you can double the proportion or get ten times the proportion. That is what we mean by enrichment.

WILLIAMS   Am I correct in understanding that uranium 235 can be either a metal or an oxide?

COCKCROFT   It can be either a metal or an oxide or it can take a variety of forms, such as nitrates.

WILLIAMS   Oxide means that it is a powder?

COCKCROFT   Quite so.

WILLIAMS   In this case a black powder?

COCKCROFT   Most likely a black powder, yes. . . .

WILLIAMS   It would be possible, would it, Dr. Cockcroft, to hand a sample of uranium 235 over in a small glass tube?

COCKCROFT   It would be possible.

WILLIAMS   And how much would about a milligram of oxide be?

COCKCROFT   Like a very small grain of sand, almost.

WILLIAMS   When it is in oxide form handling it in a glass tube would be the normal way of handling it?

COCKCROFT   Yes. . . .

WILLIAMS   And would a good description of that, when you are dealing with about a tenth of a milligram, be that it is a very thin deposit on a platinum foil?

COCKCROFT   Yes.

WILLIAMS   Where would uranium 235 enriched be found in Canada?

COCKCROFT   I would think only in the Montreal or Chalk River laboratories.

WILLIAMS   Would the quantity be appreciable?

COCKCROFT   It might amount to as much as 20 milligrams.

WILLIAMS   Would you say that was a large or small quantity?

COCKCROFT   It is a small quantity, a very small quantity.

WILLIAMS   For what purpose is it used?

COCKCROFT   It is used to study the properties of uranium 235 as distinct from the properties of uranium 238. That is, if you enrich the material you have more uranium 235 and you can study its properties separately from those of uranium 238.

WILLIAMS   Would it be correct to say that the supply of U-235 is being used for general experimental purposes by the nuclear physicists in the Council?

COCKCROFT   Enriched 235, yes.

WILLIAMS   And enriched uranium 235, can it be obtained elsewhere than in Canada?

COCKCROFT   It could only be obtained, to the best of my knowledge, from the United States' project.

WILLIAMS   Have you any idea where the supply now in Canada came from?

COCKCROFT   I was not in Montreal when that supply was obtained, but I would imagine it came from the United States' project, from the Chicago laboratory.

WILLIAMS   Is there any person in Canada, including yourself, who has full knowledge of the manufacture of the atomic bomb?

COCKCROFT   Not to my knowledge, unless Mr. Howe has, and I believe he repudiated that.

WILLIAMS   What would you say as to the care with which the people working on this matter in the United States have guarded the secret, even from the members of the National Research Council?

COCKCROFT   It has been the policy in the United States to divide their projects up into separate groups and to restrict as much as possible communication between different groups and we have had no access to the laboratory at Los Alamos where the atomic bomb was constructed, nor have we had access to the large-scale plants at Hanford or at Oak Ridge.

WILLIAMS   Have you received from them any details or technical information or drawings?

COCKCROFT   None on those subjects.

WILLIAMS   Is the set-up and the method of construction and design of those plants also something which has been kept secret?

COCKCROFT   It has been withheld from us deliberately.

WILLIAMS   Is there a distinction between plans and drawings with reference to the plants and plans and drawings or written formula with reference to the building of the atomic bomb?

COCKCROFT   Yes, I would think they would be quite different and would be kept in different compartments.

WILLIAMS   It would be important for anybody desiring to get evidence or information as to the atomic bomb secrets to know the construction of and design of plants as well as any other information that might be available?

COCKCROFT   Yes.

WILLIAMS   Nobody from Canada, so far as you know, has been in the Oak Ridge and Hanford plants?

COCKCROFT   No.

WILLIAMS   But I understand that some of the members of your department have been in one or other of the smaller experimental plants?

COCKCROFT   That is so.

WILLIAMS   You yourself have been in a large one?

COCKCROFT   I have been in the Chicago plant and in the so-called Clinton Laboratory in Tennessee.

WILLIAMS   Have any other of your associates been in the Clinton laboratories?

COCKCROFT   Yes, I would say that altogether about six people have been to Clinton.

WILLIAMS   Would Mr. May be one of these?

COCKCROFT   No, not to my knowledge.

WILLIAMS   You would be supposed to know if he was?

COCKCROFT   Yes.

WILLIAMS   Has he been in the Chicago plant?

COCKCROFT   On several occasions, yes.

WILLIAMS   What was he doing there?

COCKCROFT   He was doing experiments in collaboration with the American scientists.

WILLIAMS   Would he be able to learn anything other than what was being done in the Chicago plant?

COCKCROFT   Not unless the organization was at fault, because it was quite clearly understood by both sides that they were not to discuss any information outside of the joint interests, not supposed to discuss anything about Hanford or the atomic bomb. . . .

WILLIAMS   If May were doing experimental work in the Chicago plant would that mean that he would know everything that was being done in the Chicago plant or only part of what was being done?

COCKCROFT   Only part.

WILLIAMS   Was he working on any specific confined line of experiment when he was down there?

COCKCROFT   Yes, he was working on a definite, on quite a specific experiment.

WILLIAMS   In these smaller plants, such as the Chicago plant, they would be doing a number of different experimental jobs?

COCKCROFT   Quite a large number, yes. . . .

WILLIAMS   How does the work in the small experimental plants contrast with the work being done at Oak Ridge and Hanford?

COCKCROFT   The work at Oak Ridge and Hanford consists of very large-scale industrial processes in which they are producing materials in large quantities for atomic bombs. In a place like the Chicago laboratory they are working with minute quantities of material, perhaps a milligram or so, and studying basic properties of a particular element, such as uranium 233.

WILLIAMS   Would I be correct in saying that you who have the greatest knowledge in Canada on this matter, know only roughly the output of the Oak Ridge and Hanford plants and know generally, but not particularly, how they are constructed?

COCKCROFT   That is a correct statement.

WILLIAMS   When May would return from his Chicago trip or trips, or when you came back from your trip or trips, would there be a discussion in the National Research branch of which you are a director about the information obtained on those trips?

COCKCROFT   Yes, there would be as a rule.

WILLIAMS   In the discussions in which you took part you did not, as I understand it, disclose everything that you had learned or knew?

COCKCROFT   No.

WILLIAMS   Would the scope of the discussion depend upon whether it was a discussion between yourself and the division heads or a discussion between yourself, the division heads and the section leaders?

COCKCROFT   Yes.

WILLIAMS   The scope would be wider in your discussion with the division heads?

COCKCROFT   Yes.

WILLIAMS   But still not of the widest, and it would be narrower in your discussion with the section heads?

COCKCROFT   That is so, yes.

WILLIAMS   Have you any knowledge of the construction of the atomic bomb, as to how it is made?

COCKCROFT   My information is extremely vague. I have read the Smyth report*

WILLIAMS   You refer to the Smyth report which you were good enough to bring for the information of the commissioners?

COCKCROFT   Yes.

WILLIAMS   I will refer to that again in a few minutes. I see it is the property of Dr. Mackenzie?

COCKCROFT   That is right.

WILLIAMS   I suggest, Messrs. Commissioners, that we merely borrow it and not mark it as an exhibit.   (*To the witness*)   Would you say that May had any knowledge as to how to construct the atomic bomb?

COCKCROFT   I have no information on that subject. He might have obtained it illicitly when he was in Chicago, but it would certainly be illicitly if he had done so. I should think it was very unlikely he was told anything about it.

WILLIAMS   If he had that information he could not have got it in Canada?

COCKCROFT   No. . . .

WILLIAMS   If a sample of U-235 slightly enriched were handed over to a nuclear physicist, what use could he make of it?

COCKCROFT   He could determine the fundamental properties of uranium 235. That is, he would measure how easily this particular form of uranium could be split by a bombardment of neutrons. That is the fundamental experiment he would try to carry out.

WILLIAMS   And if this amount were handed to one of the Russian nuclear physicists, would it provide him with any basic scientific information?

COCKCROFT   Yes, it would assist them in determining this basic scientific information. It is not a very large quantity, and I would like to have considerably more than that to do an experiment properly; but at the same time it would be of some assistance.

WILLIAMS   And am I correct in understanding that the sample in question, or rather with the sample in question the physicists concerned would have to take the materials and then measure them for their physical properties?

COCKCROFT   Yes.

WILLIAMS   That would be the first thing that would have to be done?

COCKCROFT   Yes.

WILLIAMS   Would it be possible for them to have produced the U-235 in their own cyclotrons?

COCKCROFT   I would think so. We know they were constructing cyclotrons in Russia, and I would think they would have the possibility of producing it themselves.

MR. COMMISSIONER KELLOCK   And if that were so, then any sample handed to them, such as is mentioned, would simply be some more material they already had?

COCKCROFT   Yes; that is as far as U-235 goes.

---

*H.D. Smyth, *Atomic Energy for Military Purposes: The Official Report on the Development of the Atomic Bomb* (Princeton, 1945).

MR. WILLIAMS   What would you say would be behind a desire in August or July, 1945, to obtain samples of U-235?

COCKCROFT   Well, I suppose that the person who obtained it may think that it would be of some help, and he would not know with certainty that the people concerned had got sufficient samples produced by cyclotrons. He would think it would be of some help to have it.

WILLIAMS   And would you think that it would be of help to have it?

COCKCROFT   It is a little difficult to know without having information on the state of nuclear physics in Russia, which I really have not got.

WILLIAMS   Then what would you say would be behind a request for a sample of U-233?

COCKCROFT   Well, the importance of having a sample of U-233 is to demonstrate that there is the possibility at some future date of using thorium as a basic material, but I should say that this is rather a long term business, and it is of no immediate value. It is of long term value.

WILLIAMS   Would it have any immediate significance in the mind of a person endeavouring to find the secret of the atomic bomb?

COCKCROFT   No.

WILLIAMS   Then what is plutonium, Dr. Cockcroft?

COCKCROFT   Plutonium is an alternative material which has been used for producing atomic bombs. It is made by taking ordinary uranium and putting it into an atomic energy machine, such as is built at Hanford, and you change the U-233 into plutonium, and you extract the plutonium from the uranium 238 by chemical methods . . .

WILLIAMS   Then would you say the delivery over of samples of U-235 and U-233 was a matter of major importance, having regard to the Smyth report?

COCKCROFT   No, I would say that since so much was disclosed in the Smyth report, in the class of basic scientific information, the importance of passing over these samples was substantially reduced. I think they are of some value, but I would not say they were of tremendous value.

MR. COMMISSIONER TASCHEREAU   In what year was the Smyth report published?

COCKCROFT   August, 1945.

MR. WILLIAMS   The report was made by Henry D. Smyth, who I understand was a professor of physics at Princeton University in the United States?

COCKCROFT   That is so.

WILLIAMS   And he was appointed by the United States army to make a report on atomic energy for military purposes, omitting technical details?

COCKCROFT   That is so . . .

WILLIAMS   Now, generally speaking, what is the Chalk River plant?

COCKCROFT   That is an atomic energy plant which has been erected at Chalk River to study a different method of producing plutonium and uranium 233 from that used by the Americans.

WILLIAMS   Is it unique?

COCKCROFT   It is, in a sense, unique. It is similar in principle to one of the small scale equipments at Chicago, but it is a higher power unit. The Chicago units are not designed for producing any materials. This is designed for producing small quantities of materials.

WILLIAMS   Would it be important to the Russians to know the construction of the Chalk River plant, or what was being done at it?

COCKCROFT   Well, they might consider it to be important, but I do not think that anyone who wished to put up a large scale plant and feel sure of everything that has been done would choose that route in the future. They would choose a different route, and follow the Hanford route. But that is a personal opinion . . .

WILLIAMS   At that time, on August 9, 1945, [the Nagasaki bombing] was this information public property?: "It is known that the release of uranium 235 is produced to the amount of 400 grams daily at the magnetic separation plant in Clinton."?

COCKCROFT   No, I would say that that is not public property. I would say that a rough idea of the amount could be determined by reading the Smyth report, a very rough idea, but nothing like so precise an amount.

WILLIAMS   And the "Clinton" mentioned is Clinton, Tennessee?

COCKCROFT   Yes.

WILLIAMS   Then the next sentence in the communication: "The release of [plutonium] is likely two times greater (some graphite units composed on 250 mega watts, i.e., 250 grams a day)." Does that make sense?

COCKCROFT   The first part of the statement, that the release from 49 is two times greater, does not make sense. I do not believe it to be greater. It is rather obscure, and I think it is an incorrect statement, if I understand the meaning. The second part of the statement, referring to the 250 megawatts is a fairly rough estimate of the output of the Hanford atomic energy machine.

WILLIAMS   And is that of importance to be known?

COCKCROFT   It is of some importance, yes. Again, I think one gets an approximate idea of the energy of this undertaking by reading the Smyth report, but it makes rather more precise information than you got in the report.

MR. COMMISSIONER KELLOCK   That is, you get rather more precise information in the document being read to you than in the Smyth report?

COCKCROFT   Yes. . . .

MR. WILLIAMS   Would it be possible, from reading the Smyth report, for a nuclear physicist to build an atomic bomb?

COCKCROFT   No.

WILLIAMS   Is that merely because of the absence of the technical details and formulae, or would there be more missing than that?

COCKCROFT   There would be far more missing than that. In order to build an atomic bomb you require, I should think, to have a very great deal of experience, detailed experience of the work, and to have a very large staff of scientists and engineers who had worked on the actual construction.

WILLIAMS   Did May visit the Chalk River plant on any occasion?

COCKCROFT   He did, yes.

WILLIAMS   Would he be able from his visit to obtain information that would be useful to the Russians?

COCKCROFT   He would not obtain any information additional to that which he already had access to in the Montreal Laboratory, where he could see drawings of the plant, so that he would gain very little additional information by paying a visit to the plant.

240

MR. COMMISSIONER KELLOCK   The drawings that you refer to in Montreal, would they be complete?

COCKCROFT   There was a fairly complete set of drawings in the Montreal laboratory. He would not, I expect, have an opportunity of seeing all the drawings, but he would certainly have an opportunity of seeing the key drawings, because they were explained to senior members of the establishment, such as the section heads.

KELLOCK   And would he have an opportunity of copying them if he saw fit?

COCKCROFT   I suppose he might, yes. That is not impossible, that he might come back at nights and have a drawing which he could then copy; but if he were seen to be copying the drawing it would certainly arouse comment.

MR. WILLIAMS   I have read to you information disclosed to the Russians by May. If that information had been disclosed before the Smyth report was published, would it have been of greater use or value to the Russians?

COCKCROFT   I think if the Russians had not had any of the information in the Smyth report it would have been of substantially more value in giving some indication of the important lines on which work was proceeding.

WILLIAMS   Assuming that the Russians did not know until after its publication that the Smyth report was going to be published, and they were able to get the information disclosed a week or so, or two weeks, before it was published, would they think that they had something of value?

COCKCROFT   Yes, I would have thought that they would have thought that it was of some value to them. I should think so.

WILLIAMS   So in the absence of any knowledge on their part of the impending publication of the Smyth report, their inquiries addressed through their agents would be inquiries from their point of view?

COCKCROFT   Yes.

WILLIAMS   Even if the Russians did not intend to erect a plant like the Chalk River plant, would you consider that it would be of value to them to know of its construction and method of operation?

COCKCROFT   Some features of its method of operation would be of interest; yes.

MR. COMMISSIONER KELLOCK   Apart from May sitting down and making an actual copy of the drawings, could he charge his mind sufficiently with the scheme from drawings to reproduce them elsewhere?

COCKCROFT   I should think not sufficient to be of value. What he could do which would be of value would be to describe the main difficulties which were likely to be experienced in such a plant, and how we attempted to solve them.

KELLOCK   He would know that?

COCKCROFT   Yes, he would know that.

MR. WILLIAMS   Then, Doctor, if you please, I want you to direct your attention to the questions of electronically controlled shells. I understand you know something about that subject, because you worked on it in England in the early days of the war?

COCKCROFT   Yes.

WILLIAMS   Are there any documents in the Montreal laboratory with reference to such shells?

COCKCROFT   Not to my knowledge.

WILLIAMS   Is it something that is being dealt with by any part of the National Research Council?

COCKCROFT   The National Research Council had a small group working on this subject in Toronto.

WILLIAMS   And what was that group called? Has it any specific name?

COCKCROFT   No name, only it was under the charge of Mr. Pitt, of the University of Toronto.

WILLIAMS   The following is supposed to have been reported by May to the Russians, and I will read it to you.

In particular these shells are being adapted against the Japanese suicide-aviators by the American Navy. In the shell there is a small radio-transmitter with one electronic lamp (bulb) and is fed by dry batteries. The body of the shell is the antenna. The bomb explodes in the proximity of an aeroplane from the action of the reflecting waves of the plane on the transmitter. The main difficulties were found to be the manufacure of a lamp (bulb) and battery that would withstand the discharge and in determining the rotary speed of the shell, which would not require special adaptation during preparation (assembly) of the shell. The Americans have attained this result, but apparently have not handed this over to the English. The Americans have adapted a plastic covering for the battery which resists the force of pressure during the motion of the shell.

In the first place, does that communication make sense? . . .

COCKCROFT   On the whole it is a correct statement. It is not a correct statement that it was not handed over to the British.

WILLIAMS   Was it a correct statement on August 9, 1945?

COCKCROFT   No, the British had had these fuses long before that.

WILLIAMS   Then assuming that the document makes sense, has it any technical value?

COCKCROFT   Well, I would say it would correspond to the first specifications we wrote down in England in about May of 1940, and after four years of work we had not completed a satisfactory fuse, so it is really the first thing I would write down; but it does not help very much.

WILLIAMS   Have you any knowledge as to whether the Russians had done any work along that line by 1945?

COCKCROFT   No, I have no knowledge.

WILLIAMS   I take it that it would be correct to say that the experiments which you began in the United Kingdom in 1939 and 1940 would continue? As you learned more and more you would still keep on experimenting, I take it?

COCKCROFT   Yes.

WILLIAMS   And would it be correct to say that both in the realm of electronically controlled shells and in the realm of the atomic bomb, each stage is merely the beginning of another stage of experimentation?

COCKCROFT   That is so, yes, until you get something which will really work.

WILLIAMS   But even then are you scientists content with the idea that that is the best, or are you not always looking to improvements?

COCKCROFT   Not always; no.

WILLIAMS   What would you say about electronically controlled shells, then?

COCKCROFT   I would say that as far as the United Kingdom is concerned we have still got a long way to go in connection with electronic fuses.

WILLIAMS   That would apply, generally, would it not, to the United Kingdom and Canada and the United States?

COCKCROFT   Yes, I think so.

WILLIAMS   So there would be some value, would there not — and I am suggesting this to you as a layman — in knowing each stage of the development of each one of these experiments or discoveries?

COCKCROFT   Some value, yes. This is the sort of thing that you get at the very earliest stage.

MR. COMMISSIONER KELLOCK   And it would indicate, if the Russians were interested in the information in Exhibit 20-E, at the stage indicated by that exhibit, that they were lagging quite a bit?

COCKCROFT   Yes, I would think so.

MR. WILLIAMS   And furthermore, Dr. Cockcroft, would this be a fair inference; that the men who would be working to-day on this particular type of work would be likely to be the men who would be carrying on the experiments, continuing the work and hoping to make new discoveries or new adaptations of old ideas?

COCKCROFT   Well, I know that a number of people who were working on this project in England were taken off the work. As the war developed it became less important to achieve a solution.

WILLIAMS   Now let me ask you this question. I want to come back to uranium 235. I understand that it is practically impossible to say whether or not any part of the sample which May turned over came from a Canadian source?

COCKCROFT   I would think so, yes.

WILLIAMS   As I understand it, too, the samples of uranium being used in the laboratory might suffer a loss or shrinkage, either through chemical action or, as I think you put it previously, a bit of it going down the sink?

COCKCROFT   Yes.

WILLIAMS   Would you elaborate on that for a moment?

COCKCROFT   If you take U-233 as an illustration, the chemists are manipulating this. They have it in solution; they are carrying out chemical operations, and they have to transfer fluids from one flask to another, and they may leave some U-233 behind, and a small part of it may then be washed down the sink in cleaning up the apparatus.

MR. COMMISSIONER KELLOCK   So he could deliver a sample of the size indicated and it would not be missed?

COCKCROFT   That is so.

KELLOCK   Then can we sum up one part of your evidenc, Dr. Cockcroft, by saying that as far as you know it would be impossible for anybody in Canada to give away any information about the construction of the atomic bomb?

COCKCROFT   Yes, I would say that.

MR. WILLIAMS   That is all I have to ask, Messrs. Commissioners.. . .

MR. COMMISSIONER KELLOCK   As to the materials, that was U-233, and I think you said that it was altogether likely the Russians already had that?

COCKCROFT   It would be unlikely that they had U-233. It was quite likely that they would have been able to produce U-235 by their own machines, in this sort of quantity or in very small quantities. I think the U-233 is perhaps the more interesting information to the Russians, since it would indicate that we were in future likely to be able to use thorium.

KELLOCK   But, as you say, that was a long time and still is a long time proposition?

COCKCROFT   Yes.

KELLOCK   So that apart from any more definite information than is contained in the Smyth report as to the United States' plants, the furnishing of the sample of U-233 was the most valuable thing?

COCKCROFT   Yes.

MR. WILLIAMS   Might I ask this, Dr. Cockcroft. We have gone over with you what it was that May did give?

COCKCROFT   Yes.

WILLIAMS   Could it be said that he gave all he had to give?

COCKCROFT   No. I would say that he could have given much more valuable information, or he could have been much more valuable if he had written out a complete report of everything he knew.

WILLIAMS   He had more to give?

COCKCROFT   Oh, undoubtedly yes; certainly, I would say so; definitely.

WILLIAMS   Could it be said that while he had more to give, he did give as far as he was concerned quite a bit?

COCKCROFT   Yes, I would think so. It strikes me as being rather fragmentary information.

WILLIAMS   And there might of course be some leakage in the method of transmission? That is, if May were conveying information orally to somebody who was not able to appreciate it, some of the information might have got lost in transit very easily?

COCKCROFT   Yes.

WILLIAMS   And it would have been the type of information which, if conveyed orally, should have been conveyed to somebody of an equal standing in the world of nuclear physics to May, the man who was transmitting the information?

COCKCROFT   Yes, I would think so.. . .

THE TESTIMONY OF DR. RAYMOND BOYER

March 7, 1946

DR. RAYMOND BOYER, *called and sworn*

MR. WILLIAMS   Will you just tell the Commission what you did. . . . When the war started, what did you do?

BOYER   Well, as soon as war was declared I sent a telegram to the prime minister offering my services in any capacity. I don't remember exactly whether I received an acknowledgment or not, but if I received an acknowledgment that was all I heard about that.

WILLIAMS   That would be right at the beginning of the war, in September of 1939?

BOYER   That is correct. Then, also in the fall of 1939, the government set up a bureau of which Mr. E.H. Coleman was the director; I forget what it was named, but it had something to do with the work that civilians might do in the war, and I happened to be in Ottawa when the bureau was set up. I got an interview with Mr. Coleman; I think it was the first interview he granted, as a matter of fact. At that time I told him that in my opinion Russia was a factor of tremendous importance in the war, and that I thought it would be very important for Canada to know what Russia's attitude to the war was —

WILLIAMS   May I just interrupt. This was long before Russia came into the war?

BOYER   This was in September or perhaps October, but I think September, 1939.

WILLIAMS   And at that time Russia had a treaty with Germany?

BOYER   That is correct.

WILLIAMS   If I may interrupt further, I understand that you have been a member of the Communist party for some time. Is that correct?

BOYER   That is not correct.

WILLIAMS   Just explain to the Commission what your relations were?

BOYER   I have worked in organizations in which there were Communists and in which I knew there were Communists, and I have worked very closely with Communists, but I have never held a party card nor paid dues, etc.

WILLIAMS   Have you ever made contributions to the work of the Communist party?

BOYER   I made contributions.

WILLIAMS   Financial contributions?

BOYER   Yes.

WILLIAMS   And when were those made?

BOYER   I can't say when they were made.

WILLIAMS   Would they have been made prior to the time you were having your talk with Dr. Coleman, or subsequently?

BOYER   No, not prior.

WILLIAMS   So it would be subsequently?

BOYER   That is correct.

WILLIAMS   You were having your talk with Dr. Coleman in September, 1939?

BOYER   That is correct.

WILLIAMS   Now will you just carry on from there?

BOYER   And I suggested that I be sent to Russia, without any diplomatic status or anything, in order to try and find out what Russia's real attitude to the war was.

WILLIAMS   Had you reason at that time to believe that you would be received in Russia and would be able to make contacts which would enable you to do that?

BOYER   None whatsoever.

MR. COMMISSIONER KELLOCK   Did you speak the Russian language?

BOYER   I had taken some Russian lessons.

MR. WILLIAMS   Before you talked about going there?

BOYER   While I was in Europe.

WILLIAMS   And before you had your talk with Dr. Coleman?

BOYER   That is correct.

WILLIAMS   Had you any reason to think that some of the Communist people you had met there would facilitate you if you went to Russia on this expedition?

BOYER   None whatever. . . .

WILLIAMS   I understood you to say . . . that in 1939 and 1940 you were not a member of the Communist party?

BOYER   That is correct.

WILLIAMS   Have you ever been a member of the Communist party, Dr. Boyer?

BOYER   No.

WILLIAMS   Are you a member of the Labour-Progressive party?

BOYER   No.

WILLIAMS   Have you ever been a member of it?

BOYER   No.

WILLIAMS   And you said as I recollect it, that you had never paid annual dues or fees to either the Communist party or the Labour-Progressive party?

BOYER   That is correct.

WILLIAMS   However you have, as I gathered from you, given some financial support to the Communist party?

BOYER   That is correct.

WILLIAMS   What form did that take? What were the circumstances?

BOYER   Well, election funds.

WILLIAMS   And how often?

BOYER   Oh, probably three or four times.

WILLIAMS   What was the first of those occasions, do you recall?

BOYER   I think it was the by-election in August, 1943.

WILLIAMS   That was a by-election in Montreal?

BOYER   Yes.

WILLIAMS   For the federal house, was it?

BOYER   Yes.

WILLIAMS   And who was running that you were supporting?

BOYER   Fred Rose.

WILLIAMS   How much did you contribute to his campaign fund?

BOYER   I don't remember. It was probably $50.

WILLIAMS   And when was the next contribution made, and to whose fund?

BOYER   Well, I think it would be the municipal election, when Michael Buhay ran.

WILLIAMS   He was running for the city council in Montreal?

BOYER   That is correct.

WILLIAMS   As a Labour-Progressive?

BOYER   I don't know whether he used that ticket or not.

WILLIAMS   Did you know him as a member of the Labour-Progressive party?

BOYER   I knew he was. I don't know him personally, but I knew he was.

WILLIAMS   You knew he was?

BOYER   That is correct.

WILLIAMS   And you made the contribution to help him, on the basis that he was a member of the Labour-Progressive party?

BOYER   That is correct. . . .

WILLIAMS   Do you see any difference, Dr. Boyer, between the ideology of the Labour-Progressive party and that of the Communist party?

BOYER   Frankly, no.

WILLIAMS   And on that occasion, how much did you contribute to Mr. Buhay's election fund?

BOYER   Again I don't remember. I should think it would be perhaps $15 or $20.

WILLIAMS   That is the second. We have a federal by-election and the municipal election. Did you make any more contributions to campaign funds for Mr. Rose?

BOYER   Yes, in the general election in 1944 [*sic* 1945].

WILLIAMS   And how much did you contribute on that occasion?

BOYER   I should think that would again be $50.

WILLIAMS   And for the same purpose?

BOYER   Yes.

WILLIAMS   Any further campaign contributions, Doctor?

BOYER   None that I remember.

WILLIAMS   Did you at any other times or in any other ways contribute to the work of the Labour-Progressive party or the Communist party, financially?

BOYER   No. Oh, yes; I lent some money for the publication of Stanley Ryerson's last book.

WILLIAMS   And what was the amount of that?

BOYER $150.

WILLIAMS   And has that been repaid?

BOYER   No.

WILLIAMS   This is not for the purpose of prying into your personal affairs, but I understand you are a man of considerable wealth?

BOYER   Well, I do not know what you call considerable.

MR. COMMISSIONER KELLOCK   Well, anything over $10,000 a year?

BOYER   Yes, that is correct. I might add that at the same time I have contributed to the election funds of the C.C.F. party, if that is of any interest to the Commission.

MR. WILLIAMS   And the total contributions, directly or indirectly, that you have made to the work of the Communist and Labour-Progressive parties, between which you see no difference, has been election funds that would not exceed $100 all told, and a contribution toward the printing of this book?

BOYER   That is correct. . . .

WILLIAMS   You are familiar with the process that the Labour-Progressive party and the Communist party follow, of building up study groups of various individuals for purposes of studying Marxian ideology?

BOYER   Yes.

WILLIAMS   Have you ever been a member of one of those groups yourself?

BOYER   Yes.

WILLIAMS   More than one, or just one?

BOYER   Just one.

WILLIAMS   When was that?

BOYER,   That was in 1938.

WILLIAMS   In Montreal?

BOYER   Yes.

WILLIAMS   And who were the members of it; who were the members of the group; can you recall?

BOYER   Well, Stanley Ryerson; Norman and Donna Lee.

WILLIAMS   That is husband and wife, I take it?

BOYER   Yes.

WILLIAMS   And who was Mr. Lee; what did he do?

BOYER   At that time he worked in the Sun Life.

WILLIAMS   Is he still with the Sun Life.

BOYER   No.

WILLIAMS   What is he doing now?

BOYER   At present he is in the International Labour Office.

WILLIAMS   How long has he been there? Do you know?

BOYER   A few years. I don't know how long.

WILLIAMS   Can you recall any other members of the group?

BOYER   Yes. There was Paulette Benning, Scott Benning's sister. There was a girl called Currie, as I remember. That is all I recall.

WILLIAMS   How long did that group function?

BOYER   Oh, from October till the spring, I would say.

WILLIAMS   Of what year?

BOYER   Of 1939.

WILLIAMS   And what happened to it? Would you just cease?

BOYER   Yes.

WILLIAMS   And have you been a member of any group of that kind since?

BOYER   No.

WILLIAMS   Where did it used to meet?

BOYER   At various houses.

WILLIAMS   Would it be at your house at times?

BOYER   Yes.

WILLIAMS   Was it a group that had a regular monthly fee?

BOYER   No.

WILLIAMS   Or were contributions made?

BOYER   No, not as I recall it.

WILLIAMS   Did it have any organization, a chairman or treasurer?

BOYER   No.

WILLIAMS   And did you ever send a delegate to any larger group?

BOYER   No. . . .

WILLIAMS   Exhibit 128?

BOYER   Yes.

WILLIAMS   Who is that?

BOYER   David Shugar.

WILLIAMS   How long did you know him?

BOYER   I have known him since the fall of 1944.

WILLIAMS   And how well?

BOYER   No, I take it back. I met him once in 1943.

WILLIAMS   And again in 1944?

BOYER   Again in 1944; yes.

WILLIAMS   How well did you know him?

BOYER   Well; I know him well.

WILLIAMS   And do you know what his political ideology is?

BOYER   Yes.

WILLIAMS   And it is what?

BOYER   Labour-Progressive, or Communist.

MR. COMMISSIONER KELLOCK   If you know Shugar well, you must have met him more than twice?

BOYER   I did not mean to say I met him only twice. I say I met him first in 1943; then I did not meet him again until 1944.

KELLOCK   Since then you have met him frequently?

BOYER   Since then I have met him a good many times, say fifteen times.

MR. WILLIAMS   And how was it; what was the occasion that you got to know him so well?

BOYER   Through the Canadian Association of Scientific Workers.

WILLIAMS   That is an organization which was formed how?

BOYER   Well, that is how I first met Shugar. He came to Montreal in the fall of 1943, and made the suggestion that there should be such an organization formed. We talked about it all that fall and winter, but nothing happened. Then in the summer of 1944 a group of us in Montreal formed a Montreal branch, and then other branches were formed. Since that time I saw Shugar a good many times.

WILLIAMS   So it was Shugar who was responsible for the formation of the organization, which was first formed in Montreal and then branches were formed in different parts of Canada; is that right?

BOYER   Well, I would not say he was responsible. He was the first person I heard speak of it.

WILLIAMS   As far as you knew, it was his idea?

BOYER   Yes.

WILLIAMS   Is membership in that association open to any engineer or any scientist, or are there certain limitations on who may join?

BOYER   Full membership is open to any engineer or scientist who has a bachelor's degree. Associate membership is open to anyone who agrees with the aims of the association and is anxious to support its work.

WILLIAMS   What would be the number of the membership in Montreal?

BOYER   325.

WILLIAMS   And do you personally know all the members?

BOYER   No.

WILLIAMS   Would you say that a substantial number of them have Communist ideology?

BOYER   No.

WILLIAMS   Have you any idea as to what proportion of them have?

BOYER   That is very hard to say. I would say it is small.

WILLIAMS   Who is the president?

BOYER   Nationally?

WILLIAMS   No; of the Montreal group?

BOYER   Dr. P.R. Wallace.

WILLIAMS   Has he any communistic ideology in his make-up?

BOYER   Some, but definitely not —

MR. COMMISSIONER TASCHEREAU   Not enough?

BOYER   It is hard to say, but I would say he is not a Communist, although he knows a good deal about Marxism.

MR. WILLIAMS   And what are the other officers? Is there a vice-president?

BOYER   In Montreal?

WILLIAMS   Yes; I am talking of the Montreal group now.

BOYER   Yes.

WILLIAMS   Who is that.

BOYER   Dr. K.A.C. Elliott.

WILLIAMS   And what are his political leanings?

BOYER   I am unable to say. I am unable to tell.

WILLIAMS   Then has it an executive?

BOYER   Yes.

WILLIAMS   And who are on that?

BOYER   Frank Chubb was the secretary. He should have left now and resigned, but he was the secretary up till now.

WILLIAMS   And what were his political affiliations?

BOYER   Labour-Progressive.

WILLIAMS   Communist?

BOYER   Yes.

WILLIAMS   Definitely so, I imagine?

BOYER   Definitely so.

WILLIAMS   And who are the other members of the executive?

BOYER   There was Max Goldstein.

WILLIAMS   And what are his political views?

BOYER   I scarcely know him. Then there was a Mrs. Moffatt.

WILLIAMS   And how about her?

BOYER   Oh, definitely not radical, but I don't know what they would be.

WILLIAMS   Not Communist?

BOYER   No; definitely not.

WILLIAMS   Who else?

BOYER   A man called Kushranov. I scarcely know him. I have no idea what his political views are. I don't remember who the others are; I am not a member of the executive.

WILLIAMS   Can you think of any other members of the executive of the Mont-
    real branch of this association?
BOYER   I cannot, just at the moment.
WILLIAMS   Do you know if there is a branch in Toronto?
BOYER   Yes.
WILLIAMS   Do you know the president of that?
BOYER   Yes.
WILLIAMS   Who is he?
BOYER   Leon Wigdor.
WILLIAMS   Do you know anything about his political ideology?
BOYER   I know it is leftist.
WILLIAMS   Do you know any of the other members of the executive of the
    Toronto branch?
BOYER   Yes; a man called Paul Olynyk.
WILLIAMS   What about his political leanings?
BOYER   I don't know what they are, but they are not leftist.
WILLIAMS   And who else? Can you recall any others?
BOYER   In Toronto? There is a man called Buchholtz.
WILLIAMS   Do you know anything about him?
BOYER   No, I have never met him.
WILLIAMS   Then let us take the Dominion organization. Is there a Dominion
    president?
BOYER   Yes.
WILLIAMS   Who is that?
BOYER   I am he.
WILLIAMS   And who are the members of the Dominion executive?
BOYER   The secretary is Frank Margolick.
WILLIAMS   What about his political leanings?
BOYER   They are leftist.
WILLIAMS   And there is a treasurer?
BOYER   Yes. Paul Frankel.
WILLIAMS   What about him?
BOYER   L.P.P.
WILLIAMS   Labour-Progressive party?
BOYER   Yes.
WILLIAMS   And the executive consists of whom?
BOYER   There are two others; there is Dr. P.R. Wallace, whom I have already
    mentioned as chairman of the Montreal branch, and Norman Veale.
WILLIAMS   Oh, you know him?
BOYER   Yes.
WILLIAMS   And what are his leanings?
BOYER   Definitely L.P.P., Communist. He is British.
WILLIAMS   And there is an executive as well?
BOYER   That is the executive; five men.
WILLIAMS   Is Dr. Shugar a member of the association?
BOYER   Yes.
WILLIAMS   And do you know what branch he belongs to?
BOYER   Ottawa.

WILLIAMS   Do you know any other members of the Ottawa branch?
BOYER   Yes.
WILLIAMS   Just let us have the president of the Ottawa branch.
BOYER   The president is Harry Hall.
WILLIAMS   How about him?
BOYER   I think he belongs to the Social Credit.
WILLIAMS   And the other officers?
BOYER   Oh, there is Dr. Hanley.
WILLIAMS   What are his political affiliations?
BOYER   I don't know.
WILLIAMS   And is Dr. Shugar a member of the executive of the Ottawa branch?
BOYER   I don't know. I don't think so, but I am not sure.
WILLIAMS   Then will you look at Exhibit 129. Do you recognize that gentleman?
BOYER   No.
WILLIAMS   Then I show you Exhibit 142. Do you know that gentleman?
BOYER   Yes.
WILLIAMS   Who is that?
BOYER   His name is May; I do not know his first name.
WILLIAMS   Do you know him personally.
BOYER   Yes. He was a member of the Montreal branch of the Canadian Association of Scientific Workers while he was in Canada.
WILLIAMS   How well did you know him?
BOYER   I met with him as a member of the executive once a week for several months.
WILLIAMS   And did you learn during that time what his political ideology was?
BOYER   I did not learn it, I suspected that he was also Communist.
WILLIAMS   And did you know what type of work he was engaged in here in Canada?
BOYER   Yes, I knew he was in the National Research Council, on the atomic project. Mind you, the fact that it was atomic was just a rumour during the time that I knew him.
WILLIAMS   Did he ever discuss with you the work he was doing?
BOYER   Never.
WILLIAMS   Did you ever have occasion to work with him in any way?
BOYER   Never.
WILLIAMS   Your lines of endeavour were entirely apart?
BOYER   Entirely.
WILLIAMS   And he did not at any time talk to you about the work he was doing?
BOYER   Never. . . .
WILLIAMS   I should like to go a little more fully with you into your relations with Fred Rose, and certain conversations you had with him at which certain of the things you were working on were discussed. Will you tell me how the first of those occasions arose, please, and when?
BOYER   I am not sure when. I think it was early in 1943.
WILLIAMS   And how did he approach you?
BOYER   He telephoned me and asked me to go to his apartment, and asked me to reveal to him what we were doing in RDX. I told him we had worked out a new process; what materials went into that reaction — mind you, I am not

sure that this is the first time I had those conversations with him, but I also told him all the ways in which RDX were used.

WILLIAMS This was a conversation in his residence?

BOYER Yes.

WILLIAMS Just the two of you present?

BOYER Yes. His wife may have been in the apartment somewhere.

WILLIAMS But she was not present at the immediate conversation?

BOYER No.

WILLIAMS You and he were in a room by yourselves?

BOYER Yes.

WILLIAMS And did you understand from him at that time that he was asking for this information, and why?

BOYER Yes.

WILLIAMS What did he tell you?

BOYER Well, that Russia was anxious to know about it. I would like to add that at that time Dr. Ross had told me that J.R. Donald, director of chemicals and explosives in the Department of Munitions and Supply, had told him that Mr. Howe had been approached by the Russians and was willing to give the process, everything, to the Russians, but he had been prevented from doing so by the Americans.

WILLIAMS Which meant, of course, that the Russians could not get it through official channels?

BOYER That is right, but I was very anxious that the Russians should continue asking, hoping that they would get it, because I knew — I mean the information I gave was not — I mean they could not start to produce RDX with the information I gave.

WILLIAMS You were willing to give the information you did give to Mr. Rose, knowing that it would be transmitted by him to the Russians?

BOYER Yes.

WILLIAMS Did you know it was to be transmitted by him through somebody in the Soviet Embassy here in Ottawa?

BOYER That I did not know. I didn't know —

WILLIAMS But you did know it was to go to the Russians in some way or other?

BOYER Yes.

WILLIAMS He made that quite clear?

BOYER Yes.

WILLIAMS Then, just to make sure we have it, you first of all told him that a new process had been worked out?

BOYER Well, as I remember it, that was already known; that release had already been made.

WILLIAMS That is, that the newspapers had said that the Canadians had worked out a new process?

BOYER Yes.

WILLIAMS Then you told him all the chemical components of that process?

BOYER Yes.

WILLIAMS That had not appeared in the newspapers?

BOYER That is correct.

WILLIAMS So that was information which could only have been obtained either through official sources or through some persons like yourself who knew it?

BOYER   That is correct.

WILLIAMS   How many components are there in the process?

BOYER   Three.

WILLIAMS   And you gave him those three?

BOYER   Yes.

WILLIAMS   What were those components?

BOYER   Hexamine — no; there are four, actually; ammonium nitrate; nitric acid, and acetic anhydride.

WILLIAMS   That was different from the British process?

BOYER   Only by virtue of the acetic anhydride.

WILLIAMS   But it was different, by virtue of that?

BOYER   Yes.

WILLIAMS   And it was different from the American process?

BOYER   No. . . .

MR. COMMISSIONER TASCHEREAU   I understand that the American process was your process?

BOYER   That is right.

MR. WILLIAMS   They learned it from you?

BOYER   You say "your process." After the first month or two the Americans were working on it; it was no more ours than theirs.

WILLIAMS   But the process was originally developed by you?

BOYER   That is quite right.

WILLIAMS   So that at least you gave this to Mr. Rose for transmission to the Russians, the component parts of the Canadian process?

BOYER   That is correct.

MR. COMMISSIONER TASCHEREAU   Did you tell what quantity of each component should go in; the proportion of each?

BOYER   The proportion, yes.

MR. WILLIAMS   You say, Dr. Boyer, that even with that information they could not have manufactured RDX on that formula; am I correct in understanding that?

BOYER   They could have manufactured it in flasks in a laboratory, but I mean they could not build a plant around that information.

MR. COMMISSIONER KELLOCK   It would be a good start, would it?

BOYER   They could then design a plant, I imagine.

KELLOCK   In other words, there are different stages; there is the laboratory stage, the pilot plant stage and the mass production stage?

BOYER   That is correct

KELLOCK   What you gave Rose was the laboratory stage?

BOYER   That is right.

MR. WILLIAMS   And many of the Russian chemists are men of very considerable capacity, are they not?

BOYER   There is some doubt about that.

MR. COMMISSIONER KELLOCK   You were concerned only with the laboratory stage?

BOYER   That is right.

KELLOCK   So what you gave him was what you do?

254

BOYER   That is right.

MR. WILLIAMS   You told us that when you had finished your stage the engineers who were designing the plant would get in touch with you to see whether what they were designing would carry out what you had in mind, so far as your process was concerned?

BOYER   Yes, but once it goes into the plant the engineers are the men who make the decisions, really.

WILLIAMS   If the Russian chemists came to the Russian engineers with the information you gave, they could get to work and design a plant by which they could make RDX according to your formula?

BOYER   They might and they might not. I suppose the answer is yes. I mean the engineering for this reaction was quite unique. It required a different kind of reactor altogether from the ordinary reactor.

WILLIAMS   Is the doubt in your mind doubt as to the capacity of the Russian engineers?

BOYER   No.

WILLIAMS   Do you not think that if they had that formula they could design a plant, eventually at least?

BOYER   Oh, yes.

WILLIAMS   That would manufacture RDX?

BOYER   I should like the Commission to take under consideration, if it will, that by that time the chemicals which went into that process were fairly well known, not only to those working, who were working on it, because the plant at Shawinigan Falls was already in operation and once a plant begins to operate then of course carloads of material come in, hundreds of workmen are employed, and it is generally considered that it is no longer possible to keep the process secret.

MR. COMMISSIONER KELLOCK   That is as to the ingredients, but the formula is still secret?

BOYER   That formula is not, my, no; the formula was published, the formula for RDX was known in 1904, as I mentioned. . . .

KELLOCK   Using formula in my sense for the time being, that was not known in 1904?

BOYER   Oh, no.

KELLOCK   It was not known until you devised it?

BOYER   That is correct.

KELLOCK   And you say that this Shawinigan Falls plant got operating and anybody who took some trouble to find out what they were using could find out the four items you had been using?

BOYER   Definitely. In fact, one of my students who went to Shawinigan Falls was told by someone not connected with that plant what was going into the plant and what they were making.

KELLOCK   But neither that student nor anybody else could ascertain from Shawinigan Falls, except improperly, the formula of the product being made in Shawinigan Falls, using formula in the sense I am using it?

BOYER   That is correct.

KELLOCK   And that is part of the information you gave to Rose?

BOYER   That is correct.

KELLOCK   You also gave him, as I recall, the different ways in which RDX was used?

BOYER   Yes. They were not new, of course. They were worked out by the British prior to this last war.

KELLOCK   You say they were published?

BOYER   No, oh, no, they were not.

KELLOCK   They were still secret?

BOYER   Oh, yes.

KELLOCK   Perhaps we should know what you told him about that?

MR. WILLIAMS   Just go ahead and detail as much as you can of that conversation?

BOYER   I told him that RDX was used as a high explosive in the form of what is known as Composition A, which is a composition of RDX and beeswax. I told him that RDX was used in the form of Composition B, which was RDX, TNT and beeswax. I told him that RDX was used in the form of torpex, which is the same as Composition B with aluminum dust added. I told him RDX was used in the form of a plastic explosive.

MR. COMMISSIONER KELLOCK   Were those uses existing uses?

BOYER   Yes.

KELLOCK   By whom?

BOYER   By the British.

KELLOCK   And — ?

BOYER   And the Americans

MR. COMMISSIONER TASCHEREAU   And the Canadians?

BOYER   We did not make all of those four in Canada, no.

MR. COMMISSIONER KELLOCK   That information came to you in connection with the research work you were doing?

BOYER   Yes.

KELLOCK   And as a result of that?

BOYER   Yes.

KELLOCK   And it would be just as secret as the formula for RDX, using formula in the sense I have used it?

BOYER   I would not consider it so, no, since it was not new.

KELLOCK   It was not as secret?

BOYER   Let us put it this way: The Germans were using those same compositions. I think that brings the distinction out.

MR. WILLIAMS   Were the Russians?

BOYER   Not so far as I know or knew.

WILLIAMS   That was another thing they wanted to learn about?

BOYER   Yes.

MR. COMMISSIONER KELLOCK   So far as these combinations and methods of use that you have been mentioning and that you told Rose, so far as you knew at that time you were telling him something that was new to the Russians?

BOYER   That is correct.

MR. WILLIAMS   How long did that conversation take, Dr. Boyer?

BOYER   Perhaps half an hour.

WILLIAMS   Could you fix the date more accurately than you have done, the date of this conversation in Rose's apartment?

BOYER   I am sorry, I cannot.

MR. COMMISSIONER TASCHEREAU   You said it was in what year?

MR. COMMISSIONER KELLOCK   Early 1943.

BOYER   That is what I thought.

TASCHEREAU   Was Rose taking notes?

BOYER   Yes.

MR. WILLIAMS   Did you supply him with any written information?

BOYER   No.

WILLIAMS   You say that he may have talked to you about this before the meeting at his house; am I correct?

BOYER   I did not say that.

WILLIAMS   The meeting at his house was the first time that Rose asked you for secret information?

BOYER   Yes.

MR. COMMISSIONER TASCHEREAU   I understood it was not the first time; he said he had spoken to him before.

WILLIAMS   That was the impression I had.

BOYER   I had spoken to him before but not concerning RDX.

WILLIAMS   I think you gave that impression to all of us, that you may have talked to him before.

BOYER   I think I said that I did not give him all that information the first time I talked to him about RDX.

WILLIAMS   Are we to understand that the first time you talked to him about RDX was at his apartment pursuant to his request?

BOYER   That is correct.

WILLIAMS   You met him more than once at his house, did you?

BOYER   Yes.

WILLIAMS   How many times did you meet him?

BOYER   Three or four times.

WILLIAMS   During those three or four times did you discuss RDX?

BOYER   That is correct.

WILLIAMS   Did you discuss anything else with him, Dr. Boyer, of a similar nature?

BOYER   Nothing confidential. We would discuss the course of the war, any new weapons that were used, the strategy that was used and any of the technical aspects of the war, but not anything confidential.

WILLIAMS   Why was it necessary to have three or four conferences with him to give him the RDX story?

BOYER   As I say, I did not give him all that material the first time.

WILLIAMS   The material you gave him the first time you knew he was going to transmit to Russia in some way?

BOYER   Yes.

WILLIAMS   At the next meeting you gave him more information which you knew he was going to transmit to Russia?

BOYER   Yes.

WILLIAMS   Would it be three or four meetings that it took you to turn over all that material?

BOYER   Well, no; at least once he asked me whether there was anything new in RDX and I simply said, "No."

WILLIAMS   How far apart were those meetings?

BOYER   Oh, I would say six months.

WILLIAMS   Do you mean to say six months would cover the three or four meetings or would each meeting be about six months apart?

BOYER   That each would be about six months apart.

WILLIAMS   During all that time you were still working continuously on the development of RDX?

BOYER   Yes.

WILLIAMS   And each six months you would have a little more to tell him? Would that be right, would that be putting it fairly?

BOYER   No, that represents all the story that I told him.

WILLIAMS   What I am getting at is this: Could you have told all to him at the first meeting, or had developments taken place that enabled you to add to what you told him at subsequent meetings?

BOYER   I think I could have told him all of that information at the first meeting.

WILLIAMS   You think you could?

BOYER   Yes.

WILLIAMS   Even though you were still working on RDX continuously during this period?

BOYER   Because, as I say, the compositions, the way RDX was used was not new. The only new thing was that ingredient acetic anhydride, and that we knew as soon as we started.

WILLIAMS   Prior to this meeting at the house, at Rose's apartment, when he first asked you for RDX, had he shown any inclination of asking you for some information before that?

BOYER   No.

WILLIAMS   Well, when he broached this subject to you on that first occasion, when he definitely asked for information, did it come to you as a surprise?

BOYER   Yes.

WILLIAMS   But you did give it to him on that first occasion?

BOYER   Yes.

MR. COMMISSIONER TASCHEREAU   You are not sure on that; you say it might have taken two or three interviews?

BOYER   That is right. I did not give him all of that. I have told you now that I did not give him all of that on that first occasion.

TASCHEREAU   Was there a little more six months later; did you convey information also in 1944?

BOYER   Yes.

MR. WILLIAMS   And through 1945?

BOYER   No.

WILLIAMS   When did you see him last?

BOYER   Late summer of 1945.

WILLIAMS   Did you ever transmit any information of a secret nature to him other than at his own house?

BOYER   No.

WILLIAMS   You did not meet him any place else?

BOYER   No.

WILLIAMS   He did not come to your house for it?

BOYER   No. He came to our house but not—

WILLIAMS   Not for the purpose of the transmission of information?

BOYER   That is right.

MR. COMMISSIONER TASCHEREAU   Was it agreed that you would come back in six months or did he phone you for the second meeting?

BOYER   He would telephone me each time.

MR. WILLIAMS   During the interval I presume you would see him personally?

BOYER   I saw him one or twice, perhaps.

WILLIAMS   You were handing over to somebody, who was obviously an emissary of the Russians, information which your oath of secrecy forbade you to give?

BOYER   That is correct.

WILLIAMS   Would you like to tell the Commission what moved you to do that, why you did it? I mean that any statement or explanation you feel that the Commission should have, I know they would like you to make.

BOYER   I have already made a statement how Mr. Howe was willing to give it to the Russians and was not allowed to do so by the Americans. I felt throughout the work that it was unfortunate that the Russians, that there was not closer scientific liaison in connection with such information between the Russian war effort and ours. In fact I mentioned that a good many times. I was very anxious to see a technical mission, a British-American-Canadian technical mission in Russia and a similar Russian mission in Canada. I felt it was of great importance that the scientific war effort on the two fronts should be coordinated. That is all I have to say.

MR. COMMISSIONER TASCHEREAU   At that time, when you gave that information to Fred Rose, you knew that Mr. Howe did not have permission to give it to the Russians?

BOYER   Yes.

MR. WILLIAMS   You realized, Dr. Boyer, that what you were doing was contrary to the oath that you had taken?

BOYER   Yes.

WILLIAMS   Besides the information about RDX did you give Mr. Rose at any time any other secret information about any other matter for transmission to Russia?

BOYER   No.

WILLIAMS   Where was Mr. Rose living in Montreal at that time, do you recall?

BOYER   On Clark Avenue.

WILLIAMS   In an apartment house?

BOYER   Or Clark Street. In an apartment block; I think the number is 4520, but I am not sure.

WILLIAMS   Would each of those meetings be in response to a message or a telephone call from Mr. Rose?

BOYER   Yes.

WILLIAMS   Was the Russian embassy mentioned at any time in your discussion with Mr. Rose?

BOYER   No.

WILLIAMS   Was the name of Colonel Zabotin ever mentioned?

BOYER   Never.

WILLIAMS   Did you have any reason to believe you were on the books of the Russian embassy?

BOYER   None whatsoever.

WILLIAMS   There was never any suggestion of money passing from Mr. Rose or from the Russian embassy to yourself?

BOYER   No.

WILLIAMS   The question of money did not enter into it at all?

BOYER   No.

WILLIAMS   You did not know or have any reason to believe apparently that you were on the books of the Russian embassy under the cover name or pseudonym of the Professor?

BOYER   Not until two weeks ago when Inspector Harvison told me.

WILLIAMS   I would like to go over with you the various exhibits in which your name appears in the records of the Russian embassy. I want you to understand that in reading these to you I am merely reading what is written there and I do not want your feelings to be hurt by anything I say, because these are the Russian records.

In Exhibit No. 25-A we have a record of you under the cover name of Professor, and the following appears: "Frenchman. Well known chemist, about forty years." You are a Canadian of French descent?

BOYER   Yes.

WILLIAMS   And your modesty will allow you to say that you are a well known chemist?

BOYER   Not very well known, but I am a chemist.

WILLIAMS   And you are about forty years of age, or were in what year?

BOYER   I am not forty yet; I am thirty-nine.

WILLIAMS   "Works in the McGill University, Montreal." That has been true since 1941?

BOYER   Yes.

WILLIAMS   And even before that you were working in the laboratory there?

BOYER   Yes.

WILLIAMS   "Is the best specialist on explosives on the American continent." You probably—

BOYER   That is not correct.

WILLIAMS   — will say that that is a little bit wide?

BOYER   That is definitely incorrect.

WILLIAMS   We will have to allow your work to speak for itself, Dr. Boyer. "Gives full information about explosives and chemical plants." That I take it would be the information that you have detailed that you gave to Mr. Rose. You say that information you gave was with reference to RDX only?

BOYER   Yes.

WILLIAMS   Was there some discussion about the plants at which RDX would be manufactured?

BOYER   I may have mentioned that RDX was manufactured in the plant at Shawinigan Falls.

WILLIAMS   "Very rich. He is afraid to work." We do not read that to mean that you are afraid of hard work, but that you are afraid to work for the Communist party. Was that ever discussed between you and Mr. Rose, that this should be kept very secret and that you were doing it unwillingly and had a sense of fear in what you were doing?

BOYER   No.

WILLIAMS   "(Gave the formula RDX up to the present there is no valuation from the Master.)" The evidence is that Master is the cover name for a certain person in Russia and the meaning of that is, as we take it, that up to the present time they have not heard from Russia about how valuable your information is.

"Gave materials on poison gas." I understood you to say that you have not passed on any materials on poison gas?

BOYER   That is correct.

WILLIAMS   Could you give any explanation of why it was that in a record, which seems to be substantially so correct, there should be that reference to poison gas?

BOYER   Well, I could not, but Inspector Harvison suggested an answer.

WILLIAMS   What was that?

BOYER   During the interrogation. For the last year we have worked on DDT, the insecticide DDT, and I probably mentioned to Fred Rose in the course of ordinary conversation that we were working on DDT.

WILLIAMS   I see.

BOYER   And Inspector Harvison made the suggestion that that might be what — that Fred Rose relayed that information on, and they may have interpreted that as poison gas.

WILLIAMS   This entry is in the handwriting of one of the Russian embassy staff, and there is some doubt as to whether the initials which are used, which seem to be OV or DV, are the correct initials. I understood from you that you had taken lessons in Russian?

BOYER   Yes.

WILLIAMS   And that you had learned something about the language?

BOYER   Very little.

WILLIAMS   Will you look at this Exhibit 25-A and this last line, which I am showing you in the first paragraph, is the phrase in question, which has been translated as "gave about OD" or "gave materials on OD or OB or DV or OV" or translated, "gave materials on poison gas." Does that sentence mean anything to you?

BOYER   No, it does not.

WILLIAMS   Your Russian is not good enough to read it?

BOYER   No.

WILLIAMS   Then still in the record there is a suggestion that you might possibly know a person going under the name of Gini, a Jewish person going under the name of Gini in Montreal. Does that convey anything to you?

BOYER   No.

WILLIAMS   Did you ever hear of a person named Ginsberg?

BOYER   Yes.

WILLIAMS   Who is Ginsberg?

BOYER   I made that suggestion to Inspector Harvison. Reuben Ginsberg owns a chain of drug stores, or at least is part owner of a chain of drug stores.

WILLIAMS   And is he a Communist? Do you know anything about him?

BOYER   I think so.

WILLIAMS   Have you ever had any contact with him?

BOYER   I have met him three or four times.

WILLIAMS   What was the occasion of the meetings?

BOYER   I met him first at a New Year's Eve party, I think, sometime in — oh, 1942 or 1943, perhaps. Since then I have seen him once downtown, when I had lunch in his drug store, and I may have seen him once again, but that is all I recall.

WILLIAMS   Did you ever convey any information to him, or through him?

BOYER   Never.

WILLIAMS   Ever send any messages through him to Mr. Rose or anybody?

BOYER   Never.

WILLIAMS   Then also Gol, a young artist. Does that mean anything to you?

BOYER   Nothing.

MR. COMMISSIONER KELLOCK   Before you proceed to the next point, Dr. Boyer, when you gave that information to Rose, you told us that you had some information from Dr. Ross as to Mr. Howe's views as to whether or not it should be disclosed to the Russians. At the time you gave that information to Rose, did you tell Dr. Ross or anybody else in the National Research Council that you had done so?

BOYER   No.

KELLOCK   Would you have been prepared at that time to tell anybody that you had done so?

BOYER   I don't understand.

KELLOCK   Would you have been prepared to tell Dr. Ross or anybody else in the National Research Council that you disclosed that information?

BOYER   Under what circumstances do you mean? If I had been asked?

KELLOCK   If you had been asked, or would you have volunteered it?

BOYER   No . . .

MR. WILLIAMS   Then I refer you to Exhibit 35. This is a telegram, or what is believed to be a telegram, in the handwriting of one of the employees of the Russian embassy, addressed to The Director, and it reads this way: "The Professor advised that the director of the National Chemical Research Committee, Steacie told him about the new plant under construction: Pilot plant at Grand Mère in the province of Quebec." The pilot plant that you have referred to is the pilot plant for the manufacture of RDX, some three or four or five miles outside of Shawinigan?

BOYER   Yes.

WILLIAMS   That would be what; eight or ten miles from Grand Mère?

BOYER   That is possible; I am not sure how many miles there are between Shawinigan and Grand Mère.

WILLIAMS   Do you know of a pilot plant for anything at Grand Mère itself?

BOYER   No.

MR. COMMISSIONER KELLOCK   There is a pilot plant for RDX where?

BOYER   In Shawinigan.

KELLOCK   In Shawinigan itself?

BOYER   Yes.

MR. WILLIAMS   I think you said about five miles away?

BOYER   No, the pilot plant was in Shawinigan.

WILLIAMS   You know of no pilot plant at Grand Mère or anything?

BOYER   No.

WILLIAMS   Then it goes on: "This plant will produce uranium." Was that ever discussed between you and Fred Rose?

BOYER   No.

WILLIAMS   And anybody else?

BOYER   No.

WILLIAMS   Then it goes on: "The engineering personnel is being obtained from McGill University and is already moving into the district of the new plant." Does that make sense to you, even in connection with the pilot plant at Shawinigan?

BOYER   No.

WILLIAMS   Did any of the engineering personnel from McGill take part in constructing the plant?

BOYER   No.

WILLIAMS   Or in installing the equipment in it?

BOYER   No.

WILLIAMS   All that would be done, as far as the McGill people were concerned, including yourself, might be certain discussions with the engineers as to the advisability of a certain form of plant or installation?

BOYER   That is correct.

WILLIAMS   Then it goes on: "As a result of experiments carried out with uranium it has been found that uranium may be used for filling bombs, which is already being done in a practical way." Did you ever convey that information to Fred Rose?

BOYER   No, but one day Steacie did talk to Dr. Winkler and me at McGill, and did say that the Americans had spent a great deal of money on this atomic research, and he added that none of it was secret except the engineering and the chemistry. I may well have mentioned to Fred Rose what he said.

WILLIAMS   The last sentence of Exhibit 35 is: "The Americans have undertaken wide research work, having invested 660 million dollars in this business." Having in mind the information you got from Steacie; the fact that what Steacie told you is said to be set out here, and the reference to the investment of the Americans of $660,000,000 in the business, would indicate this, would it not — and I want you to correct me if I am wrong; that Rose did transmit at least part of a conversation which you had had with him, where you spoke of Steacie telling you certain things, including the investment of the Americans? That part might be an accurate transcription?

BOYER   That might be a highly garbled account of what I said.

WILLIAMS   There was a talk between Steacie and yourself and somebody else?

BOYER   Yes.

WILLIAMS   And reference was made in that talk to the amount being invested by the Americans?

BOYER   I don't know the amount.

WILLIAMS   Does the $660,000,000 register with you?

BOYER   He may have mentioned it; I don't remember.

WILLIAMS   So there is that much in it; a talk between Steacie and yourself and a third person; a large American investment for the purpose of manufacturing the atomic bomb, or experimenting with it; and would it be a fair assumption from the fact that this is in the records in the Russian embassy that Rose had transmitted the general conversation with you along those lines?

BOYER   It might well be, yes.

MR. COMMISSIONER KELLOCK   But it looks as though he had mixed up the pilot plant in connection with RDX and the pilot plant in regard to uranium; is that right?

BOYER   Yes.

MR. WILLIAMS   I am looking now at Exhibit 20-J, which is another original record from the Russian embassy. It is dated August 14, 1945, and contains this statement. Certain tasks had been given: "The tasks will be detailed to Gray, Bacon, and the Professor —" The Professor being your cover name. "— through Debouz." That is the cover name of Fred Rose. "The Professor is still on command —" A more correct interpretation is, "The Professor is still away on some job." On August 14, 1945, were you in Montreal, or were you away?

BOYER   No, I was in Montreal, That is V-J day, is it not, or very close to it?

WILLIAMS   You were in Montreal?

BOYER   That is V-J Day, is it not, or very close to it?

WILLIAMS   14th of August. (*continues*)   "Debouz will meet at the end of the month." The tasks which are referred to are set out in another telegram which does not appear to be among those which came from the cnbassy so I cannot discuss them with you. Then another original record, Exhibit No. 37, contains a rather cryptic entry. First of all it is under the heading "Professor," which means yourself, and it says: "Research Council — report on the organization and work," We do not know the date of that, but we assume it is some time around August, 1945, or it may be earlier. Were you ever asked by Mr. Rose to report on the organization of the Research Council and the nature of the work it was doing?

BOYER   No. I think I told Fred Rose one time what committees were in charge of research in the National Research Council, but that of course is not confidential information, but the nature of the work, no.

WILLIAMS   Did you mention the men at the head of the various committees?

BOYER   I do not think so; I did not know them.

WILLIAMS   You would know some of them?

BOYER   Some of them, yes. I knew Dr. Maass.

WILLIAMS   Did it ever occur to you from anything that he said on an occasion like that that he was trying to get the names of other persons he might approach in other departments?

BOYER   No.

WILLIAMS   At any time did he endeavour to get information from you as to who might be available to give information about other things in other branches of the government or in the armed services?

BOYER   No.

WILLIAMS   That time he asked you to come to his house, he asked you about a specific thing, RDX as such?

264

BOYER   Yes.

WILLIAMS   "Freida to the Professor through Grierson." Assuming for the moment that that is Freida Linden — you know who Mr. Grierson is?

BOYER   John Grierson.

WILLIAMS   And his position in 1945 was what?

BOYER   Well, I told Inspector Harvison I was not sure. I do not think he is any longer the chairman of W.I.B. [Wartime Information Board].

WILLIAMS   You do not recall the exact position he held in 1945?

BOYER   No.

WILLIAMS   One of the meanings that that is susceptible of is that Freida was to be attached to you for some purpose, either as a contact or as a means of transmitting information, and that that was to be arranged through Mr. Grierson. First of all, let me ask you this: Were you closely in touch with Mr. Grierson, were you friends?

BOYER   I have never met him.

WILLIAMS   Did you ever hear any suggestion from anybody, from Mr. Rose or anybody, that Freida might be used as a contact or means of transmitting information?

BOYER   No.

WILLIAMS   Is there any other interpretation you can suggest for that entry in the records of the Russian embassy? There is no meaning you can take out of it in any way?

BOYER   No.

WILLIAMS   Then Exhibit No. 30 contains reference to you by name. It is the only reference to you in which your name appears and not your cover name. Your name has been written in and then struck out, and the same has been done with the name of Fred Rose, it has been written in and struck out. It appears in there with reference to Dr. May whose photograph you have identified. You have told the Commission, as I understand it, that while you know May and had seen May under certain circumstances, you and he had never discussed, either his work or yours?

BOYER   That is right.

WILLIAMS   You had never learned anything from him about what he was doing, and you had never, I think you said, transmitted to him any information about what you were doing?

BOYER   That is correct.

WILLIAMS   The effect of Exhibit No. 30 in part is the setting up on the Russian files of those who were supplying information, particularly Dr. May and then your name and Rose's name is mentioned under the heading, "To think about development." Evidently at this time they were thinking about possibly developing Mr. Rose and yourself as a better means of information, and then it says: "The plant is in Grand Mère, Quebec, N13551." Does that convey anything at all to you?

BOYER   No.

WILLIAMS   Can you throw any light on it?

BOYER   Other than what is contained in the other documents, no.

WILLIAMS   You cannot throw any light on that?

BOYER   No.

WILLIAMS   As to why your name should have been written there in conjunction with Mr. Rose's and at the same time in a memo, referring particularly to Mr. May and the atomic bomb?

BOYER   No.

WILLIAMS   That sentence reads, "The plant is in Grand Mère, Quebec, N13551." Does that mean anything?

BOYER   No.

WILLIAMS   As a telephone number or code number or the name of some chemical formula or anything at all?

BOYER   No . . .

March 8, 1946

WILLIAMS   It has also been made to appear before us that other persons who were giving secret information, either directly to the Russians or for transmission to the Russians during the last few years, were either Communists or had definite Communist leanings. It would seem apparent that when Rose asked you for information as to the work that you were engaged in that he did that because he knew you for some considerable time. Would that be a fair deduction?

BOYER   Well, I have know him ever since 1938.

WILLIAMS   Not only have you known him, but you were known to him; is that so?

BOYER   I had worked in many organizations with Communists, yes.

WILLIAMS   And would it be a fair deduction to say that Rose spoke to you because he knew how you stood with regard to the Communist party?

BOYER   Yes.

WILLIAMS   Would it also be a proper inference to say that you gave Rose information because of that same Communist leaning or sympathy which you had?

BOYER   Yes, I think that is a proper inference.

MR. COMMISSIONER TASCHEREAU   When you went to see Fred Rose at his apartment or his house there to give him information, did you speak only of explosives or did you speak of anything else?

BOYER   Well, I probably discussed with him the course of the war, including technical developments of the war as I learned them in the newspaper.

TASCHEREAU   That is when you gave him the information about RDX about which you spoke yesterday?

BOYER   Yes.

TASCHEREAU   Did he give you any information?

BOYER   What sort of information?

TASCHEREAU   Well, concerning the conduct of the war, for instance; any information that he knew and that you did not know?

BOYER   We talked about the course of the war, but no technical information.

TASCHEREAU   He was in position, of course, to get information as a member of the House of Commons that you could not get?

BOYER   I suppose so.

TASCHEREAU   Did he tell you that he had information, secret information that he had obtained at the House of Commons, for instance?

BOYER   No, never.

TASCHEREAU   Did he tell you things that you did not know concerning the conduct of the war?

BOYER   Yes, but things which were in the newspaper. I presume he followed the newspapers much more closely that I did.

TASCHEREAU   So whatever he told you that you did not know, you do not know where he got it?

BOYER   Well, yes, that is correct.

TASCHEREAU   He did not give you the source of his information?

BOYER   But not technical information; he never gave me any technical information.

TASCHEREAU   What kind of information was it?

BOYER   Well, he would mention how the battle line stood, for instance, which I had no time to follow accurately.

TASCHEREAU   That first meeting was in 1940, or 1941?

BOYER   As I remember, 1943.

TASCHEREAU   The first meeting?

BOYER   As I remember.

TASCHEREAU   Concerning RDX?

BOYER   Yes.

TASCHEREAU   But you had three other meetings, you believe?

BOYER   Yes.

TASCHEREAU   They were about six months apart?

BOYER   I think so, yes.

TASCHEREAU   And every time you saw him you spoke of RDX and various other matters concerning the war?

BOYER   That is correct.

TASCHEREAU   But you do not know where he obtained that information?

BOYER   That is correct; I mean I did not ask him where he had obtained the information.

TASCHEREAU   Some of that information was unknown to you before?

BOYER   Yes, but none of it was of any importance. I mean, none of it was in my opinion — none of it could not have been obtained by reading the newspapers.

MR. COMMISSIONER KELLOCK   All this information you gave to Rose with regard to RDX, you gave to him in Montreal in his apartment?

BOYER   Yes.

KELLOCK   You spoke of this Committee for Allied Victory, and I think you said that was an organization that was organized by Communists or persons with Communist leanings; am I right in that?

BOYER   I think it may have been; I was not present at the first few meetings.

KELLOCK   Was that not your judgment later?

BOYER   Yes.

KELLOCK   There would be no question that the interests of that committee at that time and its expressed object of allied victory coincided with the interests of Canada at that time?

BOYER   In my opinion that would be so.

KELLOCK   So that there are times when the interests of the members of the Communist party or its sympathizers do coincide with the interests of Canada in which they are citizens?

BOYER   Every time so far as my work is concerned.

KELLOCK   Just let us deal with that for a minute. There was no question about that?

BOYER   That is right.

KELLOCK   In your mind, and there is none in mine. But when it came to imparting information with regard to RDX to Rose, you could not say the same thing about that, could you?

BOYER   Well, I still felt that it was of tremendous importance that there should be a full exchange of information between Russia and Canada and the United States and England.

KELLOCK   I know, but, Dr. Boyer, you have already said that the thing that influenced you in actually giving that information was your communistic sympathies, and in so doing it you knew at that time that it was the official policy of Canada not to impart that information to unauthorized persons; that is right?

BOYER   That is correct.

KELLOCK   In fact you had taken an oath not to do that very thing?

BOYER   That is correct.

KELLOCK   So in doing that in that particular instance you were put in a position where you had to act contrary to the interests of Canada as laid down officially?

BOYER   That is correct. . . .

RAYMOND BOYER, *recalled after recess*

MR. COMMISSIONER KELLOCK   One of the authorities under which we are acting as Royal Commissioners is the Inquiries Act. We have been conducting an inquiry, as no doubt you know, into what officials and other persons in positions of trust or otherwise may have communicated, either directly or indirectly, secret or confidential information, the disclosure of which might be inimical to the safety and interests of Canada, to the agents of a foreign power, and the facts relating to and the circumstances surrounding such communication.

One of the sections of the Inquiries Act, Section 12, provides that any person against whom any charge is made in the course of an investigation such as this shall be allowed to be represented by counsel. Section 13 provides that no report shall be made to the Governor in Council until reasonable notice shall have been given to the person of any charge of misconduct alleged against him and he shall have full opportunity to be heard in person or by counsel.

Up to the present you have been called before us as a witness. We have had the discretion as to whether or not counsel could appear before us on your behalf. No application so far has been made to us in any event for counsel on your behalf. If we come to the conclusion that on the evidence a charge has emerged of misconduct, then it is our duty to say to you that you have full opportunity to make any explanation or statement that you want to make, to call any evidence in addition to your own, or to have counsel appear before us on your behalf. We must do that before we can say anything in any report that we make to the Governor in Council, that in our opinion there is any misconduct of which you have been guilty.

On the evidence, and in view of your own evidence, it will be difficult for us to come to any other conclusion than that we are of the opinion that we must report that you have communicated secret information to the agents of a foreign power, the disclosure of which might be or may have been inimical to the interests of Canada. Therefore, I say to you now: Do you want to make any explanation other than you have done? Do you want to make any further statement? Do you want to call any other evidence? Do you want to have counsel appear before us on your behalf?

BOYER   Well, I am not familiar with these procedures. My wife told me when I saw her Monday night that my father had engaged counsel.

KELLOCK   Perhaps I should make it plain to you. My brother points out to me that I did not make one point clear to you. We are only a fact-finding body. We are not a court. We have no power to punish you even if we thought you should be punished. We are only a fact-finding body. We hear evidence and we form our conclusions on that evidence and report those conclusions to the Governor in Council. Whether or not a charge should be laid against you in the courts, or may be laid against you in the courts, is something with which we have nothing to do. As I say, we are just a Royal Commission. We hear the evidence, we find the facts and we make a report or reports and then our duty is finished.

If any proceedings are taken in the courts, that lies with the Governor in Council and of course should any charge be laid against you in the courts you would have the same right as anybody else to be represented there by counsel. But I am speaking only of this Royal Commission and the evidence that we have heard. It is upon that evidence that we will find and make our report. Is there anything you want to say, or do you want to have counsel appear before us?

BOYER   No, I have told you everything there is. . . .

THE TESTIMONY OF DAVID SHUGAR

March 8, 1946

DAVID SHUGAR, *called and sworn*

MR. FAUTEUX   I was asking you whether Dr. Boyer had some communistic sympathies or leanings. It has nothing to do with whatever work you have done in the past.

SHUGAR   That is too general a question to be able to answer.

FAUTEUX   Then how would you put it?

SHUGAR   To my knowledge Dr. Boyer was not a member of the Communist party, if that is what you mean.

FAUTEUX   How would you know that?

SHUGAR   I said to my knowledge. If by a Communist you mean one who advocates revolution, or the overthrow by force of the government, no; I would not think that Dr. Boyer had any opinions of that nature.

FAUTEUX   That may not be the sole definition of a Communist; there may be other definitions?

SHUGAR   It is up to you, then, to explain to me what you mean by a Communist.

MR. COMMISSIONER KELLOCK   What do you mean by a Communist? What do you understand by the term "Communist"?

SHUGAR   I would take it that a man who called himself a Communist was one who — I don't know.

KELLOCK   No idea at all?

SHUGAR   I presume one who would advocate the forcible overthrow of the government, or of a government. I am not quite sure whether that would be a definition of a Communist or not.

KELLOCK   I am asking you, what is your definition?

SHUGAR   I don't think I know enough to be able to give a definition.

KELLOCK   Have you any idea on the subject at all, as to what a Communist is?

SHUGAR   Well, from a purely — as a technical definition, I suppose a Communist is one who fully believes in all the teachings of Marx.

KELLOCK   And where do you stand?

SHUGAR   I am not a Communist. I have certain ideas about unions, about conditions, current conditions and the need for remedying them, which I believe are my right as a Canadian citizen.

KELLOCK   Oh, unquestionably. All we are interested in are the facts. That is all we want to know. Nobody is attacking your opinions. All I am asking you about is, what are they?

SHUGAR   I merely have the impression that some of these questions do not bear on the subject under discussion here.

KELLOCK   Is that why you are reluctant to answer them?

SHUGAR   No. As a matter of fact I find it a little confusing to answer such questions as, "what is a Communist?" I am not reluctant to answer anything that I can answer in a clear manner.

KELLOCK Any questions I have put to you, or any questions counsel have put to you so far you can be sure are all relevant; so if you want to go back over the ground and make any better answers or explanations, go ahead.

SHUGAR No; I would let those answers stand.

MR. FAUTEUX You stated that you were not a Communist; that is, if I understood you correctly, you said you did not share all the ideas of the Communists, or of Marx?

SHUGAR You understand what, sir?

FAUTEUX I understood you to say that if by a "Communist" I meant someone who shares all the views of Karl Marx, and believes in the necessity of world revolution, and so on, which includes the change of government, that you are not one. Is that what you meant?

SHUGAR I have not read much of Karl Marx's views. I have read some of his writings.

FAUTEUX Then the next question is, would it be fair to say that if you are not a Communist, you have Communist leanings or sympathies? Would you say that this is a fair statement, a fair way to put it?

SHUGAR (No answer)

FAUTEUX You understand my question?

SHUGAR I understand your question.

FAUTEUX Would you please answer my question?

SHUGAR (No answer)

MR. COMMISSIONER KELLOCK Why does it take you so long to answer these questions, Mr. Shugar?

SHUGAR I do not quite understand the point of it, Mr. Commissioner.

KELLOCK You do not need to understand the point of it. Just answer the question if you understand it; that is all. You are trying to look ahead and see if there is some point involved, but that is not your function. You are here to answer questions. If you do not understand the question you can ask for an explanation. If you do understand it, go ahead and answer it.

SHUGAR Would you give me an explanation of that?

KELLOCK Then I will ask you a few questions. Are you a member of the Labour-Progressive party?

SHUGAR No, sir.

KELLOCK Have you ever been?

SHUGAR No, sir.

KELLOCK Are you familiar with the Labour-Progressive party?

SHUGAR I know some of the people, I think. . . .

KELLOCK Well, Mr. Shugar, have you yourself been a member of a study group at any time?

SHUGAR Yes, I have been a member of a study group.

KELLOCK One group, or more than one?

SHUGAR One group.

KELLOCK Where?

SHUGAR Well, I was a member of a study group in Toronto.

KELLOCK In Toronto? When?

SHUGAR In 1943.

KELLOCK Is that the first study group of which you were a member or attended?

271

SHUGAR   What kind of study group would you be referring to?

KELLOCK   Communist?

SHUGAR   I wouldn't call that a Communist study group.

KELLOCK   Well, then we will go back to the question of whether the Toronto group was the first study group of which you were a member or which you attended?

SHUGAR   No, it was not, sir.

KELLOCK   Where was the first?

SHUGAR   I did used to attend some study group at McGill; the Student Christian Movement.

KELLOCK   Leaving out the Student Christian Movement, any other kind of study group before the one in Toronto?

SHUGAR   During one summer I did attend a couple of meetings of a study group on socialism.

KELLOCK   In Montreal?

SHUGAR   Yes.

KELLOCK   And what was the study group in Toronto studying?

SHUGAR   It was a study group on socialism also.

KELLOCK   The same kind of socialism as the Montreal group?

SHUGAR   No; it was really more a study of trade unionism.

KELLOCK   In Montreal?

SHUGAR   No, in Toronto.

KELLOCK   The one in Montreal, then; was that a study of Marxism?

SHUGAR   No, it was a study of a book by John Strachey.

KELLOCK   And who were the members of the Montreal group or groups?

SHUGAR   It is a long time ago. One person I remember was a Helen McMaster.

KELLOCK   Well, what about Toronto, who were the members of that group?

SHUGAR   It was composed of a few people from the Association of Technical Employees.

KELLOCK   And their names?

SHUGAR   One was Philip Dawes.

KELLOCK   Was he a Communist or a Labour-Progressive?

SHUGAR   Not to my knowledge.

KELLOCK   All right. Anybody else now?

SHUGAR   (No answer)

KELLOCK   Is that all you can think of?

SHUGAR   (No answer)

KELLOCK   Do you want a rest, Dr. Shugar?

SHUGAR   No, I don't need a rest, sir.

KELLOCK   Well, can you answer the question?

SHUGAR   (No answer)

KELLOCK   What is the trouble? Can you not think of the name, or what is the trouble?

SHUGAR   Yes, one of the difficulties is thinking of names.

KELLOCK   What is the other difficulty; that you do not want to tell the names?

SHUGAR   Well, to some extent that is correct.

KELLOCK   Well, you are obliged to tell the names, so please do not waste our time.

SHUGAR   I beg pardon?

KELLOCK   You are obliged to tell the names, so please do not waste our time. Please answer the question.

SHUGAR   Can you explain to me why I am obliged to tell you the names?

KELLOCK   Because that is the law; that you are obliged to answer any question that is put to you here.

SHUGAR   I thought any questions pertaining to the subject under discussion.

KELLOCK   Well, we decide what questions pertain to the subject under discussion. You do not need to worry about any question put to you by myself or my fellow commissioner; you are obliged to answer. So will you go ahead, unless you want a rest, if you are tired?

SHUGAR   Well, I would like to state that my legal counsel informed me that I need not answer, that I was at liberty to refuse to answer any questions.

KELLOCK   Well, I am telling you that that advice is not sound, that you are obliged to answer. So what do you say?

SHUGAR   I remember, sir, when I was administered that oath at the beginning of this afternoon, that the oath read, "questions pertaining to this inquiry."

KELLOCK   That is so.

SHUGAR   In my opinion, sir, that question does not pertain to the inquiry.

KELLOCK   But you are not the judge of that; we are the judges of that, and I have already told you that the question put to you must be answered.

SHUGAR   If I had known that I was not to be the judge of that I would have hesitated before taking the oath.

KELLOCK   Well, it would not have made any difference whatsoever; you would still have to answer.

SHUGAR   Pardon, sir?

KELLOCK   You must not waste our time. We will not have our time wasted. You are either going to answer the questions or you are not. If you are tired and want a rest, I have already told you that you can have it; but you must answer the questions put to you.

SHUGAR   Very well. Would this be considered an answer, that I would rather not answer that question?

KELLOCK   No; that is not an answer that will be accepted.

MR. COMMISSIONER TASCHEREAU   You remember what the question was?

SHUGAR   Yes, sir, I remember what the question was.

MR. COMMISSIONER KELLOCK   Then will you go ahead and answer it, please?

SHUGAR   (No answer)

KELLOCK   Well, what is it? Are you refusing to answer it or are you going to answer it? Which is it?

SHUGAR   I am at liberty to refuse to answer anything.

KELLOCK   You are not at liberty to refuse to answer. You are obliged to answer. Let there be no misunderstanding about that. I am asking you if you are refusing to answer?

SHUGAR   (No answer)

KELLOCK   What do you say?

SHUGAR   I would rather not answer that, sir.

KELLOCK   Do you say you are refusing to answer? It is not a question of your rather not answering it; it is a question of either answering it or refusing to answer. Now, which is it to be?

SHUGAR   (No answer)

KELLOCK   Which is it?

SHUGAR   (No answer)

MR. COMMISSIONER TASCHEREAU   We will have a recess for five minutes, then.

On Resuming.

MR. COMMISSIONER KELLOCK   I will ask the reporter to read the question to you, Dr. Shugar.

REPORTER

Q. Well, what about Toronto. Who were the members of that group? A. It was composed of a few people from the Association of Technical Employees. Q. And their names? A. One was Philip Dawes. Q. Was he a Communist or a Labour-Progressive? A. Not to my knowledge. Q. All right. Anybody else now?

KELLOCK   Do you understand the question?

SHUGAR   Yes, sir.

KELLOCK   What is your answer?

SHUGAR   (No answer)

KELLOCK   What is your answer?

SHUGAR   My answer, sir, is that I see no relation between that question and the matter under discussion.

KELLOCK   Very well. We will adjourn now. You will have an opportunity to think it over until to-morrow morning, and we will hear from you at half-past ten. I may explain to you that you are not the only witness that we have had regarding matters in which you have been interested; I may also explain to you that by refusing to answer, that is a contempt, and that we have the power to punish you for contempt. So you can think it over, and we will adjourn until to-morrow morning at half-past ten. . . .

March 9, 1946

MR. FAUTEUX   Assuming that Carr suggested your name as being a good source of information, you think that Carr would have suggested your name if he had any doubt about the possibility of your giving some information? To come to the point, Dr. Shugar. You can appreciate yourself that this is a file dealing with Sam Carr?

SHUGAR   Yes.

FAUTEUX   You must admit also that that man must have had some dealings with the Russian embassy to have a file in his name there?

SHUGAR   That is right.

FAUTEUX   And you find here the course of meetings and so on, and all sorts

274

of names, cover names, Frank, the Doctor, Grant and so on, and all his activities, the course of meetings, the duties of meetings, money being paid and so on. Finally we reach a page where your name is mentioned on assignments from Sam. Evidently Sam Carr is to meet you. Of course, you do not know of anyone and I do not know of anyone who could give this information except yourself. I would like personally to have your real reaction as to how you should be linked in this file of Sam Carr's with Sam Carr at the Russian embassy as being a man who could give some information there. Would you say that it would be extraordinary that Carr should suggest your name as a possible source of information on these various points?

SHUGAR   I would say it is more than extraordinary.

FAUTEUX   Pardon?

SHUGAR   I would say it is more than extraordinary.

FAUTEUX   You would say it is more than extraordinary?

SHUGAR   That is right.

FAUTEUX   You find it is there, anyway?

SHUGAR   That is right.

MR. COMMISSIONER KELLOCK   Have you any doubt as to the authenticity of the document you are looking at, Exhibit No. 19-C, or that file of Carr as being original documents coming from the Russian embassy?

SHUGAR   Well, it does seem a little fantastic to me.

KELLOCK   Fantastic, but the evidence that we have establishes to our satisfaction — I think I can say — the authenticity of these documents. I am just asking you if you have any doubt in your mind, because there are other documents as well as this. There is at least one document where your name passes between Ottawa and Moscow. I would like to know when you are considering that document in front of you whether you have any question in your mind as to the authenticity of the document.

MR. COMMISSIONER TASCHEREAU   When you wrote the Commission some time ago you said you were the victim of fabricated evidence. What is that fabricated evidence that you suspect? We are showing you all that we have.

SHUGAR   I made that statement on the basis of the interviews I was given out at Rockcliffe.

TASCHEREAU   Were you shown at Rockcliffe the documents that you are now shown here?

SHUGAR   I was shown one document that was typed and I was read to from one other. There was some document which included my name, and some questions about my address and other particulars about me. I did not see that document but it was read to me.

MR. COMMISSIONER KELLOCK   I am directing your attention to Exhibit No. 19-C. What do you say about that? Have you any reason to suggest that that is fabricated?

SHUGAR   I do not think I am in position to say, sir, because I have not the facts.

KELLOCK   You have no reason to say that it is a fabricated document, have you? If you have, I would like you to tell us because we certainly are interested in that.

SHUGAR   I can only say that I have not the evidence that is before the Commission to make a definite statement about this.

KELLOCK   All right, you cannot say one way or the other? You cannot suggest any reason to us why that document should not be regarded as an authentic document, because if you have we would like to know about it?

SHUGAR   No, I have no reason one way or the other.

MR. FAUTEUX   Now we turn to another page, which will be marked 19-D which, as you can see, is in Russian. . . .

SHUGAR   I know the Russian letters. I am a stamp collector, and I used to include Russian stamps in my collection.

FAUTEUX   You will see that the translation is headed "Task No. 2," and dated June 15, 1945. There is reference here to A.N. Veale, whom you have identified as being known to you?

SHUGAR   That is right.

FAUTEUX   "An Englishman"?

SHUGAR   That is right.

FAUTEUX   Then on the verso of this page, or on page 2 in the Russian document, what name do you read there?

SHUGAR   "Shugar."

FAUTEUX   That is you again?

SHUGAR   That is right.

FAUTEUX   How do you account for that?

SHUGAR   I cannot account for that.

FAUTEUX   It is translated "Communicate how the matter stands with the fulfilment of the former assignment for Lieutenant Shugar."
What do you say to that?

SHUGAR   I have nothing to say to that.

FAUTEUX   You have no suggestion to make?

SHUGAR   I can only draw the inference from that that somebody was expecting to get something from me.

FAUTEUX   And that someone would be who? Would that someone be Sam Carr?

SHUGAR   It could be.

FAUTEUX   In the document that we have examined for about an hour the heading was "Sam to Shugar." Do you know any other Sam than Sam Carr?

SHUGAR   Sam Gerson.

FAUTEUX   And did Sam Gerson ever inquire about your work in the way Sam Carr did?

SHUGAR   No, sir.

FAUTEUX   Other than the inquiries of Sam Carr, what other Sam did inquire about your work in the way he did?

SHUGAR   None that I know of.

FAUTEUX   All right, then.

MR. COMMISSIONER KELLOCK   (*To Mr. Fauteux*)   Exhibit 19-C was assignment No. 1, was it not?

FAUTEUX   That is right.

KELLOCK   And Exhibit 19-D speaks of "the former assignment" does it not?

FAUTEUX   Yes.   (*To the witness*)   And on this assignment No. 2 to Sam Carr, he is instructed: "Communicate how the matter stands for the fulfilment of former assignment for Lieutenant Shugar."
The information given by Carr to the Russian embassy was:
"At the present time he is working Maritime staff." That may be an expres-

sion meaning that you had left Research Enterprises Limited to go into the navy?

MR. COMMISSIONER KELLOCK   Or it might mean that the witness was in Halifax?

SHUGAR   My first impression, when that was read to me, was that it meant the Maritimes, and I pointed out that aside from the four and half weeks I spent at Cornwallis in Nova Scotia I had not made any trips to the Maritimes and I was never stationed there.

KELLOCK   But it could mean that, too, could it not?

SHUGAR   It could mean what?

KELLOCK   It could mean that you were in Halifax at that time?

SHUGAR   I guess it could; yes.

KELLOCK   Doctor, you said a moment ago that I stopped you from answering some question. There are times when, if you want to say things, you do not have to hesitate to say them. I would not like you to suggest that I stopped you from giving any answer you wanted to give. You understand that, do you?

SHUGAR   When I was interrogated out at Rockcliffe —

KELLOCK   I am speaking to you here. You said some time ago that I had stopped you from giving an answer. I do not want to stop you from giving any answer. Is that clear to you?

SHUGAR   Yes.

KELLOCK   As a matter of fact I have been waiting a long time to get some of the answers. You recognize that, do you?

SHUGAR   Some of your questions have not been too clear.

KELLOCK   Well, let us continue on this point here. Carr continued: "He has consented to work for us but with special caution." What have you to say about that?

SHUGAR   I would say that is a presumption on some person's part.

KELLOCK   And who would be that person?

SHUGAR   Whoever wrote that.

KELLOCK   Who do you think wrote it?

SHUGAR   Well, from what you have said I suppose that was written by Sam Carr.

KELLOCK   And from the exhibit that is before you, who do you think it is?

SHUGAR   Well, I believe you are in a better position to judge than I am.

KELLOCK   I am asking your opinion on it?

SHUGAR   Well, the impression you give me is that it was written by Sam Carr.

KELLOCK   I am asking what the document suggests to you?

SHUGAR   The document suggests that it was written by Sam Carr. . . .

MR. FAUTEUX   This was either written by him, or he gave the information that has been written to somebody?

SHUGAR   No, I would think that he could write Russian; either Russian or Ukrainian.

FAUTEUX   Have you any reason to suggest that Sam Carr would make a report as to your activities to the Soviet Union embassy here unless it was true?

SHUGAR   (No answer)

FAUTEUX   Do you understand my question, or is the question not clear?

SHUGAR   Would you mind repeating it?

FAUTEUX   Have you any reason to suggest why Sam Carr would make this report on you to the Soviet embassy, unless it was true? Do you understand the question?

SHUGAR   Yes, I think I understand it.

FAUTEUX   Then what is your answer

SHUGAR   I can only say that he was presuming that he could.

FAUTEUX   That he could what?

SHUGAR   That he could get information from me.

MR. COMMISSIONER KELLOCK   But what the document says, if it is a correct translation, is that you have consented to work for them.

SHUGAR   Well, that is not correct, sir. I was never asked to work for anybody.

KELLOCK   But the question you are asked is: have you anything to say as to why Carr would so report to the Soviet embassy if that were not true? That is the question you are asked.

MR. COMMISSIONER TASCHEREAU   Why would he say that you had consented to work, if it were not true?

SHUGAR   I cannot say, sir.

TASCHEREAU   You don't know?

SHUGAR   I don't know.

MR. COMMISSIONER KELLOCK   Did you agree to give him any information?

SHUGAR   No, sir.

MR. FAUTEUX   Then what he was reporting was not true?

SHUGAR   That is what I would say.

FAUTEUX   And why do you say he would do that? That was my question, in effect.

SHUGAR   I don't know Sam Carr well enough to say that.

FAUTEUX   Was there anything that you could suggest which would bring Carr to make such a report on you to the Soviet embassy?

SHUGAR   Was there anything —?

FAUTEUX   Yes; any reason. Can you find any reason why Carr would make a report on you there if it was not true? Why would he tell the Russian embassy that you had agreed, if you did not agree to work?

SHUGAR   (No answer)

FAUTEUX   Is my question clear?

SHUGAR   Yes, it is clear.

FAUTEUX   Then would you mind answering it?

SHUGAR   I am afraid I do not see the answer.

FAUTEUX   You do not see the answer?

SHUGAR   No.

FAUTEUX   You have a clear question, but you have no answer?

SHUGAR   I do not know what would be behind — the motive in making a statement like that.

FAUTEUX   Unless it was true?

SHUGAR   It was not true.

FAUTEUX   Unless it was true, I say?

SHUGAR   It was not true. . . .

THE TESTIMONY OF H.S. GERSON

March 12, 1946

H.S. GERSON, *called and sworn*

MR. WILLIAMS   When Zabotin got this list of tasks, this request for information that Moscow wanted him to get, he answered the Director at Moscow. The practice was that each telegram here was numbered with a consecutive number beginning at the first of the month and carried on, and they used to number the telegrams from Moscow. The one I have is an answer to No. 11295 from Moscow, and Colonel Zabotin says: "The tasks will be detailed to Gray, Bacon and the Professor through Debouz." Those are cover names; just as Gray is a cover name for you, Bacon and Professor are cover names for other persons, and Debouz is the cover name of the man through whom these tasks were to be given. The evidence is that Debouz is Fred Rose. Did you ever have any talks with Fred Rose about information that you were to channel through him to anybody?

GERSON   No, sir.

WILLIAMS   Think very carefully, Mr. Gerson.

GERSON   No.

MR. COMMISSIONER TASCHEREAU   Why do you hesitate to give an answer?

GERSON   He told me to think carefully. I was ready to answer right away.

MR. WILLIAMS   You realize that you are under oath?

GERSON   I am under oath here, yes, sir.

WILLIAMS   I may say that there is evidence here, Mr. Gerson, that others have told us that they passed information through Mr. Debouz.

GERSON   Never heard of the name.

WILLIAMS   I quite agree, but they knew him as Fred Rose. You still persist that you did not?

GERSON   I still persist.

WILLIAMS   Some of the tasks that were set out in the directive from Moscow were tasks that you could perform if you wished because of your connection with the Production Branch of the Department of Munitions and Supply. I put it to you that those tasks were deputed to you by Mr. Fred Rose and that you performed them?

GERSON   No.

WILLIAMS   You say no?

GERSON   I say no.

WILLIAMS   You do not wish any time to think over your answer?

GERSON   No, because the Commissioner may think I am hesitating.

MR. COMMISSIONER KELLOCK   Fred Rose knew where you were employed, did he?

GERSON   Most likely; I never discussed it with him.

KELLOCK   Never discussed any part of your work or any information in connection with that work with Fred Rose at any time?

GERSON   Not in connection with our work, no.

KELLOCK   He must have been displaying some reticence in your presence that he did not display when talking to other people?

GERSON   I am sorry. . . .

INSPECTOR C.W. HARVISON, R.C.M.P.,   *called and sworn.*

HARVISON   At the conclusion of this interrogation I told Mr. Gerson that I was suspending the interrogation for twenty-four hours, and that during that time I would like him to consider if, as a Canadian citizen, he was willing to assist his government by supplying any information in his possession regarding Soviet espionage.

The following day I had Mr. Gerson brought to my office again, and asked him if he had made any decision. He said that there were a number of personal problems connected with the decision; that he found it extremely difficult, and asked me if I could give him until the following Saturday noon to arrive at a decision.

On the Saturday noon I again had him brought to my office and asked him if he had made a decision, and he said that he had. He said that he realized that the picture ahead was very dark for him; that he had made mistakes; that he would have to face the music himself, and that he would not be able to live with himself if he gave information that so-and-so had done such-and-such; and he used the expression, if I remember well, that he would not be able to live with himself if he "put the finger on this man and that man." . . .

HAROLD SAMUEL GERSON,   *recalled:*

MR. WILLIAMS   Now, Mr. Gerson, will you come back, please. It is your duty, Mr. Gerson, to disclose to this Commission all facts within your knowledge; and the fact that it may hurt somebody else is no reason why you should not make your disclosures. You have heard what the last witness has said. Are you prepared now to be frank with the Commission?

GERSON   I have given you my testimony.

MR. COMMISSIONER KELLOCK   In the first place, you heard the evidence of the last witness?

GERSON   Yes.

KELLOCK   You heard the evidence of the last witness, the gentleman who just went out?

GERSON   You have a text; there was a stenographer in there. She took it, and there is the evidence.

KELLOCK   Do you understand the question I am putting to you?

GERSON   No, I do not.

KELLOCK   I asked if you heard the evidence of the last witness?

GERSON   I heard what Mr. Harvison said.

KELLOCK   Is what he said correct? Did he correctly say what took place in the interviews you had with him?

GERSON   To a large extent, yes.

KELLOCK   You say to a large extent. What corrections or amendments do you want to make?

GERSON   I don't want to make any amendments.

KELLOCK   All right; then you are being asked if you have anything to say in view of that situation?

GERSON   No.

KELLOCK   You have made up your mind that you will not speak; is that it?

GERSON   You have asked me questions and I have answered them. I have not made up my mind about anything.

MR. WILLIAMS   If you accepted Inspector Harvison's evidence, as you have, Mr. Gerson, who are the persons whom you did not want to identify?

GERSON   There is nobody I didn't want to identify.

WILLIAMS   There is nobody you do not want to identify?

GERSON   No. You have asked me questions, and I have answered to the best of my ability.

MR. COMMISSIONER KELLOCK   That is not what you are being asked. Will you put your mind on what you are being asked? You have said that the witness correctly stated what you told him, that you do not want to make any changes or corrections. Now you are being asked, who are the persons that you referred to, that you did not want to "put the finger on" when you used that expression to the last witness? Who are those persons?

GERSON   I don't know.

MR. COMMISSIONER TASCHEREAU   You certainly know them, because you hesitated before telling the inspector that you would not speak. So you should tell us the truth here.

GERSON   Well, I am doing that to the best of my ability.

TASCHEREAU   Oh, no, you are not. You told Inspector Harvison that you would not be able to live with yourself if you did give those names. That is what you told him; and you agreed that the inspector said the truth here. So will you please tell us what are the names of these persons; and I am suggesting to you that you are obliged to answer here?

GERSON   Well, I don't know of any names.

TASCHEREAU   Well, why did you speak that way to the inspector, then? Why did you tell him that if you gave certain names you would not be able to live with yourself? What are those names?

GERSON   I haven't any names.

TASCHEREAU   Oh, no, sir; speak the truth. You certainly have names. We know that you have. You have told the inspector that you had?

GERSON   No, I didn't.

TASCHEREAU   Yes, you did tell him.

GERSON   Pardon me.

TASCHEREAU   You told the inspector you had names and you asked for a delay before taking a decision as to whether you would reveal those names or not. You told him that on February 27, and to-day you tell us that you have no names. Do you want us to believe that, Mr. Gerson?

GERSON   (No answer)

TASCHEREAU   Do you want us to believe that? I think you should tell the truth; it will be much better for you.

GERSON   I am trying to.

TASCHEREAU   Oh, no, you are not making a very good effort now. You know some other names, and we expect you to tell us those names.

MR. FAUTEUX   What did you mean when you said that you would not be able to live with yourself?

GERSON   What did I mean?

MR. COMMISSIONER KELLOCK   You heard the question?

GERSON   I don't understand what you mean.

KELLOCK   Yes you do.

MR. COMMISSIONER TASCHEREAU   Everybody understands you.

GERSON   Maybe I am stupid.

MR. COMMISSIONER KELLOCK   No, that is one thing you are not. I will give you a certificate in that respect. Perhaps you ought to understand this, that a refusal to answer a question put to you in this Commission, which it is within your power to answer, is an offence and punishable as such. I just want to give you that information.

MR. COMMISSIONER TASCHEREAU   You told the inspector that you knew some other persons, and you wanted a few days' delay to think it over as to whether or not you would reveal the names?

GERSON   No.

TASCHEREAU   Oh, yes. The inspector told us that, and you agreed with what he said. You heard his evidence here, that if you gave those names you would be unable to live with yourself. So who are they?

GERSON   I have no names.

TASCHEREAU   Pardon?

GERSON   I haven't any names.

TASCHEREAU   You still refuse to tell them?

GERSON   I am not refusing anything. You asked me to give you names, and I haven't any.

TASCHEREAU   Why did you ask a delay for a couple of days at the barracks not long ago?

GERSON   Why?

TASCHEREAU   Yes, why?

GERSON   Just to put it off. Have you ever been questioned?

TASCHEREAU   To put off what? You said you wanted some delay to think it over, as to whether you would reveal the names or not?

GERSON   No, I didn't say that.

TASCHEREAU   Yes, that is what you said.

GERSON   No, I did not.

TASCHEREAU   That is what the inspector said, and you agreed that he was right; and you had nothing to correct in his statement? . . .

MR. WILLIAMS   It was through Dr. Boyer that you managed to get your appointment in the government service; that is right, is it not?

GERSON   Yes, sir.

WILLIAMS   And it was through you that your brother-in-law, James Scotland Benning, got an appointment in one of the government departments?

GERSON   Can I elaborate on that?

WILLIAMS   Yes?

GERSON   Do you mind?

WILLIAMS   Go ahead.

GERSON   I was sent up here — I think Mr. Lawrence will tell you that I was sent up to Ottawa for a month. When that month was up they were supposed to get somebody. They had a major there — I cannot think of his name — who was leaving and they were supposed to get somebody to replace the major. I came up here to help them out for a month. The month went by and they did not get anybody. Two months went by and they did not seem to get anybody. I suggested a couple of other people and they did not get the job and so one day, wanting to get back to Montreal, I told Colonel Ogilvie that I knew somebody who could handle the work, or I thought they could handle the work and Scott — the colonel happened to be in Montreal and he interviewed Scott and Benning came up and I was released to go back to Montreal.

WILLIAMS   So the answer to my question is "Yes." You were responsible for getting Benning into that position?

GERSON   Yes.

WILLIAMS   Have you ever gone under any other name than Harold Samuel Gerson?

GERSON   Not to my knowledge.

WILLIAMS   You are sometimes referred to as Hal Gerson, are you not?

GERSON   Yes, sir.

WILLIAMS   Have you ever been known as Harvey Gerson?

GERSON   No. Just a minute, that sounds familiar. I was not known as that, but I think there was some mail or something addressed to Harvey Gerson.

WILLIAMS   When was that?

GERSON   It was back up in when I was living in Kirkland Lake.

WILLIAMS   You were the manager of the Kirkland Lake Gold Rand Limited at Kirkland Lake, Ontario, from 1936 to 1941, were not you?

GERSON   Yes, sir.

WILLIAMS   At that time you were a member of the Communist party?

GERSON   No, sir.

WILLIAMS   You were not?

GERSON   No, sir.

WILLIAMS   Were you a member of the Communist party at any time?

GERSON   No, sir.

WILLIAMS   Have you ever been a member of the Labour-Progressive party?

GERSON   No, sir.

WILLIAMS   You knew Fred Rose in 1939, did not you?

GERSON   Yes.

WILLIAMS   He came up to Kirkland Lake in that year to raise money for the Communist party, did he not?

GERSON   I would not —

WILLIAMS   What?

GERSON   Not to my knowledge.

WILLIAMS   Did not you take a very active part when he was there in helping him to raise money for the Communist party?

GERSON   No, sir.

WILLIAMS   Did you take any part at all in helping him to raise money for the Communist party?

GERSON   Not that I remember.

WILLIAMS   In the month of September, 1939?

GERSON   1939?

WILLIAMS   Yes?

GERSON   No, sir, I do not remember that.

MR. COMMISSIONER TASCHEREAU   Will you speak louder, please?

GERSON   I do not remember.

MR. WILLIAMS   You would not say you did not?

GERSON   Yes, I would say I did not.

WILLIAMS   You would say you did not?

GERSON   Yes.

WILLIAMS   No doubt about that?

GERSON   No doubt about that.

WILLIAMS   Anybody who says differently is stating what is not true?

GERSON   Possibly.

WILLIAMS   What?

GERSON   It could be.

WILLIAMS   The answer to that must be either Yes or No, Mr. Gerson, not possibly or it could be. If anyone stated that in September, 1939, you assisted Fred Rose to raise money for the Communist party in Kirkland Lake, that must be either true or false?

GERSON   False.

WILLIAMS   False. Did you ever help Fred Rose to raise money for any organization, whatever its name?

GERSON   No, sir.

WILLIAMS   Or for any individual?

GERSON   We raised some money for China.

WILLIAMS   When was that?

GERSON   The early part of the Chinese war.

WILLIAMS   Would that be in 1939 and at Kirkland Lake?

GERSON   It was in Kirkland Lake; I do not remember the year.

MR. COMMISSIONER KELLOCK   With Fred Rose?

GERSON   No, Fred Rose had nothing to do with it. We ran a tag day with the permission of the town council.

MR. WILLIAMS   Then you stated to the Commission —

GERSON   The money was sent, pardon me, the money was sent by one of the Chinese boys to China through the bank. It was not given to any person here.

WILLIAMS   Then you stated to the Commission categorically that you never assisted Fred Rose, directly or indirectly, to raise money at Kirkland Lake for the Communist party or for any other body, organization or individual? . . . You said you have not at any time been a member of the Communist party of Canada?

GERSON   Yes, sir.

WILLIAMS   And that you have not at any time been a member of the Labour-Progressive party of Canada?

GERSON   Yes, sir.

WILLIAMS   Have you ever been sympathetic to either of those organizations?

GERSON   Ideologically, yes.

WILLIAMS   Do you see any difference between the ideology of the Labour-Progressive party and that of the Communist party?

GERSON   I don't know anything about the ideology of the Labour-Progressive party.

WILLIAMS   You said that ideologically you were sympathetic to the Communist party?

GERSON   Yes.

WILLIAMS   And you have been for how long?

GERSON   Well, I have been married fourteen years. I would say about that.

WILLIAMS   About fourteen years?

GERSON   Yes.

MR. COMMISSIONER KELLOCK   You said you had been married about fourteen years?

GERSON   Yes, because it was at that time that I had met — it was through them that I had met — through those people that I had met Fred Rose, and I had never met them before, although Fred Rose and I lived in the same neighbourhood in Cartier; that is where we lived originally.

KELLOCK   But as I understand you, as the result of coming to know your wife's people and her relations, you acquired your political ideas?

GERSON   That is right.

MR. WILLIAMS   And you have held those consistently ever since?

GERSON   Well, off and on.

WILLIAMS   And you hold them to-day?

GERSON   Well, I don't know what I hold to-day. I am pretty confused.

WILLIAMS   Did you hold them in 1942?

GERSON   I could have, yes.

WILLIAMS   Well, can you do better than that? Did you, or did you not?

MR. COMMISSIONER KELLOCK   You mean you did. Is that not what you mean?

GERSON   Pardon me, I don't mean that. I don't know what I mean. You are asking me how I felt in 1942.

KELLOCK   Well, you have already given one answer to this Commission, that for the last fourteen years you had those views. Is that right? That is what you have already said. Do you want to change that?

GERSON   Yes.

KELLOCK   All right; what do you want to say?

GERSON   Well, I mean I was in that atmosphere and got the views. I wouldn't say I held them for fourteen years.

KELLOCK   That is what you did say, and I am asking you if you want to change that?

GERSON   Yes, that is what I want to change it to.

KELLOCK   What do you want to change it to, then?

GERSON   Well, I would say off and on.

WILLIAMS   You have already said that, too. Is that all you want to say?

GERSON   Yes, sir.

MR. WILLIAMS   Were you off or were you on in the year 1942?

GERSON   I don't know, now.

WILLIAMS   How about the year 1943?

GERSON   Well, I can tell you about to-day in the same way — I don't remember how I felt in —

WILLIAMS   Well, tell us about to-day. I understood you to say a minute or two ago that you could not say about to-day. How do you feel to-day? Do you hold the ideology of the Communist party to-day?

GERSON   Well, the ideas, partly, yes.

WILLIAMS   And you are sympathetic to them?

GERSON   Some of the things they want to do, yes.

WILLIAMS   And last year, in 1945, were you sympathetic to it?

GERSON   Well, I wouldn't remember.

WILLIAMS   You don't want to say?

GERSON   I wouldn't remember that. . . .

WILLIAMS   Do you know what Lunan's political ideology is?

GERSON   No. I just considered him as a progressive. I didn't know what shade.

WILLIAMS   Would you call him a pink?

GERSON   Yes, I would call him a pink.

WILLIAMS   Which means some kind of sympathy for the Communist ideology, does it not?

GERSON   No. I have heard people in offices in the Department of Munitions and Supply talk that way, and I would not say that they had any ideology; they were just talking, that's all.

WILLIAMS   Were you one of those who used to talk about the views you held?

GERSON   Sometimes.

WILLIAMS   In the Department of Munitions and Supply?

GERSON   No, not in the department.

WILLIAMS   Or War Assets Corporation?

GERSON   No, sir.

WILLIAMS   Or Allied War Supplies?

GERSON   No.

WILLIAMS   When would you do this talking?

GERSON   When I would make an application for a job and I was turned down, and I knew why I was turned down, that would make me feel very bitter.

WILLIAMS   Is that the only time you talked about your communistic leanings?

GERSON   Those were not communistic leanings.

WILLIAMS   They were not?

GERSON   No.

WILLIAMS   Or communistic sympathies, then?

GERSON   They were anti-fascist sympathies. I was the secretary of a committee of the Canadian Jewish Congress. We were trying to fight fascism and to fight anti-Semitism. When I came down the street in Montreal and saw placards on the street, and people walking down the street with policemen leading them, carrying on practically a riot, how would you feel about it if you were a Jew?

WILLIAMS   Do you associate anti-fascism with Communism?

GERSON   Well, I think that they fight fascism. . . .

THE TESTIMONY OF ERIC ADAMS

March 15, 1946

ERIC GEORGE ADAMS, *called:*

THE SECRETARY   Take the Bible in your right hand. You, Eric Adams, swear that the evidence you give before this Commission touching the matters in question shall be the truth, the whole truth, and nothing but the truth, so help you God?

ADAMS   Yes.

THE SECRETARY   You also swear by Almighty God that you will truly answer all and every question which shall be put to you; that you will make available to the Royal Commission all the documents in your possession or control pertaining to this inquiry; and that you will not, without leave of this Royal Commission, divulge to any person any of the evidence of which you may be apprised touching the matters in question, nor any document or information coming to you touching the said matters.

ADAMS   Does that mean I have to answer questions without legal counsel?

MR. COMMISSIONER TASCHEREAU   We will let you know; we will give you the necessary information about that, Mr. Adams.

ADAMS   Well, I will not answer a question until I have legal counsel, then.

MR. COMMISSIONER KELLOCK   You will not answer what question?

ADAMS   What he just read off.

KELLOCK   It is not a question; it is an oath.

ADAMS   He asks me to swear to do something which I will not do without legal counsel.

KELLOCK   The point of it is, Mr. Adams, in order that you may understand it clearly, that it is an oath of secrecy. These sittings are being held *in camera*. You know what that means?

ADAMS   Yes.

KELLOCK   And therefore it is necessary that all persons who have any part in it — witnesses, counsel, registrar, reporters, ourselves — do not disclose anything without the consent of the Royal Commissioners. You are being asked to undertake that.

You might as well understand this now. We are not a court. We are a fact-finding body. We simply report to the Governor General in Council, and you appear here as a witness. The statute under which we act provides that if in the course of the proceedings any charge appears against you, or before we report, if that should happen, any misconduct on your part, you will have an opportunity to have counsel and make the fullest explanation you want. Of course if there should be any proceedings against you in any court, you will have the ordinary rights of any individual to counsel. But at the present time you are simply being sworn that you will keep secret unless you get permission from us any information that comes to you here, or any evidence you give here. Is that clear?

ADAMS   That part is clear, but perhaps I misunderstood the reading. I thought the first part was that I swore to answer any questions, and that is the point.

KELLOCK   Under the statute, the Inquiries Act, you are under obligation as a witness here to answer questions, just as you would be if you were in court.

ADAMS   But in court I have counsel, and here I have not.

TASCHEREAU   You will have counsel if there should be a charge preferred against you, and there is no charge against you here. You are merely a witness now. If there is to be a charge against you, you will have counsel.

ADAMS   I am not going to swear to answer questions without the benefit of legal advice. .–. .

TASCHEREAU   What part do you object to in the second oath?

ADAMS   The first part.

THE SECRETARY: "You swear by Almighty God that you will truly answer all and every question which shall be put to you —"

ADAMS   That is the point. If I say "yes" to that, I say I will answer all questions without the benefit of legal counsel, and that is what I am objecting to.

KELLOCK   That is simply the purport of the section in the Inquiries Act under which we are acting, as I explained to you a moment ago. You are here as a witness, and that statute says you must answer.

ADAMS   May I ask a question?

KELLOCK   Yes.

ADAMS   What happens if I will not answer a question without the benefit of counsel?

KELLOCK   You just have the question put to you, and if you refuse to answer we will deal with that then.

ADAMS   I see. To leave myself clear for that, I cannot swear to that section of it, then.

KELLOCK   Well then, Mr. Adams, speaking for myself all I would say is that we will direct you to answer the questions now, in the way that I have explained it to you. I have explained that this is the law; and for myself I would also direct that you keep secret any evidence you give here or anything you learn here, without our permission. If you violate that, then you do so at your own risk. If you do not want to take the oath, — have you any objection to swearing that you will keep secret what you give here in the way of evidence, and what you learn here, unless you do get our permission to disclose it?

ADAMS   No, I have no objection to that, if my understanding is correct that when I may have legal counsel, then you will give me permission to make what has gone on here available to him?

KELLOCK   That is quite clear.

ADAMS   If that is clear, sure.

TASCHEREAU   So you have taken the first oath, to the effect that you will speak the truth here?

ADAMS   Yes, I have.

TASCHEREAU   Then listen to the second one.

KELLOCK   You swear by Almighty God that you will make available to this Royal Commission all the documents in your possession or control pertaining to this inquiry, and that you will not without leave of this Royal Commission divulge to any person any of the evidence of which you may be apprised touching

288

the matters in question, nor any document or information coming to you touching the said matters.

ADAMS   I do not think I have any documents that have not been taken already, but if you would start that oath with that—

KELLOCK   Then take the Bible in your hand, please.

ADAMS   If you would start it off with that I would swear to it. It is giving evidence or documents or anything else without legal counsel that I am objecting to.

KELLOCK   Well, all right. You swear that you will not, without leave of this Royal Commission, divulge to any person any of the evidence of which you may be apprised touching the matters in question, or any document or information coming to you touching the said matters, so help you God?

ADAMS   I do, on the understanding that when I have legal counsel you will give me permission to make available what is necessary from these proceedings.

KELLOCK   Well, Mr. Adams, for myself I am not prepared to quibble with you. We have told you in the clearest terms that when you are entitled to counsel, either here or, if any charge is laid against you elsewhere, and you need counsel, then for the purpose of your counsel and your consultation or discussion with counsel for the purpose of making a full defence, you will have our permission.

ADAMS   That is fine.

KELLOCK   But I am not prepared to quibble with you about the oath. I have given you that understanding, and I have read you the oath as to secrecy. If you are not prepared to take that, there are certain penalties which follow. Are you now prepared to swear to keep these proceedings secret?

ADAMS   Yes, I do.

KELLOCK   All right. You heard the oath?

ADAMS   Yes.

KELLOCK   And you are sworn?

ADAMS   Yes.

Mr. Fauteux commences questioning the witness.

MR. FAUTEUX   What is your full name?

ADAMS   Eric George Adams.

FAUTEUX   Where were you born?

ADAMS   Hull, Quebec.

FAUTEUX   What is the name of your father?

ADAMS   C.A. Adams.

FAUTEUX   And the name of your mother?

ADAMS   Emma May Adams.

FAUTEUX   And in what year were you born?

ADAMS   1907 . . .

FAUTEUX   What school did you attend?

ADAMS   Granby High School.

FAUTEUX   And then?

ADAMS   McGill University.

FAUTEUX   You were at Granby High School from 1914 to 1925?

ADAMS   Yes.

FAUTEUX   And then?

ADAMS   McGill University.

FAUTEUX   What years?

ADAMS   1925 to 1929.

FAUTEUX   And you graduated from there with what degree?

ADAMS   Bachelor of Science.

FAUTEUX   In electrical engineering?

ADAMS   That is right.

FAUTEUX   And then?

ADAMS   The Harvard Graduate School of Business Administration.

FAUTEUX   What years; 1929 to 1931?

ADAMS   1929 to 1931.

FAUTEUX   And what degree did you obtain there?

ADAMS   Master of Business Administration . . .

FAUTEUX   What employment did you get first?

ADAMS   An advertising agency, I think it was . . .

FAUTEUX   With what firm?

ADAMS   Cockfield-Brown, in Montreal.

FAUTEUX   How long did you stay there?

ADAMS   About four years, I think . . .

FAUTEUX   And what was the nature of your employment there?

ADAMS   May I ask a question, Mr. Chairman?

MR. COMMISSIONER TASCHEREAU   What is it?

ADAMS   When I was investigated at the R.C.M.P., they had a file which seemed to be full of some misinformation, and the questions that he started to ask me there indicated that to me, and I stopped answering it, because I decided that it was not doing me any good just to clear up all the mistakes in his file. It seems to me that you are getting onto the same thing here.

TASCHEREAU   No, no; we have nothing to do with the interrogation that you underwent at the barracks. You just answer these questions that are put to you by Mr. Fauteux. This is just a preliminary, I suppose?

MR. FAUTEUX   Oh, definitely . . .

MR. COMMISSIONER KELLOCK   You do not need to know the purpose, Mr. Adams. All you have to do is answer the questions. If you have been asked some questions that indicate that somebody has an erroneous file, you just give us the correct information here. That is all we are interested in. You answer the question.

ADAMS   I would like to have legal counsel and I would prefer not to answer questions until I get it.

KELLOCK   We have the discretion at this point as to whether you shall have counsel or not, and for my part I decided that there was no occasion for you to have counsel at the present time. If any charge arises against you at some stage, then you will be given that opportunity.

MR. COMMISSIONER TASCHEREAU   No report can be made by us unless counsel has been offered to you. We cannot report against you if counsel has not been offered. You will have full opportunity of having counsel and giving all the evidence you wish before any charge can be made against you. You are just a witness and you have to answer the questions that are put to you.

ADAMS   I refuse to answer them without counsel, then.

KELLOCK   You do not refuse to answer questions en bloc. One question has been put to you, what do you say as to that?

ADAMS   No comment.

MR. FAUTEUX   Will you look at Exhibit No. 266 and say if you recognize it?

ADAMS   No comment.

FAUTEUX   Your answer is "no comment"?

ADAMS   That is right.

FAUTEUX   When did you first have employment with the Canadian government?

ADAMS   No comment.

FAUTEUX   When were you appointed to work in the Bank of Canada?

ADAMS   No comment.

FAUTEUX   Did you ever work for the Foreign Exchange Control Board?

ADAMS   No comment.

FAUTEUX   Why do you refuse to answer that question?

ADAMS   Because I am not allowed to have legal counsel.

FAUTEUX   Did you ever work for the Industrial Development Bank of Canada?

ADAMS   No comment.

FAUTEUX   Did you ever have any connection with the Russian embassy?

ADAMS   No comment.

FAUTEUX   Did you ever know or did you ever meet Colonel Zabotin of the Russian embassy?

ADAMS   No comment.

FAUTEUX   Did you ever meet Colonel Rogov from the Russian embassy?

ADAMS   No comment.

FAUTEUX   Did you have any connection whatsoever with the Russian embassy?

ADAMS   No comment.

FAUTEUX   Were you at any time interested in any spying activities for the Soviet Union?

ADAMS   No comment.

FAUTEUX   I suggest a recess at this stage . . .

THE TESTIMONY OF DURNFORD SMITH

March 19, 1946

P. DURNFORD PEMBERTON SMITH, *called*

MR. COMMISSIONER KELLOCK   Will you take the book, please, in your right hand?

SMITH   My lord, I feel that I cannot take this oath until I have seen my counsel, Mr. Aldous Aylen.

MR. COMMISSIONER TASCHEREAU   You will have to take the oath. You listen to the oath. You will have to take that and then we will discuss the matter of counsel later. You are called here as a witness and you are under obligation to attend and to be sworn.

SMITH   My lord, I have not seen my counsel for thirty-two days.

KELLOCK   That is all right. I said that you will first take the oath. There are two oaths. One is that you will speak the truth, which is the ordinary oath that any witness takes in any judicial proceeding or before any Commission. The other is that these proceedings are *in camera* and that you will keep secret anything that you tell us or anything you learn here unless you get permission from us.

SMITH   My lord, I feel it is not fair to make me testify until I have seen Mr. Aylen . . .

KELLOCK   It does not matter what your feeling is. You are here as a witness and the statute provides that you must be sworn. As I say, it is an offence not to be sworn and it is a matter for you to think over.

SMITH   Well, my lord, I feel it is a question of principle. I have been held thirty-two days. I am not a lawyer and I do not know the technicalities of the law. I am not refusing to give testimony but I do wish to see Mr. Aylen before I am questioned.

KELLOCK   Mr. Smith, let me tell you again. You are here before this Royal Commission. You must be sworn first before we listen to you at all. I am not going to listen to you unless you are sworn. As I explained to you, that is the first thing. After that, if you want to raise the question you are now discussing, raise it and we will discuss it with you but you must be sworn now. Will you take the Book, Mr. Smith? You swear that the evidence you give before this Commission touching the matters in question shall be the truth, the whole truth and nothing but the truth, so help you God?

SMITH   I swear.

KELLOCK   You swear that without leave of this Royal Commission you will not divulge to any person any of the evidence of which you may be apprized touching the matters in question, nor any document or information coming to you touching the said matters or any evidence which you shall give before this Commission, so help you God?

SMITH   I will reserve that. I will tell anything to my lawyer, Mr. Aylen.

KELLOCK   Perhaps I can explain that to you, Mr. Smith. If it should be decided that you shall have counsel, you will be given our permission to discuss anything you want to with your counsel. As a matter of fact, you will not need any permission yourself to discuss anything you want to with your counsel. We will have an undertaking from your counsel that he will not disclose, except in discussion with you, anything that you will tell him or anything that you learn here . . .

Smith is sworn. Smith was then asked to identify a photograph.

MR. WILLIAMS   Mr. Smith, that is your own photograph, is it not?

SMITH   I have asked the presiding judge a question.

MR. COMMISSIONER KELLOCK   In discussing the matter with my fellow commissioner, we do not see any reason at the moment why you should not be able to recognize your photograph, or not recognize it, just as you like, without consultation with counsel, Mr. Smith.

SMITH   I am not endeavouring to obstruct you, sir, but I realize that, nevertheless, although I am a witness, I am in a serious position.

KELLOCK   I know; but all you are being asked is whether you do or do not identify a certain photograph shown you.

SMITH   That is correct, sir.

KELLOCK   That does not require any legal advice, as far as I can see.

SMITH   It is difficult for me to be sure of that, sir.

KELLOCK   Well, Mr. Smith, under the statute, the Inquiries Act, which is one of the authorities under which this investigation is being conducted, we have a discretion as to whether we shall allow or shall not allow counsel, up to the point when any charge is made against you. There is no charge made against you as yet. Your conduct is being investigated, unquestionably; but up to the time that a charge is made, we have a discretion as to whether you shall be represented by counsel or not.

Under the same statute we may not report adversely on your conduct without you having been given an opportunity to be represented by counsel here and to make the fullest statement or explanation you care to make, or to call any evidence that you want to call; but just at the present time, while your conduct is being investigated and no charge has been made against you, we have a discretion, and as I told you when you objected to the oath this morning, if you want to raise the question at any time we will consider it.

You have raised it now. My brother commissioner and I see no reason why we should change our ruling at the present time, when you are asked as to whether or not a certain photograph is yours.

SMITH   Well, sir, I feel — I cannot rid myself of this feeling — that I know I have been held for thirty-two days, as I say. I have been questioned by Inspector Harvison. I know that whether it is correct or not he has a bulk of evidence which is alleged to connect me with certain infractions of the laws. I have the feeling that what is actually happening is that I am being questioned by a prosecution, without the advantage of legal advice.

KELLOCK   Well, that is not so. Your conduct is being investigated, but there is no question of a prosecution; there is no question of a charge.

SMITH   There is not at the present moment.

KELLOCK   That is so.

SMITH   But I have heard that all the other people appearing before this Commission have been subsequently charged.

KELLOCK   Well, that is not before us.

SMITH   Not before you, but still it follows afterwards; and here we have lawyers who are questioning me. I do not know the intricacies of the law; I may be being led into a trap, for all I know, and that is why I am asking for counsel.

KELLOCK   Well, I have explained the situation to you. The question has been put to you. You will have to make up your mind whether you are going to answer it, or whether you are not going to answer it, then after that we will give the matter consideration.

SMITH   I am afraid I am not going to answer, sir.

KELLOCK   All right. Then I think we should have a recess for a few minutes.

On resuming.

MR. COMMISSIONER KELLOCK   Well, Mr. Smith, we have decided to reserve our decision on your refusal, for the time being at least, with regard to that particular question. Will you proceed, Mr. Williams?

MR. WILLIAMS   Now, Mr. Smith, I am going to show you another photograph, which was found in the original records of the Russian embassy, and which appears in a document which is marked Exhibit 18. I am going to ask you to look at that photograph and say of whom it is a photograph.

SMITH   Mr. Chairman, I practically repeat everything I have said before. I feel this is a question of principle. We have been held without counsel, and this is a new type of procedure, I believe.

KELLOCK   No, it is not a new type of procedure; that statute under which we are acting has been in existence a good many years. The last exhibit you showed the witness was what, Mr. Williams?

WILLIAMS   It was Exhibit 18, the file from the Russian embassy; and it contains, pasted on the upper right-hand corner, a snapshot.

KELLOCK   Then where does Exhibit 119 come from?

WILLIAMS   Exhibit 119 is a photograph of the face in Exhibit 18.

MR. COMMISSIONER TASCHEREAU   It is enlarged?

WILLIAMS   Yes, an enlarged photograph of the head down to the neck.

KELLOCK   Well, Mr. Smith, I did not realize when you objected to saying anything about Exhibit 119, just where Exhibit 119 had come from. That fact is in evidence, but you can appreciate that we have heard a great deal of evidence and all of it is not in the forefront of our minds at all times. I can now appreciate, perhaps, why you desire counsel and do not desire to answer either of these questions without having an opportunity of seeing counsel.

While we have a discretion, in considering it with my fellow commissioner we believe it is a case where, in the circumstances, you should have the opportunity for which you have asked, and should have an opportunity to see your counsel and have your counsel here for the remainder of your examination before us. You mentioned the name of a counsel?

SMITH   Yes, sir; Mr. Aldous Aylen.

KELLOCK   Very well. Mr. Campbell, will you arrange to get in touch with Mr. Aylen and say that Mr. Smith would like to see him? If possible we would appreciate if Mr. Aylen could come at once, so we will be able to proceed.

MR. FAUTEUX   May I suggest that counsel be asked simply to come?

KELLOCK   Perhaps that is the better way; to simply ask him if he could come, and in the meantime Mr. Smith may retire.

WILLIAMS   Then I suggest a further recess now. . . .

On resuming.

MR. H. ALDOUS AYLEN, K.C.,   *appeared.*

MR. WILLIAMS   Messrs. Commissioners, Mr. H. Aldous Aylen, K.C., is here. When Mr. Smith asked to be permitted to consult him this morning, that was arranged. Mr. Aylen will tell the Commission what the advice is that he has given to his client. I take it that the question is whether your client will answer the question that has been put to him.

AYLEN   Messrs. Commissioners, my client is quite ready and willing to answer any questions which may be put to him.

MR. COMMISSIONER KELLOCK   Mr. Aylen, you are going to remain?

AYLEN   With your permission.

KELLOCK   May we just have your undertaking as these proceedings are *in camera* that you will not disclose anything that you learn as a result of acting here except with the consent of the Commission. That consent will be given in case it should be necessary for you to use it elsewhere.

AYLEN   That is understood, Mr. Commissioner. . . .

The proceedings continued . . .

MR. COMMISSIONER TASCHEREAU   Mr. Smith, surely you can recall if you wrote these documents, 26-Y, 26 Z and 26-X?

SMITH   No, sir.

TASCHEREAU   Six pages and you would not recall it?

SMITH   I don't recall it, sir.

MR. COMMISSIONER KELLOCK   There is something you said I should like to understand. I should like to understand your evidence. You have said that this Exhibit 26-Y resembles your handwriting, and that it might be your handwriting, as I understood you, and you also said you did not think it was. Will you tell us why you do not think it is?

SMITH   Well, I will, sir, yes. It is very difficult for me in view of what little I know of what has been presented here to make a perfect theory of it. It is my impression that somebody has forged my writing and possibly wished to make it appear that I wrote these documents.

KELLOCK   All right. Have you any other reason for thinking that it is not your handwriting?

SMITH   Just that I do not recall ever writing it.

KELLOCK   You do not recall ever writing it. Now, any other reason?

SMITH   I don't know any other reason.

KELLOCK   Would you go so far as to say if it is a forgery it is a good or bad forgery?

SMITH   I would think, sir, it is a good forgery.

MR. COMMISSIONER TASCHEREAU   A good imitation.

MR. COMMISSIONER KELLOCK   Can you suggest any reason why anybody would want to forge your handwriting to documents such as these? . . .

SMITH   May I inquire from my counsel whether it is correct to answer that question?

MR. COMMISSIONER TASCHEREAU   What is the question?

REPORTER   (*Reads*)   "Q. Can you suggest any reason why anybody would want to forge your handwriting to documents such as these?"

MR. AYLEN: I think you should try to answer that.

SMITH   My guess is possibly someone was making money from the number of people he could implicate, and that possibly he or some person acting for him was able to get hold of this material and forge my handwriting.

MR. COMMISSIONER KELLOCK   I should like to understand that.

SMITH   To go further, I have heard of, although I have not been allowed to see the newspapers —

KELLOCK   Speak up.

SMITH   I have heard, although I have not been allowed to see the newspapers that much of this information has been provided by Mr. Gouzenko. I am wondering whether he had any advantage in turning in people as implicated in this work and therefore took some means to get my handwriting forged.

KELLOCK   I see.

SMITH   But I don't —

KELLOCK   Just a minute. What is present in your mind is that if anybody forged these documents it was Gouzenko. Is that right?

SMITH   I don't know that, sir, but it is a possibility.

KELLOCK   I am understanding you correctly when I say that the person that you have in your mind as the possible forger is Gouzenko?

SMITH   Yes, or an agent of Gouzenko.

KELLOCK   Or an agent of the same person, and that Gouzenko was being paid something for that purpose?

SMITH   I don't know, sir.

KELLOCK   Would you have any idea who would be paying Gouzenko to utter such forgeries, any forgery?

SMITH   I don't know, sir.

KELLOCK   Well then, Mr. Smith, apart from the question of forgery, if it is not a forgery then it must follow that the documents are in your handwriting from what you say even if you do not recall, as you say, writing them? Would that be so?

SMITH   I am not certain those are the only alternatives.

KELLOCK   They are the only alternatives you can think of at the moment?

SMITH   At the moment, yes.

KELLOCK   All right. Perhaps I could tell you for my part, Mr. Smith, that I have no question in my mind that there is anything forged about these documents. There is no question whatsoever.

296

MR. COMMISSIONER TASCHEREAU   And I fully concur in that.   (*To the witness*)
Are you still hesitant as to whether or not you wrote this document?

SMITH   No, sir, I believe I did not write this document.

TASCHEREAU   You persist in that?

SMITH   Yes.

TASCHEREAU   It may be you or it may not be you? That is what you believe?
It is a possibility that it may be you?

SMITH   I don't believe I wrote it.

TASCHEREAU   No, but that is what you said some time ago, that it is very similar to your handwriting, and am I to take it there is a possibility you wrote
it if it is not a forgery?

SMITH   I answered I did not think those are the only alternatives, sir.

TASCHEREAU   It has got to be a forgery or it is not.

SMITH   It might not be a forgery by the mechanism which I have suggested.

TASCHEREAU   But with any mechanism you wish, it is written by you or it is
not written by you. If it is not written by you it is a forgery; if it is not a forgery
it is written by you?

SMITH   I suppose.

TASCHEREAU   So there is a possibility that you wrote that. If we take into
account what is written there, the knowledge that is displayed there and the
similarity of your own handwriting, there is a great possibility that you wrote
this?

SMITH   I suppose you could call it a possibility.

TASCHEREAU   Would you not go further than a possibility, a probability?

SMITH   No, sir, I don't think so.

TASCHEREAU   But, as a matter of fact, you do not deny it under oath?

SMITH   I do not believe I wrote it, sir. . . .

March 20, 1946

P.D.P. SMITH,   *recalled*

MR. ALDOUS AYLEN, K.C.,   *present.*

MR. COMMISSIONER KELLOCK   At this stage my co-commissioner and myself
would like to say that in any case where prosecution may be had in relation
to the subject matter of this inquiry the oath of secrecy taken by witnesses and
the undertaking of counsel not to divulge to any person any of the evidence
of which they were apprised touching the matters in question, nor any document
or information coming to them touching the said matters shall cease to have
effect to such extent as may be needed to ensure to any accused the exercise
of the right of full answer and defence and to enable any witness to give evidence
in any of such prosecutions.

MR. WILLIAMS   Mr. Smith, your counsel, Mr. Aylen, says that you wish to add
something to one of the answers you gave yesterday with reference to the radio
set?

SMITH   That is correct.

WILLIAMS   Will you speak up, please, and just say what it is you want to add?

SMITH   Gentlemen, since last night when we were talking about the microwave zone position indicator, I have recalled that I believe this set was at one time considered for sale to the Soviet government. Although I did not see them, I understand that certain Russian officers were taken through the set. I think that that could be checked up by either going to the N.R.C. authorities or to Brigadier Wallace or Dr. D.W.R. McKinley.

MR. COMMISSIONER KELLOCK   So far as you are concerned were you ever given any instructions that any information with regard to that might be given out by you to any person outside the National Research Council?

SMITH   No, sir, I just thought this might be relevant and mentioned it. . . .

MR. WILLIAMS   Now, Mr. Smith, these three documents which are before you and which we have gone over are documents that were found in a brief case owned by Lieutenant-Colonel Rogov in a room in the Russian embassy on the 5th September, 1945. Have you any explanation or idea as to how these three actual documents were in that brief case and in that room in the Russian embassy on that date?

SMITH   No, sir, I have not.

WILLIAMS   You can give no explanation whatsoever?

SMITH.   No, sir.

WILLIAMS   I am going to show you a photograph which I have already shown you. I am going to ask you to consider it very carefully and tell the Commission whether you do not know the man who is represented there by the photograph?

SMITH   I do not know that man, sir.

WILLIAMS   Would it make any difference, do you think, if he were not represented with a uniform on? I cover everything but the face and again ask you to look at that photograph.

SMITH   I cannot recognize that face, sir.

WILLIAMS   You cannot recognize that face. I am going to tell you, Mr. Smith, that that is a photograph of Lieutenant-Colonel Rogov, and that there is evidence before the Commission that not only were you introduced to Lieutenant-Colonel Rogov but that you spent some time in his company. With that information, what do you say?

SMITH   I still cannot recognize that photograph.

MR. COMMISSIONER KELLOCK   What do you say about that information?

SMITH   I do not believe I have ever met Lieutenant-Colonel Rogov, sir.

MR. WILLIAMS   Were you ever introduced to a man who was going by the name of Jan?

SMITH   I do not believe so, sir.

WILLIAMS   Were you ever introduced by Gordon Lunan to a man named Jan with whom you took a trip in a motor car in the city of Ottawa?

HALPERIN   I do not believe so, sir.

WILLIAMS   Will you say you did not and were not?

SMITH   I am reasonably sure that I did not.

MR. COMMISSIONER KELLOCK   What is that?

SMITH   I am reasonably sure that I did not, sir.

MR. WILLIAMS   Can there be any possible doubt in your mind on the subject, Mr. Smith?

SMITH   Not unless I suffer from amnesia, sir.

WILLIAMS   Well, you are not suggesting that you suffer from that, are you?

SMITH   No, sir.

WILLIAMS   If Mr. Lunan says that he did introduce you to Rogov, known as Jan, and that you spent some time in Rogov's company with Lunan, what do you say about that?

SMITH   I have no explanation.

WILLIAMS   Is it or is it not a fact?

SMITH   I maintain that I did not see him.

WILLIAMS   You maintain that you did not see him, so that if Mr. Lunan has said, as he has, before this Commission, Mr. Smith, that that is so; is he telling the truth or is he not telling the truth?

SMITH   I think he must be mistaken.

WILLIAMS   You think he must be mistaken. We will see, perhaps if we can throw a little more light on this. . . .

Mr. Smith, I am putting before you another document, an original document which came from the Russian embassy and which is a file on a man who was identified by them with the cover name of Back. It has been filed as Exhibit No. 17. The evidence before this Commission is that that was the cover name of Gordon Lunan, and Mr. Lunan himself has admitted it. I am drawing your attention to a sheet, Exhibit No. 17-B, which you will observe consists of a sheet of paper with a Russian heading typewritten on and then pasted on that sheet is another sheet of completely typewritten material. You see that?

SMITH   I do, sir.

WILLIAMS   The translation of the Russian heading is, "Scheme of the Research Group." The evidence before this Commission is that a duplicate of the part typewritten in English was given to Gordon Lunan and he has admitted that that is so. It reads, "The scheme of your group —" which is Lunan's group, "— will be approximately such as it is shown below." Then there is a diagram showing Jan at the top. The evidence before the Commission, Mr. Smith, is that Jan is the cover name of Rogov. Then the next one on the diagram is G. Lunan whose nickname, as they know it in Russian, or cover name or pseudonym, is Back. This is the file on Back, otherwise Gordon Lunan. Then working under him are three men, one Isidor [Israel] Halperin, who is given the nickname of Bacon. Another is Doruforth Smith, which is a misspelling of your name with the nickname of Badeau. Then there is Ned Mazerall who is given the name of Bagley. Then it goes on:

You only will know me (as Jan) but nobody else.
2. What we would like you to do:
a. To characterize the scales and works carried out at National Research and also the scheme of this department.
b. To conduct the work of "Bacon", "Badeau" and "Bagley."
It is advisable to put the following tasks to them separately:
Bagley

That is Mazerall.

— to give the models of developed radio sets, its photographs, technical (data) facts and for what purpose it is intended. Once in three months to write the reports in which to characterize the work of Radio Department, to inform about the forthcoming tasks and what new kinds of the models are going to be developed.

Bacon — to give the organization and characters of Valcartier Explosives Establishment's direction. To write the report on subject: "What kind of the work is this organization engaged in?" If possible to pass on the prescriptions (formula) of explosives and its samples.

Badeau —

That is the name given to you, Mr. Smith.

— to write the report: What kind of the work is his department engaged in and what departments it is in contact with (by work).

All the materials and documents to be passed by Bagley, Bacon and Badeau have to be signed by their nicknames as stated above.

If your group have the documents which you will not be able to give us irrevocably we shall photograph them and return them back to you.

I beg you to instruct every man separately about conspiracy in our work.

In order not to keep their materials (documents) at your place, it is advisable that you receive all their materials (documents) the same day you have the meeting with me.

To answer all the above questions we shall have the meeting on March 28.

P.S. After studying burn it.

Now, Mr. Lunan says that he got a duplicate of that document and that he carried out the instructions given in it. There are in this same file, Exhibit No. 17, reports typewritten by Lunan, according to his own admission, and given by him to Rogov in which he reports on each one of the three men in his group. On the 28th March this is what he reported about you: "Badeau lives at the furthest end of Hull." Was that true?

SMITH   I live at Wrightville.

MR. COMMISSIONER TASCHEREAU   What exhibit is that?

WILLIAMS   Exhibit No. 17-D.

SMITH   I live at Wrightville which is at the far end of Hull.

WILLIAMS   "And works during the day out of town." Where did you work during the day when you were in the National Research Council?

SMITH   Mostly at the field station.

WILLIAMS   Where is that?

SMITH   That is near the Metcalfe Road, south Ottawa.

WILLIAMS   It is outside of Ottawa?

SMITH   Yes, sir.

WILLIAMS   "— and out of reach at lunch times." Was that true?

SMITH   Yes, sir.

WILLIAMS   "And other times convenient to me. My house is out of the question for meeting (and typing) purposes as I have two others living with me." That was a fact, was it not?

SMITH   I presume so.

WILLIAMS   "We shall probably solve these difficulties as we gain practice in the work. The following notes describe in detail progress made with each individual on each task set." Remember this was written on the 29th March, 1945. First he deals with Badeau, which is the cover name for you:

> Badeau: warmed up slowly to my requests and remained non-committal until he had checked independently on my bona fides. Once satisfied he promised to cooperate. He is preparing the report on his dep. as requested, also a full report on organization and personnel, interlocking deps. etc. of NDC.

That is a misprint for N.R.C.

> plus any other information he thinks useful. These reports are promised to me for Apl 9. I am unable to get them any sooner.
> Discussing the work of NDC in general.

Again that should be N.R.C.

> Nadeau [Badeau] informs me that most secret work at present is on nuclear physics (bombardment of radio-active substances to produce energy).

That was true, was it not?

SMITH   Yes, I believe it was.

WILLIAMS   You are sure it was, Mr. Smith?

SMITH   In view of the presently known news, yes, sir.

MR. COMMISSIONER KELLOCK   I do not understand that last answer. You were asked if that was true. You were asked if that was true at that time, not if it was true now. The statement is, "Badeau informs me that most secret work at present is on nuclear physics (bombardment of radio-active substances to produce energy)." Was that true at that time that that was most secret?

SMITH   I think so.

KELLOCK   Did you know it at that time?

SMITH   I do not think I knew it at that time.

KELLOCK   You had an idea, is that what you mean?

SMITH   I could not really be sure how long I had an idea.

MR. WILLIAMS   "This is more hush-hush than radar and is being carried on at University of Montreal and at McMaster University at Hamilton." That was true, was it not?

SMITH   I think so, sir.

WILLIAMS   "Badeau thinks that government purchase of radium producing plant is connected with this research." That referred to Eldorado, did it not?

MR. COMMISSIONER KELLOCK   Or the Chalk River plant.

WILLIAMS   Chalk River was built, Mr. Commissioner.

KELLOCK   "Government purchase" would be Eldorado, yes.

WILLIAMS   (*To the witness*)   That was true, was it not?

SMITH   Well, I assume it was.

WILLIAMS   That is, you knew that the government had purchased the Eldorado plant? Everybody knew that.

SMITH   Well, if it was in the papers, yes.

WILLIAMS   You knew it, did not you?

SMITH   It is a long time back, sir. I cannot remember how long I have known it.

WILLIAMS   That is the best answer you can make?

SMITH   I am afraid so.

MR. COMMISSIONER KELLOCK   I would like to understand that. You learned at the time that the government had purchased Eldorado, did you?

SMITH   Truly, I cannot remember.

KELLOCK   It is known to you this morning, is it?

SMITH   No, I know I have known it for some time but I cannot remember when I acquired this information.

KELLOCK   Do you read the newspapers?

SMITH   Fairly regularly, yes.

KELLOCK   And in raising that you are suggesting that you did not know at the time the newspapers were carrying that report?

SMITH   No, sir.

KELLOCK   There was a good deal of publicity about it, is that right? Do you recall that?

SMITH   I cannot recall it, but if you say so —

KELLOCK   I am not saying anything; I am asking you. Do you not recall that there was a good deal of publicity about it?

SMITH   I cannot say I recall it but there must have been.

MR. WILLIAMS   You did associate in your mind the purchase of the Eldorado plant with research in respect of radio-active substances to produce energy?

SMITH   That I certainly cannot recall.

WILLIAMS   "In general, he claims to know of no new developments in radar, except in minor improvements in its application." In March, 1945, did you know of no new developments in radar except in minor improvements in its application?

SMITH   That is quite possible; I cannot be certain of it.

WILLIAMS   Then part of this document says: "With regard to photographs and biographical notes on Bagley and the others, Bacon and Badeau will provide them with their reports. I will supply Bagley's later. Bacon is a mathematics professor from Queen's University at Kingston, now a major in the Army. Badeau is an electrical engineer who has worked in the engineering department of the Bell Telephone Company at Montreal. Fuller details later." Are you an electrical engineer?

SMITH   No, sir, I am a physicist.

WILLIAMS   Have you any electrical engineering degree?

SMITH   No, sir.

WILLIAMS   Have you ever done work as an electrical engineer?

SMITH   I have been communications engineer in the Bell Telephone.

WILLIAMS   You worked in the engineering department of the Bell Telephone Company at Montreal?

SMITH   Correct, sir.

WILLIAMS   And you did work that an electrical engineer would do?

SMITH   Yes, sir. . . .

MR. COMMISSIONER KELLOCK   What are your political associations, Mr. Smith?

SMITH   Well, I have no official political associations, sir. I do not belong to any party.

KELLOCK   Have you — ?

SMITH   I sympathize with the labour movement a good deal.

KELLOCK   What do you mean by "the labour movement"?

SMITH   Trade unions.

KELLOCK   Have you had some dealings with members of the Labour-Progressive party from time to time?

SMITH   I may have. I don't really know.

KELLOCK   You have more capacity to give vague answers than any witness we have had before us. There is a great deal of answering of that kind, that you might have, and so on. Do you not know?

SMITH   I don't know anybody I could name offhand of my friends who is actually a member of the Labour-Progressive party.

KELLOCK   I am not thinking about members, because there may be some question about when a person is a member and when he is not. I am asking you if you had associations with members of the Labour-Progressive party from time to time?

SMITH   No, sir, as far as I know.

KELLOCK   Have you ever known a member of the Labour-Progressive party?

SMITH   I don't believe I do know any members.

KELLOCK   Did you ever belong to any study group?

SMITH   I belonged to the Quebec Committee for Allied Victory, when I was in Montreal. . . .

MR. WILLIAMS   In referring to Shugar's evidence at page 1999, he was asked these questions and made these answers:

> Q. In the study group you had in Ottawa, we have the information that besides you there was Durnford Smith, Gordon Lunan. . . .
> A. I remember the names. . . .

What do you say as to that evidence?

SMITH   Well, all I can say, sir, is that the others appeared to think it was a group or some very definite organization, but I had not thought so.

MR. COMMISSIONER KELLOCK   But you did attend a group, whether it was a definite organization or not, with these other named persons in Ottawa?

SMITH   Yes, sir, I certainly have met them.

KELLOCK   That is not my question at all, Mr. Smith?

SMITH   All right; I will say yes.

KELLOCK   You did attend groups? How often were you in such groups, having in mind that Lunan says it met every two weeks?

SMITH   I suppose that is approximately correct, sir.

KELLOCK   And over what period were you meeting with these groups periodically?

SMITH   I can't recall how long this has gone on, sir.

KELLOCK   Would it be years?

SMITH   I suppose so, sir.

KELLOCK   Ever since you came to Ottawa?

SMITH   No, sir.

KELLOCK   Well, would it be two years, three years, four years? What do you say?

SMITH   Well, to my best memory it would be between two and three years.

KELLOCK   Was any money collected in those groups at any time, Mr. Smith?

SMITH   I think money was collected for the purchase of papers.

KELLOCK   For the purchase of what?

SMITH   Papers.

KELLOCK   What kind of papers?

SMITH   Papers such as the *Canadian Tribune*, the *New Masses*, and papers like that.

KELLOCK   We have heard about the *Canadian Tribune*. What is the *New Masses*?

SMITH   *New Masses* was an American publication.

KELLOCK   Of the Communist party?

SMITH   Well, it was certainly very sympathetic to them.

KELLOCK   And there is no doubt about where the *Canadian Tribune* stands, is there?

SMITH   It is a publication of the Labour-Progressive party, sir.

KELLOCK   And would you agree that that is the Communist party of Canada?

SMITH   Well, it is the nearest thing there is to such.

KELLOCK   Do you know any difference between the Labour-Progressive party and the Communist party?

SMITH   Well, I imagine that would be a question of constitution and rules and so on.

KELLOCK   I did not ask you what you imagine; I asked you if you knew any difference, or was it just a change of name?

SMITH   Well, that, sir, I don't know.

KELLOCK   All right. I just want to know what you know. This money that was collected; how much was it; 10 cents or a quarter or a dollar?

SMITH   In that order of magnitude; one or two dollars.

KELLOCK   About that much; and was that collected at each of these meetings?

SMITH   That I couldn't recall.

KELLOCK   Was it collected frequently?

SMITH   Yes, sir, I think so.

KELLOCK   And was it used for any other purpose except buying these papers you have mentioned?

SMITH   I don't think so, sir.

KELLOCK   To whom did you pay your money?

SMITH   I really can't recollect.

KELLOCK   You cannot recall anyone that you paid your money to?

SMITH   No, sir. . . .

KELLOCK   Then, Mr. Smith, instead of all this long process, is it not a fact that these groups that you attended were made up of people who were either members of or were sympathetic towards the Communist or Labour-Progressive party?

SMITH   Not as members, but I think they were probably sympathetic.

KELLOCK   And that included yourself?

SMITH   Oh, yes.

KELLOCK   There is no reason at all that I know of why you should not have any opinion that you want to have. All I am interested in is, what the opinion was, because it is quite relevant here; I can tell you that.

SMITH   Yes, sir. . . .

MR. WILLIAMS   . . . according to the Russian embassy, Mr. Smith, in addition to the meeting which they believe they had with you and Captain Lunan on July 5, and which Captain Lunan says took place, they had other meetings with you. Still looking at your own file now, Exhibit 18, we find under the date of August 18, 1945, "Urgent meeting on photographing. He just returned from the United States." Exhibit 285, Mr. Smith, shows that on July 29, 1945, you went to Cambridge, Massachusetts, to the Massachusetts Institute of Technology and the Bell Laboratories, and were away a week. So that on August 18 you had practically just returned from the United States, had you not?

SMITH   Yes, sir.

WILLIAMS   It goes on: "Didn't bring anything; for the next meeting he will bring his account of the trip to the United States and other material which we designate. He could not take any photographs. He has only a photo apparatus and nothing more." That was a fact; you just had the ordinary photo apparatus; camera and darkroom equipment?

SMITH   As we mentioned.

WILLIAMS   As we mentioned before. And what do you say about that meeting? Did you meet Colonel Rogov or anybody from the Russian embassy, whether you knew his name or not, on August 18, 1945, and report to him about your trip to the United States?

SMITH   I have no memory of meeting anybody from the Russian embassy.

WILLIAMS   Will you deny that you met anybody from the Russian embassy on August 18, 1945?

SMITH   I am sure I didn't meet anybody.

WILLIAMS   Does that mean you will deny it?

SMITH   Yes, sir. . . .

WILLIAMS   Let us look now at exhibit 20-P and 20-P-P. Exhibit No. 20-P, which is a document written in Russian, Mr. Smith, is in the handwriting of Col. Zabotin. It is signed by his cover name, which was Grant. It is addressed to the director at Moscow and it is dated the 27th of August, 1945. This is what Col. Zabotin is telling Moscow. Remember the date, the 27th of August, 1945.

We have received from Badeau 17 absolutely secret —

And we could interpret it "top secret" —

and secret documents (British, American and Canadian) on the question of magnet, radio locators for field artillery, three secret scientific research journals of 1945. Altogether about 700 pages. In the course of the day we were able to photograph all the documents with the help of the Leica and the photofilter. In the next few days we will receive almost the same amount of documents for 3 to 5 hours and with one ribbon (film) we will not be able to do it. I consider it necessary to examine the whole of the library of the scientific research council.

Then he goes on: "Your silence on My No. 256 may disrupt our work on photographing the materials. All materials have been sent by mail in turn." That is in rotation as they were received. You will notice that this telegram bears a number, and the evidence is that they started to number their telegrams at the beginning of the year, and numbered them through, or the beginning of the month, and numbered them through. We have telegram 266 but we have not telegram 256 which was an earlier one.

Now, first of all, Exhibit 20-PP, referring to 17, absolutely secret, a secret document of that kind, giving a pretty good description of all of the documents which you took out of the documents library of the National Research Council in August, does it not?

SMITH   It might possibly be considered so, sir.

WILLIAMS   We have just gone over a whole pile of them, Mr. Smith; would you not agree with me that that was a pretty good sort of description of the documents you were getting out of the library?

SMITH   I would say it might possibly be, sir.

WILLIAMS   That is as far as you wish to go. Have you any explanation or idea about why Colonel Zabotin should be telling the director in Moscow that he had, the Russian embassy here, had got from Durnford Smith these secret documents?

SMITH   I have not, sir.

WILLIAMS   And you can make no suggestion of any kind whatsoever to help the Commission?

SMITH   I am afraid not, sir.

WILLIAMS   Bearing in mind that Badeau was the name they had given to a man named Durnford Smith, they had given him credit for doing a lot of work, had they not?

SMITH   Possibly, sir. . . .

WILLIAMS   I have read to you Captain Lunan's statement as to the meeting which he says took place between you, Rogov and himself, given under oath here before the Commission. What do you say as to that, Mr. Smith?

SMITH   I say I know nothing about it.

WILLIAMS   You say that it did not happen?

SMITH   Not as far as I was concerned.

WILLIAMS   That you had no part in such a meeting?

SMITH   That is correct.

WILLIAMS   And that what Captain Lunan is saying is made up entirely out of whole cloth and absolutely untrue?

SMITH   It must be a mistake of some sort, sir.

WILLIAMS   It is either true or false, now which is it? Captain Lunan's story that I have just read to you is either true or false; which do you say it is?

SMITH   It is certainly not true.

WILLIAMS   Do you say it is false?

SMITH   It must be.

WILLIAMS   False from beginning to end?

SMITH   I do not know from beginning to end.

WILLIAMS   I have read it to you, you have heard it; is there any truth in what Captain Lunan said?

SMITH   I cannot vouch for it.

WILLIAMS   You doubt it?

SMITH   Yes.

WILLIAMS   I ask you if there is any truth in Captain Lunan's story that I have just read to you, any truth at all?

SMITH   I do not know that there is any truth in it.

WILLIAMS   You do not know; it relates to yourself?

SMITH   Certainly. I do not know about being there.

WILLIAMS   Will you swear you were not there?

SMITH   I am sure I was not there.

WILLIAMS   Why should Captain Lunan come here under oath and tell the Commission you were; have you any idea?

SMITH   No, sir.

WILLIAMS   You have no idea; you have no suggestion to make as to why he should do it?

SMITH   I am afraid not, sir. . . .

WILLIAMS   How close were your relations with Mr. Halperin?

SMITH   He was a friend of mine.

WILLIAMS   A very close friend of yours, was he not?

SMITH   He is a good friend of mine.

WILLIAMS   And you see each other frequently?

SMITH   Reasonably so, sir.

WILLIAMS   You and he were good enough friends for you to know what his political affiliations were, were you not?

SMITH   I know what his sympathies were, sir.

WILLIAMS   You knew as a matter of fact he was very sympathetic to the Communist party in Canada and the Labour-Progressive party in Canada?

SMITH   I would certainly not have thought he was unsympathetic.

MR. COMMISSIONER KELLOCK   According to the evidence they are one and the same thing.

WILLIAMS   Yes. Mr. Commissioner.   (*To the witness*)   You know more than that, do you not? You know that he was so sympathetic to the Communist party of Canada and its ideology that he would be willing to take part in Lunan's group, do not you?

SMITH   No, I did not know that.

WILLIAMS   You did not know that, but did you tell Captain Lunan that he was?

SMITH   No, sir. . . .

WILLIAMS   Then we will come back to Exhibit 17, Exhibit No.17-I, which is the assignment. No. 5 contains this: "Figure out what NDC stands for." The explanation of that sentence, Mr. Smith, is that by a typographical error Captain Lunan had written "NDC" for "NRC" which he corrected here before the Commission.

"Ask Badeau whether he can obtain uranium and 235. Tell him to be very careful. If he can, tell him to write in detail about this radium producing plant." Were you ever asked to obtain uranium 235?

SMITH   No, sir.

WILLIAMS   You are a physicist, are you not?

SMITH   I am.

WILLIAMS   And you know what uranium is being used for at the present time in connection with the atomic bomb?

SMITH   Yes, sir.

WILLIAMS   That is a problem in nuclear physics, is it not?

SMITH   That is right, sir.

WILLIAMS   And you say that nobody ever asked you to obtain uranium 235?

SMITH   I have no recollection of that.

WILLIAMS   "Badeau asks a decision about changing over for the work on uranium." Did you ever ask anybody at the Russian embassy to communicate with Moscow to give approval for your changing over from the work you were doing to doing work on uranium?

SMITH   No, sir.

WILLIAMS   "There is a possibility that he could enter either by invitation or by suggesting it himself but he must be warned that they are very careful about selecting workers and keep them under strict observation." Have you any comment to make on that?

SMITH   No, sir.

WILLIAMS   Then coming to the last page, these are the conclusions by the gentleman in the Russian embassy reporting to Moscow: "It is not recommended that Badeau should transfer into the uranium industry but is to develop the work in research more broadly. In the future with the object of more efficient direction, it is expedient to detach him from Back's group and to transfer him on independent contacting." Did you ever discuss that with Rogov?

SMITH   No, sir.

WILLIAMS   If Captain Lunan's story is true, Mr. Smith, he arranged for you to meet Lieutenant-Colonel Rogov, which he says you did, and the original secret records from the Russian embassy show, as I have already shown you, that you were detached in that sense from Lunan's group and you did have meetings personally with Colonel Rogov — I say if Lunan's story is true. Did those things happen? Did you have meetings with Rogov?

SMITH   No, sir.

WILLIAMS   Not at any time?

SMITH   No, sir.

WILLIAMS   Whether you knew him by the name of Rogov or by any other name?

SMITH   No, sir.

WILLIAMS   Mr. Smith, can you explain to the Commission how every one of these secret records from the Russian embassy checks in every material part with the facts that have been disclosed and that have been shown to you in your particular case if they were not genuine?

SMITH   I have no explanation at the moment.

WILLIAMS   Do you think if you thought that over for a while that you could dig up an explanation?

SMITH   (No audible answer.) . . .

MR. COMMISSIONER KELLOCK   Mr. Smith, you had a responsible position in the National Research Council?

SMITH   Yes, sir.

KELLOCK   Where were you born?

SMITH   In Westmount.

KELLOCK   Quebec? Then you went to university; then to the Bell Telephone Company, and the National Research Council. You have your master's degree, and you are working on your doctor's degree?

SMITH   Yes.

KELLOCK   You had pretty good prospects of advancement in your work?

SMITH   Fair, sir.

KELLOCK   We have some evidence, which I think has been drawn to your attention, that one of your superiors down there had formed a pretty favourable idea of your ability and training. Do you recall that?

SMITH   Yes, sir.

KELLOCK   In the light of those facts I would like to ask you what appealed to you in the Communist philosophy. What attracted you?

SMITH   Into studying it, sir?

KELLOCK   Yes, or becoming sympathetic toward it?

SMITH   Its logic, sir.

KELLOCK   Could you amplify that for me?

SMITH   Not very easily, sir.

KELLOCK   Do I understand from that, that you think its philosophy is reasonable? Is that what you mean?

SMITH   Yes, sir.

KELLOCK   And it appeals to your reason?

SMITH   To some extent, sir.

KELLOCK   Well, I never hope to get a very definite answer from you, Mr. Smith, but that is as far as you will go?

SMITH   Yes, sir.

KELLOCK   When did you first become interested in it?

SMITH   I suppose I first heard of such things when I was in college.

KELLOCK   In university?

SMITH   Yes, sir.

KELLOCK   You first heard of it then. From what source did you hear of it?

SMITH   From Dr. McCrae, sir.

KELLOCK   Who was he?

SMITH   He was one of the research students in Montreal.

KELLOCK   One of the research students?

SMITH   Yes, sir.

KELLOCK   A student along with you?

SMITH   I guess his position was senior to that of student. He was a research worker.

KELLOCK   Would you call him a lecturer?

SMITH   No, sir; I don't think he had any such position.

KELLOCK   He had some staff position?

SMITH   Yes, sir.

KELLOCK   How far back does that go?

SMITH   Into the 1930's.

KELLOCK   Then from that time on your interest has been steady, has it?

SMITH   Well, I wouldn't say — it is a little hard to answer that, sir.

KELLOCK   You have always had the interest since that time?

SMITH   Well, certainly sympathetic since then, sir.

KELLOCK   And you have been associated with other Communists during those years?

SMITH   No, sir, I don't think that I have been associated with other Communists.

KELLOCK   You have been with these study groups?

SMITH   Yes.

KELLOCK   Did you attend any study group in Montreal?

SMITH   No, sir. Whether you would call those people Communists or not —

KELLOCK   Well, either Communists or with communistic leanings. That is what I mean.

SMITH   I see.

KELLOCK   You have associated yourself with such people over the years?

SMITH   I have never avoided them.

KELLOCK   I did not ask you that, Mr. Smith. I think that is avoiding my question. I say you have associated yourself with them?

SMITH   Yes, sir.

KELLOCK   I don't know why you spar so much, Mr. Smith.

SMITH   I am sorry, sir.

KELLOCK   I do not think it is doing your position any good at all; in fact rather the contrary, to my way of thinking. All right; I wanted to understand that from you. Now I want to understand this also from you, if I can. Some of the witnesses that we have had, whose names have been referred to during your examination, have been a good deal more frank with the Commission than I think you have. My impression at the moment, to use your expression, is that you have not been completely frank, and that you are in a position to say a good deal more if you will.

I am going to suggest to you, subject to what my brother commissioner says, that you think the matter over a little further. I suggest that you give the matter some further thought, and you will have an opportunity to say anything further that you may have to say in the light of your further thought.

But I would like to ask you this. Can you think or can you suggest to me any reason why any person in your position should have given any information, secret information, to the Russians or any other foreign power, apart from the fact that you were sympathetic to the Communist philosophy? You see, you swore an oath of secrecy. I am not asking you now to admit that you did anything, but I am trying to get this from you, if I can.

Take a person in your position. He swears an oath of secrecy. He is born and brought up in this country; he has had the experience you have had; he has attained the position you have attained; he acquires communistic leanings that you say you have acquired. Can you suggest any reason why such a person would furnish information of a secret nature, that he had sworn not to furnish, to a foreign government; can you suggest any other reason apart from the fact that he was sympathetic toward the Communist philosophy? I would like to have you answer that, if you will?

SMITH   No, sir.

KELLOCK   You cannot suggest any other reason?

SMITH   No, sir, not at the moment.

KELLOCK   All right. Then I suggest that you think the matter over, and perhaps we will hear from you in a few days, Mr. Smith. We will be engaged on some other matters, and if you want to come back and make any statement to us at any time, just make that information known to Mr. Maclaren or Mr. Aylen, and they will be here if you want to come. We will provide an opportunity for you if you want to come.

MR. COMMISSIONER TASCHEREAU   At any time. . . .

THE TESTIMONY OF ISRAEL HALPERIN

March 22, 1946

ISRAEL HALPERIN, *called*

MR. COMMISSIONER KELLOCK   What is your full name?

HALPERIN   Israel Halperin.

KELLOCK   You swear that the evidence —

HALPERIN   Before you swear me, would you mind telling me who you are?

MR. COMMISSIONER TASCHEREAU   Well, we are the Royal Commission appointed by the government to investigate particular matters. What is your name?

HALPERIN   Israel Halperin; it is the basic right of every Canadian citizen to have access to legal counsel; therefore I ask you for access to legal counsel.

KELLOCK   Just a minute; you are before us in the character of a witness, and you must be sworn first; and then the matter which you have raised — we will consider that.

HALPERIN   I am here against my will.

KELLOCK   Of course you are.

HALPERIN   And I have the right to know under which laws I am governed.

KELLOCK   Well, may I see the Order-in-Council; I am showing you a copy of the Order-in-Council P.C. 411, passed pursuant to the provisions of the War Measures Act. Have you seen that already?

HALPERIN   I have not!

KELLOCK   All right; you read it then, if you like.

HALPERIN   Thank you; may I be advised as to the meaning of the term "*sub judice*"?

KELLOCK   It means that it is under consideration by somebody such as a court or a royal commission that we are.

HALPERIN   Does this Commission have the status of a court?

KELLOCK   We are a Royal Commission pursuant to the Inquiries Act passed by the Parliament of Canada.

HALPERIN   Can I be cited for contempt of court?

KELLOCK   You can be, yes.

TASCHEREAU   Yes.

KELLOCK   For contempt of this Commission, you can; I do not know what cited means in that connection unless committed.

HALPERIN   Is it legal under the law of Canada?

TASCHEREAU   The Commission can do that.

HALPERIN   I will change that question; under what laws am I compelled to make any answer whatsoever?

TASCHEREAU   We will read you the law. . . . (*Taschereau reads*)   . . . so that means that we have the power to enforce the attendance of witnesses, to compel them to give evidence, and that in the course of this investigation, it is in our own discretion to grant permission to a witness to have counsel; and that we cannot report against a person unless we have given him the opportunity of having counsel. For the moment, you are a witness here and you are obliged to take the oath, and to give the evidence, and answer the questions that are being asked of you.

HALPERIN   Does that word "compulsion" — is it to be understood to include physical compulsion?

TASCHEREAU   We have the permission; we are under the law; we have the power to compel you to speak.

HALPERIN   Does that include physical intimidation?

TASCHEREAU   That means that we have the same powers to compel witnesses to speak as if we were an ordinary civil court.

HALPERIN   I am afraid I am not proficient. .

TASCHEREAU   Under the civil law, we could compel you to speak and to answer the questions legally put to you.

HALPERIN   I would like a direct answer to my question: Are you empowered to use physical intimidation?

TASCHEREAU   Not physical intimidation; but we have the power to punish you if you do not answer.

HALPERIN   But you have not the power at this investigation to impose any type of physical intimidation, is that correct?

TASCHEREAU   Now I have told you everything that I have to tell you; now you have got to take the oath that is provided by law.

KELLOCK   Are you ready to be sworn?

HALPERIN   No, I am not.

KELLOCK   Will you read that before?

HALPERIN   I will read this.

KELLOCK   You may note that the witness is reading the Order-in-Council appointing the Royal Commission, P.C.?

MR. FAUTEUX   P.C. 411.

HALPERIN   While I am reading this, I may remind you that you have refused —

KELLOCK   You have nothing to remind us; if you have any questions to ask, after, we will answer you. We do not want any impertinence.

HALPERIN   I am a citizen; I intend absolutely no impertinence, but merely to ascertain my legal rights and naturally I ask such questions.

KELLOCK   You will have all the legal rights you are entitled to, so you need not worry about that.

HALPERIN   I have been held five weeks.

KELLOCK   Just go ahead and read, please. Have you read the Order-in-Council?

HALPERIN   I have read part two of it, is that all you wish me to read?

KELLOCK   I gave you P.C. 411 and asked you read it.

HALPERIN   I have read section two of that pamphlet.

KELLOCK   I did not say anything about section two; I gave you a copy of this, of these two pages. Have you read them?

HALPERIN   I have.

KELLOCK   Are you ready to be sworn?

TASCHEREAU   I want to impress upon you that this Commission is a fact-finding body and we have to report to the Governor General in Council as to the facts that we find here; under the act it is our discretion as to whether or not a witness may have counsel; but we cannot report to the Governor General in Council if we come to the conclusion that there is a charge against you, unless you have had the full opportunity of the benefit of counsel. Is that clear to you?

HALPERIN   I have to tell you, gentlemen, that it is my decision to make no further statement beyond the one I am making to you now until I have the opportunity to have access to legal counsel.

TASCHEREAU   To legal counsel?

HALPERIN   Yes, sir.

KELLOCK   Are you ready to be sworn?

HALPERIN   No, sir.

KELLOCK   I think we should have a recess.

TASCHEREAU   We will have a recess for a few minutes.

At Dr. Halperin's insistence, the Commission agreed to permit his counsel, Senator Arthur Roebuck (Liberal, Ontario), to attend the hearings. Because Senator Roebuck was out of town, Dr. Halperin's evidence was postponed.

March 27, 1946

SENATOR A.W. ROEBUCK, K.C.,   *appeared.*

MR. WILLIAMS   Mr. Halperin is coming in.

MR. ROEBUCK   Before he comes in, tell me why I am here. Are you going to question Halperin?

MR. COMMISSIONER KELLOCK   No. We think we had better tell you when Halperin is here, and then you will have an opportunity to say what you wish.

ISRAEL HALPERIN,   *called*

MR. COMMISSIONER KELLOCK   Senator Roebuck, the witness refused to answer questions put to him by counsel for the Commission, saying that he wished to be advised by his counsel, and then he told us that you were his counsel. For that reason you were communicated with, and the witness would like to have an opportunity of consulting with you in regard to his obligation to answer. You will have an opportunity now to retire and consult with him.

I want to point out to you that these proceedings are *in camera*, and we have in all cases asked for the undertaking of counsel that they would not disclose what they learned from their clients or in here until such time as may be necessary, should it ever be necessary. Then an application can be made here and the proper leave will be given. That situation can be explained to you later, but in the meantime could we have your undertaking?

MR. ROEBUCK   Oh, yes, by all means. One does not like to give undertakings, but you have been taking them from others. Usually the discretion of counsel is sufficient. Then there is this factor, too, that these proceedings will be discussed in Parliament; and while I will not divulge what goes on here, I wish to be entirely free to discuss the situation as I know it outside of what I learn here.

KELLOCK   Quite so.

MR. COMMISSIONER TASCHEREAU   Anything you learn from other sources —

ROEBUCK   Quite so; I cannot tie my hands in my public capacity; but as far as this is concerned — of course. Now, could you give me a copy of the order?

KELLOCK   Mr. Campbell will furnish you with that.

TASCHEREAU   Then we will have a further recess.

ISRAEL HALPERIN,   *called*

HON. ARTHUR ROEBUCK, K.C.,   *appeared.*

MR. COMMISSIONER TASCHEREAU   Were you sworn?

MR. ROEBUCK: I think I ought to make a very short statement of explanation. Following the interview, this morning, I have had a long conference with Mr. Halperin, and I have gone over with him, as far as I know, the picture that presents itself here; and I have said to Mr. Halperin, and he agrees with me, that, as a civil servant, and as a citizen of Canada, in view of the serious nature of the allegations, the situation he is in, he is in duty bound to give all the assistance possible to this Commission. He has decided to do so.

MR. COMMISSIONER KELLOCK   Thank you. You will take the book, then, Mr. Halperin, and stand — take the book. You swear that the evidence you give before this Commission touching the matters in question shall be the truth, the whole truth, and nothing but the truth, so help you God?

HALPERIN   Yes.

ISRAEL HALPERIN,   *sworn*

MR. COMMISSIONER KELLOCK   There is another oath, Senator Roebuck, arising out of the fact that these proceedings are *in camera*. Mr. Halperin, you swear by Almighty God that you will truly answer all and every question which shall be put to you; that you will make available to the Royal Commission all the documents in your possession or control pertaining to this Inquiry; and that you will not, without leave of this Royal Commission, divulge to any person any of the evidence of which you may be apprised touching the matters in question, nor any document or information coming to you touching the said matters?

HALPERIN   That is an oath I would prefer not to take.

   Dr. Halperin objected to the second oath, and a prolonged legal discussion took place concerning his ability to reveal secret information to the Commission, and whether his evidence would be protected by the Evidence Act. Eventually, however, Halperin conceded. . . .

HALPERIN   I think my objections are rather vacuous.

MR. ROEBUCK   You are perfectly justified in making them. You heard the oath, and you swear. Kiss the book. . . .

MR. FAUTEUX   Did you communicate to anyone not authorized in the army or outside it any information at any time about the work that you were doing in the organization of your department or any part of it?

HALPERIN   Well, I would like to answer that question quite carefully. My own principal in the university had lunch with me once and asked me what I was doing. He did not mean to ask for secret information, and I did not understand that question that way. I told him I was helping to organize an army research and development establishment which I told him would play quite an important role.

FAUTEUX   Is that all you told him?

HALPERIN   I cannot recall the exact words.

FAUTEUX   That is the substance of what you told him?

HALPERIN   That sort of thing; I only mean to point that out to show you I did not — if you want a clear-cut answer I did not go around giving out secret information.

FAUTEUX   I did not ask you that. I asked you if you communicated any of the information I outlined to you?

HALPERIN   No technical information.

FAUTEUX   My question was not technical information. . . . You mentioned something you told your principal. Apart from that did you communicate any of that kind of information to anybody?

HALPERIN   Nothing that I would consider was either at that time or at this time as being misconduct.

MR. COMMISSIONER KELLOCK   Well, I do not think that answers my question in view of your previous answers that you had very little knowledge of what should be kept secret, so I would like you to answer the question I put to you. I would still like you to answer the question I put to you. Make it as full as you like, but I want an answer to it, please.

HALPERIN   I did not imply that I had no knowledge of what should be kept secret. In fact, as I have already said, there were occasions on which my opinion was requested on whether things, specific things should be kept secret or not. All I said was that I was not familiar with any printed material which specified certain things as being secret and certain things as not being secret. . . .

March 28, 1946

MR. ROEBUCK   Before I came here I had intended to make a submission to the Commission as a result of some thought during the evening. It was to this effect, that the questioning which has already gone on makes it quite clear that this is an inquisition so far as the witness is concerned, not just an ordinary general inquiry under the Act.

MR. COMMISSIONER KELLOCK   I do not understand that, Senator.

ROEBUCK   Shall I —

MR. COMMISSIONER TASCHEREAU   Would you make that a little clearer?

ROEBUCK   Yes. I shall make it clear by my subsequent remarks. That being so, I was going to submit that a clear statement of what is alleged against the witness should be given to him so that he would know what it is he is meeting, and not to be open to broad general questions that have no relevancy; that

316

is, that the questions that have no relevancy to the accusations alleged against him, and not just showing all his life from the time he was born up until the present moment. That was my intention when I came here, but I think the situation has changed since I saw my client, and I believe he has something that he wishes to say to the Commission.

HALPERIN   Gentlemen, the ideas that have been expressed by the senator are precisely my own. On thinking over the kind of questions that have been asked I have come to the conviction that this is in effect a prosecution with a charge not yet laid. I feel that I prefer to have a charge laid in open court and avail myself of the usual procedures. . . .

ROEBUCK   Let me make my position clear. I told you in my opening remarks that I had come with a certain thought in mind and I thought it was right to express that thought that the accused should be informed of what there is against him.

KELLOCK   He is not the accused.

ROEBUCK   That was to be the tenor of my remarks. However, I told you that the circumstances had changed since my arrival. Now I am not in a position to say what advice I have given to my client, as you know, but it should not be assumed that he is acting on my advice; he is acting on his own. We came in here yesterday, and as you know yesterday afternoon I told you that he had come to the conclusion he should assist this Commission to the extent of his ability, and we proceeded on that basis. I thought he should be informed of that one little change. My position has not been changed. The picture only is changed, and the witness is telling you in what degree it is changed.

KELLOCK   As far as I am concerned all that can be said at the present time is that your client's conduct is being investigated under the terms of the Order in Council, and therefore the questions are being put to him to that end. There is no charge made against him.

ROEBUCK   Now he is acting on his own.

KELLOCK   Proceed, Mr. Fauteux.

MR. FAUTEUX   Mr. Halperin, you explained yesterday that you were connected with the organization of C.A.R.D.E. Would you mind telling this Commission in what way you were connected with that organization?

HALPERIN   I am sorry, my statement still stands, the statement that I made to the Commission.

KELLOCK   Well, let us have the situation clear. You have counsel here. Your counsel has not objected to the question. Are you objecting, Mr. Roebuck?

ROEBUCK   Counsel is withdrawing. I do not see anything else for me to do.

KELLOCK   All right, Senator Roebuck, thank you.

ROEBUCK   Does that change your situation so far as you are concerned? May we have a recess, Mr. Commissioners?

KELLOCK   Yes.

On resuming

MR. COMMISSIONER KELLOCK   Mr. Halperin, we all thought we would make the situation clear to you. You do not apparently seem to appreciate the position. No charge has been made against you. This Commission is a fact-finding body.

We have no power to punish you even though we thought you had been guilty of something. Our function is to hear the evidence and to report the facts as we see them. Now, we can tell you this, that in the Soviet embassy at Ottawa certain documents exist which have now been placed before this Commission in which your name appears. Those documents indicate that certain information was given by you to the Soviet embassy through Gordon Lunan. For your further information counsel will show you at least one of these documents and you will be asked to say what you have to say about the situation. Mr. Fauteux, would you show the document? After you have seen the document, Mr. Halperin, if you want to retire again for the purpose of consulting with Mr. Roebuck we will offer you that opportunity. If you do not want to retire then we shall proceed.

MR. FAUTEUX   I am exhibiting to you first of all Exhibit 17, more especially 17-B.

MR. COMMISSIONER TASCHEREAU   Which is a translation.

FAUTEUX   Which is the original document. Exhibit 17-B is the original document composed of one typewritten page of English which was pasted to a sheet of paper in the original file which is actually before you and a translation of the Russian heading appears on Exhibit 17-B on the left-hand side.

ROEBUCK   "Scheme of the Research Group."

FAUTEUX   That is correct.

TASCHEREAU   That was prepared by —?

FAUTEUX   That file was prepared by Colonel Rogov of the Russian embassy.

KELLOCK   The particular document the witness is looking at was delivered by Rogov to Lunan.

TASCHEREAU   The assignment of Rogov.

WILLIAMS   The duplicate of it.

FAUTEUX   The other documents having been given to Lunan, this one being a copy from the embassy. The instructions to Lunan as appear in the lower part of the document was to burn the duplicate of the document which was given to him, but this one remained in the embassy.

TASCHEREAU   And was filed here by Gouzenko.

FAUTEUX   That is right.

TASCHEREAU   You have also there the cover names of each individual who was to work under Lunan.

FAUTEUX   In the same exhibit there are also other documents where you are mentioned, as you can see. I am pointing out to you especially Exhibit 17-E. Exhibit 17-E, which you are now reading, was written by Lunan as being his report of a contact with you to Mr. Rogov of the Soviet embassy.

HALPERIN   I notice some other paragraphs back here. Am I permitted to read them — a paragraph on the previous page which apparently gives the same word "Bacon." Am I permitted to read it too?

KELLOCK   Yes. Perhaps we should not take the time for you to read all these documents now. We are exhibiting to you the nature of these documents. Now, counsel wants to ask you certain questions about them.

FAUTEUX   You understand the gist of the information that is suggested by this exhibit?

HALPERIN   I have seen the exhibit.

KELLOCK   Are you ready to proceed?

HALPERIN   If I may do so without any prejudice to the proceedings I should certainly speak to my counsel.

KELLOCK   All right. We shall have a short recess. . . .

On resuming.

MR. FAUTEUX   If the witness can explain to us now what C.A.R.D.E. was?

HALPERIN   It was chiefly intended to be a rocket establishment.

MR. COMMISSIONER KELLOCK   Will you please speak up?

HALPERIN   I am sorry. It was chiefly intended to be a rocket establishment, to do work on rockets.

MR. COMMISSIONER TASCHEREAU   Rockets?

HALPERIN   In effect it was. I made a vague statement a little while ago, that something was suggested for an expanded improvement. That suggestion, was, in effect, a suggestion for a large-scale rocket research group building, with all sorts of features, and, although the plans were somewhat modified, it was still considered, certainly by myself, and I think by my associates, that its primary importance would lie in the doing of rocket work. For that reason — shall I go on with this?

FAUTEUX   Oh, yes.

HALPERIN   For that reason we accelerated those features of the establishment which would assist rocket work. I myself was instrumental in sending a cable overseas to facilitate the building, and to get opinions in order to facilitate the building of a certain little building for making pressure measurements of rockets. There had always been there a ballistics — there had been this group of research scientists, whose chief work consisted of internal and external ballistics' theory calculations, carrying out experiments in that field. . . .

ISRAEL HALPERIN,   *recalled.*

HALPERIN   Messrs. Commissioners, I previously made protests against the type of procedure, and you undertook, I understood, to let me see what there was being held against me so I could know what was going on. I was shown a couple of documents, but given no particular opportunity to speak about them; and then the questions proceeded to be of the same type of questions which did not particularly seek information but were of a prosecutional type, which tried to get me by trickery to commit myself —

MR. COMMISSIONER KELLOCK   You can stop right now. Do not use that kind of language here. I will not put up with it, personally.

HALPERIN   I am sorry; I withdraw those words.

KELLOCK   All right. You are here as a witness. You have a counsel here. You will listen to the questions. If your counsel thinks any question is improper, he will object and we will rule on it.

HALPERIN   In that case I will ask my counsel to withdraw and stand on my own, because I refuse to go on with this kind of thing.

MR. COMMISSIONER TASCHEREAU   I did not hear that?

HALPERIN   I refuse to go on with this kind of thing.

MR. ROEBUCK   And he asked his counsel to withdraw, so I am withdrawing.

KELLOCK   We are sorry to see you go, Mr. Roebuck.

319

Mr. Roebuck withdrew.

MR. FAUTEUX   Will you look at Exhibit 387, and say whether you recognize that?

HALPERIN   I am sorry; I refuse to go on with the inquiry and I will not repeat that. That is definite. . . .

MR. COMMISSIONER TASCHEREAU   Would you exhibit to the witness, one after the other, the documents concerned, and if he refuses to answer, the reporter will take note of that. Show him one after the other, the various exhibits which concern him.

MR. COMMISSIONER KELLOCK   Do you understand, witness, that by refusing to answer you commit an offence, which is contempt, for which you can be punished? You understand that, do you? It does not matter whether you understand it or not; I am telling you.

HALPERIN   I am sorry, I refuse to go on with this procedure. . . .

Mr. Fauteux read evidence into the record.

MR. COMMISSIONER TASCHEREAU   What is your answer to what Mr. Fauteux read you?

HALPERIN   That it is a lot of rubbish. I don't know this man Lunan, and I certainly didn't give him or anybody else any information to be communicated to a foreign power.

TASCHEREAU   You do not know Lunan?

HALPERIN   That is right.

TASCHEREAU   You swear that?

HALPERIN   Yes, to the best of my remembrance I don't know Lunan.

TASCHEREAU   Do you swear that you don't remember having met him, or do you swear that you do not know him, under your oath?

HALPERIN   To the best of my remembrance I don't remember ever meeting him.

TASCHEREAU   You know what an oath is?

HALPERIN   I took it. I may say that I saw a picture of Lunan in a newspaper, and I certainly don't recognize any person like that.

TASCHEREAU   You never spoke to Lunan? Is that what you swear?

HALPERIN   I made my answer, sir.

TASCHEREAU   Did you ever speak to him?

HALPERIN   I refuse to go on with this cross examination. . . . I must say that I now withdraw from the oath which I gave.

TASCHEREAU   Oh, no; you cannot do that.

HALPERIN   I do it.

TASCHEREAU   You cannot do that. You are here as a witness.

HALPERIN   Am I here by compulsion?

TASCHEREAU   You are not here by compulsion.

HALPERIN   Then I will walk out of the room.

TASCHEREAU   No; you will stay here.

HALPERIN   Unless I am held here by compulsion, I will leave the room.

Whereupon the witness left the witness chair and walked to the door.

TASCHEREAU   No, you are not leaving the room.

HALPERIN   Then I have to tell you that I consider the oath invalid, and will feel perfectly free to inform all of Canada exactly what happened from now on; and I certainly will.

TASCHEREAU   (*Resumes questioning*)   Have you anything to add?

HALPERIN   Simply that I will not go on with this.

TASCHEREAU   To any further questions which are put to you? Is that your answer?

HALPERIN   That is my answer.

TASCHEREAU   Mr. Fauteux has to read to you all the exhibits concerning you that are in the record here. Do you wish those exhibits to be read to you?

HALPERIN   I would have liked them to be read to me when I started.

TASCHEREAU   Do you wish Mr. Fauteux to read those exhibits to you?

HALPERIN   I have no interest in going on with this procedure.

TASCHEREAU   Can I take your answer, then, as a negative answer?

HALPERIN   I will answer no further questions, sir.

TASCHEREAU   No further questions?

HALPERIN   (No answer.)

MR. FAUTEUX   Is there any explanation that you would care to give?

HALPERIN   I have already given it.

FAUTEUX   Any further statement?

HALPERIN   I will give no further statement; beyond the statement I now make, I will not open my mouth here again.

MR. COMMISSIONER TASCHEREAU   Then that will be all.

Whereupon the witness retired.

THE TESTIMONY OF J. SCOTT BENNING

March 23, 1946

J.S. BENNING, called

BENNING   You examine me on the basis of certain facts and presumably prepare a charge on the basis of those facts.

MR. COMMISSIONER KELLOCK   Not necessarily. We just express our opinion on those facts and find what we think the facts are.

BENNING   It would be reasonable to believe that your opinion would be predicated on the facts elicited in the interrogation here.

KELLOCK   Certainly.

BENNING   Then on that basis one would stand, let us say, to put it politely, not condemned but suspect in the country on the basis of the Commission ruling or recommending a charge. Be that as it may, what follows that, after one is committed and brought in front of a magistrate and the evidence is laid — presumably the evidence that will be laid by the Crown will be based on the facts elicited here. Then the court case that follows, where a man is convicted of being guilty or where he is released as innocent, there will always be a suggestion in the minds of people that two judges of the Supreme Court of Canada examined this man and in their estimation he is guilty.

KELLOCK   We have not heard the evidence.

BENNING   Let me proceed.

KELLOCK   We do not know what our views will be; we have not heard the evidence. We are not in the habit of forming our opinion in advance.

BENNING   I am assuming — that is the way I started this — I am assuming that you recommend that I be charged and brought in front of a magistrate presumably, and I am committed for trial on the basis of the evidence presented by the Crown. Then I am brought into court and tried. Now in the event of my being declared innocent, is it not a fact on the ground — you probably will not answer this question — is it not quite possible that the Canadian people will say, "This man escaped this charge on the basis of legal technicalities but none the less at the original examination presided over by two judges of the Supreme Court they found sufficient evidence to book him and commit him for a charge or recommend a charge."? You see the point I am trying to make, gentlemen, is that despite the fairness of this particular procedure, a point I am not willing to debate at the moment, whether I am declared guilty or innocent, and I will be declared innocent, I am going to have for the rest of my life, if you recommend me for a charge, a slur on my reputation; it will be shot, my name will be gone. I am not fooling myself on that score one little bit because I as an ordinary, common Joe on the street, would say if I were out on the street and somebody else was in here, "That man had a smart lawyer and he got away; otherwise he never would have been picked up to begin with."

KELLOCK   All that is happening at the moment is that you are being asked to be sworn and I personally do not see what connection that has with what you are saying now. We are here to hear your evidence, that is part of our duty; our duty is to hear your evidence. Your duty is to give that evidence. What somebody may think about you because you are here is something neither you nor we can help.

BENNING   No, but the connection, the obvious connection is that if this evidence is given in secrecy you presumably are at liberty to take what particular portion you like of the evidence to lay your charge, to recommend the laying of your charge, and I am not in position to contradict that until such time as you are prepared to give me permission.

MR. COMMISSIONER TASCHEREAU   You will be in position to contradict all that; you will be given the full opportunity of defending yourself here.

BENNING   Here?

TASCHEREAU   Yes.

BENNING   I am assuming after I leave this room I have to keep my mouth sealed. I cannot even tell my counsel what proceeded in here.

TASCHEREAU   Oh, yes, we will release you.

KELLOCK   You will have that permission from us. . . . What is troubling you?

BENNING   Well, I think it should be rather obvious. Five weeks plus two days and the abrogation of all civil rights.

KELLOCK   We are not going to discuss anything of that kind. What is troubling you about the oath?

BENNING   I think I made that sufficiently clear. The thing that troubles me about this oath is the fact that I cannot as a citizen state exactly what proceeded here to whomever I shall desire. I find it difficult to understand, gentlemen, to be frank. I mean I am aware that there is a tremendous amount of publicity with regard to this matter. . . .

MR. WILLIAMS   Exhibit 122, — is that the photograph of anybody you know?

BENNING   Gordon Lunan.

WILLIAMS   How long have you known him?

BENNING   I think I first met Lunan some time around 1938. Those were the days of the Spanish Medical Aid, China Relief, the League against Fascism and War.

WILLIAMS   You and he were interested in all those organizations?

BENNING   I do not quite like the wording of that question — "you and he were interested in that." I was what you would call a parlour pink, I believe, or as some of the more orthodox would call an arm-chair Bolshevik.

MR. COMMISSIONER KELLOCK   A Communist?

BENNING   No, not a Communist.

MR. WILLIAMS   That was in 1938 — to 1939?

BENNING   It might have been 1937 and 1938 — sometime around the latter part of 1937. I think it conceivably could have been; the Spanish civil war was still on, some time around there.

WILLIAMS   Yes. And you described yourself as a "parlour pink"; are you still a "parlour pink"?

BENNING   No, a liberal with a small "l."

WILLIAMS   A liberal with a small "l." You also used the term "arm-chair Bolshevik." Are you an "arm-chair Bolshevik" now?

BENNING   No, not after the pact.

WILLIAMS   Not after the pact — what is that?

BENNING   I think we will all recollect that in 1939, when the famous train of history hit another curve, and the Russians signed an historic agreement with the Germans, I am afraid I found that last bit of meandering a little too strong for my stomach.

WILLIAMS   But when that pact was turned down in 1942 [*sic*, 1941], did that make any difference in your "arm-chair Bolshevik" ideas?

BENNING   No, not any essential difference. I hold no particular brief for the Russians, one way or the other. I think that they probably did a magnificent job during the war, but then, so did all the Allies.

WILLIAMS   In referring to yourself, at one stage, as an "arm-chair Bolshevik," would you say that that indicated an interest on your part in the Marxist ideology and economic ideas?

BENNING   Well, if I have the permission of the commissioners, perhaps if I just gave you a sketch, I would say, from the time I left high school up.

WILLIAMS   Yes. Just try to speak a little more deliberately and raise your voice a little, Mr. Benning.

BENNING   Yes. In 1930, when I was still in high school, in my last year —

MR. COMMISSIONER KELLOCK   How old are you now?

BENNING   I will be 33 in June. I became rather an ardent pacifist, to the point that I refused to join the high school cadet corps, which resulted in a slight argument with the principal over the right of the individual to select what course, to select a particular course in that field.

From then on I was acutely interested in various topics and became quite interested in the question of national minorities. I was rather aware of anti-Semitism, particularly in the province of Quebec and in Montreal, due to the fact that my features are of a somewhat Semitic cast. Therefore I was probably a bit more aware of it than the average gentile or Christian, call him what you will.

Naturally my mother was always adamant on one particular subject: that a man should never be judged by his race, colour or creed; that everyone had a dislike of individuals but only as individuals, not as people of a particular colour or a particular political or religious conviction.

I think shortly after that I did a fair amount of reading, mostly of a left wing nature. I started off with — I think the first book that made a real impression on me was Beverley Nicholls' *Cry Havoc*. From there I graduated to *The Merchants of Death*. After that I read some of Laski and some of Strachey. Several times I started to read Marx, but I must admit that it proved a bit too cumbersome. The same with most of the more orthodox of the Communist writers, with the possible exception of another book that remained very clearly in my mind; I think it was called: *The Coming Struggle with Fascism* written by R. Palme Dutt.

On the basis of that particular kind of reading I gravitated, let us say, more naturally to people holding rather liberal viewpoints, and thus became quite interested at one time in the Civil Liberties League or Union, I forget what the Montreal one was called. I think the Toronto one was Union and the Montreal one was League, or vice versa. I attended some of their meetings. From there I was interested in the Spanish Relief Committee. I am not entirely sure, mind you, of some of the various names, but the rough idea is the same; and the Chinese Relief Committee; and in the closing stages, before the war finally broke, the League against War and Fascism; and during that period I ran into Lunan, and I did a certain amount of work such as stuffing envelopes, and things of that nature. But I am afraid I did not allow it to interfere with my normal social activities.

KELLOCK   What do you mean by "stuffing envelopes"?

BENNING   Oh, well, they would send out various broadcasts warning the Canadian people of the war and telling them — quite justifiably, in my estimation — that non-intervention was a farce, that it was the beginning of the war, and so on, etcetera; and they would run them off on the mimeograph machines, and we would shove the darned things in envelopes and send them out on mailing lists.

KELLOCK   Who did this?

BENNING   The League against War and Fascism, I think, did; I am pretty sure the Spanish medical relief or Spanish Medical Aid Committee.

KELLOCK   Who were these people?

BENNING   I had my own suspicions, and later they were pretty well-founded, that they were composed equally of people who sincerely believed in it, with no particular axe to grind, and a fair sprinkling of people who I found out later were Communists.

KELLOCK   Who were they?

BENNING   I forget most of their names now, because the only way you could tell them was that they were the people who seemed to do most of the work. If I would go in and help in stuffing from 12 to 1 on Sunday afternoon, and drop back after at 5 or 6 to pick up a friend and go on to a cocktail party, they were still there stuffing.

MR. WILLIAMS   Were you ever a member of the Communist party in Canada?

BENNING   No, sir, I was not.

WILLIAMS   Were you ever a member of the Labour-Progressive party of Canada?

BENNING   No, sir, I was not.

WILLIAMS   You never joined either of those?

BENNING   No, sir; I never joined either of the parties.

WILLIAMS   So it was in work of that kind that you first ran into Gordon Lunan?

BENNING   Yes. It was not work, but associations with those people, that I first saw Sam Carr. I heard him speak at a Labour Day rally in the Queen's Hotel in 1938.

MR. COMMISSIONER KELLOCK   Did you regard Lunan as one of the Communists or otherwise?

BENNING   No, I did not. I regarded him as quite an active person, and quite a sincere person, but at no time did it dawn on me that he was a Communist.

KELLOCK   What about Poland?

BENNING   The same answer would go there. Fred I saw around less often. I quite considered them as being very much as I was, interested onlookers, interested with them to do a certain amount of work in things that they believed in.

MR. WILLIAMS   Then will you look at Exhibit 123. Is that the photograph of anybody you know?

BENNING   No, that does not look familiar at all to me.

WILLIAMS   Do you know a man named Mazerall, Ned Mazerall?

BENNING   No. I never heard the name before.

WILLIAMS   Then Exhibit 124. Is that the photograph of anyone you know?

BENNING   That is Fred Rose, M.P.

WILLIAMS   Do you know him personally?

BENNING   Oh, about the same way that I know Sam Carr. I have heard him speak, and I have bumped into him at these cocktail parties and musicales that the left wing circles used to hold to raise funds for — what was the Communist paper called in those days? I think it was *The Clarion*, and then it became *The Tribune*. They had various fund-raising stunts. . . .

WILLIAMS   Do you recall attending a meeting at Miss Agatha Chapman's house, where you attended as representative of one of these small study groups, at which there were representatives of some five or six other Ottawa groups, which met to discuss questions of policy?

BENNING   What type of study group are you referring to there, sir?

WILLIAMS   I am referring to study groups that have been described by witnesses here as Communist cells?

BENNING   Well, my answer to that is no, sir.

WILLIAMS   Did you belong to any small groups in which the Marxist ideology and economic principles were discussed?

BENNING   Again my answer to that would be that I have, in the days in Montreal, belonged to an organization or a study group that was known as the left book club, where we discussed the current publications and most of them, or I should say all of them, were of a left wing character; and the odd time I have been to Agatha's house and we have had casual discussions. My wife and I have dropped in, and there were other people there, and we have discussed things casually; but it was never on a regular or fixed nature.

WILLIAMS   Are you aware that at these study groups, the ones I am referring to, which have been described here as Communist cells, small fees are paid to a treasurer and then by the treasurer paid into a central fund?

BENNING   I could well believe it.

WILLIAMS   You say you could well believe it. Are you not aware of the fact that that is the way these study groups work?

BENNING   The study groups that I have been associated with, we have been solicited for funds for *The Tribune*, and things of that nature, but I was not aware of the fact that the funds were being used for the advantage of any specific political party.

WILLIAMS   There is evidence here, Mr. Benning, that you and Mazerall and a number of other people met at Agatha Chapman's house in Ottawa in 1943, each of you representing one of these study groups which, as I say, have been described as Communist cells here, and that that meeting and those meetings were meetings of representatives of these groups. What do you say to that?

BENNING   I say it is false, sir.

WILLIAMS   And I think you have told us already that you never knew Mazerall?

BENNING   I have never known Mazerall.

WILLIAMS   Were you ever a member of a study group? That is, a study group composed, among others, of Eric Adams, Miss Willsher and Matt Nightingale?

BENNING   No, sir.

WILLIAMS   So that any evidence to that effect before the Commission would be wrong?

BENNING   Yes, sir, as far as I am concerned.

MR. COMMISSIONER KELLOCK   Were any of those persons members of the study group to which you belonged, or a group to which you belonged?

BENNING   Well, again, pardon me, sir, I object to the emphasis on the word "group." A couple of times I dropped in casually on invitation, and as it will to some people, the conversation gravitates in a certain direction, and to be quite frank I was always, always have been and expect always to be, interested in matters dealing with political economy and allied topics. . . .

KELLOCK   Did you ever give any information to [Nikolai] Zheveinov? [TASS correspondent]

BENNING   Consciously or unconsciously I have not given any information in writing, by word of mouth to anybody but authorized officials of the Canadian government and even then only the ones I have given information to are the ones that I was directly directed by my immediate superiors to turn information of any nature whatsoever over to.

KELLOCK   Now, Mr. Benning, can you suggest any reason why a record from the Russian embassy that was never to see the light of day should credit you with having given information through those channels?

BENNING   Yes, I could. I have given this matter a considerable bit of thought. As a matter of fact, I took occasion to re-read certain portions of *Out of the Night.** I realized that an awful lot of the book was a complete fabrication, but there were certain portions about it that were authentic. It is not unusual, as far as I can gather in other reading I have done, in espionage to create the raising — I grant you that this is fiction or fact according to the credence that any individual wants to put into it — but I find it in several books, presumably written as facts, that when a nation or a party who is resident in a country, such as this, let us say, desires certain material things that his salary does not provide for, it is a comparatively simple operation for him to find out who the people are, where they could possibly be located and then put their names down as persons from whom they are receiving information from and presumably paying money for it. Presumably when their immediate chiefs come over and they are asked, let us say, in this case, "Who is this man Foster? What is his position? What has he done?" it is an authentic person, it is not a fictitious name. That is one explanation that went through my mind after my interrogation by Inspector Anthony.

KELLOCK   Just let us follow that up a little. Quite a substantial number of these records relating to a large number of people have been produced and in those records there is information as to money being paid to some of them. But throughout so far as Foster is concerned, whoever he may be or whether it is James Scotland Benning or anybody else, there is no indication that he was taking money. So that the records which have been established to be authentic beyond any question and have been checked in practically every detail —

BENNING   Which records are those?

*by Carl van Vechten

KELLOCK   These original records from the Russian embassy. They do not indicate that Foster was one of the men to whom money was either offered or imparted. Leaving out the money question, could you suggest any reason why they should credit, James Scotland Benning, with giving information other than from the factors of sympathy with the political ideals of the Communist party? I am only throwing that out as a suggestion. What this Commission has to do is to try to find out what all this means. Would you say that might be a fair suggestion?

BENNING   Well, I mean on the basis of your remark, that the Commission is entirely satisfied that this is an authentic record from the Soviet embassy's secret files of espionage workers, I am afraid you leave me cold because the only possible reason that I could ever think of that my name should have been used was from the viewpoint of the financial end, that the individual who is presumably claiming that I worked for them could mark down "Paid Benning" or Foster, $100 or $50 or $25," or whatever the case may be.

KELLOCK   And then stick it in his own pocket?

BENNING   And stick it in his pocket.

KELLOCK   That is eliminated in this case. Let me tell you this: in each case so far where it has been suggested that money was paid, with only two exceptions the persons who have otherwise admitted the authenticity of the record as it related to them, have denied getting money, so it is possible money was knocked down, but in this case of Foster there is no suggestion in the record that money was paid. Eliminating the possibility of money, why should the records credit you at least with having given information? Have you any other suggestion that you would like the Commission to consider or that would throw any light on this?

BENNING   The only other suggestion I might make is that — I grant you it is rather difficult to make it in reference to that — if I had or Foster — if Foster had not been already credited with giving information I would suggest that as at various times my left wing sympathies were quite perceptible, I might have been suggested as a person who might be amenable to doing that kind of work.

KELLOCK   That you could be recruited?

BENNING   Correct, but in the light of the fact that I have given information about the fleet and air force and army I find that their methods must be extremely imaginative because the information I dealt with, with very few exceptions, could be got by anybody who wanted to take enough time to clip the newspapers intelligently. They could have got most of it in the end.

KELLOCK   I have here another record, Exhibit 22, in the Russian original. It refers to other persons, and amongst others, Sam Carr and Ernst. With the same qualifications as to name, you notice this is what it says about you. "Foster, Englishman." Meaning Anglo-Saxon. "Assistant to the Superintendent of the Department of Distribution of War Production with the Ministry of Munitions and Supplies. Gave material about war material, guns and other kinds of supplies. Obtaining other work with promotion. Can give better materials. He is contacting with Martin" — which is Zheveinov. Then there is a word "our.". Do you read Russian?

BENNING   No.

KELLOCK   "Our," meaning that he belongs to the Soviet. There again is another independent entry which deals, so far as the Russian embassy was concerned, with Foster or J. Scotland Benning?

BENNING   Yes, sir, but assuming the possibility I was guilty of this I do not think I would be quite so careless as not to at least tell them exactly where I did work. There is no such position as "Assistant to the Superintendent of the Department of Distribution of War Production."

KELLOCK   That is a Russian's attempt to describe the position.

BENNING   Oh, I see.

KELLOCK   This is a translation from the Russian original. The document was written in Russian by these men, written in Russian for their own information. They would get it from somebody who told them in English and then they would write down in the Russian the way they translated it.Then we have had to translate it back from the Russian.

BENNING   It gives a rather odd meaning.

KELLOCK   It gives a rather odd meaning, but at least you were with the Ministry of Munitions and Supply.

BENNING   That is correct.

KELLOCK   And you were doing work in connection with economics and statistics of war production?

BENNING   That is correct.

KELLOCK   So that the poor Russian has not made such a bad hand of it. The point is not that so much, the point is why in this second document should they have credited you with giving material about war materials, guns and other kinds of supplies?

BENNING   I wish I knew.

KELLOCK   You cannot think of any?

BENNING   No, I am afraid not. . . .

KELLOCK   First of all, let me ask you: Did you ever supply documents to anybody to transmit to the Russian embassy to be forwarded to Moscow?

BENNING   I certainly did not.

KELLOCK   Now, first of all, let me ask you, did you ever supply documents to anybody to transmit through the Russian embassy to Moscow?

BENNING   I certainly did not, sir.

KELLOCK   Did you ever supply documents to be copied for transmission to the Russian embassy?

BENNING   I did not.

KELLOCK   Did you ever make summaries of documents?

BENNING   The answer again is no. . . .

KELLOCK   Now, then, this document, Exhibit 16, opposite item 156, calls attention to the fact that Gerson is the secretary of that meeting of which the document being sent was the minutes; and the ordinary inference from that is that this is the real document; that they would be able to get lots more documents concerning meetings of which Gerson was the secretary. It is a fine source of information. But Mr. Benning has handed it to us. That is what they say.

BENNING   Well, I prefer if you use the name Foster, sir.

KELLOCK   Well, I will tell you why we use the name "Benning." It is because we have evidence that in the Russian embassy at Ottawa they had a dossier on you, and we know what that means: your name, your biography, and all that sort of thing; your real name and your cover name; so that in the Russian embassy at Ottawa there was a file on you, and you were James Scotland Benning, and your cover name was Foster; and in any document apart from the file on you, where you were referred to, the name which was used was Foster. So this document, Exhibit 16, says a copy of these minutes of a meeting, of which Gerson was the secretary, was "handed to us by James Scotland Benning." My question to you is, that being so stated in the document, which nobody was ever intended to see but the Russians in Ottawa and the Russians in Moscow, why would that statement be made if it were not based on fact? I have said to you, "put yourself in our position and deal with that question." We want any help you can give us. You have been doing a lot of smiling and laughing and treating this thing as a joke, but it is not a joke, Mr. Benning.

BENNING   I can fully appreciate that, Mr. Commissioner.

KELLOCK   All right, then; you answer the question, please?

BENNING   I am afraid I cannot answer that question, because I do not know the answer to it. All I can do is reiterate my complete innocence of any complicity with regard to this matter.

MR. COMMISSIONER TASCHEREAU   We have evidence from one person from the embassy, who says this:

> Q. Do you know who Foster is? Is that a cover or a nickname?
> A.   A nickname.
> Q. And do you know whose nickname it is?
> A.   Scott Benning.
> Q. How do you know that Foster was Scott Benning?
> A.   I read the file compiled on him by Gouseev.
> Q. And that file was also in the safe in Room 12?
> A.   That is right.
> Q. And that disclosed the real name and the cover name?
> A.   Yes.
> Q. The file would be kept under which, the real name or the cover name?
> A.   Always the nickname.
> Q. On the cover of the file?
> A.   Yes.

BENNING   I am afraid I cannot find a reason for it. I certainly would like to. . . .

TASCHEREAU   You would agree also that it is your duty to assist the Commission in every conceivable way to get to the bottom of this whole story?

BENNING   Yes, sir.

TASCHEREAU   As I mentioned earlier, at the time the oath was being discussed, there are a lot of names that I have mentioned to you that appear in the documents I have shown to you, and many other names as well, Mr. Benning.

Now, I have put to you from time to time the question as to whether you could suggest any reason why you should be given credit for certain activities and doing certain things. First of all you suggested that somebody might be taking credit for having paid money to you and, to use an expression we all understand, was knocking down the money himself.

I have explained to you that there is no suggestion in any of these documents that you, directly or indirectly, have been offered or have taken money, as far as we can see. I am telling you that the suggestion is made that other people have received money, and some of them have admitted it. So in your case there is no suggestion that Foster, whoever he might be, was taking money for anything that he was doing, so that thought must be put to one side.

Now, having in mind everything that has been put before you here, can you make any suggestion that would help this Commission in connection with the work it has to do?

BENNING   No. I am sorry I cannot. I will have to refer to the final statement I made to Inspector Anthony, sir.

I say with all sincerity that in my lifetime, at various times, I have been, as probably thousands of others have, toyed with various radical ideas. I have never joined the Communist party. I have never been a member of it. I have never been a member of the Labour-Progressive party. To the best of my ability I have tried to be a good Canadian. I have not ever, consciously or unconsciously, given by word of mouth, written document, transcribed document, in part or in whole, any information to anybody other than people that I knew were authorized to receive it in the government. How this whole thing has occurred — I am forced to admit the same thing I admitted to Anthony, when he said, if I was on the other side of the desk how would I regard it, and I concede that in the light of the various documents that have been attributed to me and the chain of events looks more than coincidence. But I solemnly declare that in no way am I responsible; in no way is there any complicity — I do not know if that phraseology is correct — in no way have I done anything to aid or abet in this particular or in all these particular instances.

I grant you it looks damned black that my name is found there, and I think you mentioned, sir, that not only my name but a complete dossier is there. I concede those points, and it costs me an effort to say it, but I concede perhaps you are right to charge me on the basis of that evidence.

But I do swear by all that I regard as sane and just that I am not guilty of it, and I regret that I cannot give you any suggestion as to how it might have occurred. I have given it a great deal of thought, and I assure you from the bottom of my heart if I could do it, not only as a Canadian citizen but also in an effort to salvage my name, my reputation and my future I certainly would do it. . . .

THE EVIDENCE OF AGATHA CHAPMAN

March 29, 1946

MISS AGATHA CHAPMAN, *called and sworn*

Agatha Chapman was asked about a study group she attended.

MR. COMMISSIONER KELLOCK   And at this group did you study Marxism?

CHAPMAN   We would sometimes read some Marxism, but most of our discussions would be on current topics.

KELLOCK   I was not asking you about anything else. At these groups I asked you if you would study Marxism?

CHAPMAN   We did sometimes discuss Marxism.

KELLOCK   Quite frequently?

CHAPMAN   Sometimes — I do not know what you call frequently. We usually got ourselves so involved in discussions on current developments.

KELLOCK   Would you collect any moneys?

CHAPMAN   We would sometimes take collections for special occasions.

KELLOCK   For what?

CHAPMAN   We took a collection one time for the Windsor strike.

KELLOCK   That is the Ford strike?

CHAPMAN   Yes.

KELLOCK   Any other moneys collected for any other purpose?

CHAPMAN   Let us see. We took one for the Aid to Russia at one time, the Canadian Soviet Friendship Council.

KELLOCK   Anything else?

CHAPMAN   No; I don't remember any.

KELLOCK   Any moneys collected to buy papers or periodicals or books?

CHAPMAN   We would sometimes if somebody was going to Montreal or Toronto — they would get some papers for us.

KELLOCK   What papers?

CHAPMAN   We would like to read *National Affairs Monthly*, for instance. You cannot get it — some of us — you cannot get it on the newsstands.

KELLOCK   *National Affairs Monthly*; is that a paper or a periodical?

CHAPMAN   It is a magazine.

KELLOCK   Who publishes that?

CHAPMAN   I am not sure actually who publishes it. I read it in the Bank of Canada library myself.

KELLOCK   What organization is responsible for it?

CHAPMAN   I think it is not the official organ of the Labour-Progressive party.

KELLOCK   But it is an organ, is it?

CHAPMAN   I don't know whether it is an organ. I know people connected with it.

KELLOCK   All right, Miss Chapman, you are not doing anything. We have the paper here. Any other papers or books?

CHAPMAN   Sometimes they would bring *New Masses*, too, which is a United States' paper.

KELLOCK   *New Masses.* Is that also a communistic paper?

CHAPMAN   I believe you would call it communistic.

KELLOCK   Would you call it communistic?

CHAPMAN   Well, I know it is understood to be communistic. I do not understand the question, whether I call it communistic.

KELLOCK   I think you understand it well enough. Anything else, now?

CHAPMAN   No.

KELLOCK   Miss Chapman, did you hold any office in this study group?

CHAPMAN   No. . . .

MR. COMMISSIONER TASCHEREAU   Are you sure about Adams?

CHAPMAN   As I say, it was up at my house — Adams was at my house and we used to discuss things, if you call that a study group.

MR. FAUTEUX   I am exhibiting to you a number of issues of *National Affairs*. That is the periodical you have been referring to, is it not?

CHAPMAN   Yes.

FAUTEUX   You can find by whom it is published?

CHAPMAN   Yes.

FAUTEUX   The National Committee of the Labour-Progressive party?

CHAPMAN   That is right.

FAUTEUX   It is very clear, is it not?

CHAPMAN   That is right.

FAUTEUX   You knew that?

CHAPMAN   When I said it was not the organ I did not know whether it was the official organ, whether it speaks officially or not. I knew it was connected.

FAUTEUX   And can you read that at page 194: "We did not follow the American example; on the contrary, the Communist party being outlawed by the King government we established the Labour-Progressive party, with a Marxist program and utilized the possibilities and the widespread progressive sentiment to strengthen our party and extend its influence." You knew that, too?

CHAPMAN   I read it there.

FAUTEUX   I am asking you do you know that the Labour-Progressive party is the current label for the old Communist party?

CHAPMAN   I do not think they have made any secret about it.

MR. COMMISSIONER KELLOCK   That is not the question you are asked. Would you answer the question?

CHAPMAN   Yes, I understand —

KELLOCK   You would save a lot of time if you would answer the question directly.

MR. FAUTEUX   Will you answer the question?

CHAPMAN   Yes, I understand that.

FAUTEUX   You knew that?

CHAPMAN   I know it, yes.

FAUTEUX   You knew it since when?

CHAPMAN   Oh, I do not remember when I knew that.

FAUTEUX   But it has always been to your knowledge?

CHAPMAN   It was my understanding.

FAUTEUX   And to make it clear Miss Willsher testified here when she was asked what qualification was needed to belong to any of these groups, especially the one she was with, the group to which you belonged yourself:

Q. What was the qualification?
A.   Interest in the same kind of study.
Q. Interest in communistic writings and teachings?
A.   Yes.

Is that right?

CHAPMAN   That is putting it more specifically.

MR. BEAMENT   (*Miss Chapman's counsel*)   I do not understand whether Mr. Fauteux is asking whether that is what Miss Willsher said or whether that is the opinion of this witness.

FAUTEUX   I am asking the opinion of the witness.

CHAPMAN   You are asking me whether it is my opinion that the groups were for that purpose?

FAUTEUX   You agree with that?

CHAPMAN   I would not have put it like that. I would say the people who discussed these things in the study groups at different times were people who were interested in a great many things, and particularly in what is going on in the world, and were interested in the Communist approach as well as others.

MR. COMMISSIONER KELLOCK   At least in the Communist approach?

CHAPMAN   Not only.

KELLOCK   I say "at least." Is that right?

CHAPMAN   I beg your pardon?

KELLOCK   Would it be right to say "at least in the Communist approach," to use your language?

CHAPMAN   Well, they were interested in that and other approaches. They were studying. The groups were discussion groups or informal discussions.

MR. COMMISSIONER TASCHEREAU   Would you say they had communistic leanings?

CHAPMAN   I would like to have communistic leanings defined. I am not too clear what it means myself. . . .

MR. FAUTEUX   Were there regular dues collected in these study groups?

CHAPMAN   No.

FAUTEUX   We have information that some were requested to pay $1 a month?

CHAPMAN   No.

FAUTEUX   Were there any sorts of contributions?

CHAPMAN   Not where I was. As I described, there were special contributions for special occasions. Sometimes we would decide we would like to take up some money, as I gave an example, for the Windsor strike, and we might take it up over a period of months.

FAUTEUX   You gave the names of certain persons belonging to one group and you stated you belonged to several groups?

CHAPMAN   At different times.

FAUTEUX   What are the other groups?

CHAPMAN   Well, a while ago there was a group or a couple of study groups here

334

called the Fellowship for a Christian Social Order. I was connected with it, and we used to have discussion groups.

FAUTEUX   What else?

CHAPMAN   I belonged to the Canadian Soviet Friendship Council. I am on the executive.

FAUTEUX   What else?

CHAPMAN   Those are all that have any formality that I can think of now. I belong to the Ottawa Public Affairs Council. . . .

MR. COMMISSIONER KELLOCK   As far as you are concerned are you a Communist?

CHAPMAN   No, I am not a Communist.

KELLOCK   Are you sympathetic?

CHAPMAN   I am — I do not know how to describe myself. Let us say I am progressive in my sympathies. That is how I would describe myself, and if you want to define progressive —

KELLOCK   No, I cannot define anything for you. I am just asking something about you and your opinions which are your own, but they are also facts, and we are interested in facts. You say you are not a member of the Communist party or Labour-Progressive party but would you describe yourself as sympathetic towards the aims of that party?

CHAPMAN   Is this question relevant?

MR. BEAMENT   Do you know what the aims of the party are? I do not.

KELLOCK   The witness can answer the question any way she likes, Mr. Beament. The witness is not putting the questions. She is answering them.   (*To the witness*)   You can answer any way you like.

CHAPMAN   I described my sympathies as progressive.

KELLOCK   If you want to parry and dodge the question, that is your privilege, too, but I put the question to you. What do you say? I am not asking for idle pastime. I want to get through with this investigation, but your opinions are facts, and we are interested in facts.

CHAPMAN   Let us put it this way. There are certain aims, as I have read in magazines you showed me, and so on, of the Labour-Progressive party which I am sympathetic with. To say I am sympathetic with their aims in general is putting it too broadly. I cannot commit myself to that question.

KELLOCK   Well, you would say you are interested?

CHAPMAN   In so far as they agree with me about what will make a better world.

KELLOCK   All right, Miss Chapman. We will have to form our opinion from the other evidence. That is as far as you want to help, is it, on that subject?

CHAPMAN   In regard to my own opinions that is all I feel I can say. . . .

335

SAM CARR'S FAILURE TO APPEAR

April 15, 1946

MR. FAUTEUX   Inspector, will you call Sam Carr?

INSPECTOR LEOPOLD   Sam Carr is not present.

MR. COMMISSIONER TASCHEREAU   Has Mr. Carr been called?

FAUTEUX   The inspector called Sam Carr and Sam Carr does not answer.

TASCHEREAU   There was no answer, Inspector?

LEOPOLD   No answer, sir.

TASCHEREAU   A subpoena has been served upon him?

FAUTEUX   I wish to file the original of a copy of a subpoena which has been served, as well as a copy of the Order of the commissioners. I should like to read into the record a copy of an original letter which was delivered by hand at the same time as the subpoena was served with the order. This reads:

> Justice Building,
> Ottawa, 10th April, 1946
>
> Dear Sir,-
>
> The Royal Commissioners appointed under the above named Order in Council have instructed me to advise you that certain evidence placed before them indicates that you have engaged in certain activities which they are investigating and to notify you that they desire you to appear before them immediately and that you will be given full opportunity to be heard and to be represented by counsel should you so desire.
>
> This letter is being written to you because so far it has proved impossible to locate you to serve you personally with a subpoena which the commissioners issued to require your appearance before them. An order has been made to serve you substitutionally however.
>
> Your appearance on 15th April next is required under the subpoena which has been issued pursuant to this order.
>
> Yours very truly,
> W. Kenneth Campbell
> Secretary to the Commission.
>
> Sam Carr, Esq.,
> 74 Rusholme Road,
> Toronto, Ont.

TASCHEREAU   That is to his domicile?

FAUTEUX   That is to his domicile. I might say on this point that there is a return sworn to on Exhibit No. 483, which is the original of the subpoena, and the order. I might as well read that:

> I, H.P. Mathewson, Inspector, Royal Canadian Mounted Police, of the city of Toronto, make oath and say that I did on Thursday, the 11th

day of April in the year 1946, serve the within named Sam Carr with a true copy of the within subpoena by leaving it for him at his most usual place of abode to wit 74 Rusholme Road, Toronto, Ontario with his wife Mrs. Julia Carr an inmate thereof apparently not under sixteen years of age and at the time of such service I exhibited to Mrs. Julia Carr the within original subpoena.

(Signed) H.P. Mathewson

Sworn before me at the City of Toronto, this 11th day of April in the year 1946.

(Signed) C.A. Lynn

A Justice of the Peace for the County of York. . . .

THE EVIDENCE OF FRED ROSE

April 26, 1946

FRED ROSE, *called*

JOSEPH COHEN, K.C.   )
MARCUS FINER   )   *Representing*
ALEX HILL, K.C.   )   *Mr. Rose.*

MR. COHEN   Gentlemen, since we left I have spent as much time as I could in examining into this question. I have read as carefully as I could the Inquiries Act which is the basis of the Order in Council which created this Commission, and I have read too the extended powers that you have apart from the Inquiries Act under the Order in Council.

I have seen that you have all the rights and powers of a civil tribunal together with the extended rights as to procedure that you have in your Order in Council. The stand that I must take this morning is the same that I took before you the other day.

I do not wish to reiterate but we feel that the effect of testifying before this civil tribunal will have directly the effect of removing from the Witness Rose the protections that the Criminal Code and the jurisprudence has surrounded the person of an accused once he is before a court. May I use also the term "sanctity of his position," that he cannot be compelled by any criminal court to testify against himself or give evidence which will disclose the nature of the defence that he intends to make before the actual date on which he makes his defence.

If that be the case, then with all the respect that I have for the Commission I say that you, having the powers of a civil tribunal, will be doing indirectly what no judge in a criminal court can do directly. I have had occasion to examine into the use that has been made of depositions taken before this Commission and the testimony of other people in their own trials before the criminal court and also in the trials of others before the criminal court and, therefore, gentlemen, I must say that we firmly believe that we should not testify until the trial of Rose is completed after May 20.

MR. COMMISSIONER KELLOCK   Have you any authorities to support the position you take?

COHEN   I have none except what I consider to be the basic rights of an accused which stem from the Magna Charta, which I am not going to read or refer to except by name, and which have been hallowed by jurisprudence ever since our Code has been put into effect.

MR. COMMISSIONER TASCHEREAU   We take it that Mr. Rose refuses to be sworn?

COHEN   That is the position Rose has been advised by counsel to take.

TASCHEREAU   All right, we will consider it.

COHEN   While I am on my feet may I put in, for the purpose of the record, the fact that it is common knowledge as well as a judicial fact that Rose is a member of Parliament representing the Montreal constituency of Cartier and as such he has certain rights of immunity.

KELLOCK   While the house is in session, but it is not in session.

COHEN   I suggest that the law is that he has those rights of immunity for forty days before the house is in session and for forty days after the house is in session.

KELLOCK   Immunity from arrest, but that is not the point here. It is only a question of testifying.

COHEN   Immunity from arrest with all its —

KELLOCK   The principle is quite different, as I understand it.

COHEN   I am not going to argue this question before you. This is a matter which is directly within the jurisdiction of the Commission. You are sitting with the powers of a civil tribunal and I suggest that all the rules of civil law in connection with the immunity of members of Parliament are quite clear that a member has immunity from arrest in a civil matter.

TASCHEREAU   You understand that we have the powers that are given to us under the Act and in addition we have the powers of a civil court for the purpose of compelling a witness to speak.

COHEN   As I said before, you have the powers under the Inquiries Act and you also have the powers under the Order in Council which, as I said, go far beyond the Inquiries Act. But I do not think they go so far beyond the Inquiries Act as to remove from a member of Parliament his right of immunity from arrest in a civil matter.

KELLOCK   All I am pointing out to you, Mr. Cohen, is that there is no question of arrest at the moment; it is a question only of testifying.

COHEN   I did not say there is.

KELLOCK   Let us not talk about something that is not relevant.

COHEN   Since you intend to deliberate on the matter I thought I would make these remarks to you so that you would have our position completely and fully before you.

KELLOCK   I was simply asking if you had any submissions that were relevant. There is no question of arrest; it is a question only of testifying.

COHEN   I have tried to make my position clear.

KELLOCK   That is all you wish to say?

COHEN   That is all I can say.

WILLIAMS   Messrs. Commissioners, there are two matters that occur to me following what has been submitted by my friend. While I know that he is speaking with the full approbation of his client who is here before the Commission, after all it is the client who has to take the responsibility of taking the advice of counsel, I respectfully suggest to the Commission that Mr. Rose himself should state whether he declines to be sworn.

TASCHEREAU   I think the Bible should be offered to Mr. Rose.

THE SECRETARY   Take the book in your right hand, Mr. Rose.

ROSE   I refuse to be sworn.

WILLIAMS   Then in his latter remarks my friend made some reference to immunities. I suggest that for the purpose of this record it should be clearly stated on Mr. Rose's behalf or by Mr. Rose himself that he claims whatever immunities he may be entitled to as a member of the House of Commons so that the Commission may know exactly where it stands.

COHEN   I do not know whether that is an appropriate request to make in view of the fact that it is a submission in the law which is properly made by counsel. I am speaking not only for myself but for the other counsel, Mr. Finer of

Montreal and Mr. Hill of Ottawa, who, I believe, approve of the legal propositions I have made.

KELLOCK   If your client hears you and does not dissent, I suppose he approves.

COHEN   I hope he will not disallow what I have said because that might bring in serious adjustments.

KELLOCK   We have had that here.

WILLIAMS   That was not exactly my point. My suggestion is that he should say definitely now that he is or is not relying on any immunities to which Mr. Rose may be entitled.

COHEN   Perhaps I can put it this way. I tried to make it clear to the commissioners that Rose is a member of Parliament. The question of sanctions by this Commission may arise in your minds, and properly so. A question of law, the question of immunity exists in the circumstances and I have pointed out to the Commission that that question of immunity should be considered by the Commission if and when they consider sanctions in connection with the refusal of Rose to testify.

KELLOCK   As I understand the point Mr. Williams is raising, when you speak of immunity you are speaking about immunity from arrest which may arise if this Commission decided to impose sanctions on your client for refusing to be sworn, but the point is that there is no immunity existing at this moment which frees your client from the obligation to be sworn and testify before this Commission.

COHEN   No, the question of immunity arises after his refusal to be sworn.

TASCHEREAU   All right.

KELLOCK   Anything else, Mr. Williams?

WILLIAMS   I have nothing else to add, Messrs. Commissioners.

TASCHEREAU   We will consider that.

COHEN   We will await your pleasure.

Short recess ensued.

MR. COMMISSIONER TASCHEREAU   Well, Mr. Cohen, we have had the opportunity of considering your objection. As you know, this investigtion has been going on for a number of weeks, and the evidence shows that Mr. Rose has been guilty of misconduct in connection with the subject-matter which we have been investigating. We wanted to give Mr. Rose an opportunity to come here and answer to those charges; but in view of the attitude which he now takes, and in view of the fact that he has refused this opportunity, we feel free to report to the Governor General as we deem fit.

COHEN   That is exactly within the terms, I think, of Section 13 of the Inquiries Act.

TASCHEREAU   That will be all, thank you.

Whereupon the witness withdrew.

MR. WILLIAMS   I suggest, Messrs. Commissioners, that the sittings be adjourned. . . .

THE EVIDENCE OF JOHN GRIERSON

May 13, 1946

MR. JOHN GRIERSON, *called and sworn*

MR. WILLIAMS   Have you any objection to telling us your own political leanings? First of all, are you a Communist or communistically inclined?

GRIERSON   I would be delighted. I have been a public servant now for a matter of eighteen years. I was trained in the classical Whitehall school. I have been first and last a public servant, that is, a civil servant. Now, that meant in the Whitehall sense that you have no party and having no party, I have never had party affiliations. A party should not affect one's public job, particularly in the kind of work I have done, because I have always been concerned with government information.

I emphasize the Whitehall angle because the rules there and the feelings there are much stronger, the philosophy is much tougher than one sees, for example, in Washington, where they permit the public servant to take actual part in political affairs; tougher even, I think, than you have here.

May I tell you a little story to illustrate? I remember once meeting a principal political leader in this country who asked me, "What are your political views?" I said, "My political views are to be as progressive as is possible within the machinery of the constitution, that is, within the machinery of government." My views are the ones every public servant should hold. They must be subject, not just to the government in power but any sanctions for the public service are applied not by the government in power but by the consensus of the whole government, that is, the House of Commons. I hold that it is one's duty to press as far as possible the progressive legislation of the country, but within the firm and very strict rules.

For example, I served under many governments and I may say that I have had the confidence of high governmental leaders in many parties or different parties. I have found the ironical situation in my own work, that it is possible to be more progressive under the Conservative government of England than under the Labour government of England. That is a curious point.

WILLIAMS   I gather from what you say that it was your procedure to apply your personal political views in the course of your duties in the manner you have described?

GRIERSON   I graduated in political philosophy under Farrow. I spent ten years in political philosophy in the university and I picked up a little, I suppose, in the course of that time. In the university my views — may I state them?

WILLIAMS   I want you to.

GRIERSON   I would follow Mr. Truman's speech on Saturday. He said that the only defence against an attack on democracy is the creation and development of the science of human relationship. He was simply following along the lines of Mr. Roosevelt who did not live to carry out his ideas.

My idea is that there are great forces working in the world. I rank them, not in order of importance, as the Catholic church, international socialism and Liberal democracy. I believe very strongly and very firmly that anything that is done to better the understanding of what lies behind those basic ideas in the world will represent an advance for civilization.

Therefore, I would say that it behooves us to understand what lies behind Catholicism, what lies behind international socialism and what lies behind Liberal democracy. My own philosophy is that Liberal democracy represents one-half or one third, Catholicism represents one-third and international socialism represents one-third.

In the matter of political philosophy the issue is this: those of us who have been trained and who are dyed in the wool Liberal democrats say that there cannot be any economic freedom if there is no political freedom. On the other hand, those who believe in international socialism say that there cannot be any political freedom unless there is economic freedom.

WILLIAMS Would you say then that the effect of all that is that you are not a member of the Communist party?

GRIERSON Oh, no.

WILLIAMS That is officially. What would you say about subscribing to any of their views? Would you say that your inclinations were of the leftist variety. . . .

GRIERSON Not at all; I do not think that way. I am entirely a person who is concerned with the establishment of good international understanding. Therefore, I am concerned with the floating of all ideas. I mean, I get as much from Gobineau as I get from Marx.

WILLIAMS Let me put it to you this way. A number of the witnesses who have appeared before us have admitted that in breach of their oaths of secrecy, they have passed over to the Russians information which they knew they should not have passed over. Some of them have justified it, or attempted to justify it on the ground that there was a higher duty than their oaths and obligations of secrecy, because they felt that they were helping to accomplish something in the world. Would you express your views on that attitude?

GRIERSON I would like to have this even stronger than anything I have said. As, shall we say, a student from a Whitehall stable, I believe the firm rule should be that if they take an oath in the public service then that oath must be respected in the public service, if the integrity of the public service is to be maintained. Not only that; I add to that, that where clear and present danger has been proven, the interest of the state is paramount. These are fundamental in my own philosophy.

WILLIAMS Then let me ask you this. The evidence before the Commission is that one of the favourite methods of recruiting was to get people into these Communist study groups, or some of the witnesses have described them as Communist cells; and the evidence equally is that many of the prime movers in this work, members of these study groups, the recruiters, were employees of the Film Board. Have you any comment to make on that?

GRIERSON No. I don't know what the evidence is, but they were a pretty good group down there. Of course I was all for the exchange of ideas. I wanted them to be as broad and as bright as possible, in so far as they were handling serious matters, of necessity. They were handling the problems of Canada, both national and international, and I wanted them to have a grasp of the full implications of those problems; and any studies they did were — I favoured any grouping for study, as I would anywhere in the world; but that they were used for partisan political purposes, I have no reason to believe. I should like to mention to the French members of the Commission that one of the things I was keenest on all the way through was breaking down this division inside Canada, and I think the Film Board did more than any department in this country to concentrate on the study of the French by the English and of the English by the French. We did a really good job of bringing the people together.

WILLIAMS   That is apart from the point I am trying to develop with you.

GRIERSON   Did I answer the point?

WILLIAMS   No, and I should like to follow it up. I want to make the situation perfectly clear. There has been proved here before the Commission the existence of an astonishingly large number of Communist cells masquerading as study groups. There has been proved here before the Commision that an astonishingly large number of persons working in those cells and drawing other people into them were employees of the Film Board. I am not talking about the public work of the Film Board; I am asking you whether, first of all, you would have any knowledge that that was going on; and, if you had not, how you could explain that so many of them —?

GRIERSON   An astonishingly large number?

WILLIAMS   Yes; how you could explain that so many members of the Film Board would be engaged in these activities?

GRIERSON   First of all, I am surprised that — definite partisan political activity?

WILLIAMS   Oh, definitely; subversive political activities.

GRIERSON   It makes me choke a little. I can only say this. Naturally, in recruiting for the Film Board I was reaching out of the sky for the people, as you know, in the sense that many people had gone to the Army, and I had not much access in the latter years to that clique of people. I was dealing with 4-F'ers too, almost exclusively, in the last two or three years. I had not much choice. I went for the brightest I could get, because I had to train them fast. Remember, you had very few people in this country who knew films or the handling of films. I had to go simply on the quality and brightness and the quickness of apprehension, because I really had to train people in something like three or six months.

WILLIAMS   And did you have no reason to suspect from your contacts with these people that some of them might be active workers for the Soviet Union, in subversive activites in Canada?

GRIERSON   If I had dreamed of it I would certainly have fought it.

WILLIAMS   And did you sense at any time that kind of atmosphere or an extremely leftist atmosphere in the personnel of the Film Board?

GRIERSON   No. I had a sense of atmosphere of progressive thought, we will say, in the vague sense we have used it before, that was very good for Canada. . . .

THE TESTIMONY OF WILLIAM WHITEHEAD, METROPOLITAN POLICE, LONDON.

May 14, 1946

MR. FAUTEUX   Reference has been made in several documents brought from the Soviet embassy by Igor Gouzenko and filed before this Commission to a person known under the cover name of Alec, and identified by Gouzenko as being Dr. Alan Nunn May?

WHITEHEAD   Yes, sir.

FAUTEUX   Further evidence actually established that Dr. Alan Nunn May had been charged in England under the Official Secrets Act in connection with his actions as disclosed in these various exhibits. My question would be this: Are you aware of that case? Did you hear about that case in England?

WHITEHEAD   I arrested Dr. Alan Nunn May.

FAUTEUX   I am exhibiting to you a photograph which has been filed as Exhibit 142?

WHITEHEAD   Yes, that is him.

FAUTEUX   You recognize Alan Nunn May?

WHITEHEAD   Yes, sir.

FAUTEUX   Could you inform the Commission what happened to his case?

WHITEHEAD   Yes, sir. He appeared at the Central Criminal Court on May 1, 1946, before Mr. Justice Oliver, he pleaded guilty to an offence charging him as follows:

> That on a date in 1945, being now within the jurisdiction of the under-mentioned court, in the said district, did, for a purpose prejudicial to the safety and interests of the state, communicate to some person unknown certain information which was calculated to be or might be directly or indirectly useful to an enemy, contrary to section 1(1)(c) of the Official Secrets Act, 1911.

After he had pleaded guilty and the Attorney General had summarized the facts of the case, the defending barrister put in a plea for leniency. The judge said:

> Alan Nunn May, I have listened with some slight surprise to some of the things which your learned counsel has said he is entitled to put before me: the picture of you as a man of honour who had only done what you believed to be right. I do not take that view of you at all. How any man in your position could have had the crass conceit, let alone the wickedness, to arrogate to himself the decision of a matter of this sort, when you yourself had given your written undertaking not to do it, and knew it was one of the country's most precious secrets, when you yourself had drawn and were drawing pay for years to keep your own bargain

with your country — that you could have done this is a dreadful thing. I think that you acted not as an honourable but a dishonourable man. I think you acted with degradation. Whether money was the object of what you did, in fact you did get money for what you did. It is a very bad case indeed. The sentence upon you is one of ten years' penal servitude.

FAUTEUX   Were you present when that sentence was given?
WHITEHEAD   I was present, sir.
FAUTEUX   And when the facts you have disclosed took place?
WHITEHEAD   Yes, sir; in court; when the facts were disclosed in court.
FAUTEUX   So you have personal knowledge of that?
WHITEHEAD   Certainly, sir. . . .

THE CLOSE OF THE COMMISSION'S HEARINGS

June 27, 1946

MR. WILLIAMS   Messrs. Commissioners, as far as counsel are able to say there is no further evidence to be submitted to the Commission. Certain translations have been made which are being used in the report and I suggest that they be filed as Exhibit 601, and if it meets with the approval of the commissioners that the evidence now be noted as closed.

MR. COMMISSIONER TASCHEREAU   We will now adjourn for the completion of the final report.

The Commission adjourned.